DETROIT'S STREETCAR HERITAGE

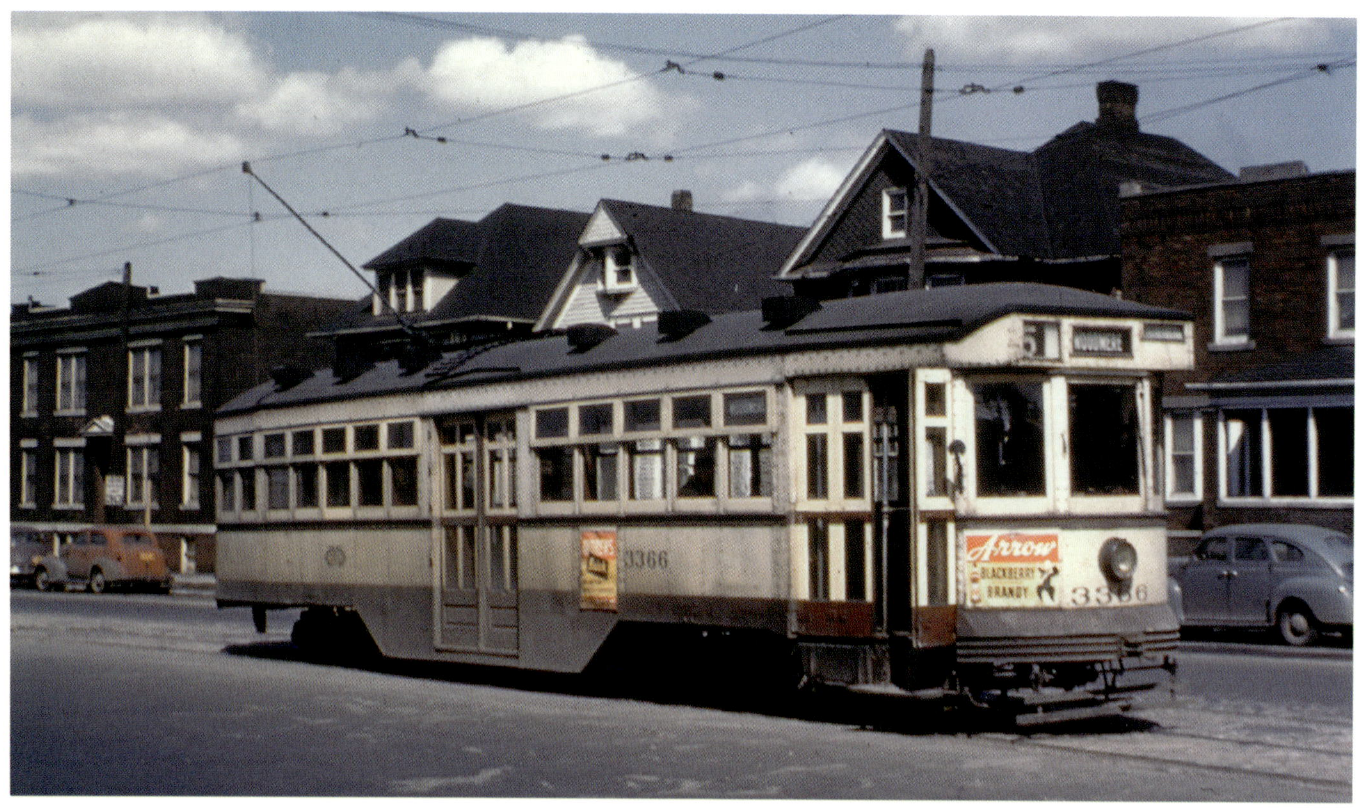

Detroit, Department of Street Railways (DSR), car No. 3366 is on Fort Street at Woodmere Street in 1950. This was one of seventy-five Peter Witt-type cars, Nos. 3350–3424, built by St. Louis Car Company and delivered in 1922. Powered by four General Electric type 265 motors, each car seated fifty-two passengers and weighed 37,660 pounds. (*Clifford R. Scholes collection*)

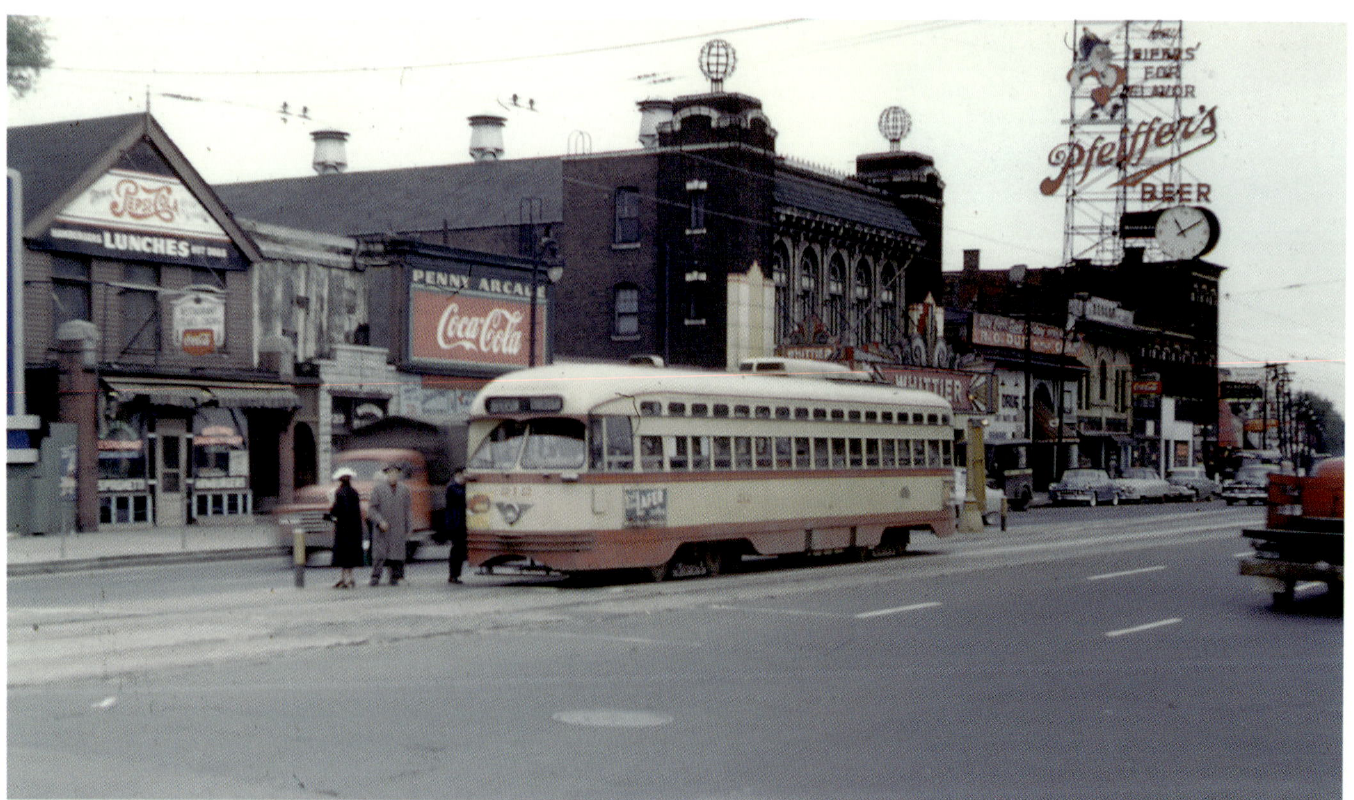

In 1953, Jefferson Avenue at Grand Boulevard is the location of DSR car No. 212. Weighing 39,000 pounds and seating fifty-four passengers, this was one of fifty-three Presidents' Conference Committee (PCC) cars, Nos. 181–233, built by St. Louis Car Company and delivered during August–October 1949. Each car was powered by four General Electric type 1220 motors. (*Clifford R. Scholes collection*)

DETROIT'S STREETCAR HERITAGE

KENNETH C. SPRINGIRTH

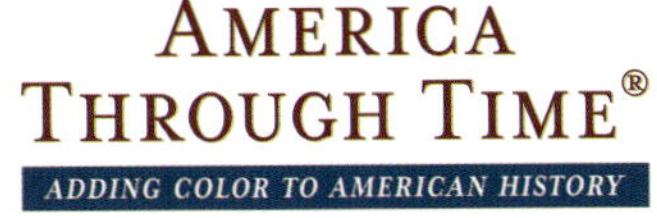

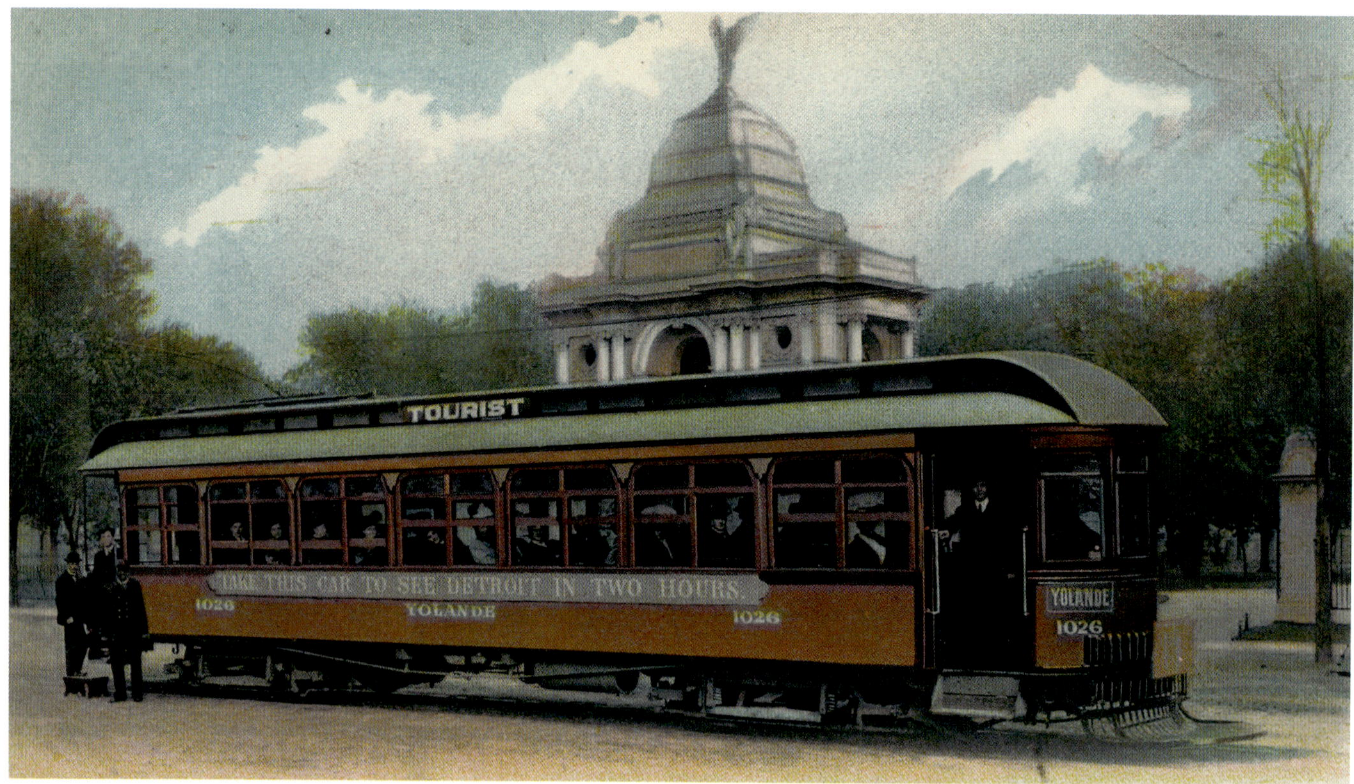

Posing at the three tiered limestone Hurlbut Memorial gate entrance to the Water Works Park on East Jefferson Avenue and Cadillac Boulevard in Detroit, excursion car No. 1026 "Yolande" proudly advertises "Take this car to see Detroit in two hours" in this postcard scene. Powered by four Westinghouse type W56 motors, this car was built by Detroit United Railway (DUR) in 1901 and seated fifty-three passengers. For a 25-cent fare, the car could be boarded at any street along its circular route, which included manufacturing plants, residential areas, and Water Works Park. Detroit city water commissioner Chauncey Hurlbut died in 1885 and left a significant amount to beautify Water Works Park, of which $30,000 was used in 1894 to build the Hurlbut Memorial Gate. In 1975, the gate was listed on the National Register of Historic Places.

On the top portion of cover: On August 16, 1953, Detroit, Department of Street Railways (DSR), Peter Witt-type car No. 3874 is at the Jefferson and Wayburn Avenues terminal in the City of Grosse Point Park, which borders on Detroit in Wayne County, Michigan. Powered by four General Electric type 265 motors, this was one of sixty-four cars, Nos. 3851–3914, built by St. Louis Car Company in 1930. Weighing 37,200 pounds, each 8.5-foot-wide by 48.5-foot-long car seated fifty-two passengers. (*Bob Crockett photograph—Clifford R. Scholes collection*)

On the bottom portion of cover: DSR car No. 272 is at the Griswold and Atwater terminus of the Woodward line in downtown Detroit on August 16, 1953. The 50.5-foot-long PCC car was built by St. Louis Car Company in 1949. This was one of 183 PCC cars sold to the municipal street railway system of Mexico City during 1953–1956. (*Bob Crockett photograph—Clifford R. Scholes collection*)

Back cover: Open summer car No. 247 is on Jefferson Avenue and Griswold Street in downtown Detroit in September 1996 on the Washington Boulevard Trolley, later known as the Detroit Citizens Railway. This car was built by J. G. Brill Company in Philadelphia for Lisbon, Portugal, in 1900 and arrived in Detroit in 1975. The line, part of the revitalization program for Washington Boulevard, began operation on September 20, 1976 and made its last run on June 21, 2003. (*Clifford R. Scholes collection*)

America Through Time is an imprint of Fonthill Media LLC
www.through-time.com | office@through-time.com

First published 2018

ISBN 978-1-63499-072-1

Typeset in Utopia Std
Printed and bound in England

Published by Arcadia Publishing by arrangement with Fonthill Media LLC

For all general information, please contact Arcadia Publishing:

Telephone: 843-853-2070
Fax: 843-853-0044
E-mail: sales@arcadiapublishing.com
For customer service and orders:
Toll-Free 1-888-313-2665

www.arcadiapublishing.com

Contents

Acknowledgments

Thanks to the Erie County (Pennsylvania) Public Library system for their excellent inter-library loan system and the Detroit Public Library Main Library on Woodward Avenue in Detroit, Michigan, for their wonderful collection of Detroit streetcar books, plus their excellent reference department that helped identify buildings along Woodward Avenue. Numerous pictures were purchased from Clifford R. Scholes. Thanks to Brookville Equipment Corporation for providing information and the photograph of the first QLINE car No. 287 delivered to Detroit. Thanks to Birdsall H. Nichols for the use of his pictures. Books that served as excellent reference sources were *Detroit's Street Railways Volume I: City Lines 1863–1922* by Jack E. Schramm and William H. Henning; *Detroit's Street Railways Volume II: City Lines 1922–1956* by Jack E. Schramm and Thomas Dworman; *PCC cars of North American* by Harold E. Cox; *The Tramways of Portugal* by B. R. King and J. H. Price; Electric Railroaders Association's various issues of *Headlights*; *Modern Tramway* January 1977 issue; and *Motor Coach Age* January–February 1991, March–April 1992, and May–June 1993 issues.

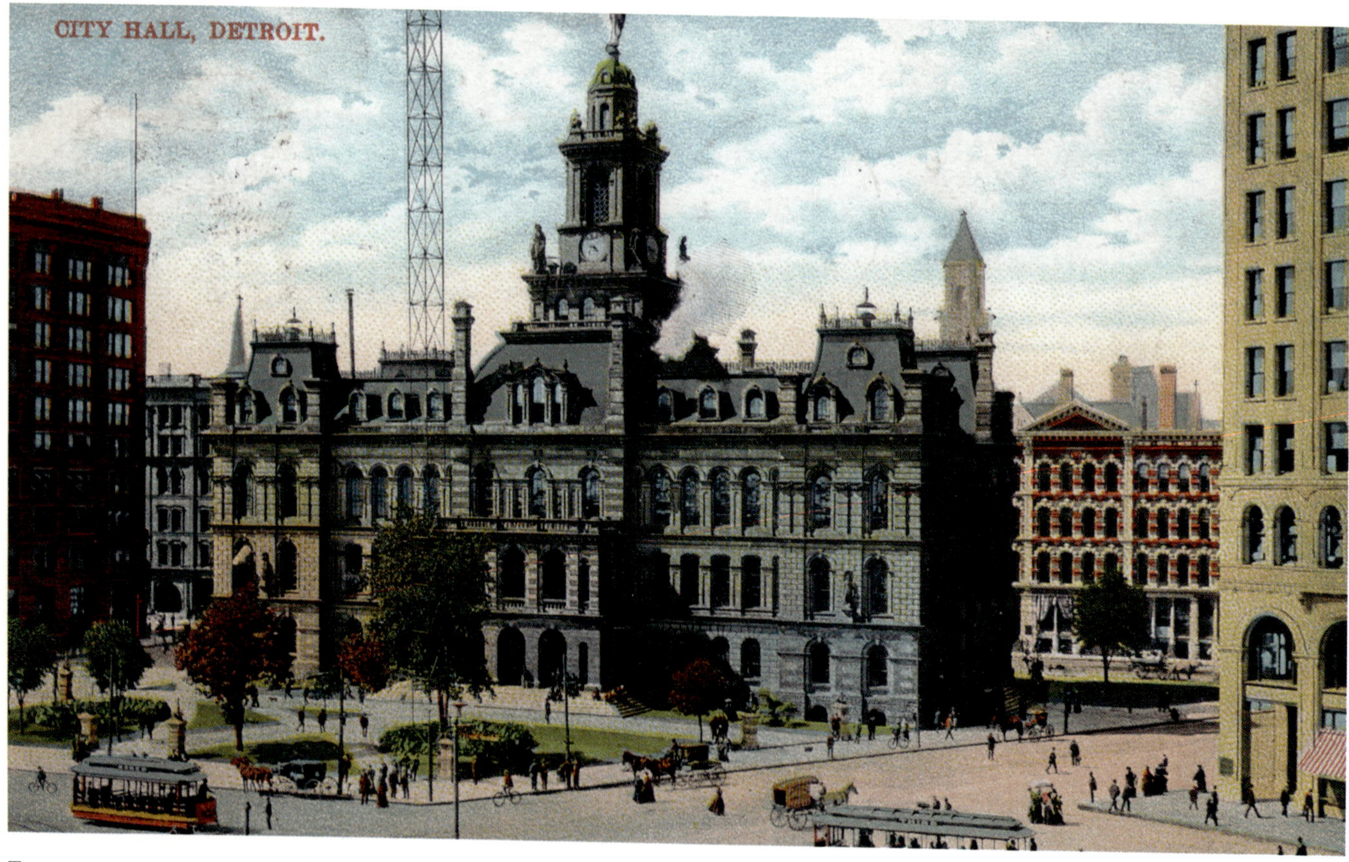

Two open summer cars are in this postcard postmarked August 26, 1909 showing the Detroit City Hall, which was located on the west side of a park area known as Campus Martius, bounded by Griswold Street on the west, Michigan Avenue on the north, Woodward Avenue to the east, and Fort Street on the south. On December 30, 1900, all of Detroit's streetcar systems were consolidated into the Detroit United Railway. Designed by architect James Anderson, the Detroit City Hall was built by N. Osborn & Company of Rochester, New York, in 1871, at a cost of $379,578. The foundation was laid in 1867, and the new city hall was dedicated on July 4, 1871. The 200-foot-long by 90-foot-wide three-story building, with its 180-foot-high tower, featured an Italian Renaissance revival architectural style, characterized by arched windows and horizontal bands of stone to visually separate the floors. Although some building improvements were made in 1953 to address fire code concerns, a new City-County Building was built and a parade of officials went from the Old City Hall to the new City-County Building on July 21, 1955. Demolition of City Hall began on August 14, 1961 and was completed on September 18, 1961.

Introduction

Detroit's first public transit service began in May 1847 on a 2-mile omnibus line on East Jefferson Avenue that quickly failed. A second attempt was made in 1850 on Jefferson Avenue, plus a line on Woodward Avenue from the Detroit to Adams, which also failed. A third company started service in 1853 and was moderately successful. On August 4, 1863, the Detroit Street Railway began regular horsecar service on Jefferson Avenue from Third Street to Mt. Elliott. Horsecar routes expanded in Detroit. A dreaded horse disease hit Detroit on October 25, 1872, and there was no horsecar service for several days. As Detroit grew, horsecar companies extended lines into new neighborhoods. However, using electric power to propel the streetcar would soon supersede the horsecar because horses were prone to disease, horse droppings polluted streets, and horses were very slow.

On August 22, 1892, the Detroit Citizens Street Railway opened an electric streetcar line on Jefferson Avenue from St. Antoine Street to Baldwin Street. The Woodward line was converted to electric operation in mid-December 1892, followed by the Mack line. Detroit Mayor Hazen S. Pingree wanted a 3-cent fare with a free transfer, and the Detroit Citizens Street Railway countered by stating the company could not break even with that fare proposal. On November 21, 1894, Mayor Pingree announced that an agreement had been reached with the new Detroit Railway Company, which had been granted a thirty-year franchise with a low fare of eight tickets for $.25 from 5:45 a.m. to 8 p.m. and six tickets for $.25 for the rest of the day. In return for those low fares, the city agreed to maintain the tracks and could buy the lines when the franchise expired at a price determined by arbitration. The Detroit Railway began service on their Crosstown and Belle Isle line on July 8, 1895 and was sold to the Detroit Electric Railway on July 29, 1896. Officers of the Detroit Citizens Railway obtained full control of the Detroit Electric Railway on January 4, 1897.

In 1897, the Citizens Traction Company was formed as a holding company for the purpose of consolidating all of the Detroit streetcar lines. Mayor Pingree became governor of Michigan on January 1, 1897 and intended to also be Mayor of Detroit. However, the Michigan Supreme Court ruled against him and he resigned as Mayor. On November 9, 1899, the final horsecar run was made, and all of the lines had been converted to electric streetcar operation.

It was announced on December 30, 1900 that all of the Detroit area streetcar systems had been consolidated into the Detroit United Railway (DUR). E. W. Moore and H. Everett of the Everett-Moore Syndicate obtained full control of the Detroit United Railway by February 15, 1901 and now had 1,500 miles of rail systems under their control or under construction. Since they had overextended their funding, banks called in their notes on February 5, 1902, and the Everett-Moore Syndicate went into bankruptcy. The number of passengers increased from 55,378,918 in 1898 to 148,840,835 in 1908.

In 1909, the City of Detroit formed a "Committee of Fifty" to study transit needs and determine the valuation of the system. They recommended a subway be built, but the "Committee of Fifty" resigned in 1910 because they could not agree on the valuation of the system. Voters approved a Charter Amendment in 1913 for municipal ownership of the DUR. A Detroit Street Railway (DSR) Commission was created under that act on July 29, 1913, and its first members were John Dodge, Partner Dodge Brothers Motor Car Company; James Couzens, General Manager Ford Motor Company; and William Mahon, Vice-President of the American Federation of Labor. During 1915, a report of Detroit's transit needs by Barclay, Parsons, & Klapp was submitted to the DSR Commissioners, which recommended a 6-mile Woodward Avenue subway, eliminate through routings of lines, and add large trailer cars to make two-car trains. Although the subway was never built, the DUR separated the Fort line into two routes, the Michigan and Gratiot lines were separated, and purchased larger cars Nos. 3000–3099 during 1915–1917 and trailers Nos. 5000–5199 during 1915–1917. The city offered to purchase the DUR for $24.9 million on February 23, 1915. Although DUR directors and stockholders accepted the offer, the offer was withdrawn on March 31, 1915 because of newspaper concerns. Detroit Mayor James Couzens (Mayor from 1919–1922) won approval for his Municipal Operation (MO) plan, which began on February 1, 1921, under which new lines were built and 250 Birney trolley cars were purchased. On April 17, 1922, voters approved purchase of the DUR by the city, which resulted in the city taking over the system for $19,850,000 on May 15, 1922. Under city hall management, the system would favor buses, and streetcar service ended on April 8, 1956.

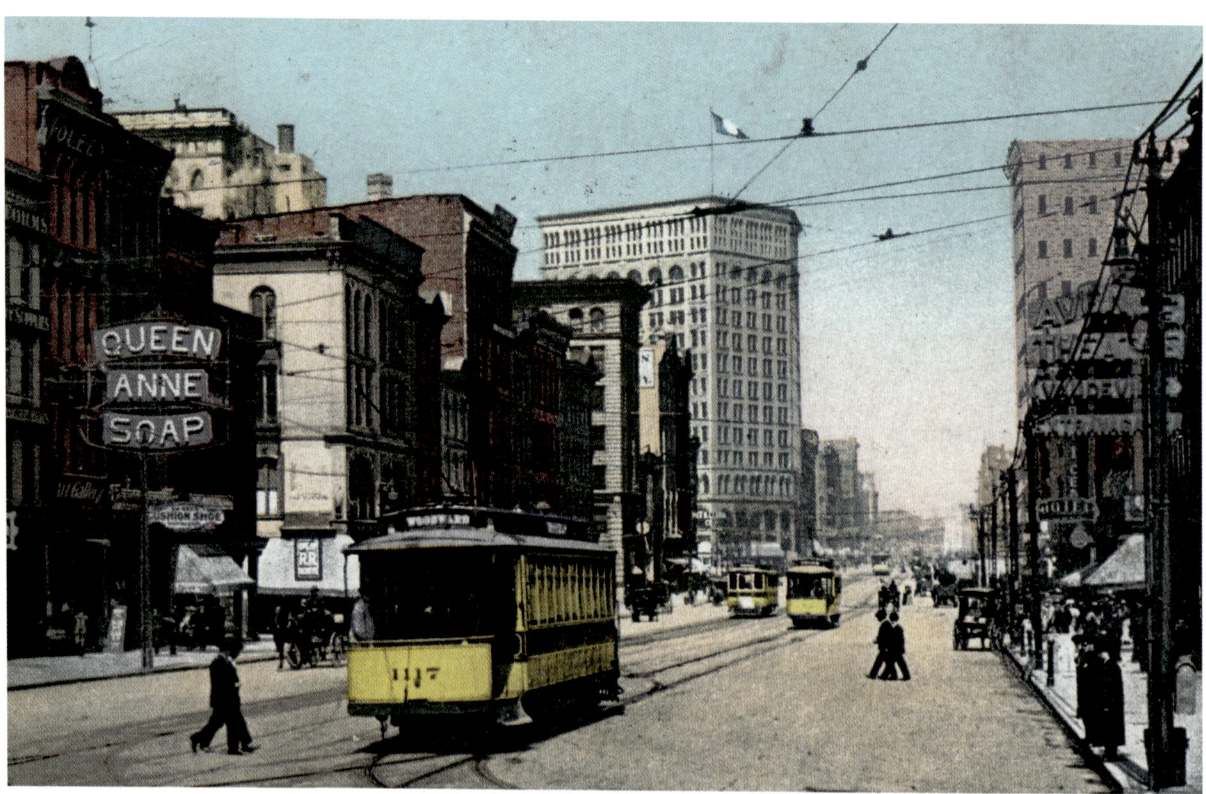

Above: Detroit United Railway (DUR) Company streetcar No. 1117 is northbound on Woodward Avenue at Congress Street in this postcard postmarked May 25, 1908. This was one of thirty-five cars, Nos. 1103–1137, built by J. G. Brill Company in 1904. Each car weighed 37,300 pounds and seated forty passengers. Behind the two distant streetcars in the center of the picture was the fourteen-story Majestic Building, designed by Daniel H. Burham & Company. The completed building, dedicated on October 4, 1896, required 3,000 tons of structural steel and iron, and more than 2 million bricks. The building closed on July 14, 1961. According to HistoricDetroit.org by Dan Austin, "The Majestic closed for good on July 14, 1961 when Butler's Shoes became the last tenant to move out." The building was demolished in 1962.

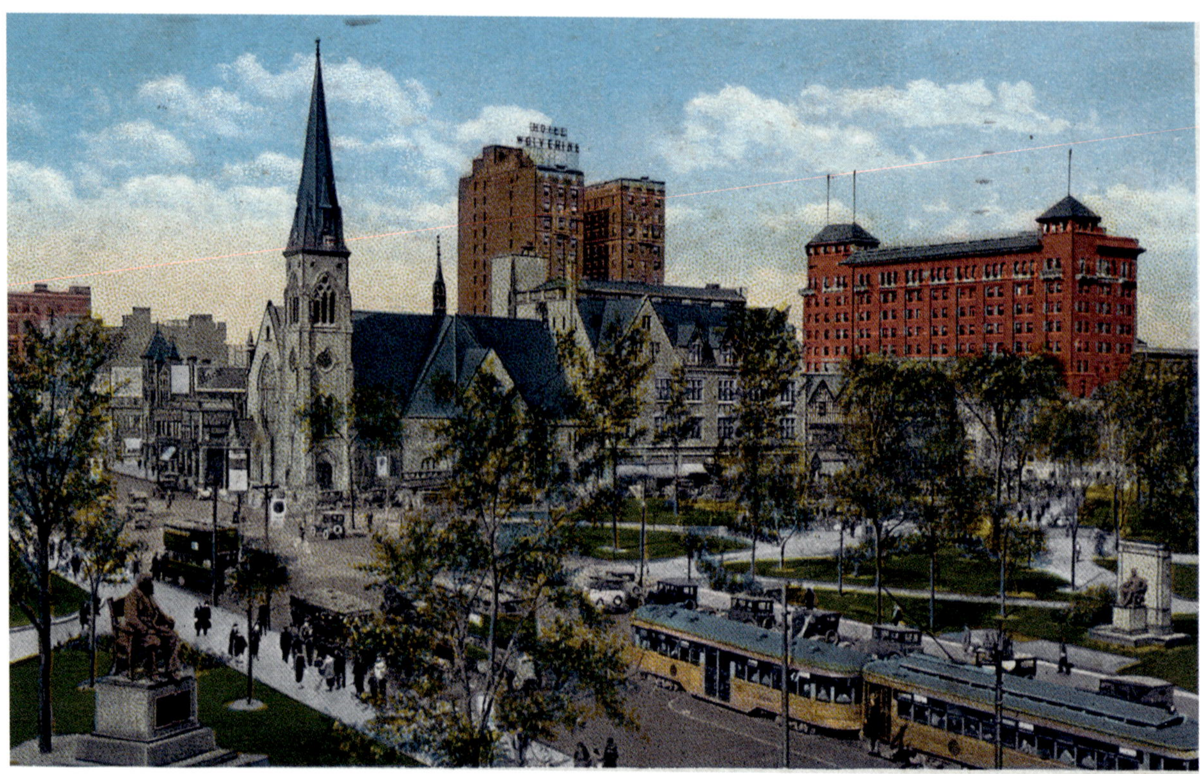

Previous page, below: A two-car DUR train of streetcars is southbound on Woodward Avenue with the Central United Methodist Church at East Adams Street, shown on the left side of the postcard postmarked June 17, 1938. The church was constructed in 1866 in a Tudor Revival architectural style characterized by its steeply pitched roof and Gothic architectural style characterized by its pointed windows and a sense of great height. It was designated a Michigan State Historic site in 1977 and listed on the National Register of Historic Places in 1982.

Right: The multistory Kresge building at the corner of Woodward Avenue and State Street in downtown Detroit is shown in this postcard postmarked August 18, 1914. Sebastian Spering Kresge along with J. G. McCory and Charles J. Wilson opened the first S. S. Kresge dime store in Detroit, and this store was served by numerous DUR streetcar lines.

Below: Three DUR streetcars are shown on Woodward at Gratiot Avenue and Farmer Street in front of the Detroit Public Library in this postcard postmarked September 11, 1912. The cornerstone was laid on May 29, 1875, and the excellent building was formally dedicated on January 22, 1877. This library housed 200,000 volumes and was accessible by frequent streetcar service.

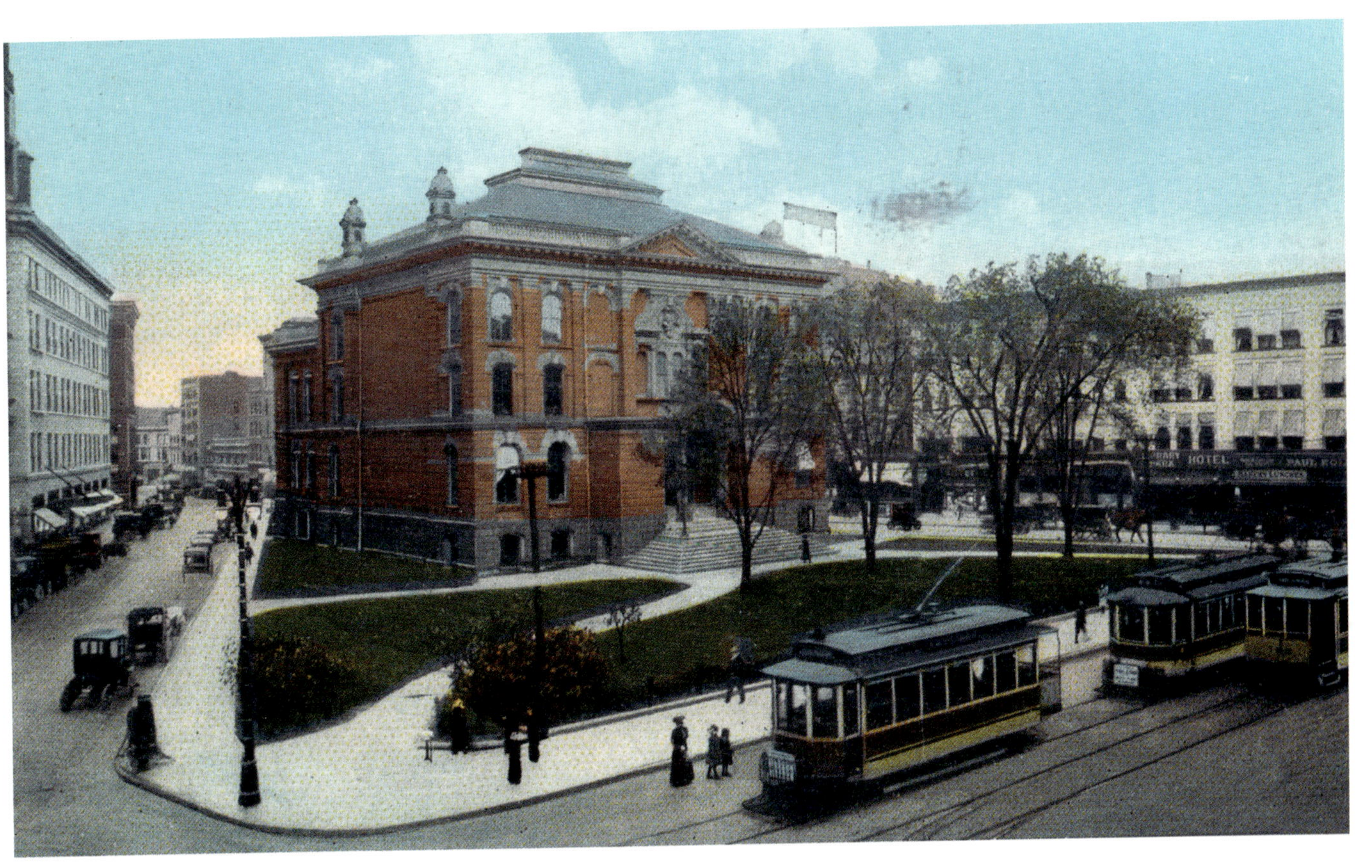

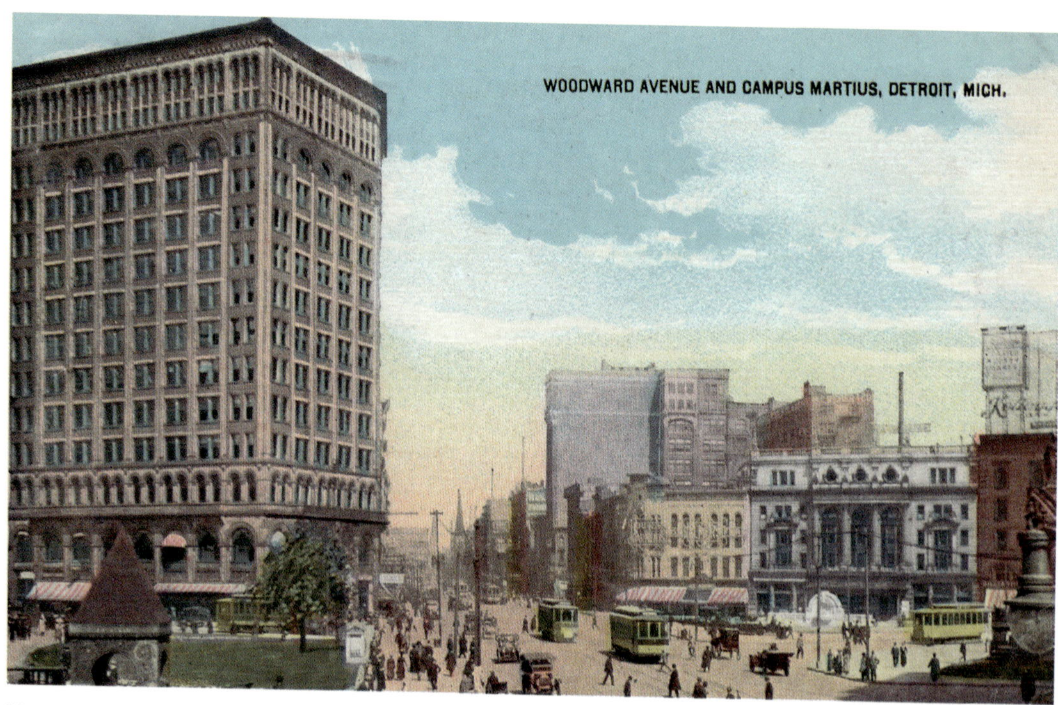

Numerous DUR streetcars are shown in this postcard postmarked July 11, 1917 on Woodward Avenue at the Campus Martius Park. This park is the point of origin of Detroit's coordinate system. For example, 7 miles north of this point is Seven Mile Road. On the left is the stunning Beaux-Arts-style (characterized by a flat roof, deep cornices, and arched windows), fourteen-story Majestic Building located at Woodward and Michigan Avenues that was dedicated on October 4, 1896 and closed on July 14, 1961. The building was demolished and replaced by the twenty-five-story First Federal Building, which opened in 1965.

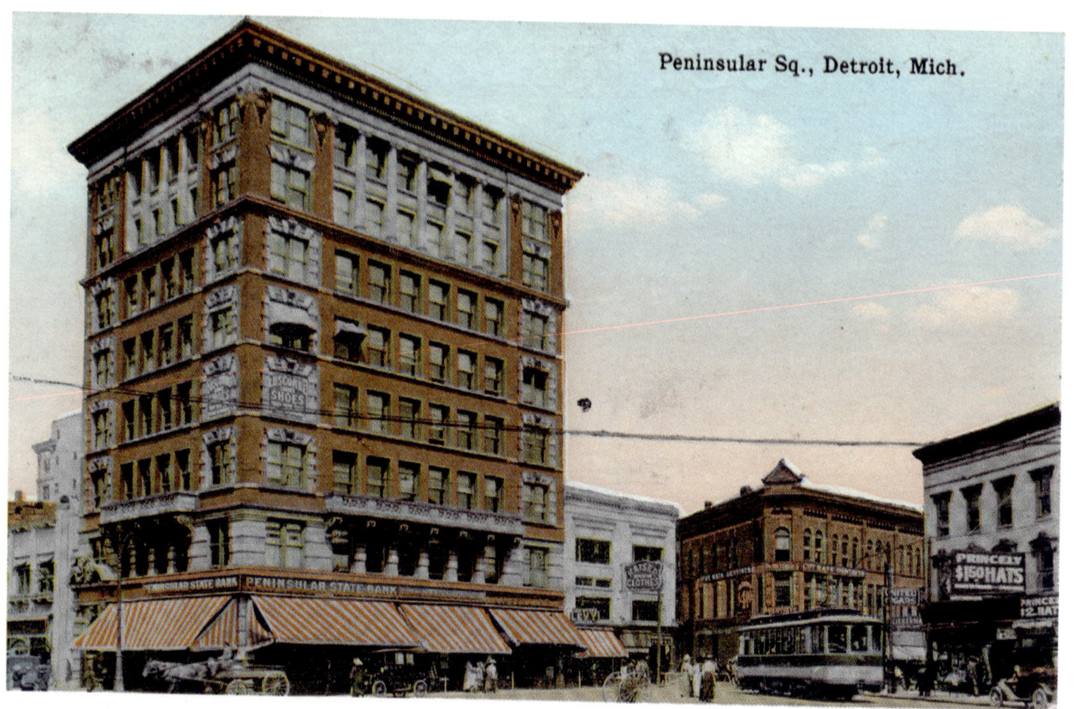

In this postcard postmarked February 1, 1915, a DUR streetcar is passing by the eight-story, red brick and cream terracotta, Beaux-Arts-style Breitmeyer-Tobin building, located on Broadway and Gratiot. This building was constructed in 1906 at a cost of $120,000 by John Breitmeyer & Sons. Under new ownership in 1926, the building was renamed the Peninsular State Bank Building. In 1941, the Peninsular State Bank went into receivership. After Benjamin Tobin acquired the building in 1944, the name was changed to the Tobin Building. In 2008, the building was sold to Beal Properties and became the Beal Building.

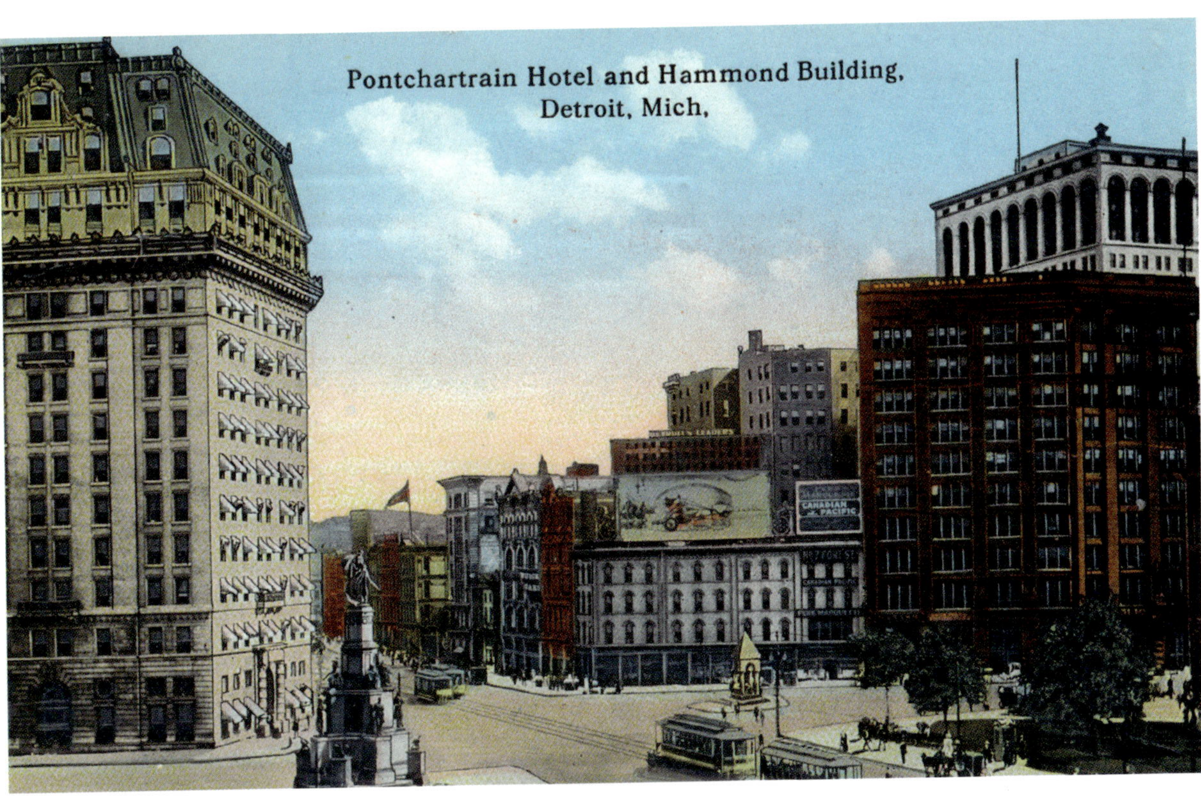

The ten-story luxurious Pontchartrain Hotel (opened on October 29, 1907 and demolished in 1920) on the southeast corner of Cadillac Square and Woodward Avenue is on the left, and the red stone and brick ten-story Hammond Building (the city's first skyscraper, completed in 1889 and demolished in 1956) on the southeast corner of Griswold Street and West Fort Street is on the right in this postcard postmarked August 7, 1914.

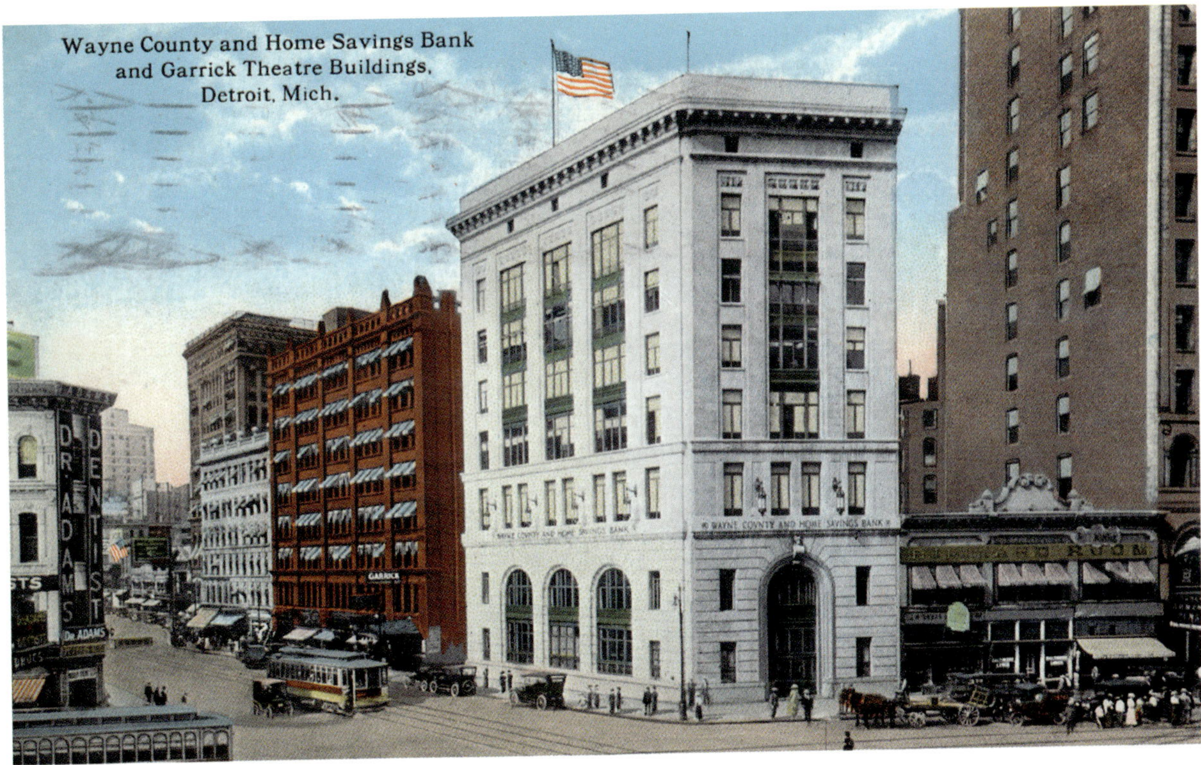

Two DUR streetcars are in this postcard scene around 1910, with the red brick Garrick Theatre (opened October 31, 1887, closed on August 11, 1938, and demolished in 1929) on Griswold Street and the white faced Wayne County and Home Savings Bank (opened December 20, 1915) at the corner of Griswold Street and Michigan Avenue.

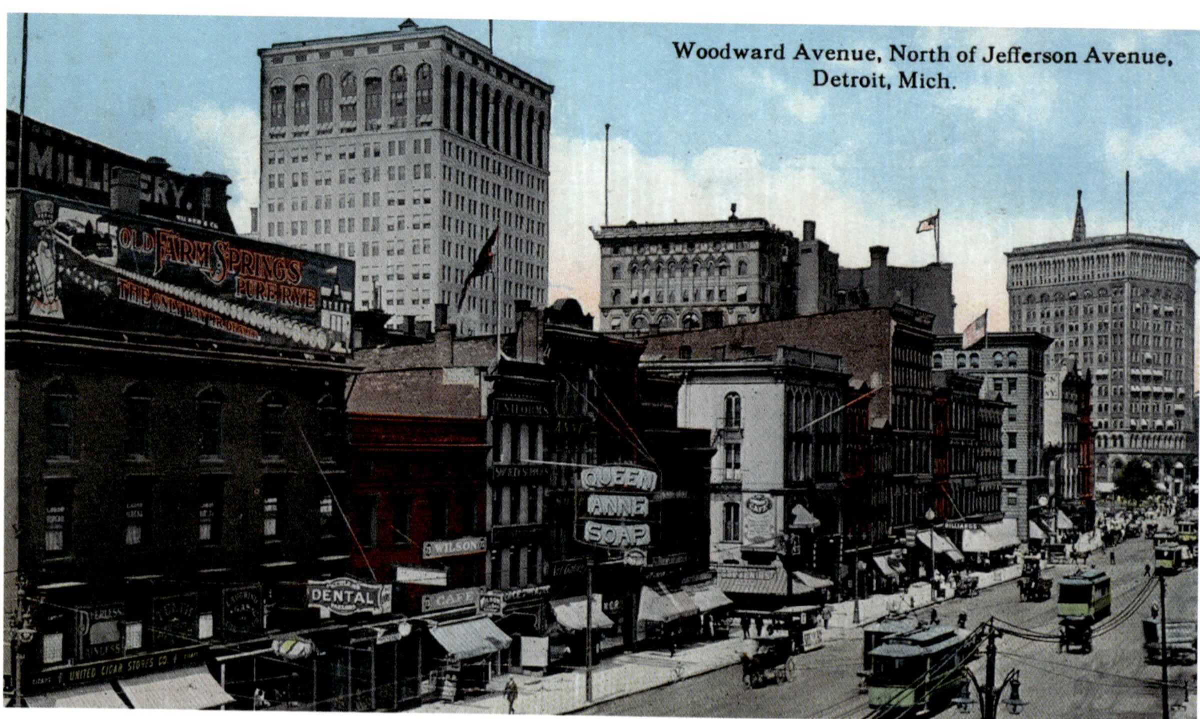

Many DUR streetcars are traversing Woodward Avenue north of Jefferson Avenue in this postcard postmarked August 26, 1912. Woodward Avenue, running northwest away from the Detroit River, was named for Judge Augustus Brevoort Woodward who had been appointed territorial judge in Michigan Territory after the 1805 Detroit fire. Woodward laid out a vision for Detroit, including the roadway that was later named after him.

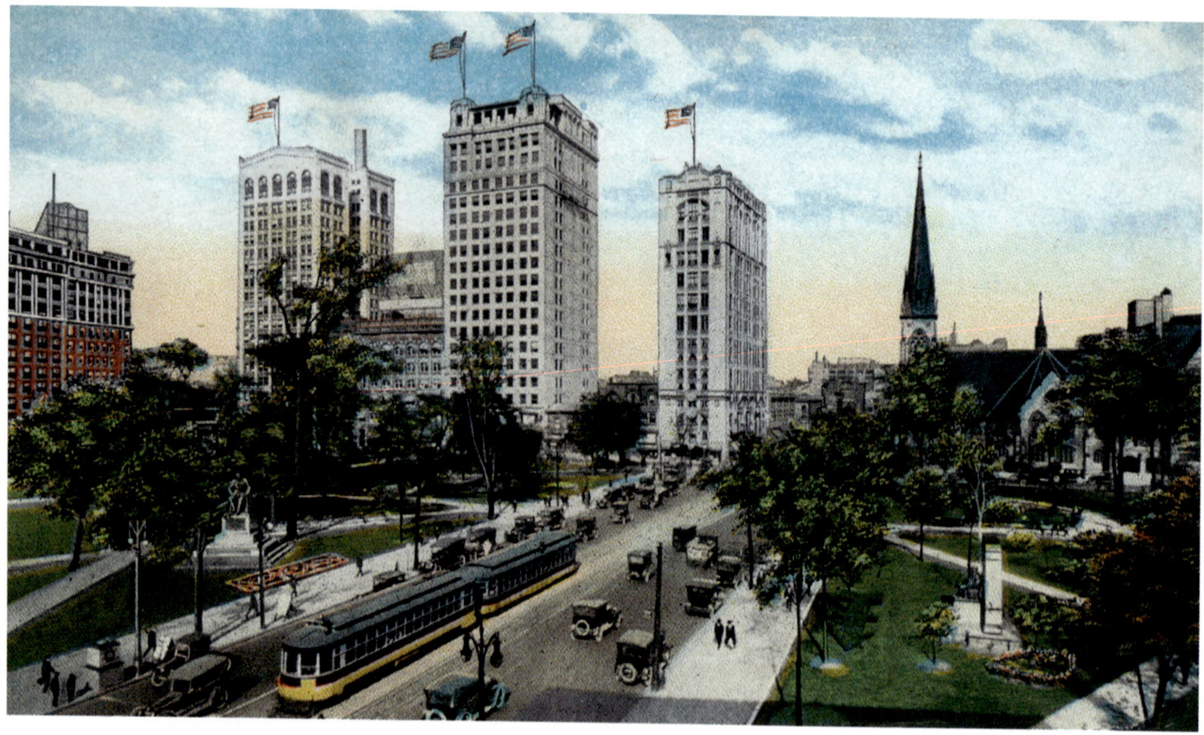

A two-car train of streetcars is on Woodward Avenue at Grand Circus Park and Adams Avenue in this postcard scene postmarked May 2, 1923. *From left to right*: The building with the United States flag is the eighteen-story, white-bricked Kales Building that was once the S. S. Kresge headquarters and became a 119 residential apartment complex in 2004; the middle tall building with the two flags was once the headquarters of the Stroh Brewery Company; at the corner of Adams Street and Woodward Avenue, the building with one flag on the roof is the Fyfe Building, named after Richard H. Fyfe who had a large shoe store on the first floor; and the Central United Methodist Church steeple is on the right side of the postcard.

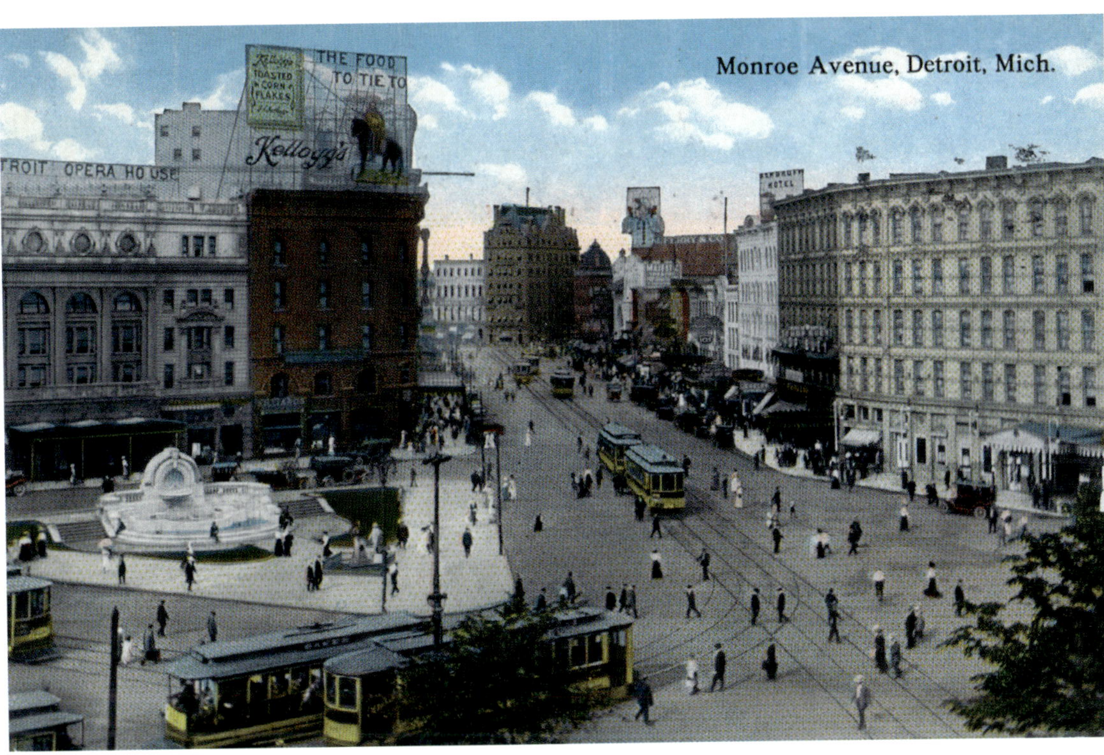

Two DUR streetcars are passing on Cadillac Square, while several streetcars are on Monroe Avenue in this postcard postmarked April 2 1916. On the left is the second Detroit Opera House. A fire destroyed the first opera house and central business district on October 7, 1897. The opera house was rebuilt and reopened on September 12, 1898. Monroe Avenue, originally Detroit's amusement thoroughfare, is in the center of the postcard view.

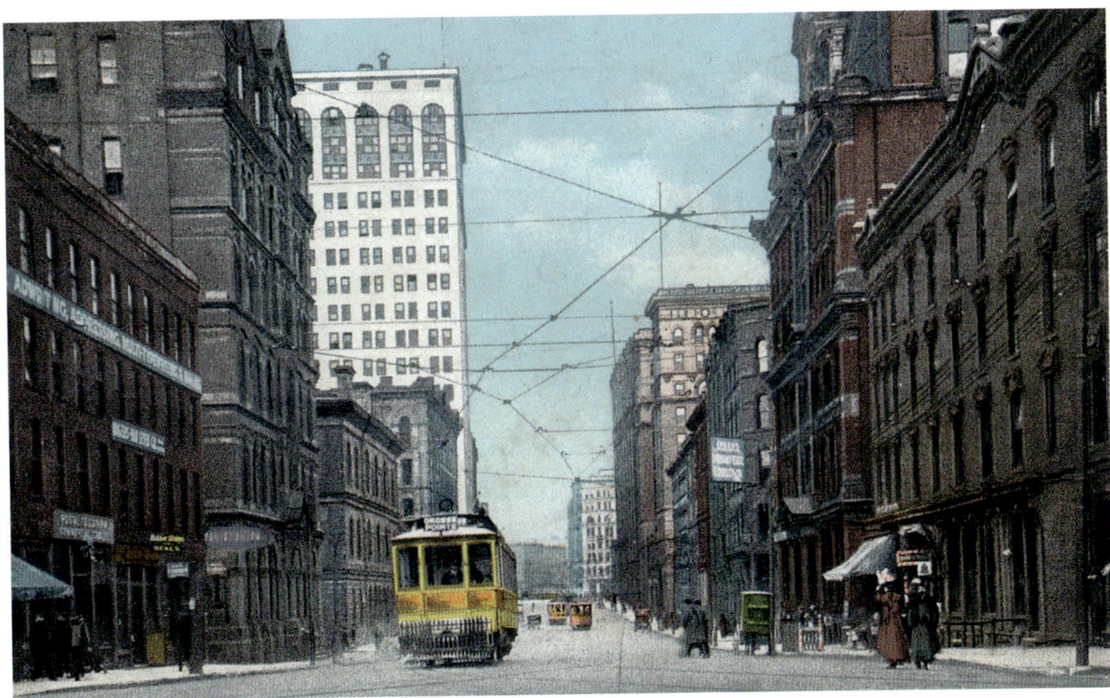

A streetcar is on Griswold Street, signed for Grosse Pointe, in this postcard scene around 1915. Griswold Street, a major north–south street, passes through Detroit's financial center. The white terracotta nineteen-story building behind the streetcar is the Ford Building, designed by architect Daniel H. Burnham. It was completed in 1908. By 1990, the Ford Building had deteriorated, and its occupancy rate declined to 38 percent. On April 11, 1991, the building was put up for auction. Tom Paglia Jr., real estate lawyer and golf course investor, submitted the only bid of $1.35 million, which was accepted. The building has been restored.

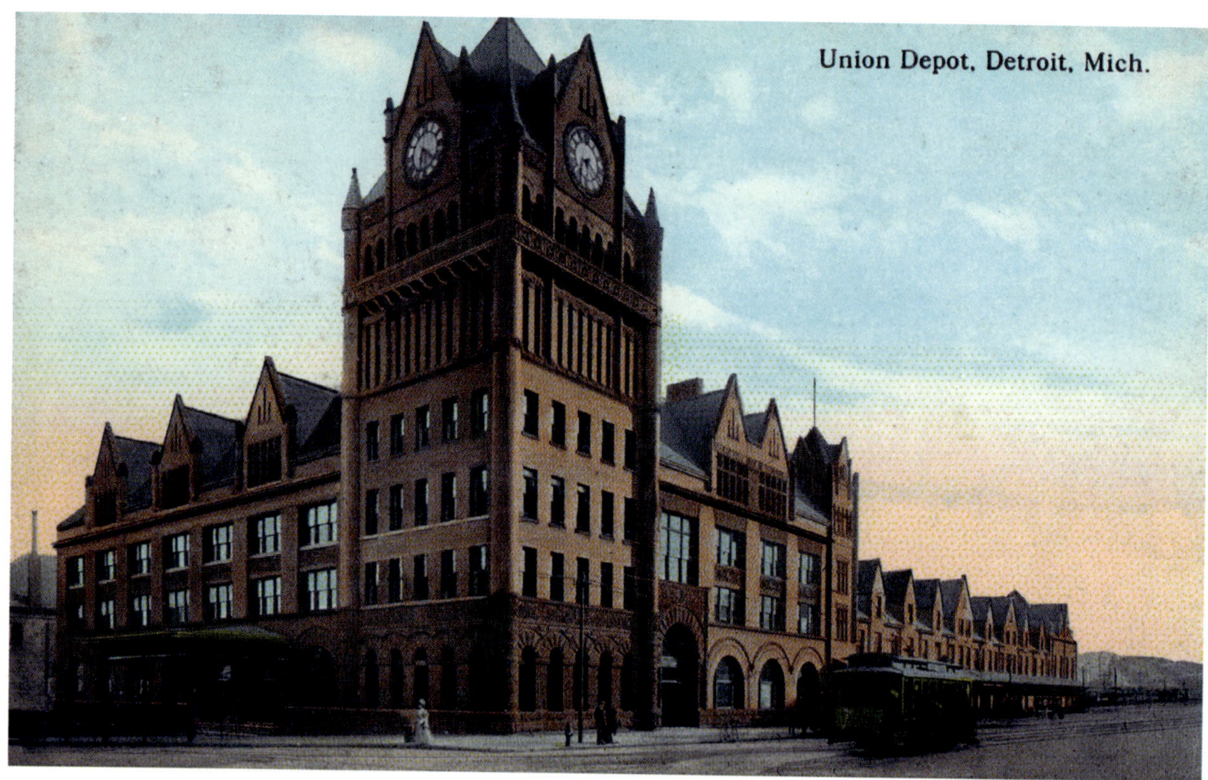

Located at the corner of Fort and Third Streets, the Union Depot (with its Romanesque Revival architectural style, characterized by arches over windows and entranceways plus thick masonry walls) is the location of a DUR streetcar in this postcard postmarked June 11, 1914. The station was opened on January 21, 1893. It was used by the Pennsylvania Railroad, Pere Marquette Railway, Baltimore & Ohio Railroad, and Wabash Railroad. Dwindling ridership resulted in the closure of the station on April 30, 1971, and it was demolished in January 1974.

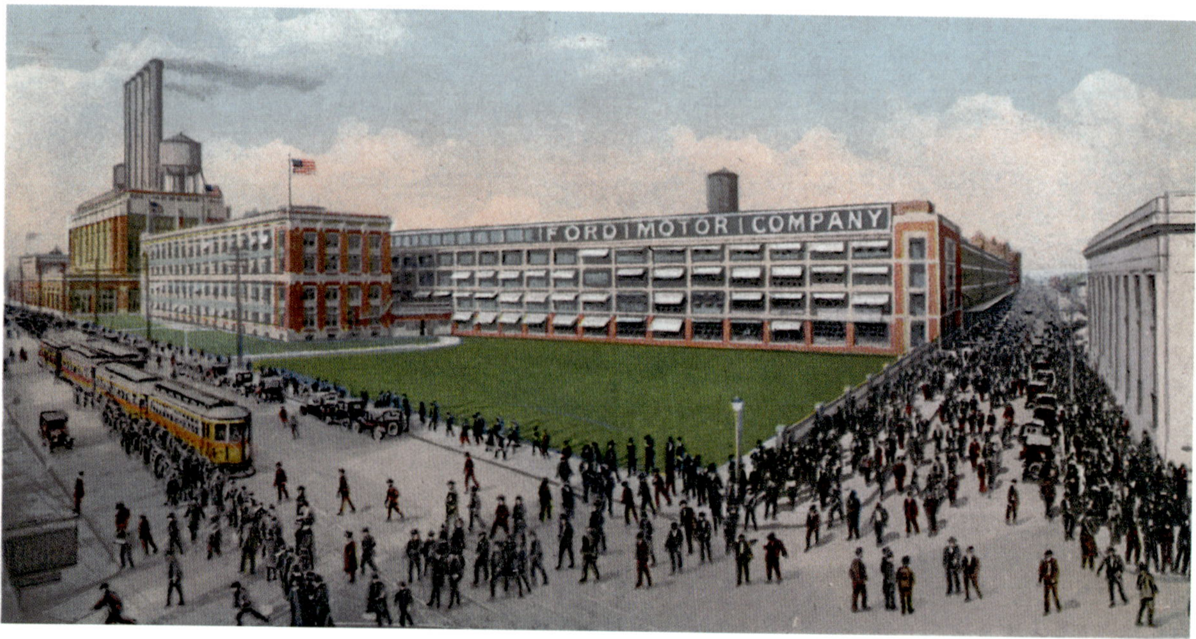

Four DUR streetcars are at the Highland Park Ford Motor Company Plant located at Manchester Avenue and Woodward Avenue in Highland Park, Michigan, in this postcard scene around 1920. On January 1, 1910, the Ford Motor Company shifted operations to the Highland Park Plant. Most of the employees traveled to and from the plant by streetcar. By December 1, 1913, a continuously moving assemble line went into operation that reduced the assembly time of a completed automobile from 728 minutes to ninety-three minutes. Model T automobile sales increased from 5,986 in 1908 at $850 each to over 1 million in 1924 at $260 each. That was one of the factors that ultimately contributed to the decline in streetcar ridership.

1

Detroit Street Railways History

When the Detroit Department of Street Railways (DSR) began municipal ownership and operation of all streetcar lines with the city on May 15, 1922, it was the first large United States city to own and operate its public transit system. The Detroit Street Railway (DSR) Commission, formed on July 29, 1913, made high level policy decisions. Commissioners, appointed by the Mayor, were civic leaders and were not required to be street railway experts. The DSR operated 1,457 cars on 363 miles of track with twelve car houses and 4,000 employees. Only fifty of the 250 Birney cars that had been delivered in 1921 were retained. The long conflict between the city and DUR resulted in minimal track maintenance. With the concern that the city would set a low price for the streetcar system when it was taken over by the city, the DUR refrained from making major investments.

In the push for municipal ownership, promises were made to extend transit lines into new areas. However, the increased costs of building new streetcar lines and improvements in bus manufacture shifted from extending streetcar lines to extending bus lines. A World War I ordinance plant on Lynch Road had been served by a new DUR streetcar line. After the war ended, ridership declined, streetcar service was discontinued in October 1921, and the trackage was removed. The ordinance plant became the Dodge Export plant, and DSR opened its first bus line on November 19, 1922 on Lynch Road to serve it; however, charging a 5-cent fare with no transfers, DSR could not make the line profitable, and Detroit Motorbus took over the line on November 23, 1923. Trackage was relaid, and streetcar service was restored on November 8, 1924. DSR opened its first permanent bus line on January 1, 1925 as an extension of the Mack streetcar line operating from Hart loop to the Detroit city limits at Cadieux Road. As a hint of the future, Detroit City Councilman Fred Castator expressed concern over DSR policy favoring buses over streetcars, noting in a January 18, 1927 letter to Detroit Mayor John W. Smith that although 60 percent of passengers rode streetcars, about $2 million had gone into a competing bus system.

Another area of concern was jitney service, which began in Detroit in 1922. By November 15, 1921, Detroit had 1,424 licensed jitneys. On October 24, 1928, the DSR obtained a ruling from the Michigan Supreme Court allowing the city to remove jitney operators from the streets. With jitneys carrying an estimated 80,000 passengers daily, the Michigan Supreme Court on October 24, 1928 reaffirmed its ordinance prohibiting jitney operation and leaders of two associations representing the majority of jitneys ordered jitney service to cease on October 26, 1928. DSR had 100 additional streetcars available for this decision, plus had on loan twenty-five buses from the American Car Foundry in advance of the twenty-five buses on order. Additional sixteen-passenger parlor motor coaches (buses) were ordered, with General Motors Corporation providing forty and Dodge-Graham providing 120.

The 1929 stock market crash severely hit Detroit, with large numbers of workers out of a job with no place to go, resulting in a dramatic decline in DSR ridership from 396,454,184 in 1929 to 189,674,348 in 1933. Plans for a 33 percent fare increase from 6 cents to 8 cents, effective from March 1, 1930, met with such massive public opposition that fares remained unchanged through the depression and World War II. In 1932, DSR reduced salaries by 50 percent. Service reductions were made that resulted in layoffs of motormen, conductors, and car house employees. On June 27, 1933, the DSR and the City of Detroit began a bond refunding program whereby $8,255,000 in bonds that were scheduled to mature between February 14, 1935 and June 30, 1935 were refinanced to mature in 1950 without changing the interest rate. Many employees voluntarily reduced their work week from seven to six days or from six to five days. Government funding became available to create jobs for unemployed workers during the depression. One project resulted in the installation of a rear door on thirty-eight Peter Witt type streetcars to speed up unloading. This required an additional lever that was controlled by the conductor. The United States Government established a Civil Works Administration (CWA), under which the DSR received financial assistance in 1934 to overhaul and repaint 500 streetcars, upgrade seating on eighty-seven streetcars, plus overhauled trucks and motors on 624 streetcars. It should be noted that most of the shop employees were hired by DUR and had a tradition of quality workmanship.

The Depression, which had been gradually easing, became worse in 1937, and effective from March 28, 1938, the Crosstown, Mount Elliott, and Fort-Kercheval streetcar lines had buses substituted for streetcars from 7 p.m. to 4 a.m. on weekdays and Saturdays, and all day on Sundays and holidays. This occurred because of the union's unwillingness to use one-man cars on night and Sunday runs. While the buses were one-man operated, in the first several years of DSR operation, all of the streetcars except the Birney cars were two-man operated. The first one-man Peter Witt car, No. 3386, was placed into service on the Northwest Belt line on July 22, 1924 and nine more Peter Witt cars were converted to one-man operation. With looming large-scale layoffs because of the Depression, the union took a stand against one-man streetcars. Scotten line streetcar service was discontinued on March 20, 1933. By 1939, the same rail/bus service was used on twenty streetcar lines. Three streetcar lines were completely converted to bus operation: Myrtle on October 11, 1937; Van Dyke on February 14, 1938; and West Jefferson on April 23, 1938. While the Myrtle and Van Dyke lines were lightly used Birney car lines, the West Jefferson line could have been a viable streetcar line according to an October 31, 1937 report, which showed the line was operating at a $1,300 loss with two-man operation, but under a one-man operation, it would have shown a $25,000 profit. That same report showed a $1,400 loss as a one-man bus operation, requiring twenty buses, seating twenty-five passengers, to replace the twelve streetcars. A major sewer-related pavement collapse contributed to its conversion to bus operation. The East Lafayette line, which operated the system's last Birney cars, was converted to bus operation on February 28, 1939. In 1940, only the Woodmere, Michigan, and Baker lines remained with 100 percent streetcar operation. A 1940 DSR Commission report noted that while the percentage of one-man cars was 0.5 percent in Cleveland and 2.3 percent in Detroit, it was 51.3 percent in Philadelphia, 91.4 percent in Boston, and 100 percent in Pittsburgh and Buffalo.

In an October 25, 1938 report to the DSR Commission, General Manager Fred Nolan (who had risen rapidly through the ranks from a clerk checking cement bags in the storage yards becoming Acting General Manager on January 16, 1934 and full General Manager in June 1934) did not recommend the purchase of Presidents' Conference Committee (PCC) cars because they would have required major expenditures for roadway and maintenance equipment; additionally, he felt that the DSR streetcar system would disappear long before the fifteen years needed to amortize the investment in PCC cars. In the years before World War II, no new streetcars were purchased. One new car (No. 401, the "Blue Streak") was built in the shops, with parts and equipment from scrapped Birney cars. It went into service on October 31, 1934 on the Woodmere line. The car was not deemed satisfactory, and no additional streetcars of this type were built. In contrast, in the three years ending June 24, 1937, DSR purchased 847 buses seating twenty-one to twenty-five passengers and thirty-two buses seating forty passengers.

When the United States entered World War II, the government ordered that lines served by joint rail-bus operation would revert back to only streetcar operation. Many of the out of service older cars were back in the shops for rehabilitation. As cars became available, joint rail-bus lines went back to 100 percent streetcar operation. Ridership increased from 189,151,678 for the year ending June 30, 1941 to 377,699,295 for the year ending June 30, 1945. Both the shop employees, maintaining streetcars to handle the huge increase in riding, and the women, hired to serve as conductors and car operators, did an excellent job during the war years.

After World War II ended on September 2, 1945 with the surrender of Japan, Detroit transit riding remained high; however, as automobile production increased, public transit riding declined. Recognizing that the existing streetcar fleet needed to be replaced, the DSR ordered two Presidents' Conference Committee (PCC) cars, Nos. 100 and 101, from the St. Louis Car Company in August 1945, and they were delivered in September 1945. These were actually part of Pittsburgh Railways Company's 1600 series cars that were diverted to Detroit. Detroit Mayor Edward Jefferies appointed a board to study and provide solutions for Detroit's transportation needs. The board's February 1945 report recommended a network of radial expressways plus a crosstown superhighway. The center section of each new road would have a high speed rail line operated by multiple unit streetcars. Some of the existing streetcar lines would be converted to trackless trolley operation. Streetcars and trackless trolleys would enter a subway at the edge of the central business district and come to a new underground Cadillac Square terminal. While miles of expressways were built, the rail lines and downtown subway were never built. The Oakman car line, operating from the Ford Highland Park plant to Dearborn (Michigan Avenue), was the first streetcar line after World War II to be converted to bus operation on December 9, 1945. DSR issued its own report in November 1946, calling for high-speed bus routes operating on expressways that would terminate in four new off-street underground terminals in downtown Detroit. The report proposed the purchase of eighty PCC cars for the Woodward line, and all of the other lines would be converted to bus operation. Buses became trapped in expressway traffic and became slower than most of the local bus routes. The Hamilton line was converted to bus operation on April 28, 1947.

On December 18, 1946, the DSR Commission approved the discontinuance of the Grand River Avenue streetcar line based on DSR General Manager Richard Sullivan's presentation that the state and city planned to repave Grand River Avenue; the need to rebuild the terminal to accommodate more buses; and the fact that express buses and streetcars operating on Grand River Avenue resulted in an expensive duplication of service as well as an inefficient use of street space. Detroit City Council approved a four-month trial period of bus service on Grand River Avenue, and the DSR was required to retain the rail facilities in case a decision was made to reinstate streetcar service. Buses replaced the Grand River Avenue streetcars on May 5, 1947. The city began paving over the track that day, and streetcar service never resumed on the Grand River Avenue line.

On June 23, 1947, the street operator's union approved the use of one-man cars, contingent on a pay increase and that no employees with twenty or more years of service would be affected. Between May and August 1947, St. Louis Car Company delivered thirty-nine PCC cars (Nos. 102–140) followed by another thirty-nine PCC cars (Nos. 142–180), which were delivered between August and October 1947. Buses replaced streetcars on the Crosstown and Harper lines on October 26, 1947, which allowed the city to change portions of Forest and Warren Avenues to one-way traffic. On June 24, 1948, buses replaced Grand Belt streetcars. On July 18, 1948, route Fourteenth streetcars were replaced by the Linwood bus and route Woodmere streetcars were replaced by the West Jefferson and Springwells shuttle buses. At a cost of $2.7 million, 106 PCC cars (Nos. 181–286) were ordered from the St. Louis Car Company in April 1949. PCC car No. 181, the first car received in late August 1949, appeared in a Labor Day parade. The remaining PCC cars were received before the end of October 1949. Even with the arrival of new PCC cars, the Fort (Westside) line was converted to bus operation on June 23, 1949 followed by Charlevoix on July 17, 1949, and Kercheval on December 15, 1949. On January 15, 1950, one-man operated PCC cars entered service, with the issues over one-man operation resolved. The Gratiot and Michigan lines were consolidated on November 13, 1950.

The 1951 report of the Transportation Survey Department of the General Motors Corporation, Truck and Coach Division recommended that 148 high-capacity, fifty-one passenger General Motors Corporation diesel buses be acquired to convert the Trumbull, Mack, Clairmount, Oakland, and Mt. Elliott lines with the one man Peter Witt cars released from these routes replacing the two-man Peter Witt cars on the Baker line. Following a two-month-long strike of operating, employees in the first half of 1951, buses took over the Mt. Elliott, Oakland, and Trumbull lines on June 19, 1951, followed by Clairmount on July 29, 1951, and Mack on November 11, 1951. The changeover of these five lines to bus operation resulted in the scrapping of 106 Peter Witt cars, three snow sweepers, and one money car. With the deterioration of the Baker line requiring an estimated $1 million for repairs, the DSR Commission approved on February 26, 1952 to convert the Baker line to bus operation, which occurred on April 6, 1952.

Only three streetcar lines remained: Jefferson, Gratiot-Michigan, and Woodward. The last use of Peter Witt cars was in tripper service for the 1953 Christmas season. On February 7, 1954, streetcars made their final runs on the Jefferson line, with thirty-two PCC cars transferred to the remaining two lines. The Michigan section of the Gratiot-Michigan line made its last streetcar run on September 7, 1955.

On March 25, 1956, at 4:40 a.m., Department of Street Railways (DSR) PCC car No. 210 completed the final regular service run on the Gratiot line. The last streetcar line in the city of Detroit and the state of Michigan was Woodward, which completed its last regular service run when PCC car No. 233 pulled into the Woodward carbarn at 5:56 a.m. on April 8, 1956. Later that day, DSR sponsored a parade of twenty-four PCC streetcars, carrying about 2,000 passengers. The last car in that parade (PCC No. 237) pulled into the carbarn around 5:30 p.m. DSR sold 150 PCC cars to Mexico City for $4,000 and the final thirty-three PCC cars for $3,000 each. For each car, the contract required the car body to be repaired and painted inside and exterior; clean, repair, and test the electrical equipment; check and re-machine wheels where necessary; lubricate the car; and conduct a running test. Each car was wired to enable reverse operation. An inspector from Mexico conducted a rigorous inspection on each car, which sometimes resulted in extensive rework. The last PCC car (No. 185) was shipped to Mexico City on July 19, 1956. With the amount of rehabilitation needed underestimated, DSR absorbed $500 costs per car in repairing the cars for Mexico City.

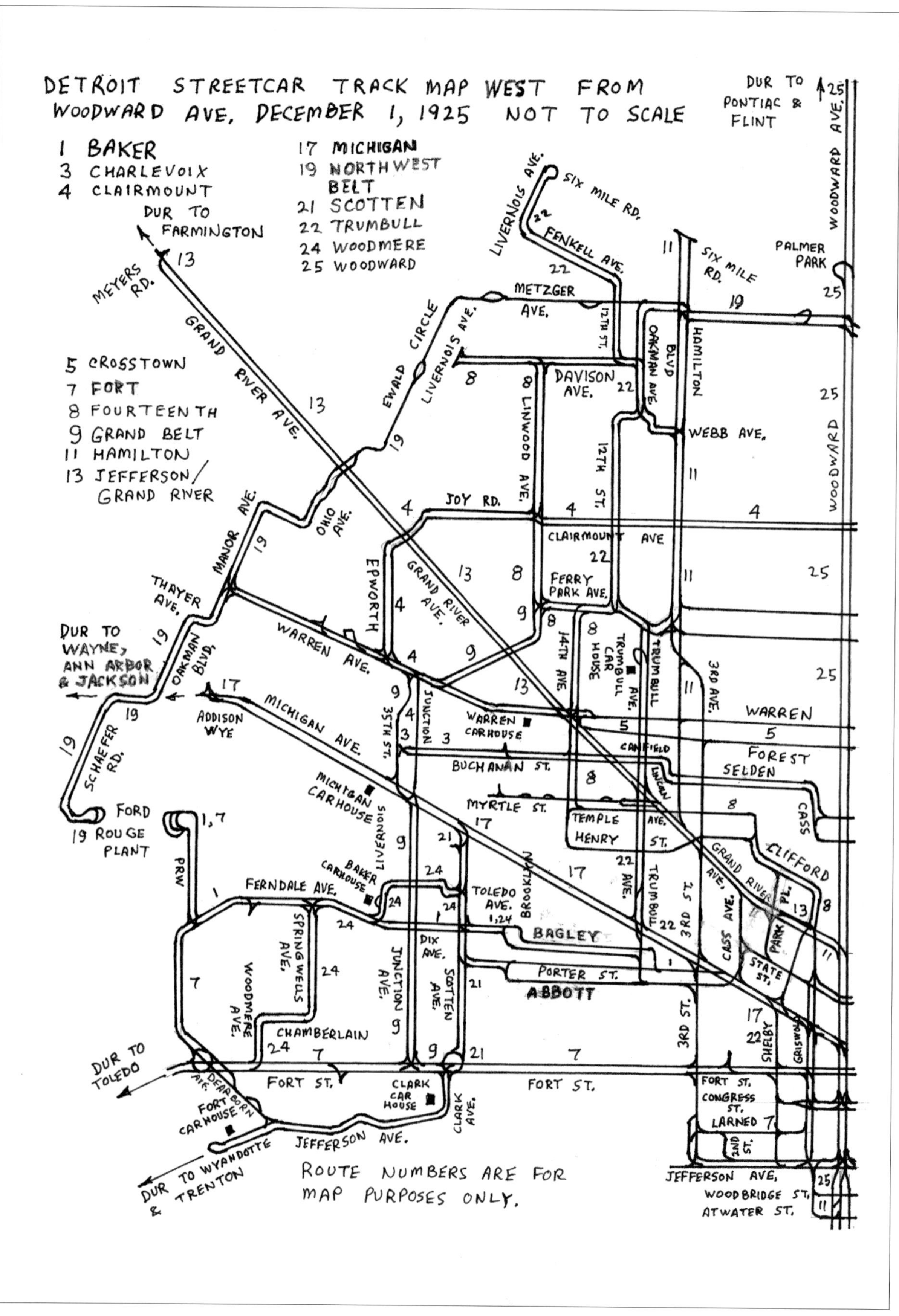

This map shows Detroit Department of Street Railway track on December 1, 1925, west from Woodward Avenue. The route numbers are for map purposes.

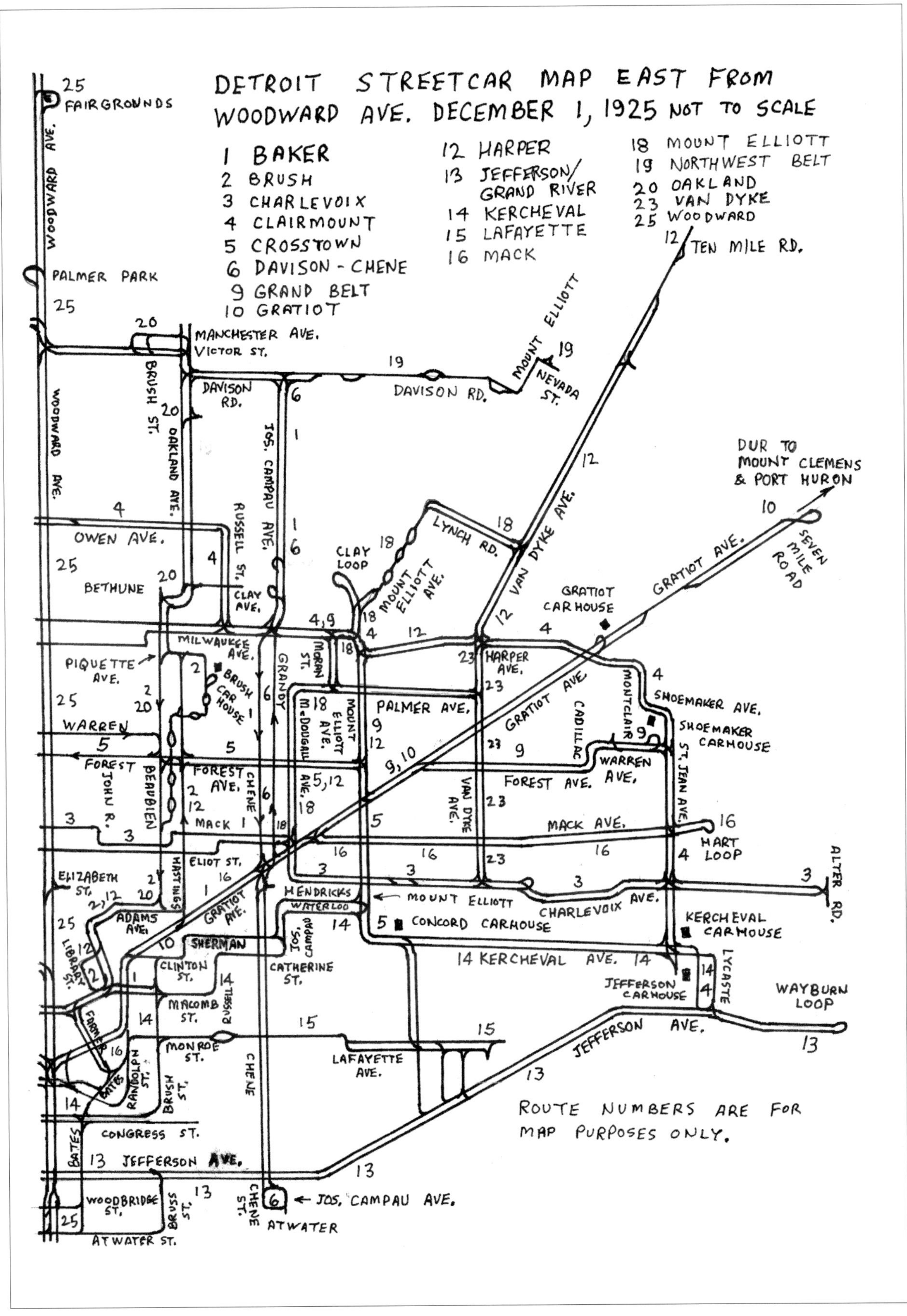

This map shows Detroit Department of Street Railway track on December 1, 1925, east from Woodward Avenue. The route numbers are for map purposes.

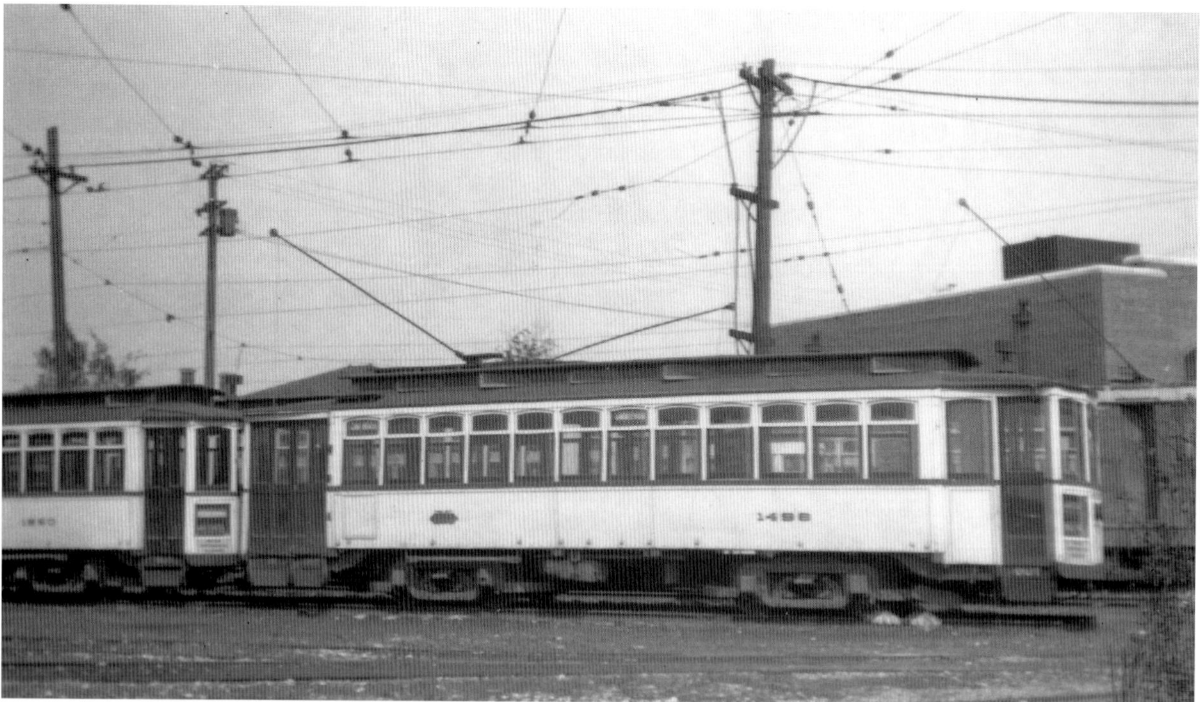

On September 8, 1937, Detroit Department of Street Railway (DSR) car No. 1498 (one of fifty cars, Nos. 1475–1524, built by G. C. Kuhlman Car Company in 1912 and powered by two General Electric type 210 motors) and car No. 1650 (one of fifty cars, Nos. 1650–1699, built by G. C. Kuhlman Car Company in 1910 and powered by two Westinghouse type 310 motors) are at the East Jefferson car house. In 1937, DSR operated over 1,300 streetcars, housed in seven car houses: Baker, Coolidge, East Jefferson, Gratiot, Shoemaker, Woodward, and Wyoming. (*Bob Crockett photograph—Clifford R. Scholes collection*)

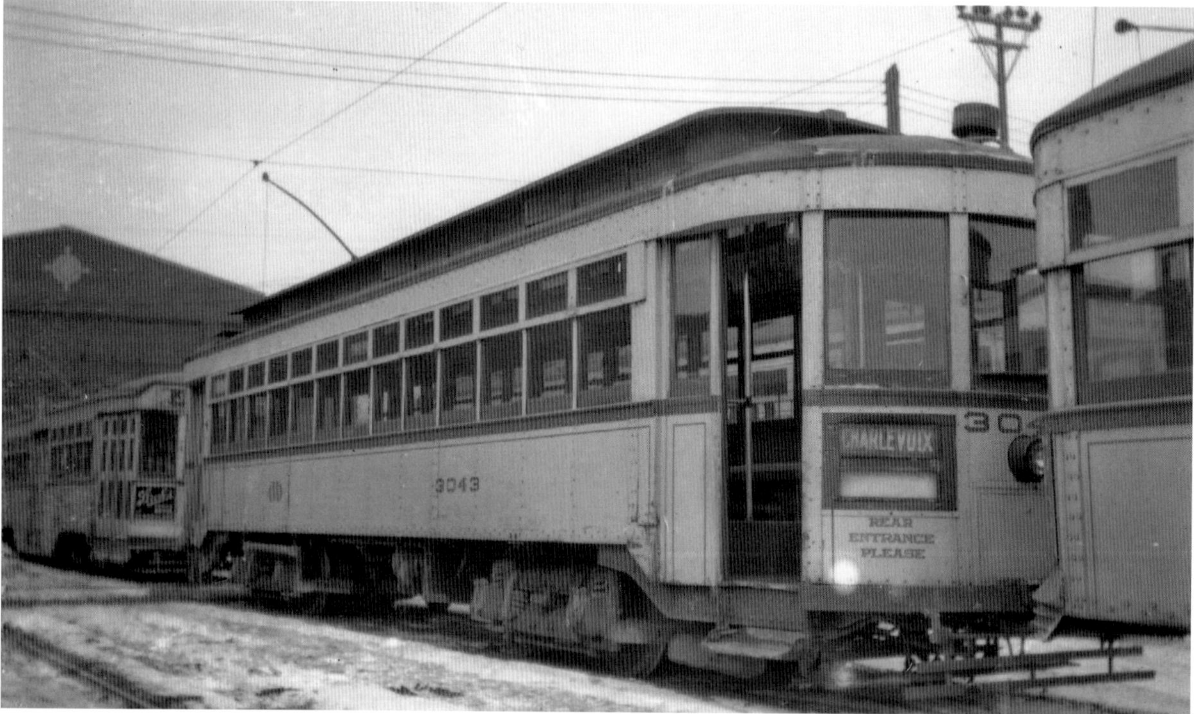

The East Jefferson car house on East Jefferson Avenue and St. Jean Street is the location of car No. 3043, in the lineup with other cars on January 28, 1939. Powered by four General Electric type 203L motors, this was one of twenty-five cars (Nos. 3025–3049) built by G. C. Kuhlman Car Company and delivered in 1916. Each car weighed 48,000 pounds and seated forty-six passengers. The East Jefferson car house opened in 1904 and closed on September 5, 1951, with cars moved to Gratiot car house. (*Bob Crockett photograph—Clifford R. Scholes collection*)

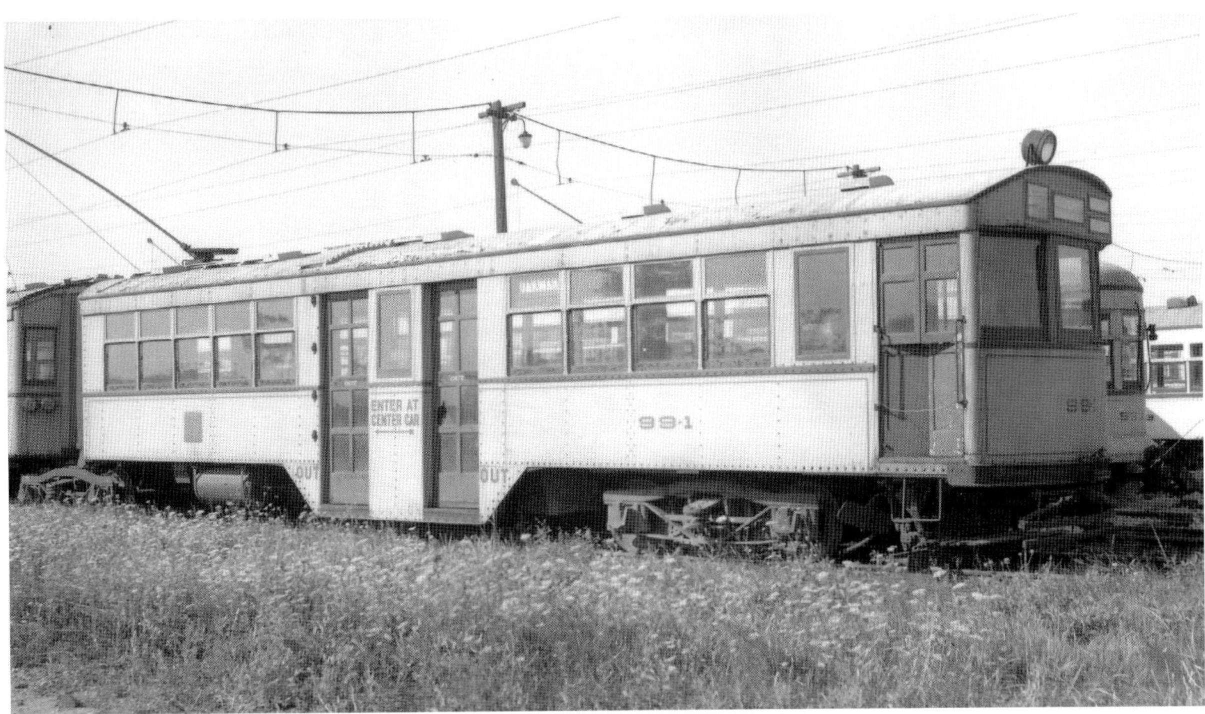

DSR articulated car No. 99-1 is waiting for the next assignment at the Highland Park–Woodward car house on October 17, 1939. This was one of three articulated trains, originally numbered 5000–5002, built by Cincinnati Car Company and delivered in 1923. The cars were later numbered 4000–4002 and renumbered 99-1, 99-2, and 99-3. Each train was powered by four General Electric type 275 motors, weighed 75,000 pounds, and seated 134 passengers. (*Bob Crockett photograph—Clifford R. Scholes collection*)

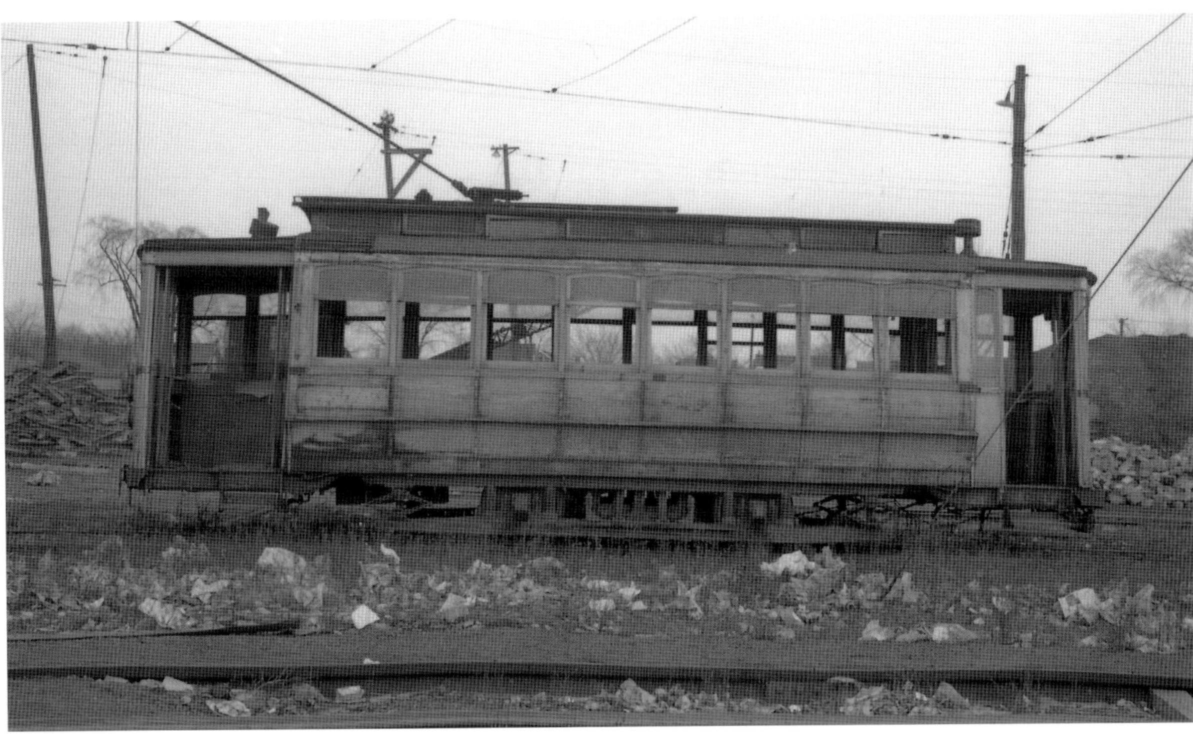

Rail grinder car No. X-37 is at the Coolidge car house on December 8, 1946. Built by American Car Company in 1912, the car was powered by two General Electric type 203 motors and weighed 27,700 pounds. The car was originally passenger car No. 927 and seated twenty-eight passengers. It was rebuilt by DSR in 1926, and was retired in 1947. (*Bob Crockett photograph—Clifford R. Scholes collection*)

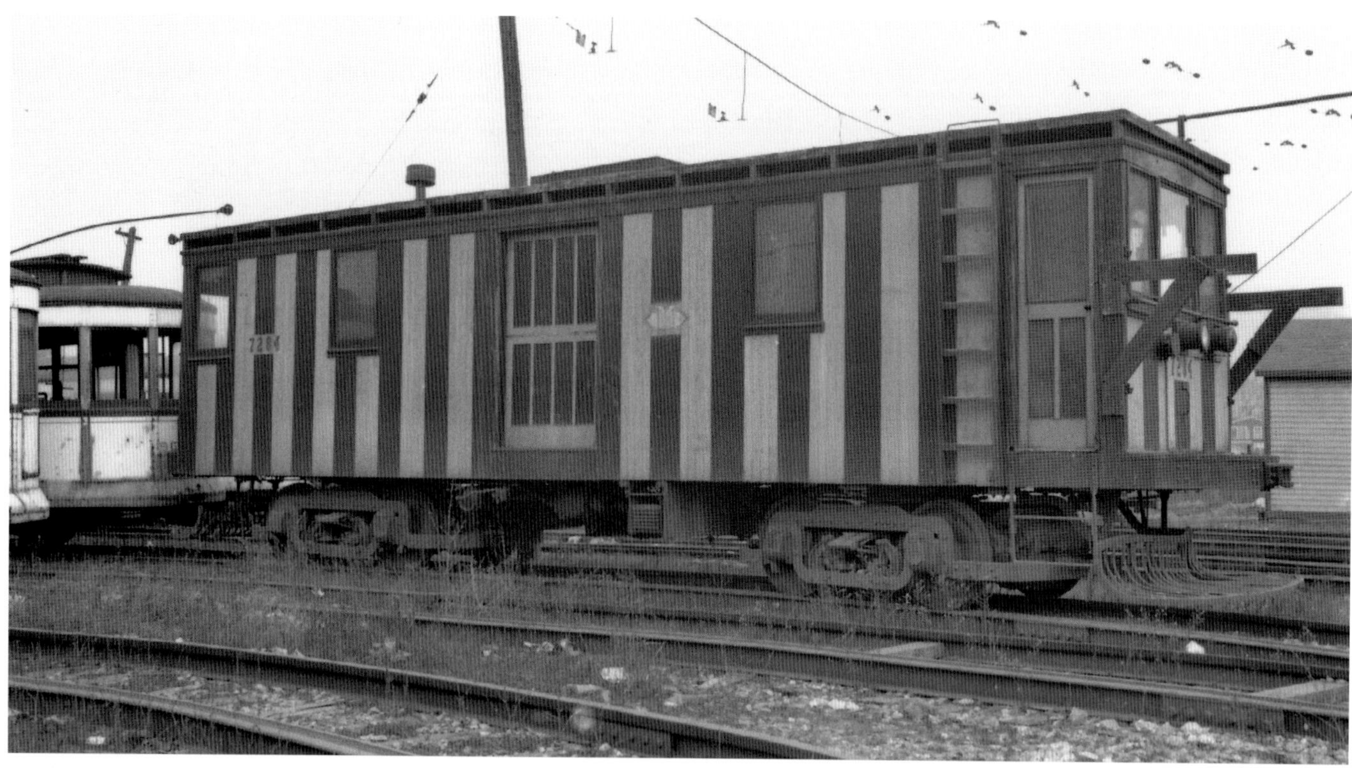

Wyoming car house is the location of line car No. 7284 on December 8, 1946. Powered by two Westinghouse type 38 motors, this car was built by Niles Car & Manufacturing Company in 1916. The Wyoming car house at 5170 Wyoming Street in Dearborn, Michigan, opened on March 3, 1930. It temporarily closed on June 20, 1948; reopened on October 2, 1949; and the car house portion closed on September 7, 1955. (*Clifford R. Scholes collection*)

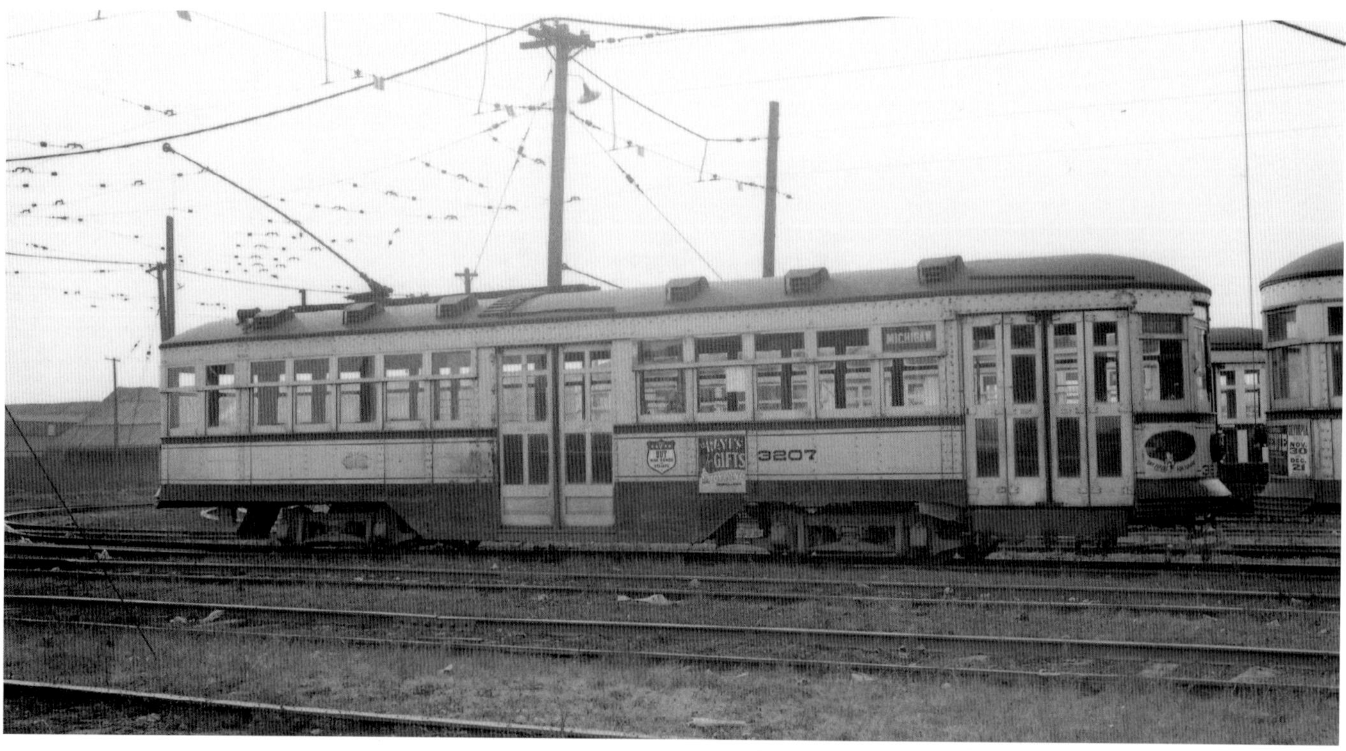

On December 8, 1946, Peter Witt type car No. 3207 is at the Wyoming car house. This was one of fifty cars (Nos. 3200–3249) built by G. C. Kuhlman Car Company and delivered in 1921. Each car was powered by four General Electric type 265 motors, weighed 37,320 pounds, and seated fifty-two passengers. These cars were originally numbered 1000–1049 and renumbered 11000–11049. (*Bob Crockett photograph—Clifford R. Scholes collection*)

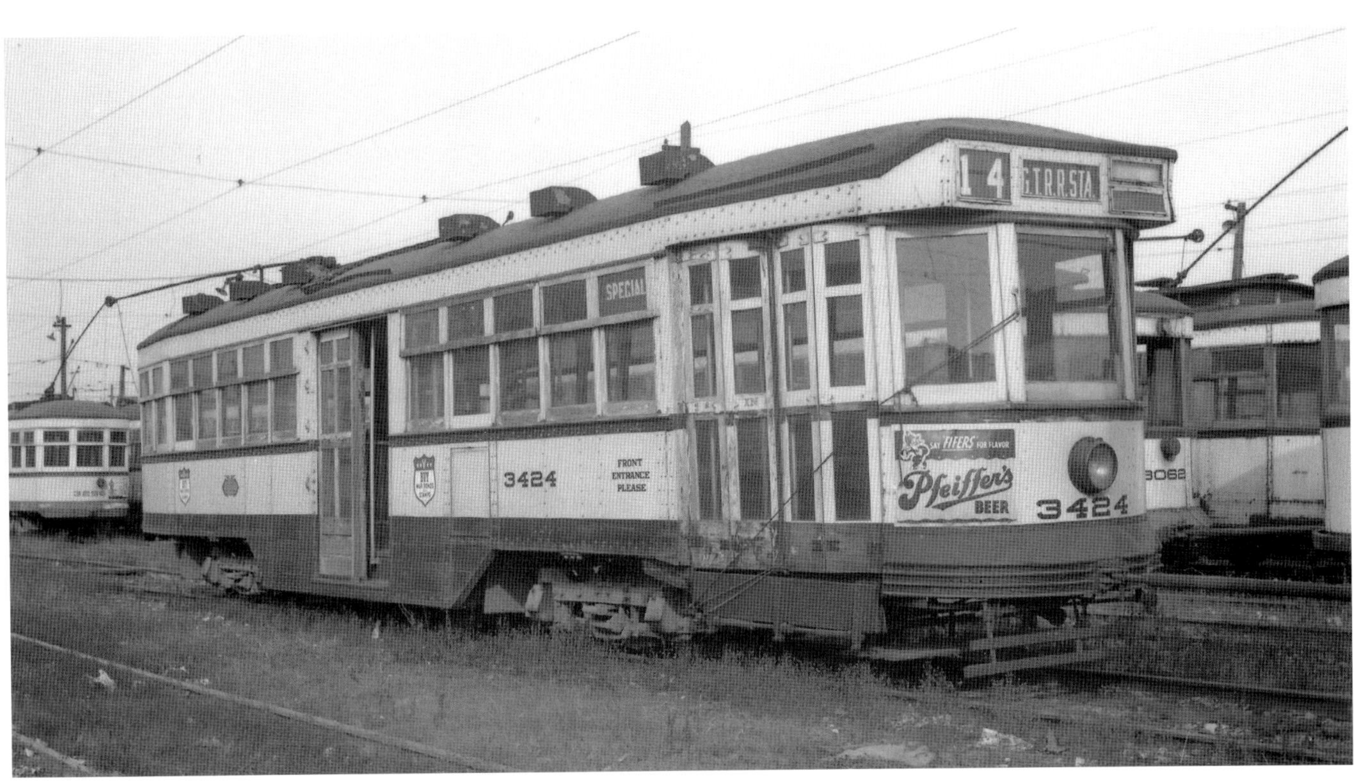

Peter Witt type car No. 3424 (built by St. Louis Car Company and delivered in 1922) with a small visible portion of car No. 3062 (on the right, built by G. C. Kuhlman Car Company and delivered in 1917) and behind the back of Peter Witt type car No. 3256 (built by G. C. Kuhlman Car Company and delivered in 1922) are at the Wyoming car house on December 8, 1946. (*Bob Crockett photograph—Clifford R. Scholes collection*)

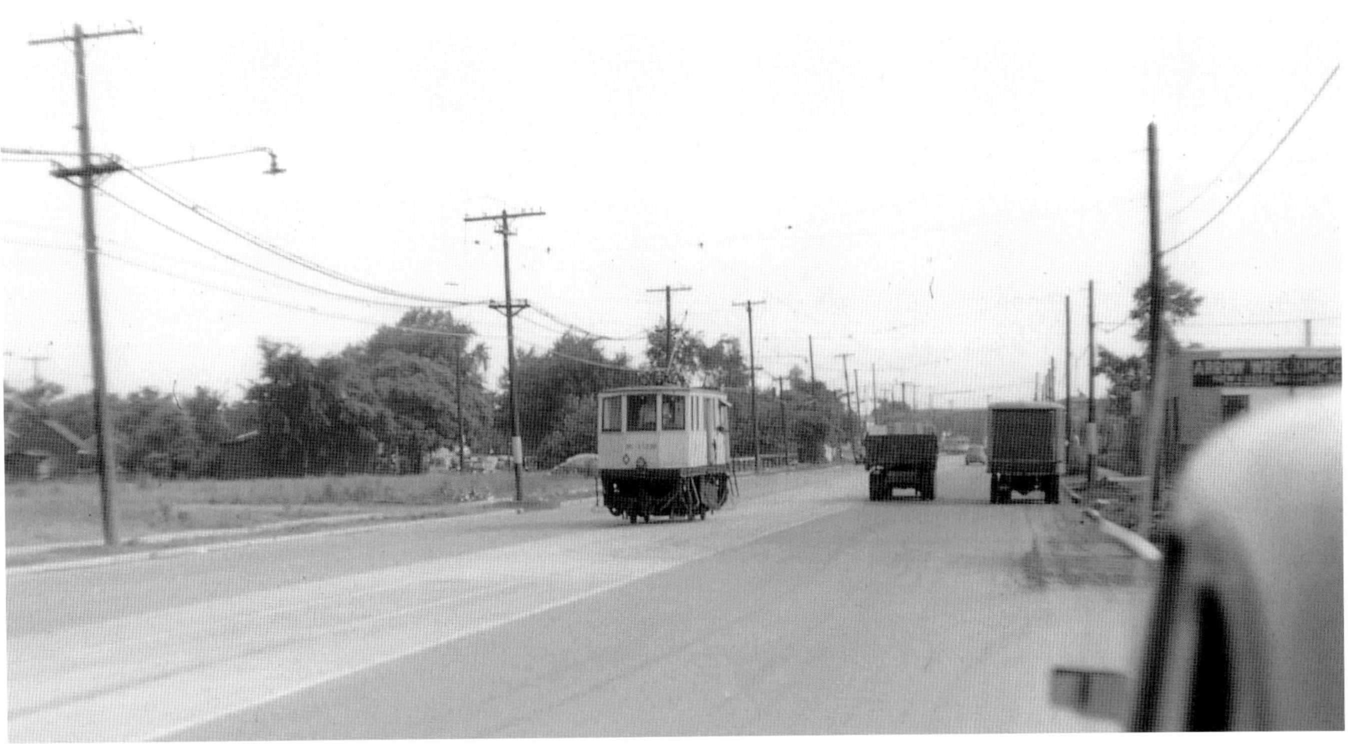

On a June 21, 1951 summer day, double-ended snow sweeper No. X-102 is on Wyoming Avenue near the car house. Built by Mc-Guire Cummings Manufacturing Company in 1924, the snow sweeper weighed 37,080 pounds and was powered by two General Electric type 203 motors. (*Bob Crockett photograph—Clifford R. Scholes collection*)

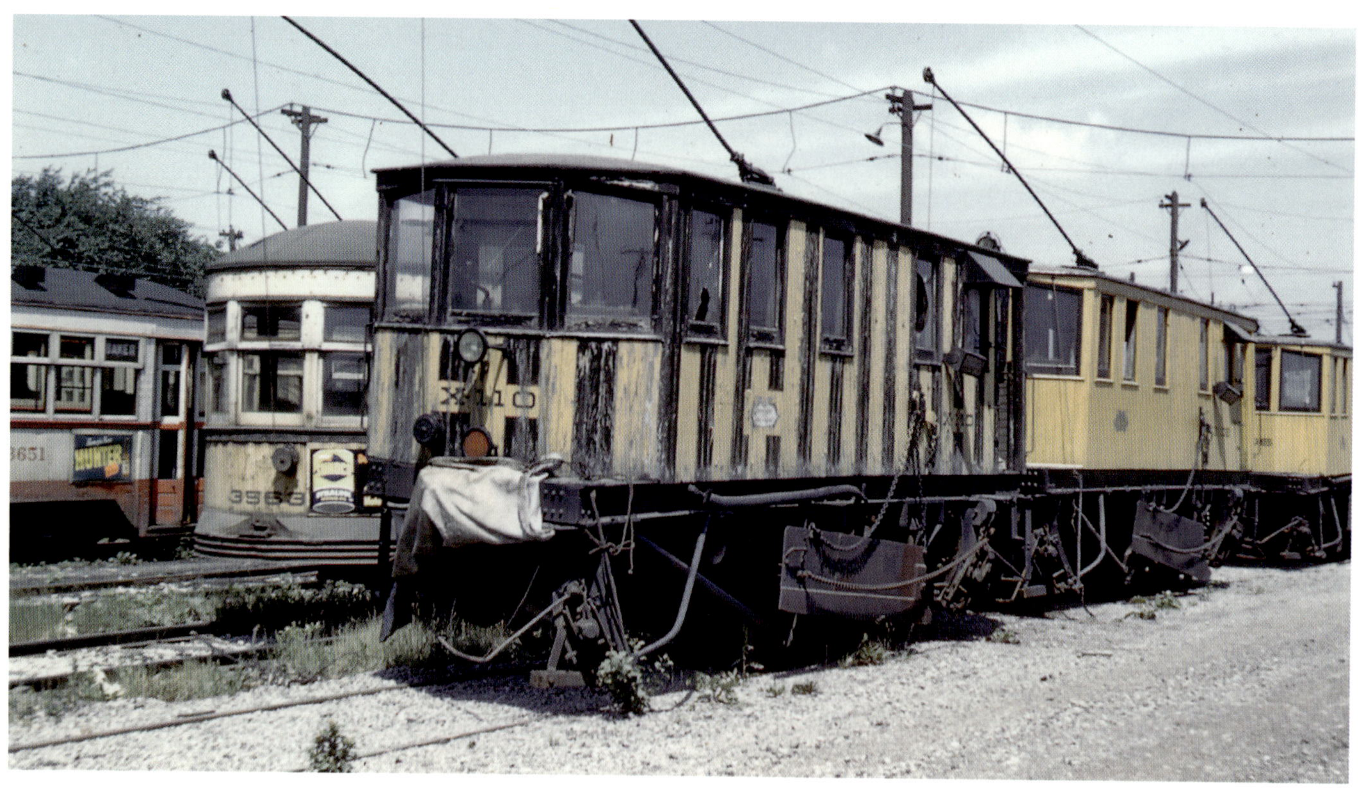

Two snow sweepers, Nos. X-110 and X-108, plus car No. 3563, all built by Mc-Guire Cummings Manufacturing Company in 1924, are at the Wyoming car house on June 27, 1951. (*Bob Crockett photograph—Clifford R. Scholes collection*)

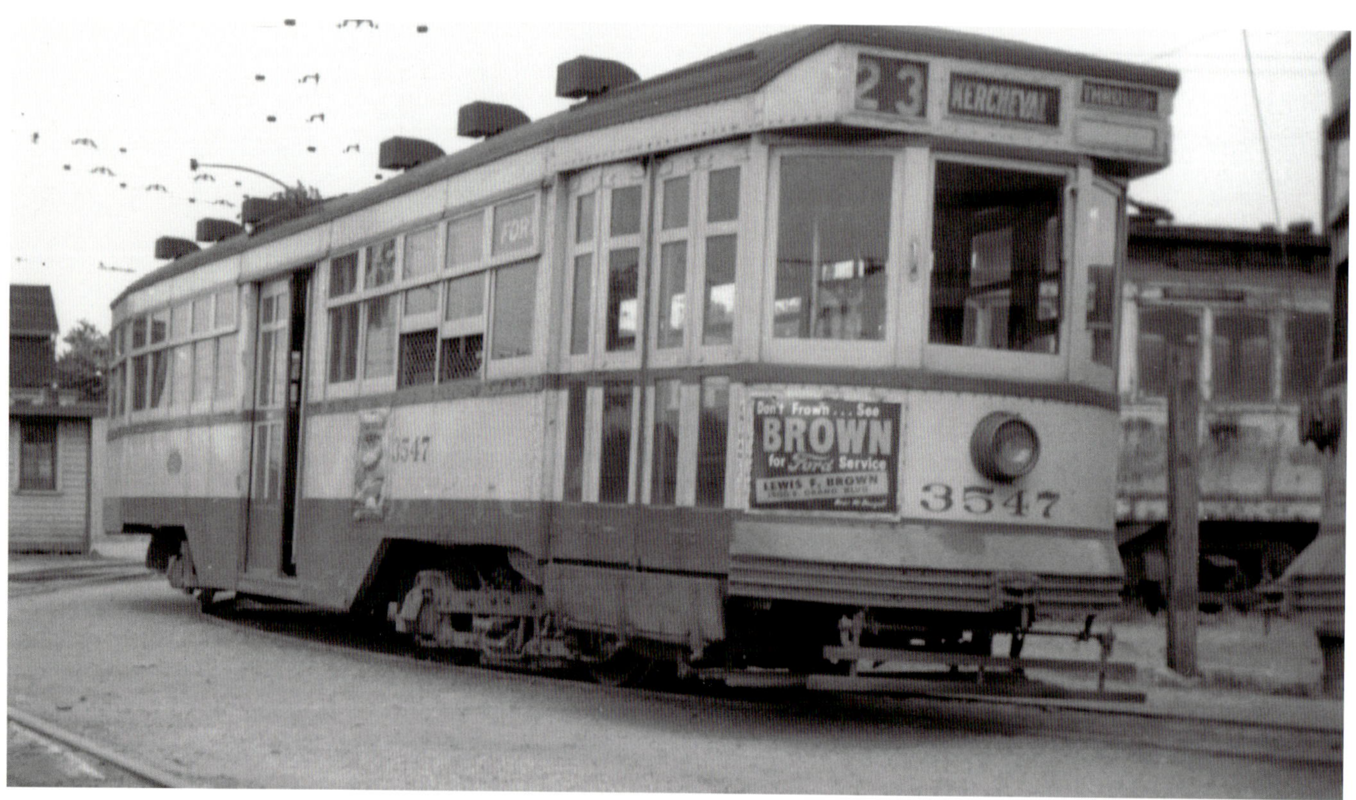

On July 5, 1947, Peter Witt-type car No. 3547 is at the Wyoming car house ready for duty. This was one of fifty cars (Nos. 3500–3549) built by Osgood Bradley Car Company and delivered in 1923. Weighing 36,000 pounds, each car was powered by four General Electric type 265 motors and seated fifty-two passengers. (*Richard Wagner photograph—Clifford R. Scholes collection*)

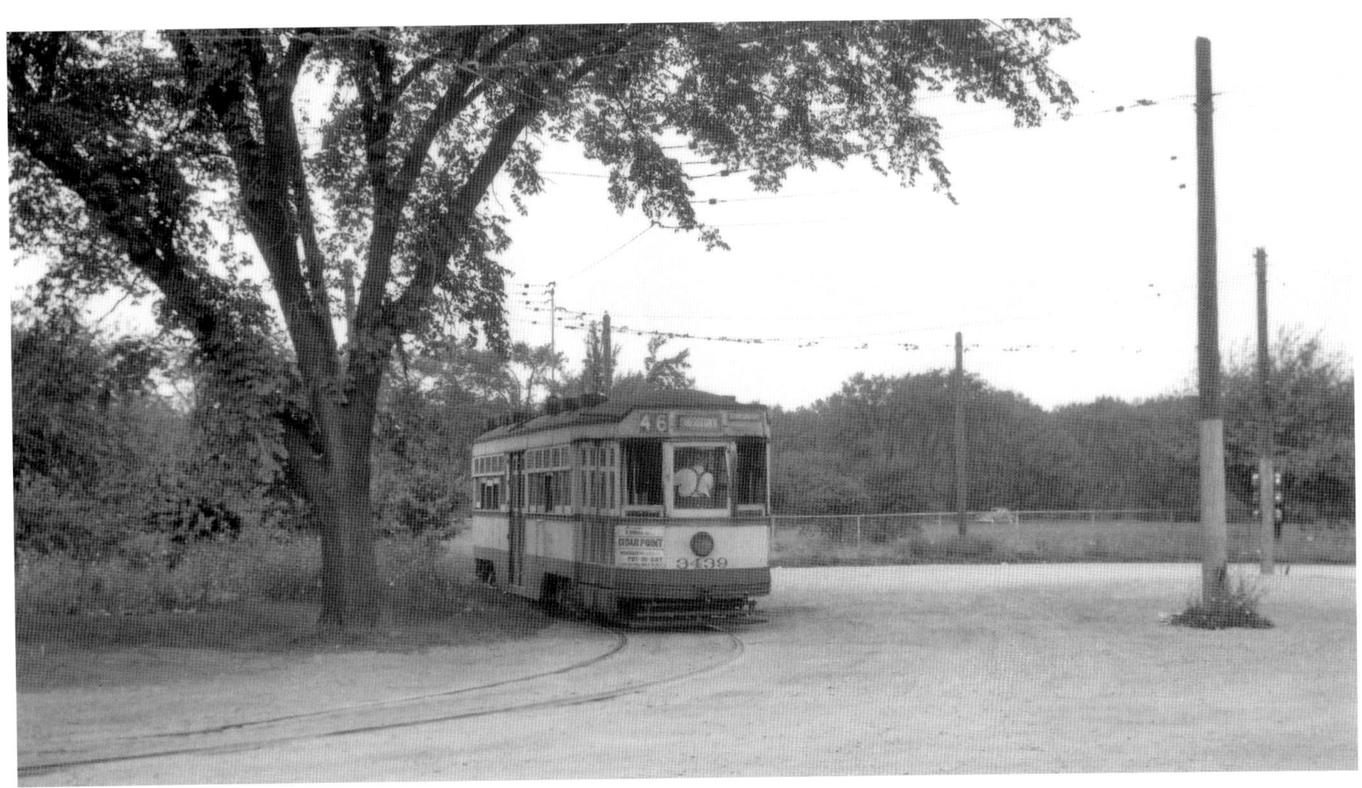

The Warren Avenue and Pierson Street terminal is the setting for DSR car No. 3439 on August 27, 1947. This was one of twenty-five Peter Witt-type cars (Nos. 3425–3449) built by McGuire Cummings Manufacturing Company and delivered in 1922. Each car was powered by four General Electric type 265 motors, weighed 37,660 pounds, and seated fifty-two passengers. (*Bob Crockett photograph—Clifford R. Scholes collection*)

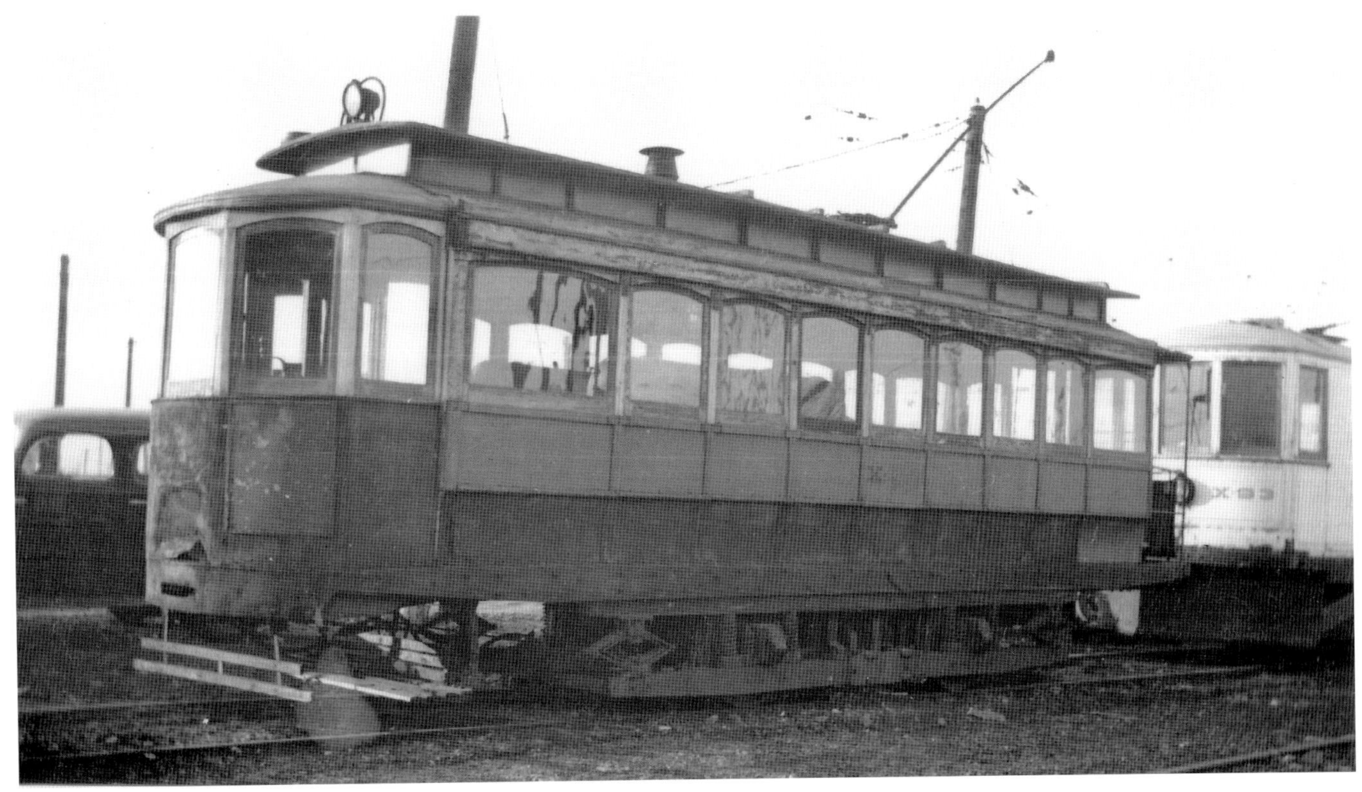

In 1947, air compressor car No. X-81 (built by DUR in 1904 and later rebuilt by DSR) and supply car X-93 (built by DUR in 1911 and rebuilt by DSR in 1929) are at the Highland Park–Woodward Avenue shops. (*Bob Crockett photograph—Clifford R. Scholes collection*)

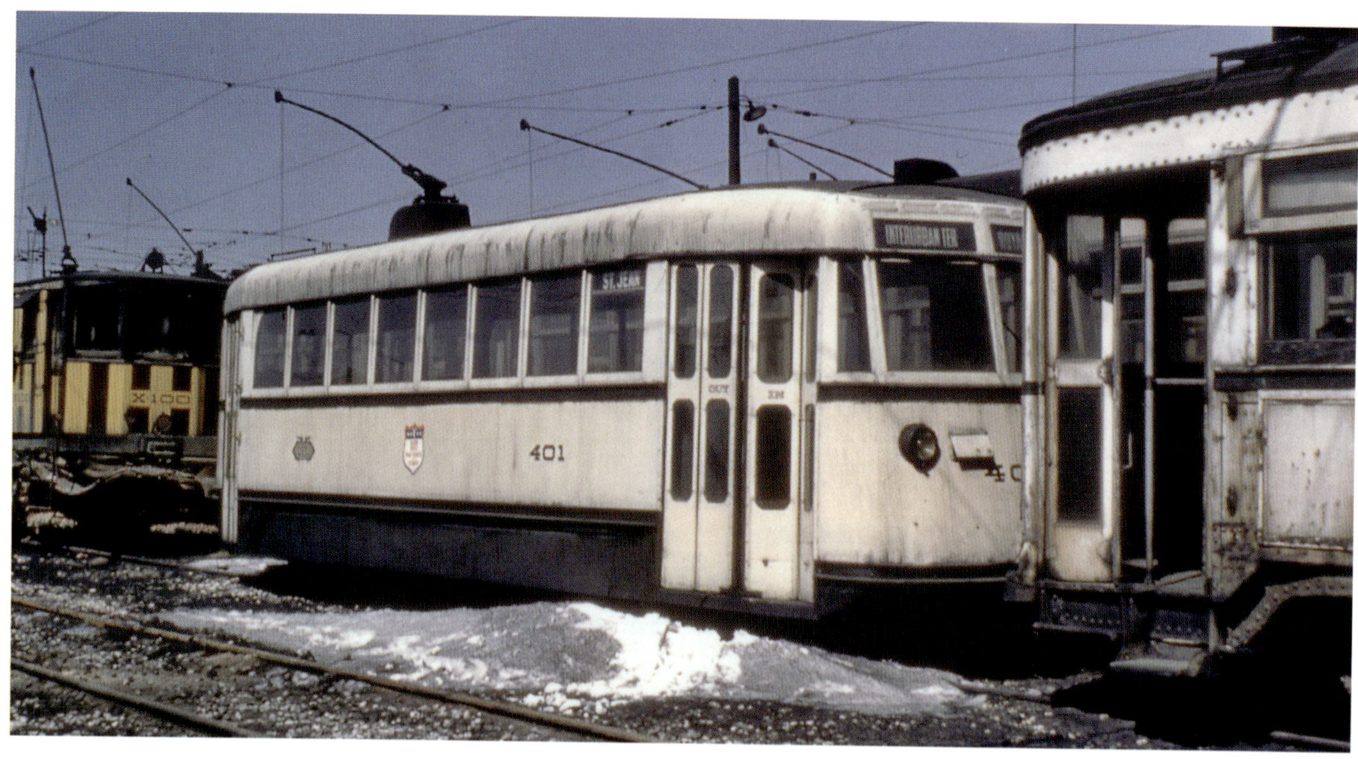

In 1947, one of a kind experimental car No. 401 (built by DSR in 1934, with welded sides, safety glass windows, and a streamlined body, it was powered by four Westinghouse type 508 motors, weighed 24,000 pounds, and seated thirty-nine passengers) and snow sweeper X-100 (a 1924 product of McGuire Cummings Manufacturing Company) are awaiting the next assignment at the Baker car house. (*Bob Crockett photograph—Clifford R. Scholes collection*)

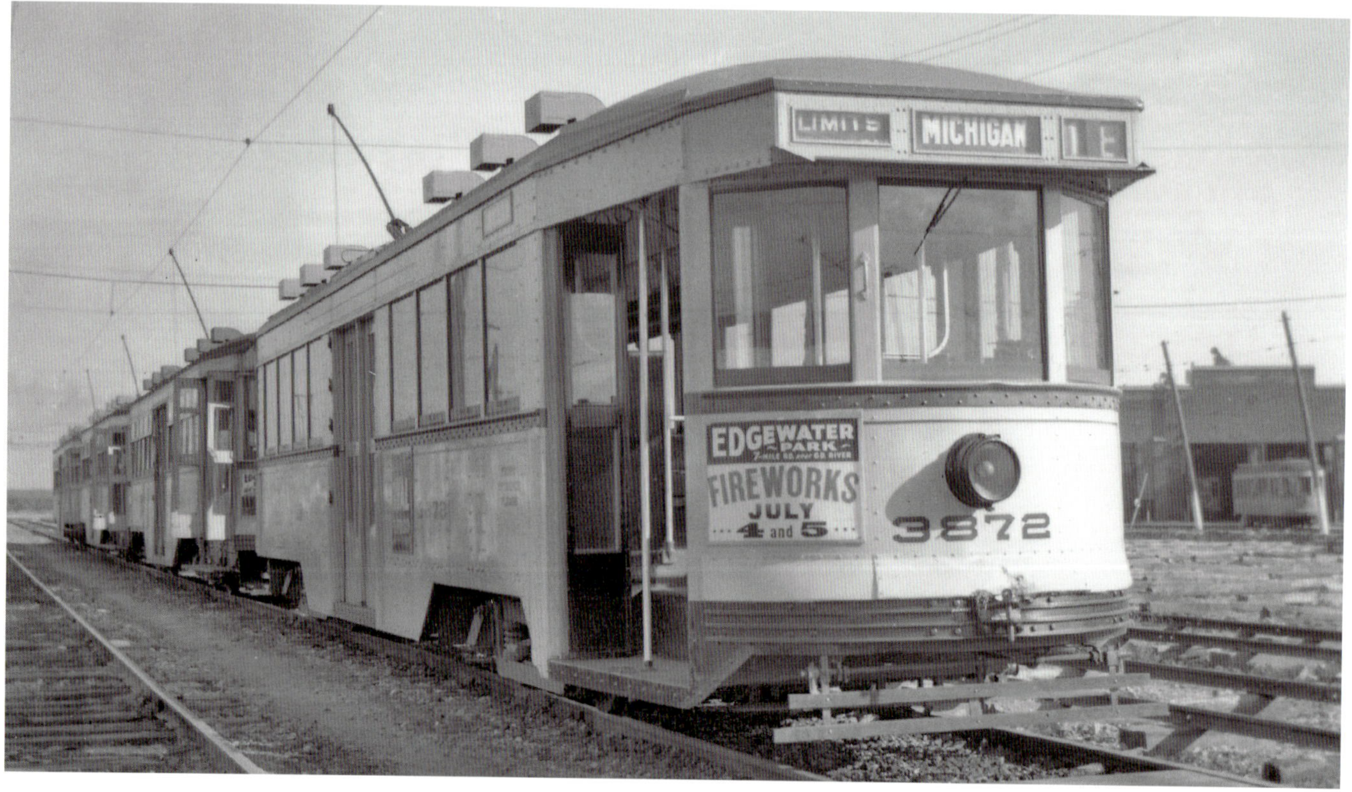

Peter Witt-type car No. 3872 is heading the lineup of cars at the Wyoming car house in 1947. This was one of sixty-four cars (Nos. 3851–3914) built by St. Louis Car Company and delivered in 1930. Each car was powered by four General Electric type 265 motors, weighed 37,200 pounds, and seated fifty-two passengers. (*Bob Crockett photograph—Clifford R. Scholes collection*)

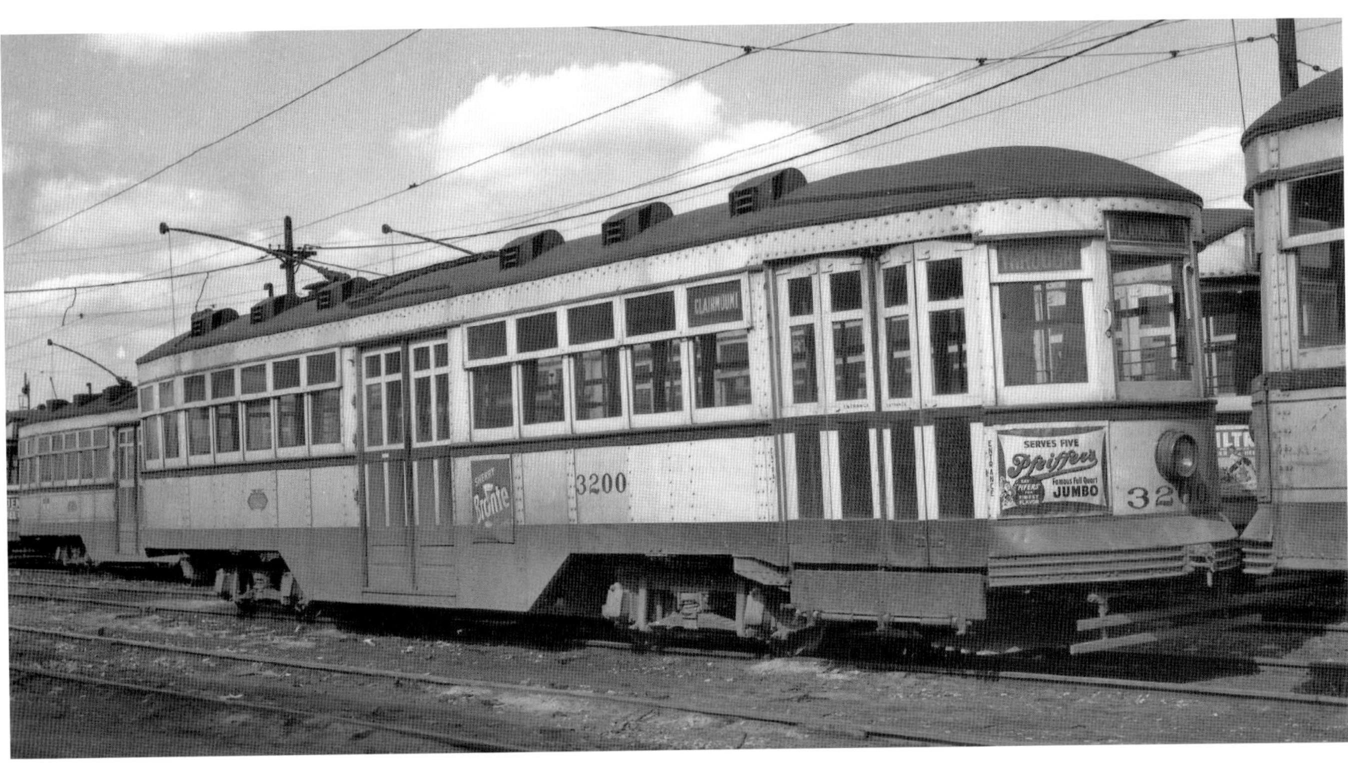

Baker car house is the location of Peter Witt-type car No. 3200 on March 30, 1947. This was in the first group of Peter Witt cars purchased (Nos. 3200–3249) from G. C. Kuhlman Car Company in 1921. The last Peter Witt cars (Nos. 3961–3980) were purchased from St. Louis Car Company in 1930. Detroit's Peter Witt fleet Nos. 3200–3980 totaled 781 cars. (*Bob Crockett photograph—Clifford R. Scholes collection*)

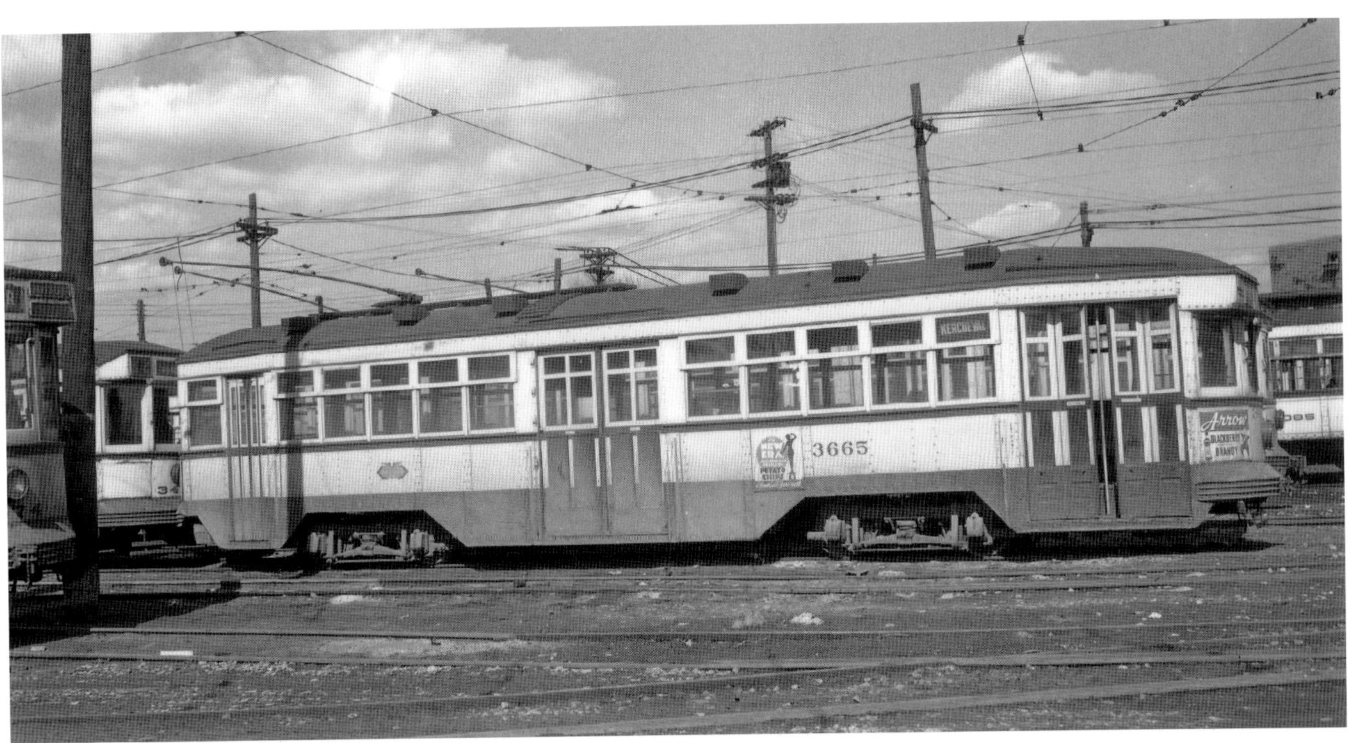

On March 30, 1947, Peter Witt-type car No. 3665 is at the Baker car house. This was one of forty-five cars (Nos. 3655–3699) built in 1927 by G. C. Kuhlman Car Company. Powered by four General Electric type 265 motors, each car weighed 37,580 pounds and seated fifty-two passengers. With the need to create jobs for the unemployed during the Depression, the United States Government provided funding for a DSR project to install rear doors on the Peter Witt cars to speed up exiting passengers. Car No. 3665 was one of thirty-eight Peter Witt cars to receive rear doors. An extra lever on the conductor's left controlled the rear doors. (*Bob Crockett photograph—Clifford R. Scholes collection*)

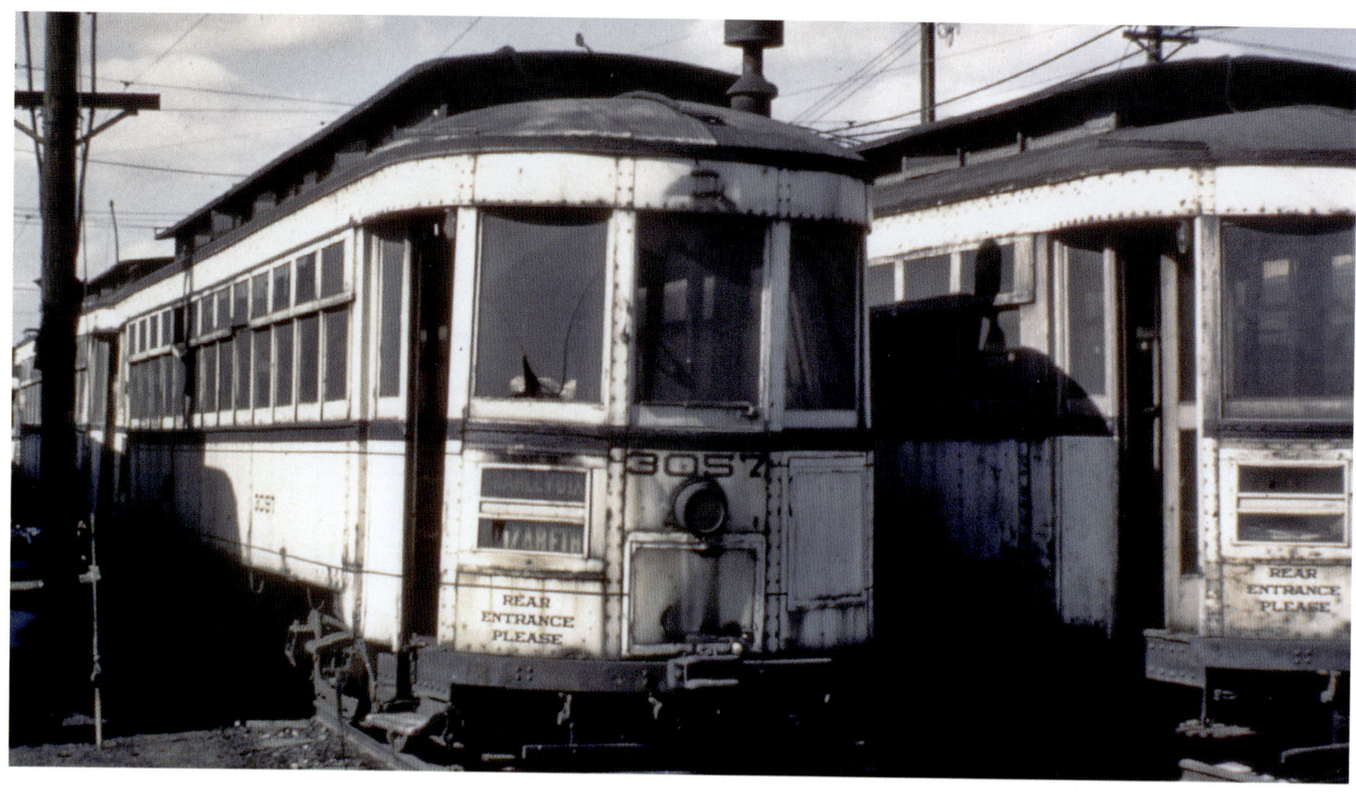

In 1950, weathered car No. 3057 is at the Baker car house. G. C. Kuhlman Car Company built twenty-five of these deck roof cars (Nos. 3050–3074) in 1917 for Detroit United Railways (DUR). Heated by coal, each car was powered by four General Electric type 203L motors, weighed 48,000 pounds, and seated forty-six passengers. (*Bob Crockett photograph—Clifford R. Scholes collection*)

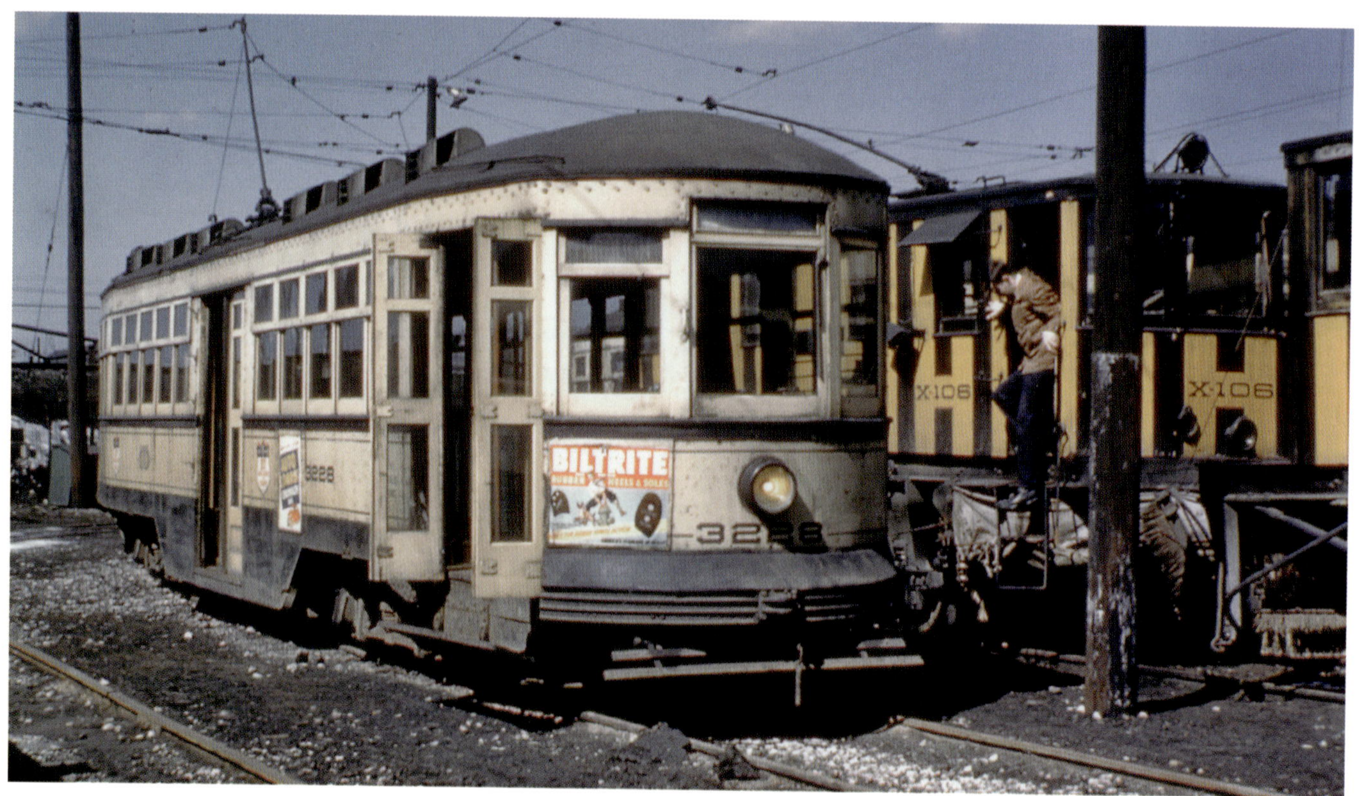

Baker car house in 1950 is the location of DSR car No. 3228 (G. C. Kuhlman Car Company in 1921) and snow sweeper No. X-106 (built by McGuire Cummings Manufacturing Company in 1924). The Baker car house, located on Livemois Avenue at W. Vernon Highway, opened in 1917 and closed on October 2, 1949. (*Bob Crockett photograph—Clifford R. Scholes collection*)

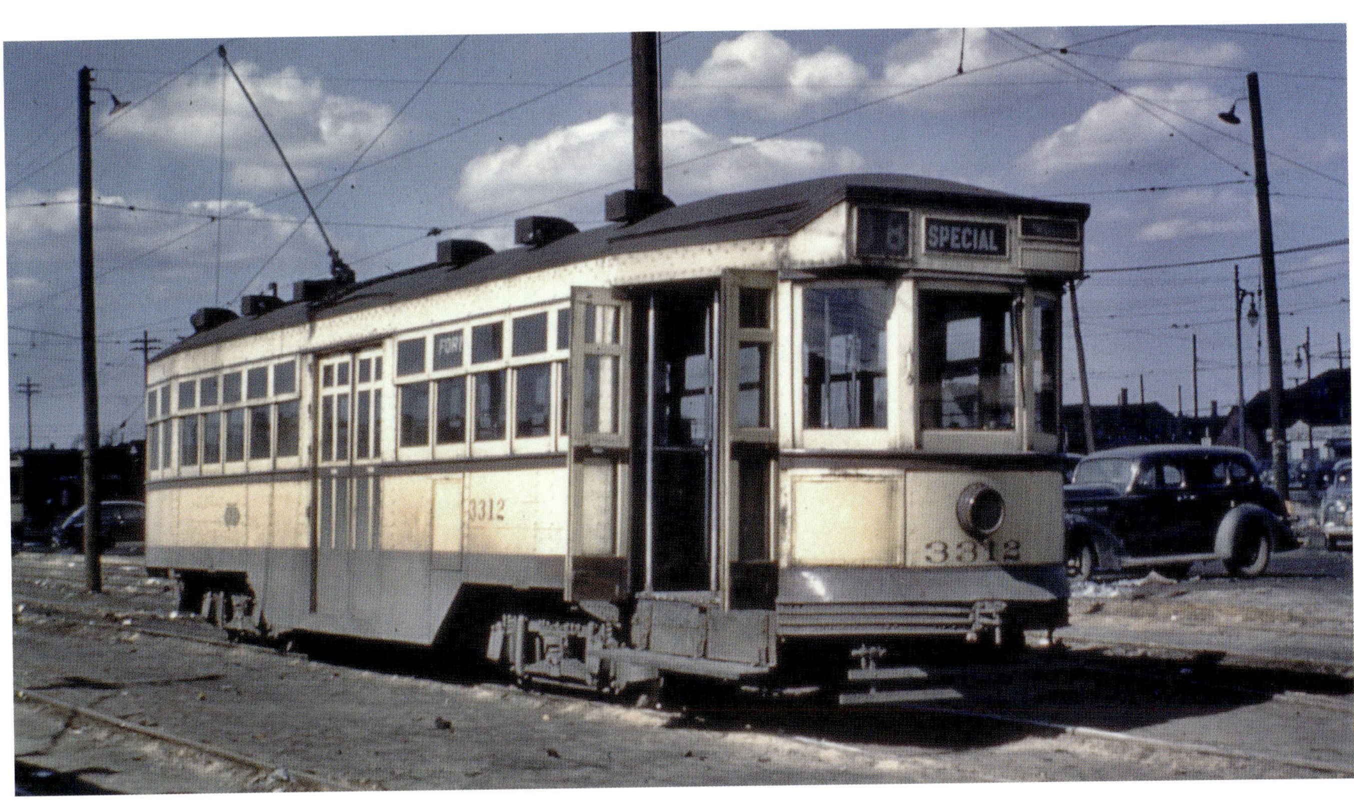

On a sunny day in 1950, Peter Witt-type car No. 3312 is ready for the next assignment at Baker car house. This was one of 100 cars (Nos. 3250–3349) built by G. C. Kuhlman Car Company in 1922. Weighing 37,660 pounds, each car was powered by four General Electric type 265 motors and seated fifty-two passengers. (*Bob Crockett photograph—Clifford R. Scholes collection*)

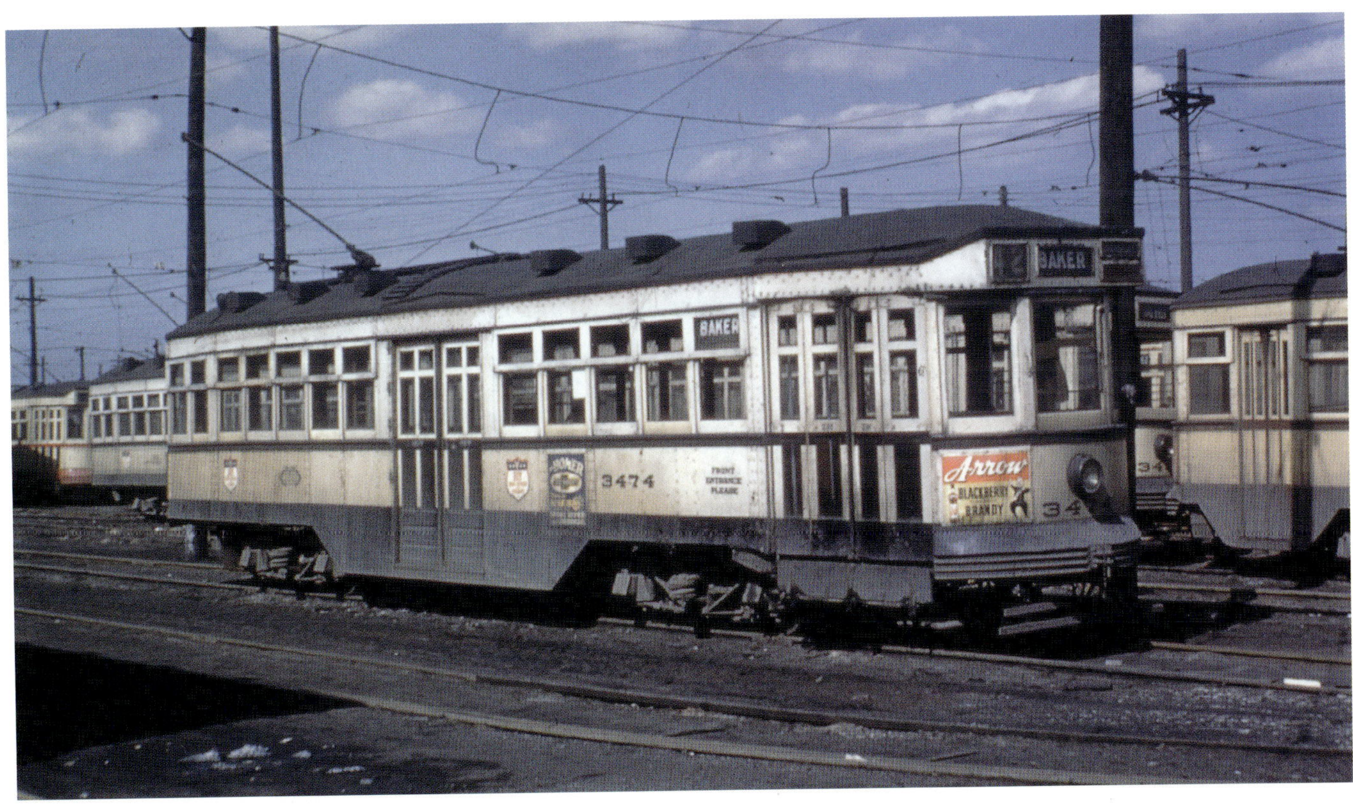

In service for twenty-seven years when this picture was taken in 1950 at the Baker car house, Peter Witt-type car No. 3474 is one of fifty cars (Nos. 3450–3499) built in 1923 by Mc-Guire Cummings Manufacturing Company. Powered by four General Electric type 265 motors, each car weighed 37,320 pounds and seated fifty-two passengers. (*Bob Crockett photograph—Clifford R. Scholes collection*)

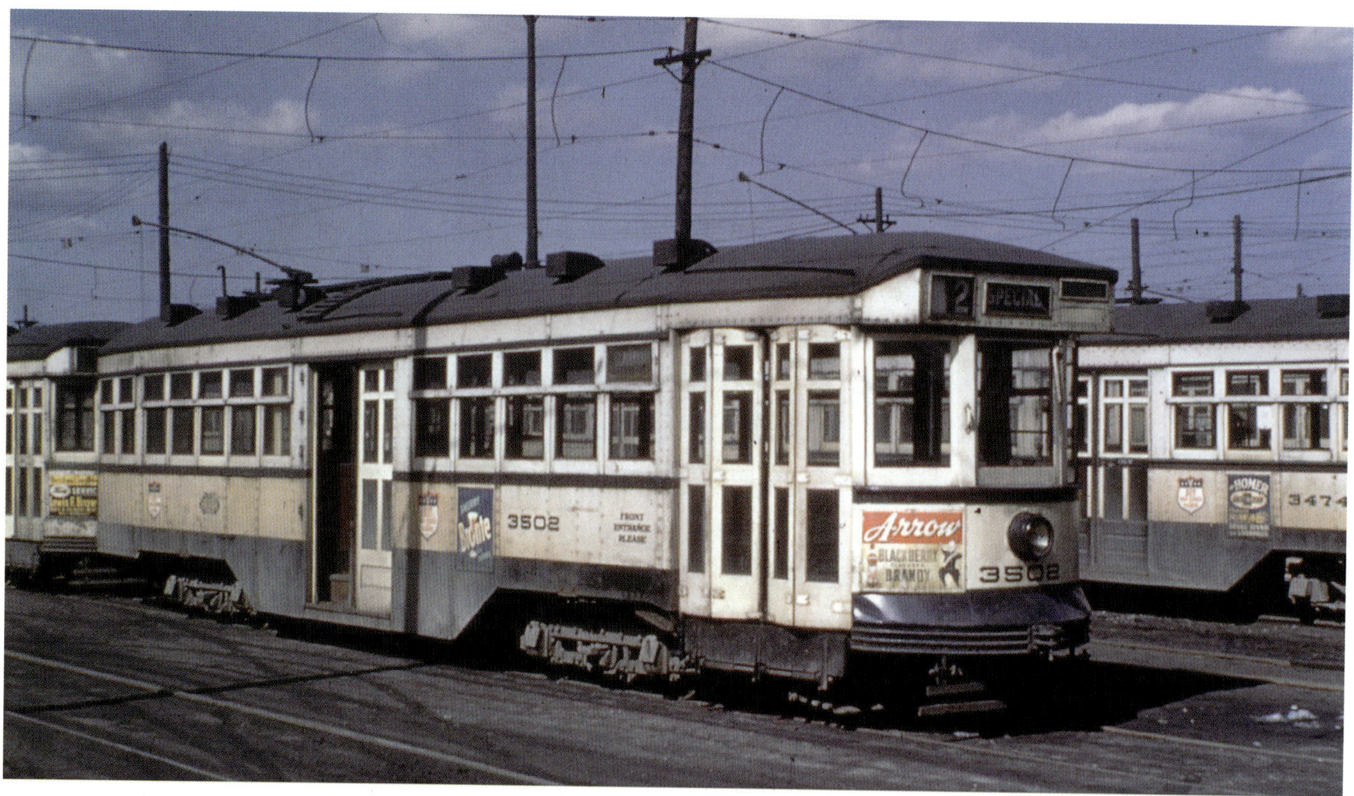

The Baker car house is the location in 1950 of Peter Witt car No. 3502 (built by Osgood Bradley Car Company in 1923); to the right, a small portion of car No. 3474 (built by McGuire Cummings Manufacturing Company in 1923) can be seen. When this picture was taken, both of these cars had been in service twenty-seven years. (*Clifford R. Scholes collection*)

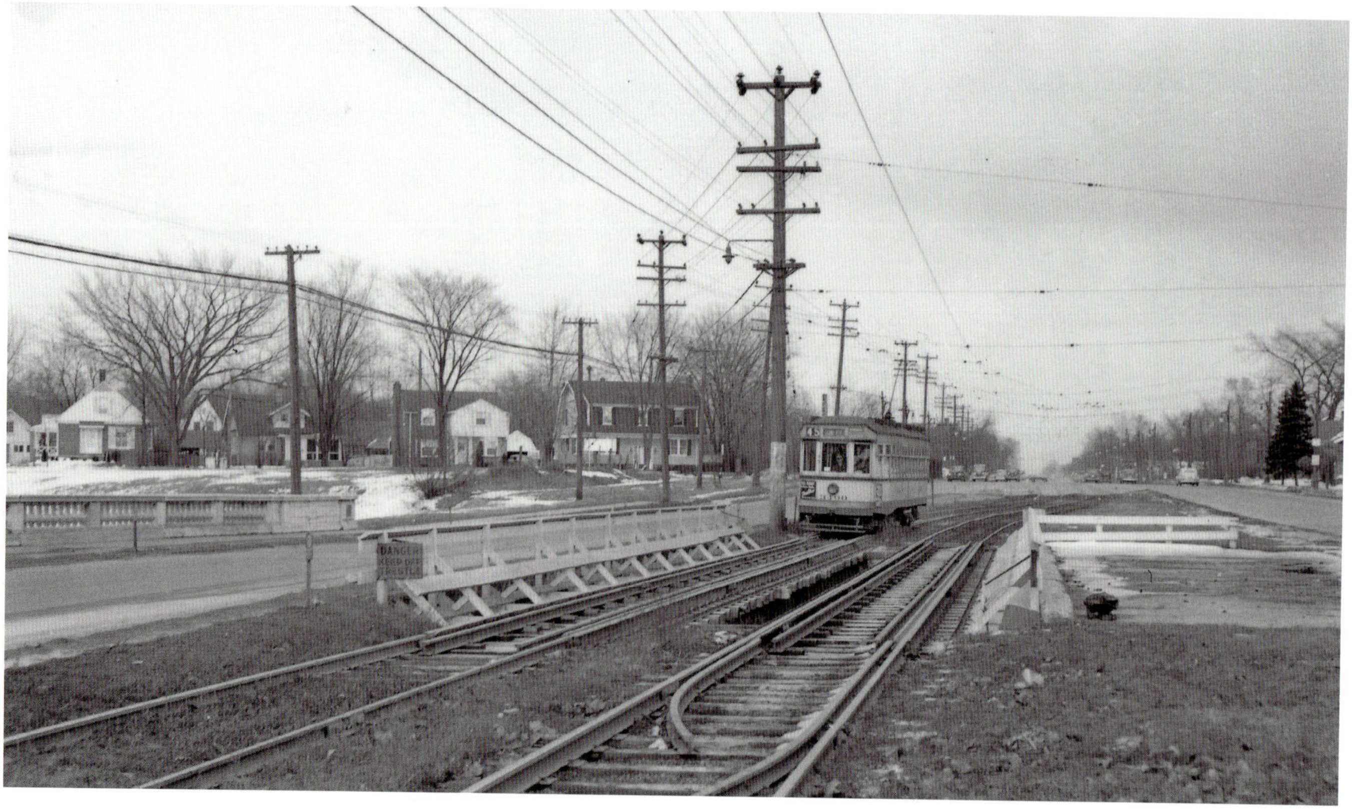

Grand River Avenue at River Rouge bridge is the location of car No. 3490 on March 8, 1947. (*Bob Crockett photograph—Clifford R. Scholes collection*)

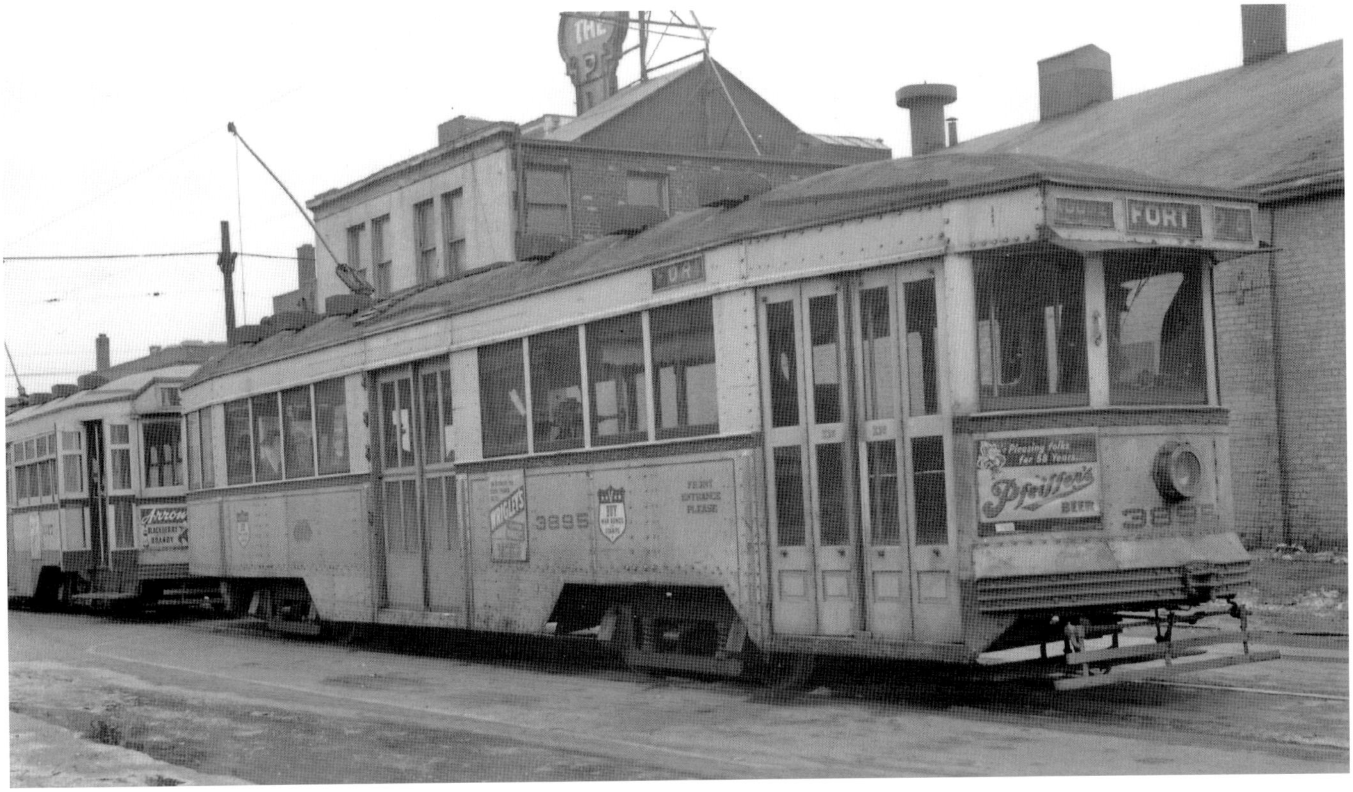

Peter Witt-type cars Nos. 3895 and 3317 are at the Lycaste Street and Jefferson Avenue terminal loop on February 15, 1947. On car No. 3895, note the square destination sign on the upper front of the car in contrast to the curved upper front destination sign on car No. 3200 in the top picture on page 27. (*Bob Crockett photograph—Clifford R. Scholes collection*)

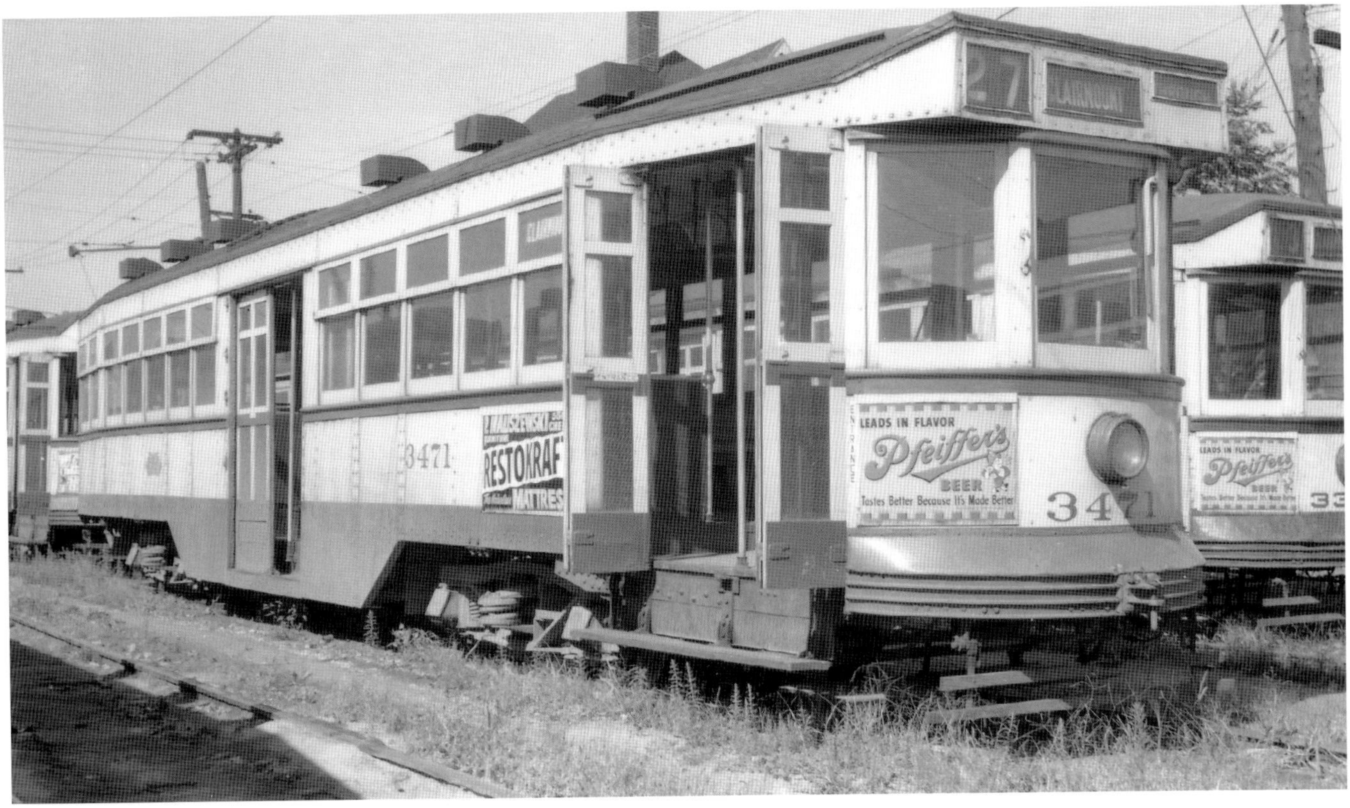

On September 10, 1949, Peter Witt-type car No. 3471 (built by McGuire Cummings Manufacturing Company in 1923) is in the lineup of cars at the East Jefferson car house. (*Bob Crockett photograph—Clifford R. Scholes collection*)

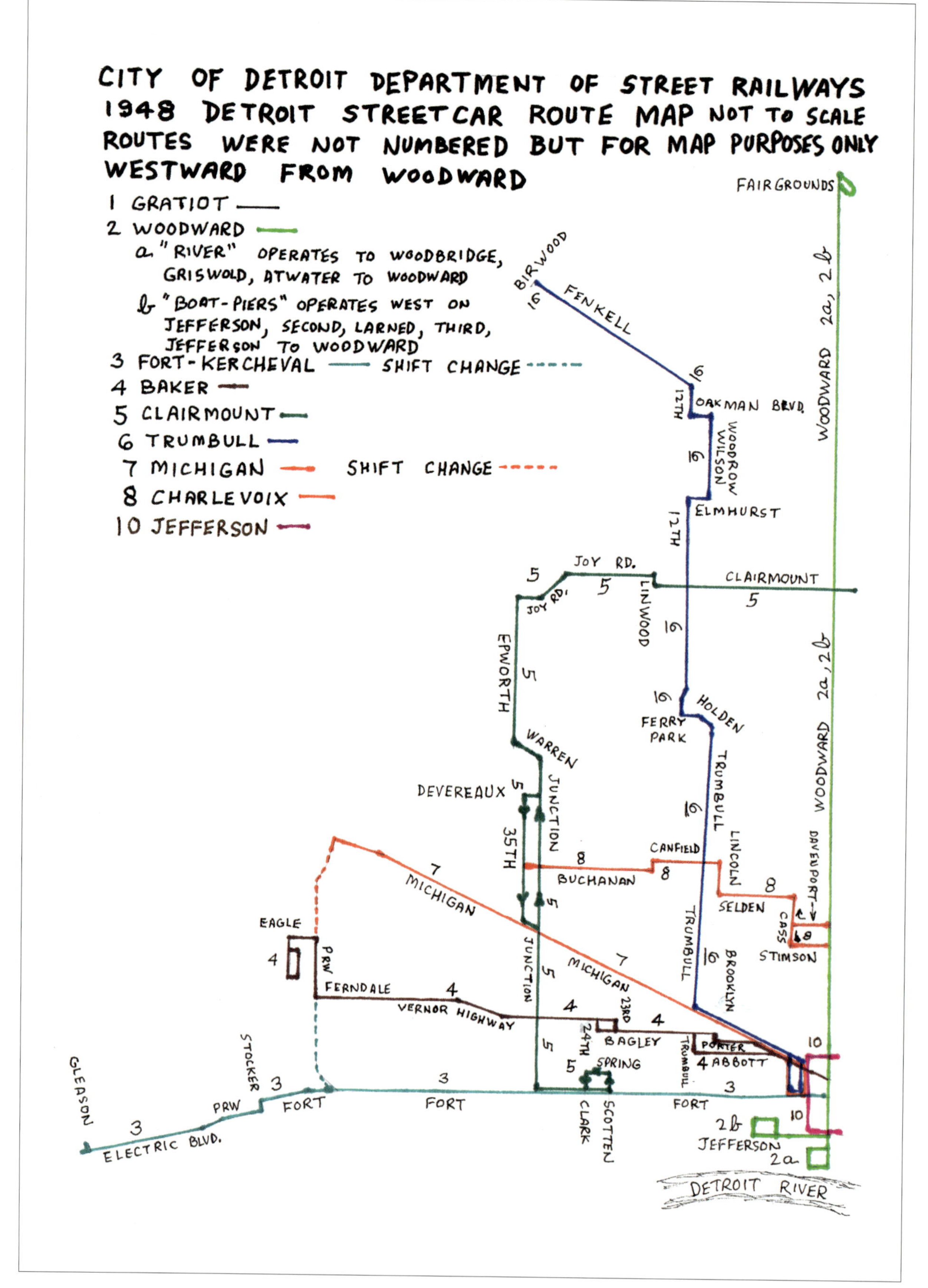

This 1948 map of the City of Detroit Department of Street Railways shows streetcar service west from Woodward Avenue. The route numbers were only for map purposes.

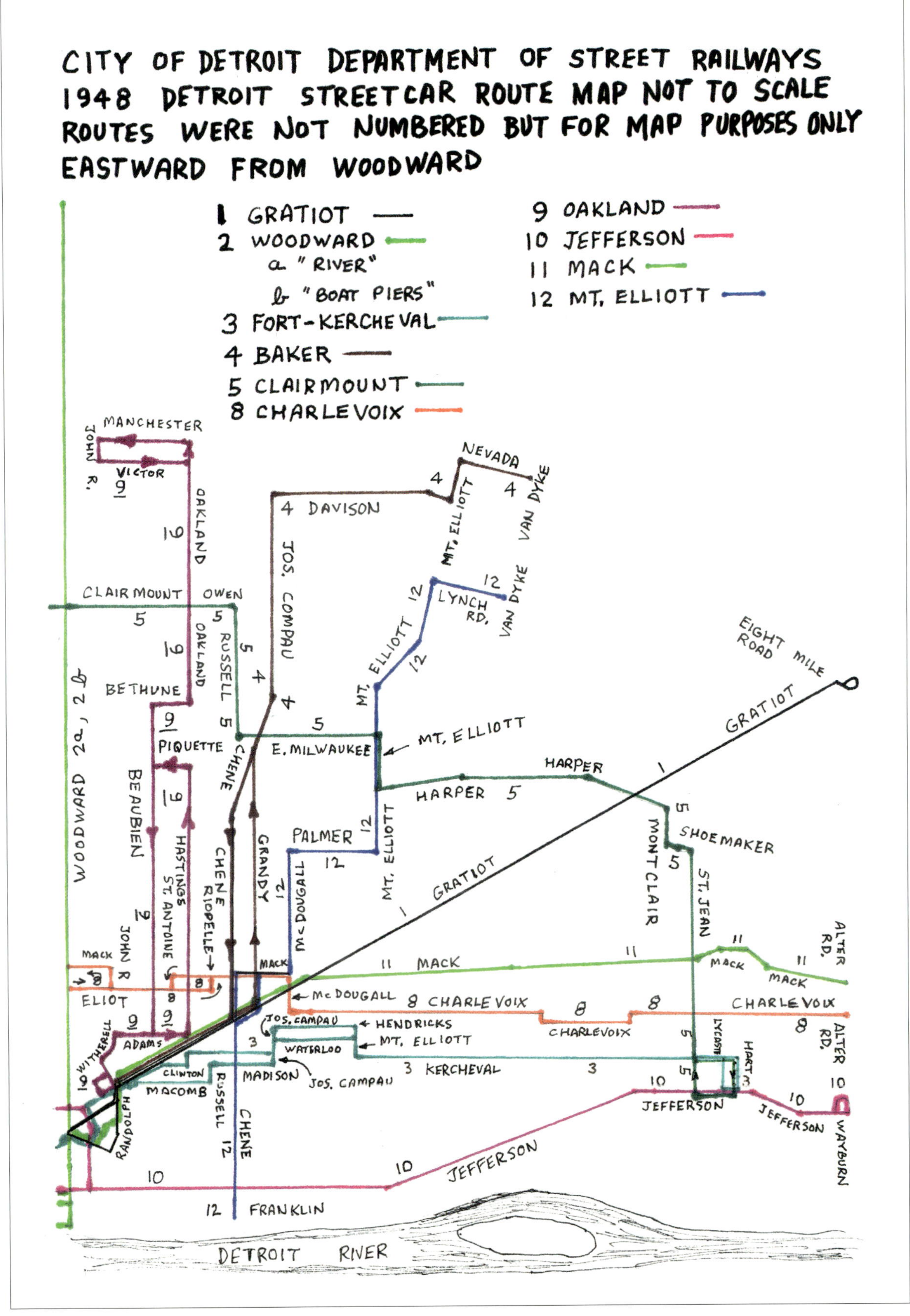

This 1948 map of the City of Detroit Department of Street Railways shows the streetcar service east from Woodward Avenue. The route numbers were only for map purposes.

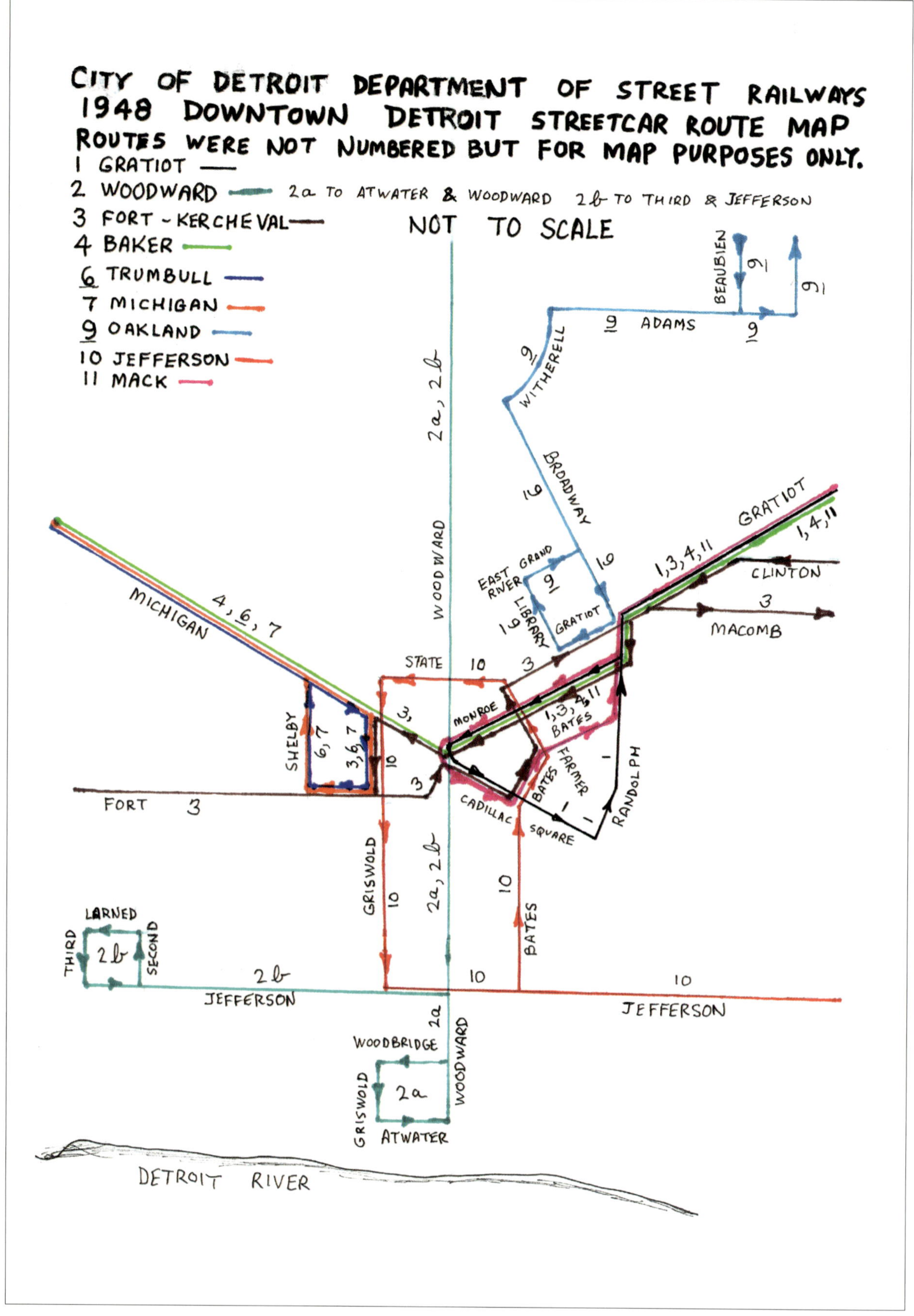

In 1948, downtown Detroit still had extensive streetcar service. Woodward, Gratiot, and Michigan were very busy streetcar corridors in the downtown area. On the evening of April 8, 1956, Detroit became an all bus system.

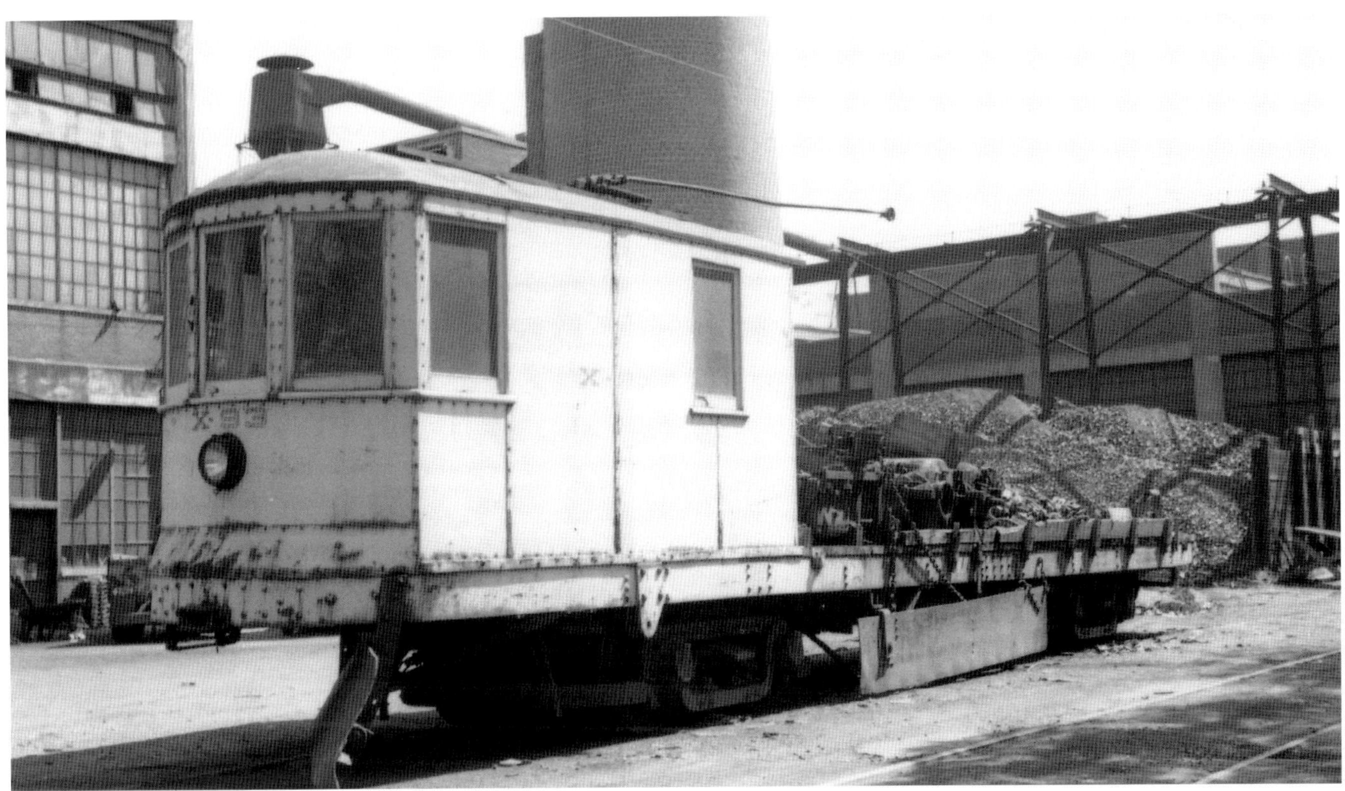

On September 10, 1948, supply car No. X-93 is at the Highland Park–Woodward Avenue Shops. This car was built by DUR as a supply car in 1911 and was rebuilt by DSR in 1929. Powered by four General Electric type 203 motors, the car weighed 43,320 pounds. (*Bob Crockett photograph—Clifford R. Scholes collection*)

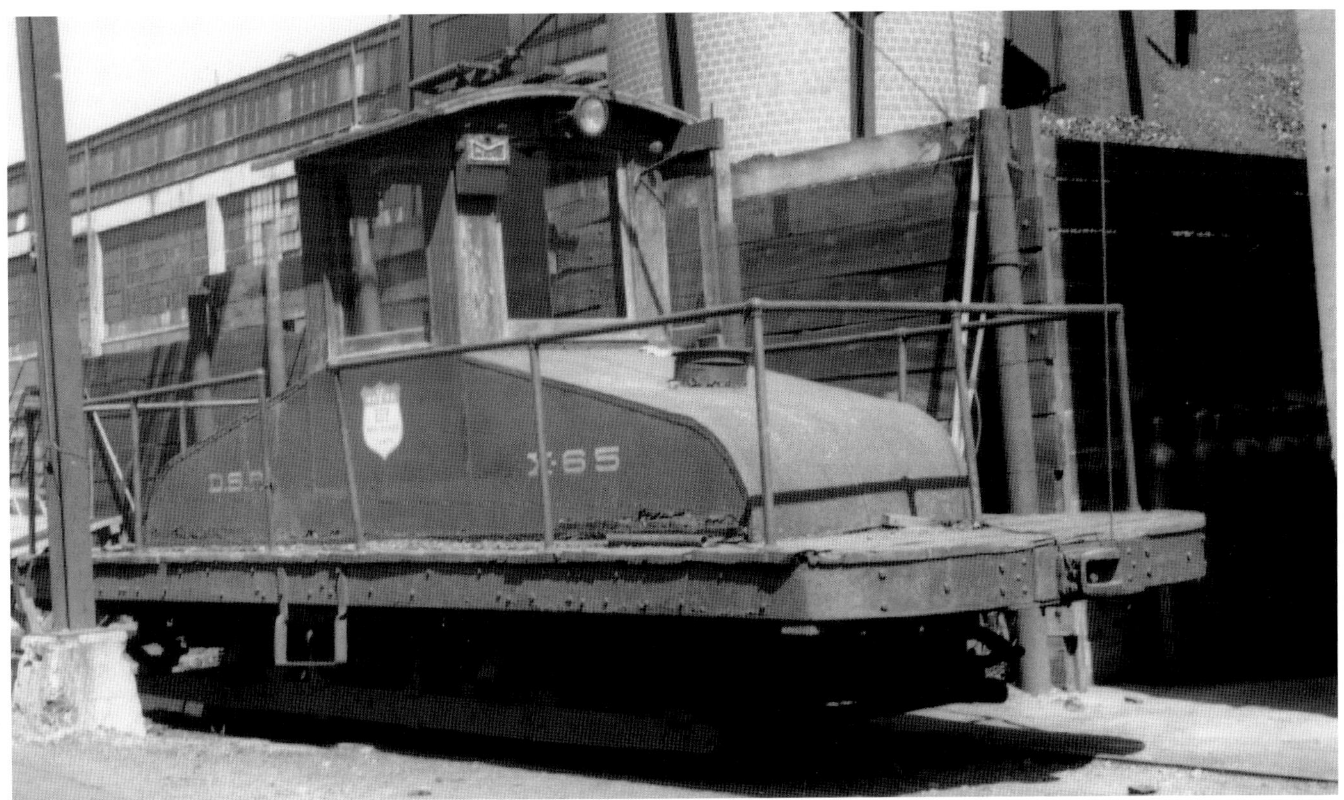

Steeple cab car shifter X-65 is at the Highland Park-Woodward Avenue shop on September 10, 1949. This was originally built by Cincinnati Car Company in 1906 and was rebuilt by DSR in 1924. (*Bob Crockett photograph—Clifford R. Scholes collection*)

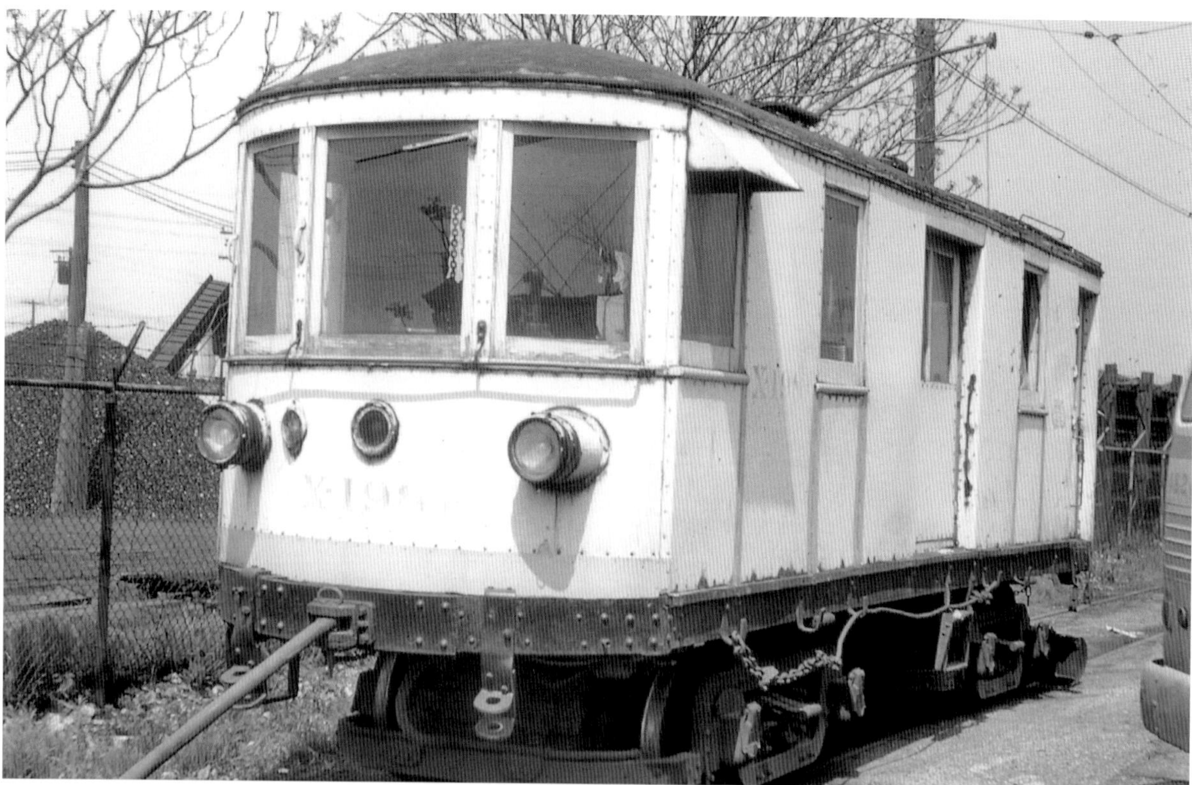

The Highland Park Shops is the location of wrecker car No. X-1981. This was originally steeple cab locomotive No. 1981 built in 1914 by DUR. It was rebuilt in 1922 by DSR into a wrecker. (*Bob Crockett photograph—Clifford R. Scholes collection*)

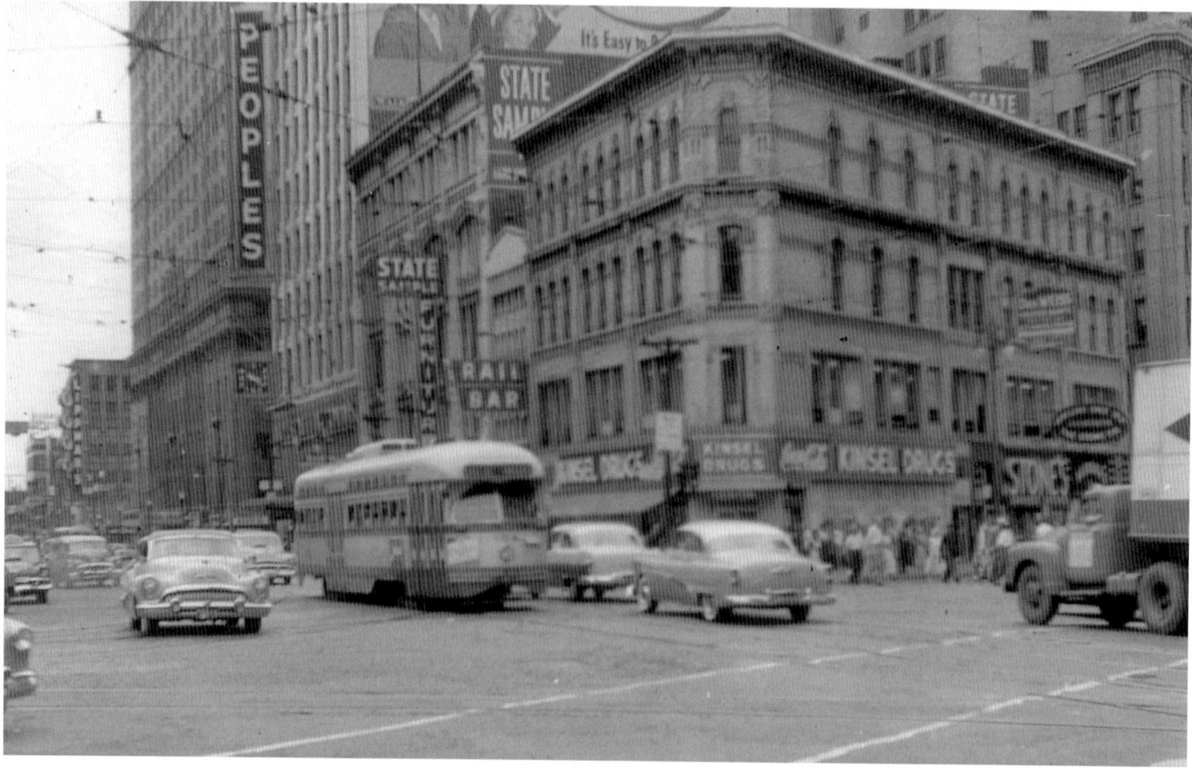

On June 21, 1952, DSR Presidents' Conference Committee (PCC) car No. 154 is on Michigan Avenue and Griswold Street in downtown Detroit. This was one of thirty-nine cars (Nos. 142–180) ordered in September 1945 from St. Louis Car Company, and they were delivered in August–October 1947. Powered by four Westinghouse type 1432 motors, each 48.5-foot-long car weighed 36,000 pounds and seated fifty passengers. (*Clifford R. Scholes collection*)

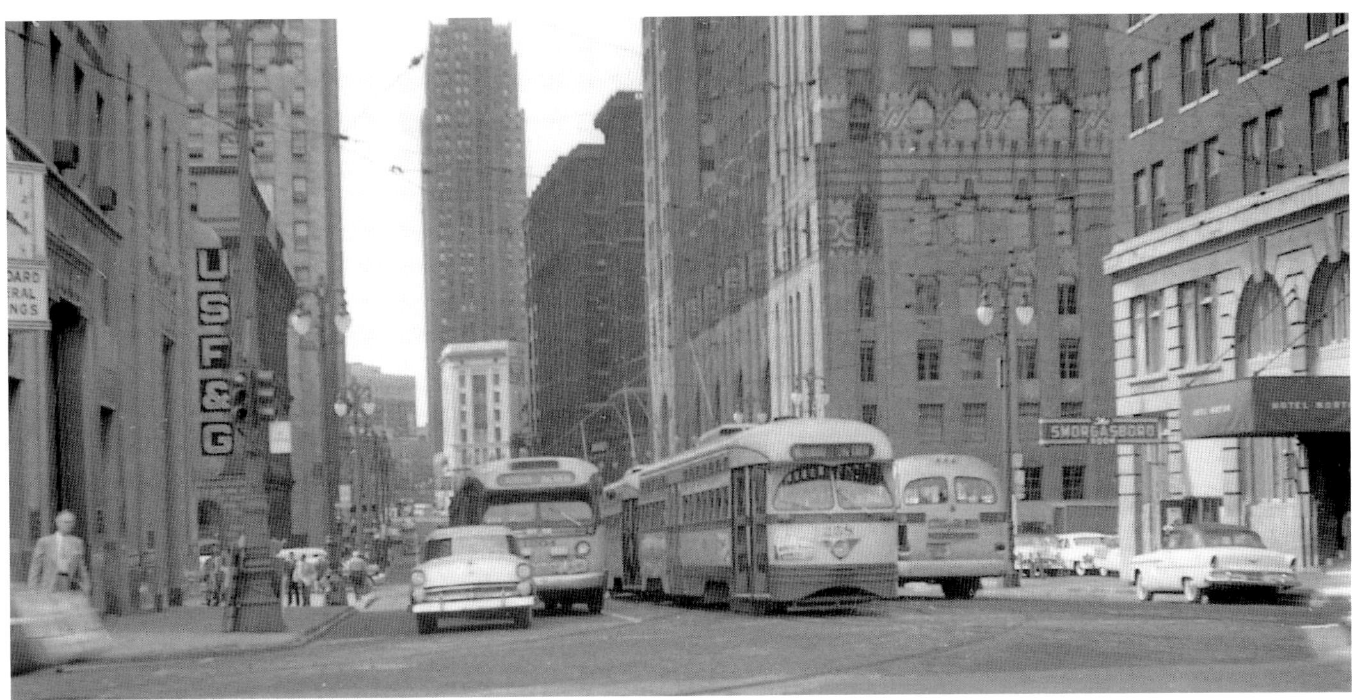

Griswold Street and Jefferson Avenue is the location of PCC car No. 258, one of fifty-three cars (Nos. 234–286) built by St. Louis Car Company and delivered in August–October 1949. Weighing 39,000 pounds, each 50.5-foot-long car was powered by four Westinghouse type 1432K motors and seated fifty-four passengers. To the left is DSR bus No. 1204, which was one of twenty-five model TDH-5105 ("T" is transit bus, "D" is diesel, H is hydraulic automatic transmission, 51 is the seating capacity, and 05 is the bus series) buses (Nos. 1201–1225) purchased in 1953 from General Motors Corporation. (*Clifford R. Scholes collection*)

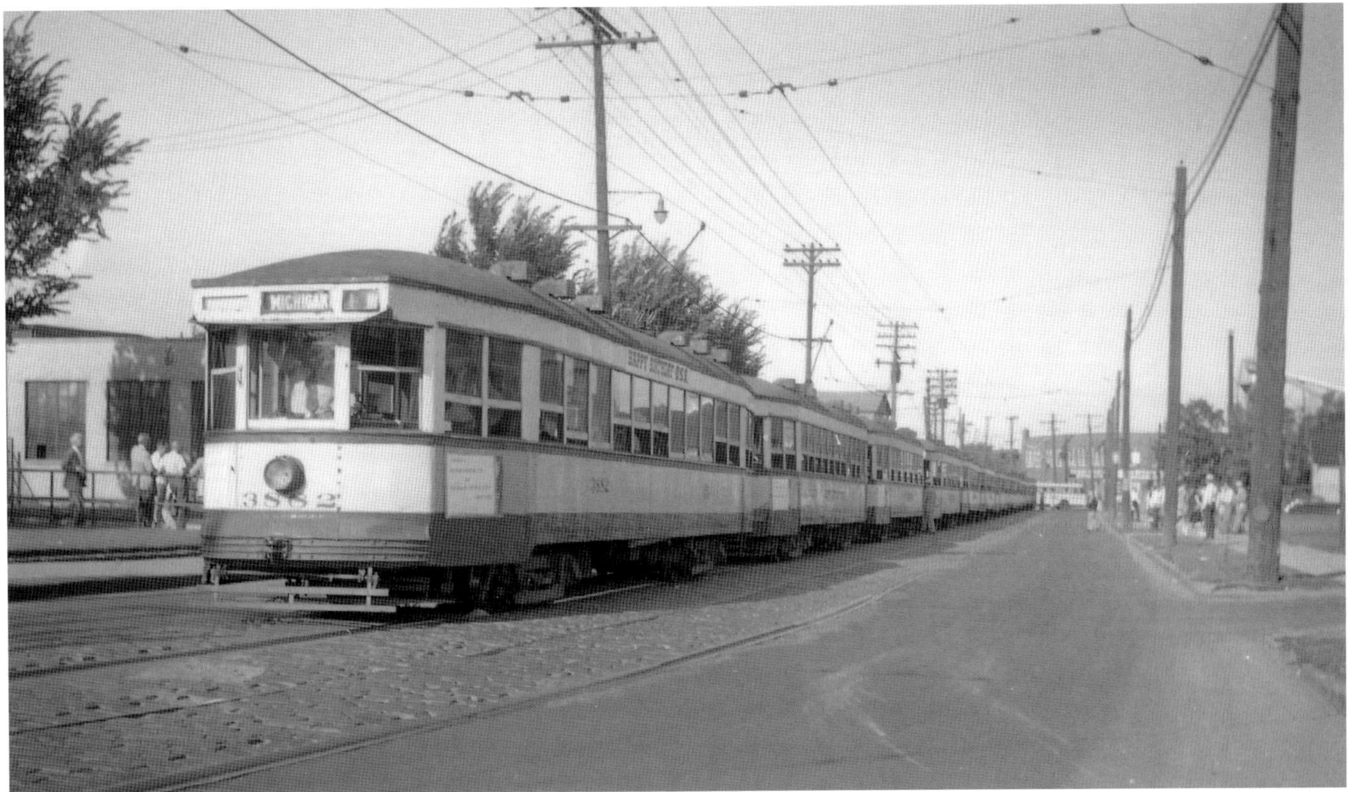

On August 16, 1953, Peter Witt-type car No. 3882 and nine other cars are at Jefferson and St. Jean Avenues, commemorating the ninetieth anniversary of street railway service in Detroit. On August 4, 1863, the Detroit Street Railway began horsecar service on Jefferson Avenue between Third Street and Mt. Elliott. (*Clifford R. Scholes collection*)

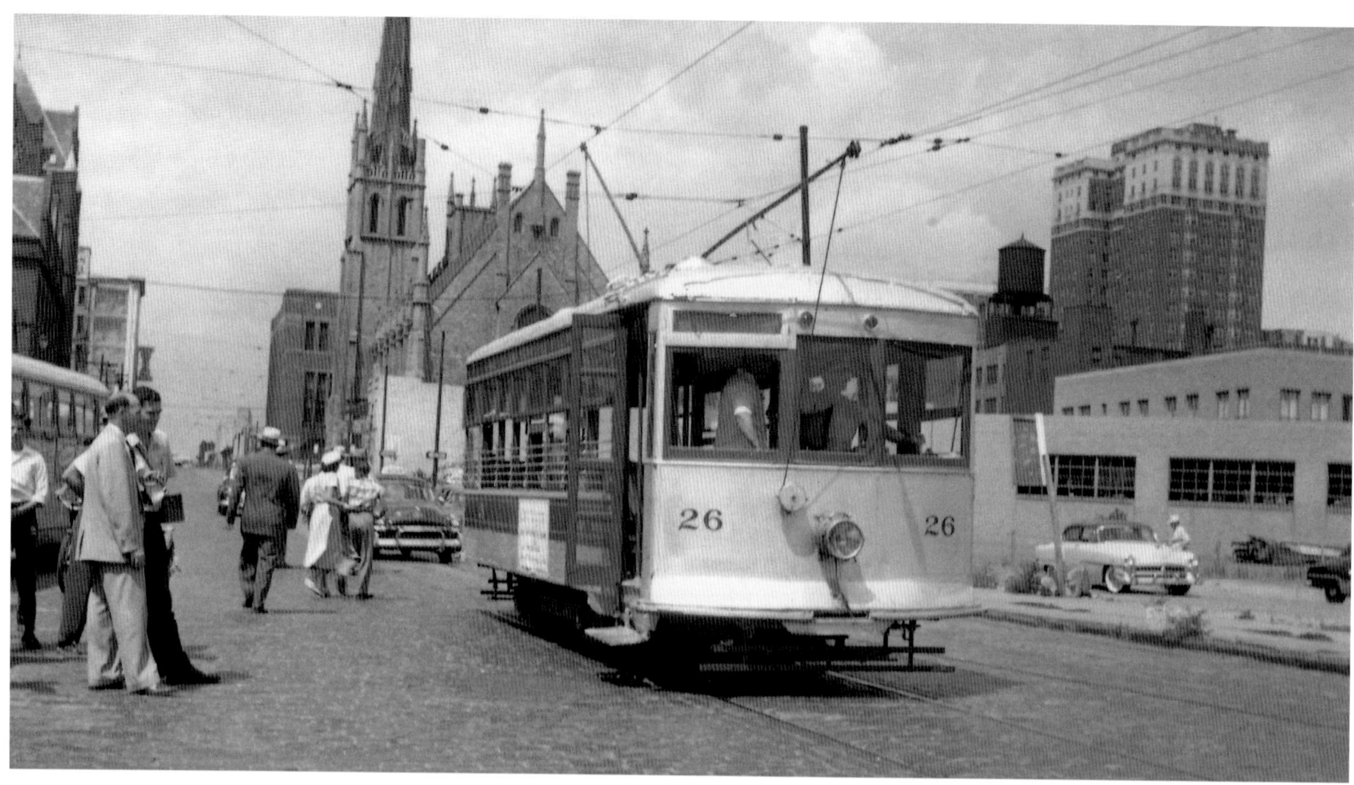

On August 16, 1953, Birney-type car No. 26 is at Third and Larned Streets for a ceremony before heading to the Henry Ford Museum in Dearborn, Michigan. This car was originally No. 7 built in 1922 by the American Car Company for the Cheyenne Electric Railway and used until 1924. It became No. 26 at the Fort Collins Municipal Railway from 1924 to 1951. (*Clifford R. Scholes collection*)

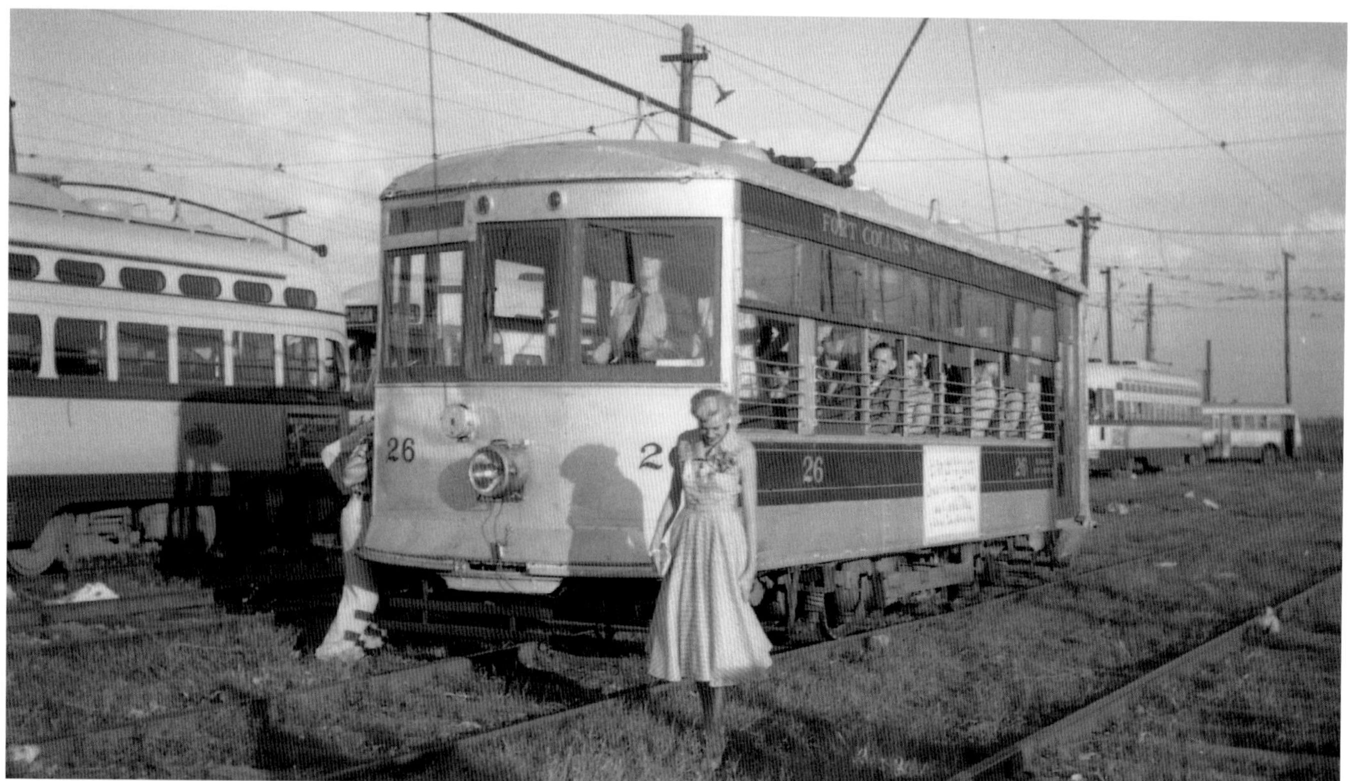

The Highland Park–Woodward Avenue car house on August 16, 1953 is the location of "Miss DSR" in front of former Fort Collins Municipal Railway car No. 26, celebrating the ninetieth anniversary of the DSR. This car was sent to the Henry Ford Museum in Dearborn, Michigan. (*Clifford R. Scholes collection*)

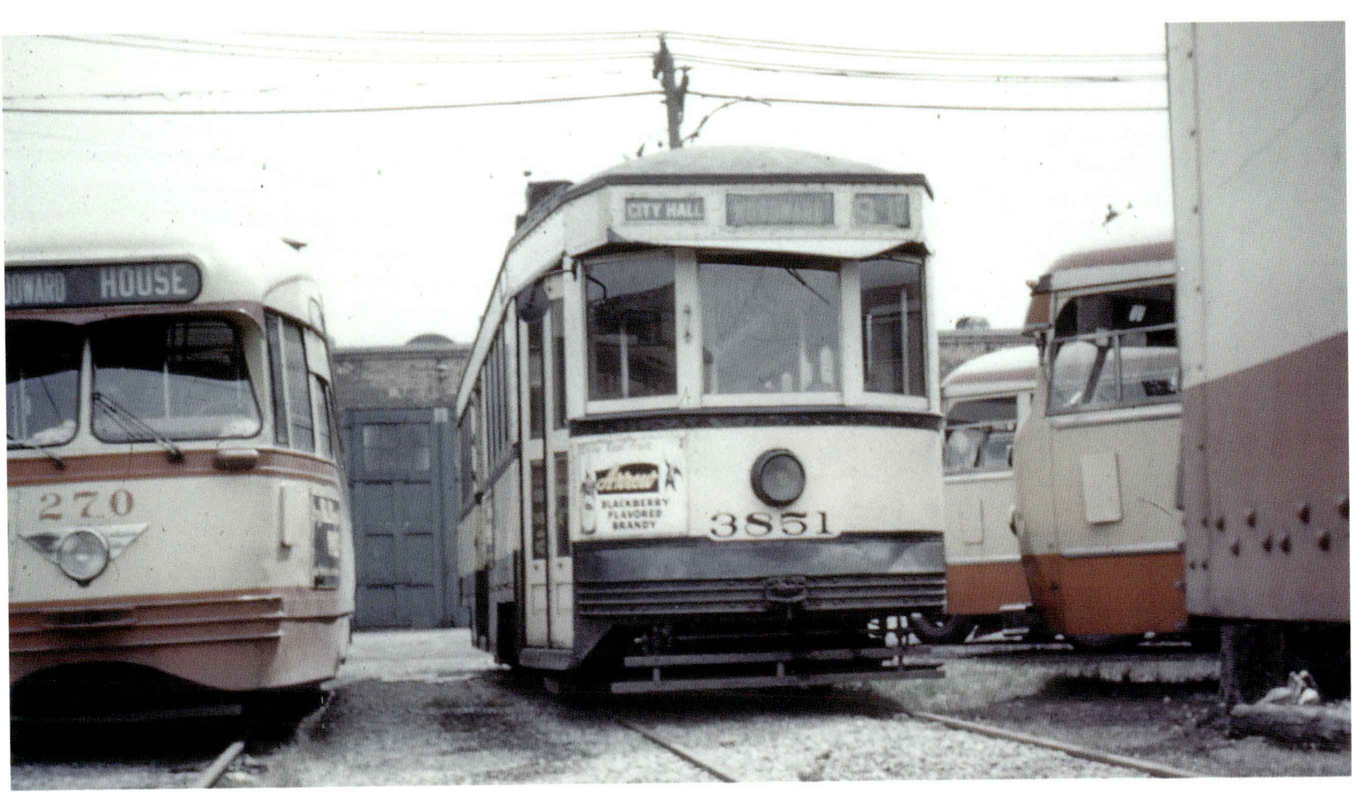

The Woodward Avenue car house is the location of Peter Witt type car No. 3851 and PCC car No. 270 in 1953. (*Clifford R. Scholes collection*)

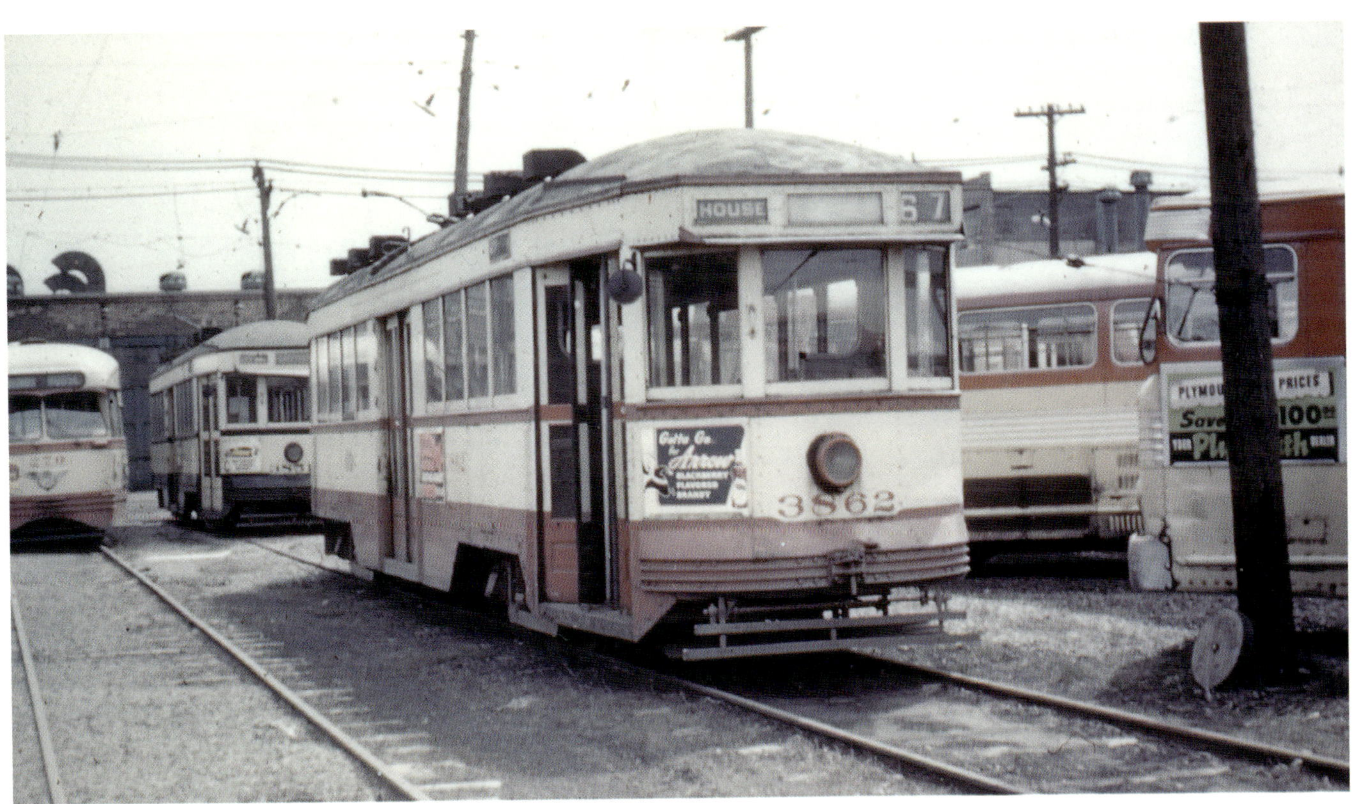

Peter Witt-type car No. 3862 is at the Woodward Avenue car house in 1953. Behind it is Peter Witt car No. 3851 and to the left of it is PCC car No. 270. Located on Woodward Avenue at Manchester Street, the Woodward car house opened in 1910 and closed on October 16, 1955. Streetcars were temporarily moved to the adjacent Highland Park terminal. All DSR streetcar service ended on April 8, 1956. (*Clifford R. Scholes collection*)

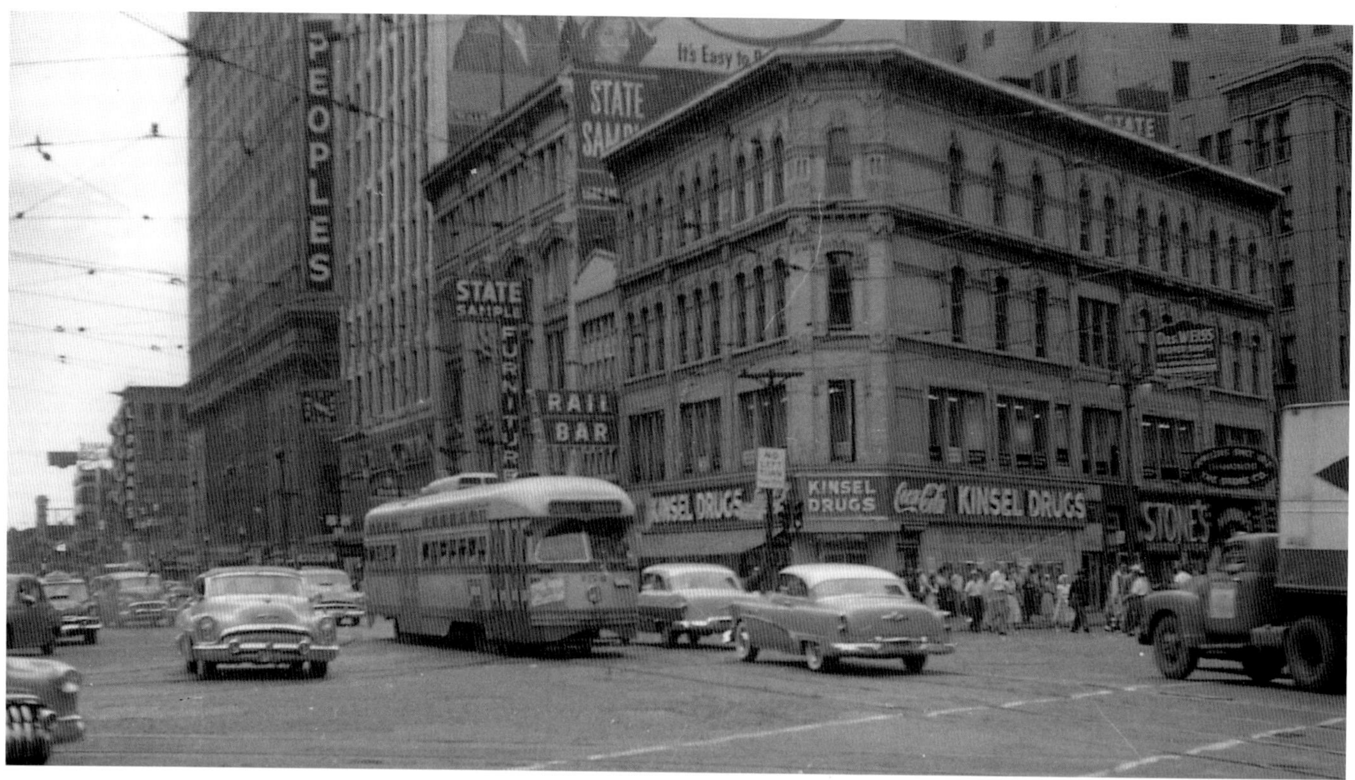

PCC car No. 154 is on Michigan Avenue crossing Griswold Street in downtown Detroit in this busy 1953 scene. With a loss of industrial and working-class jobs, Detroit's population declined 61.4 percent from 1,849,568 in 1950 to 713,777 in 2010. In 1950, Detroit, Department of Street Railways operated 463 streetcars, 2,088 buses, and sixty trackless trolleys, and carried 331,782,828 passengers. By 1974, Detroit Department of Transportation had 1,025 buses and ridership declined to 85,450,000. (*Clifford R. Scholes collection*)

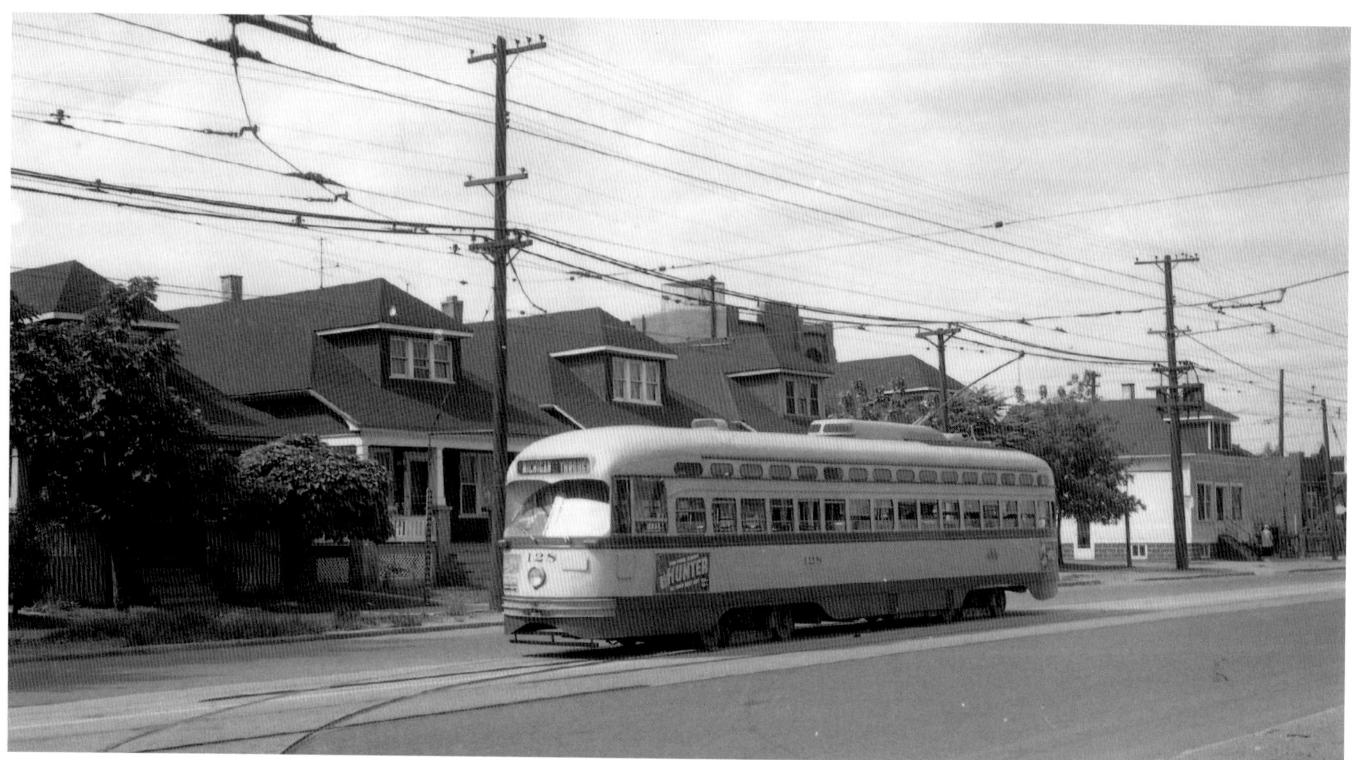

Wyoming Avenue at the car house is the location of PCC car No. 128 on December 5, 1955. This was one of thirty-nine PCC cars (Nos. 102–140) ordered on September 1945 from St. Louis Car Company and were delivered May–August 1947. Each of the 48.5-foot-long cars were powered by four General Electric type 1220 motors, weighed 36,000 pounds, and seated fifty passengers. (*Clifford R. Scholes collection*)

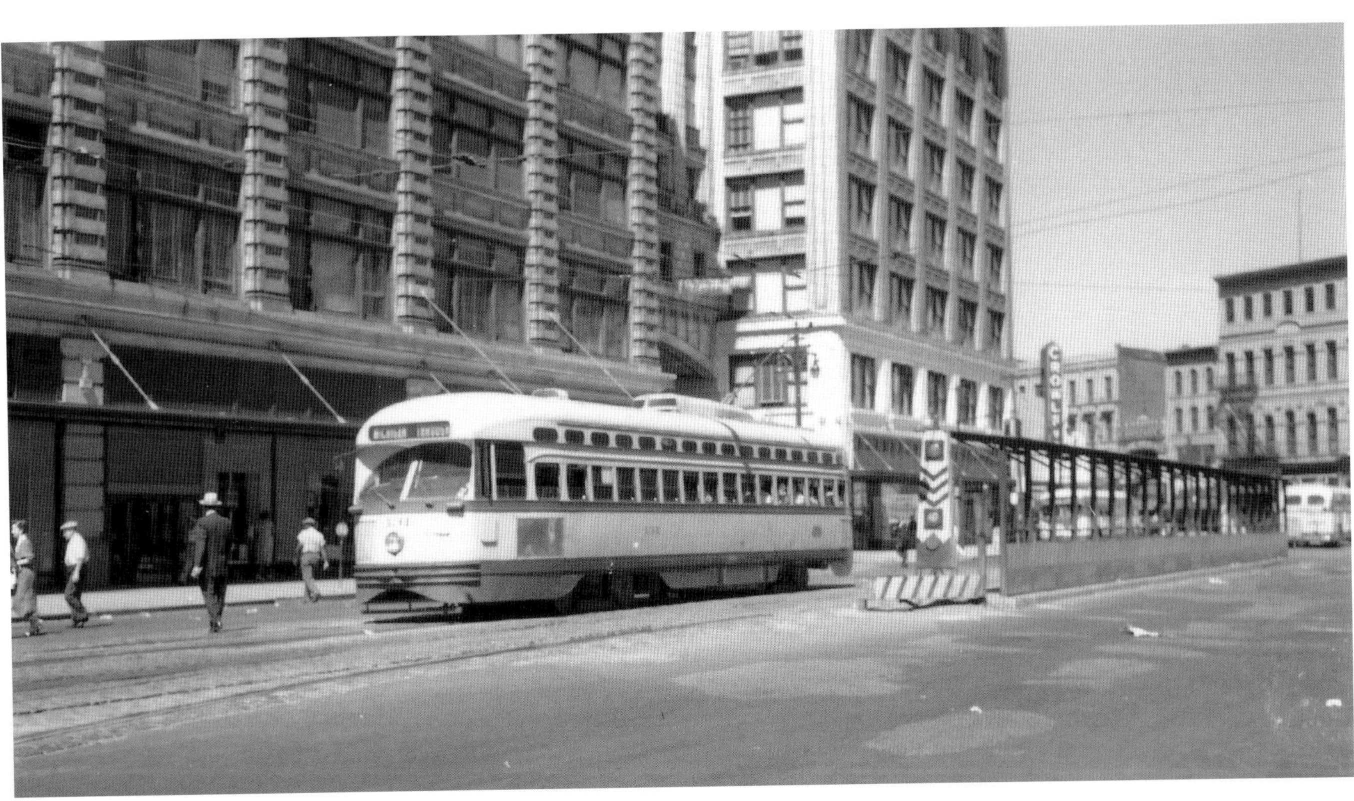

On September 5, 1955, PCC car No. 131 is on Monroe Avenue near Farmer Street in downtown Detroit. The small "standee" windows above the windows were for viewing by standing passengers. Cars Nos. 102–180 had a 30-degree slope in the front windshield design to prevent interior light glare from reflecting back at the motorman at night. (*Clifford R. Scholes collection*)

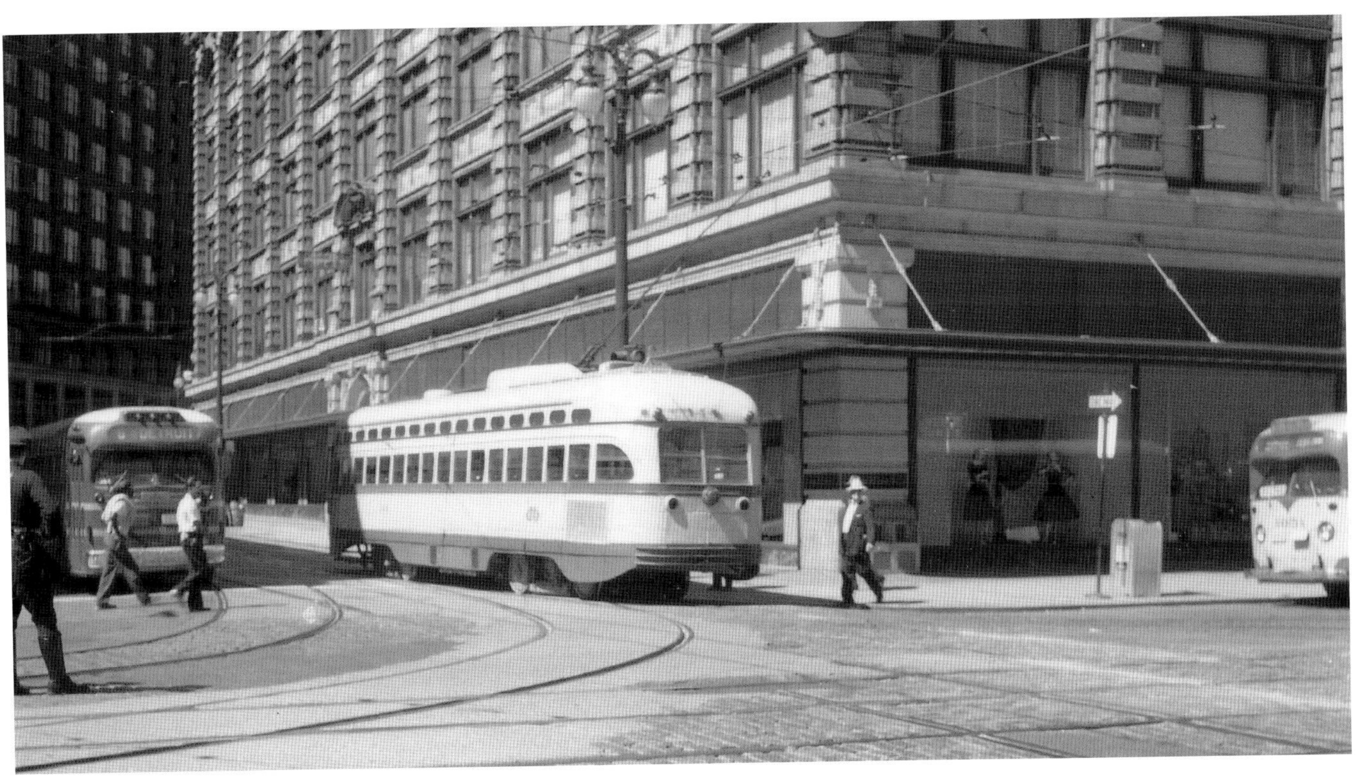

PCC car No. 144 is on Farmer Street, having just crossed Monroe Street, on September 5, 1955. The Michigan section of the Gratiot–Michigan line made its last streetcar run on September 7, 1955, leaving only two streetcar lines in Detroit: Gratiot and Woodward. By the end of 1955, DSR had 1,761 buses, 185 streetcars, and 140 trackless trolleys. (*Clifford R. Scholes collection*)

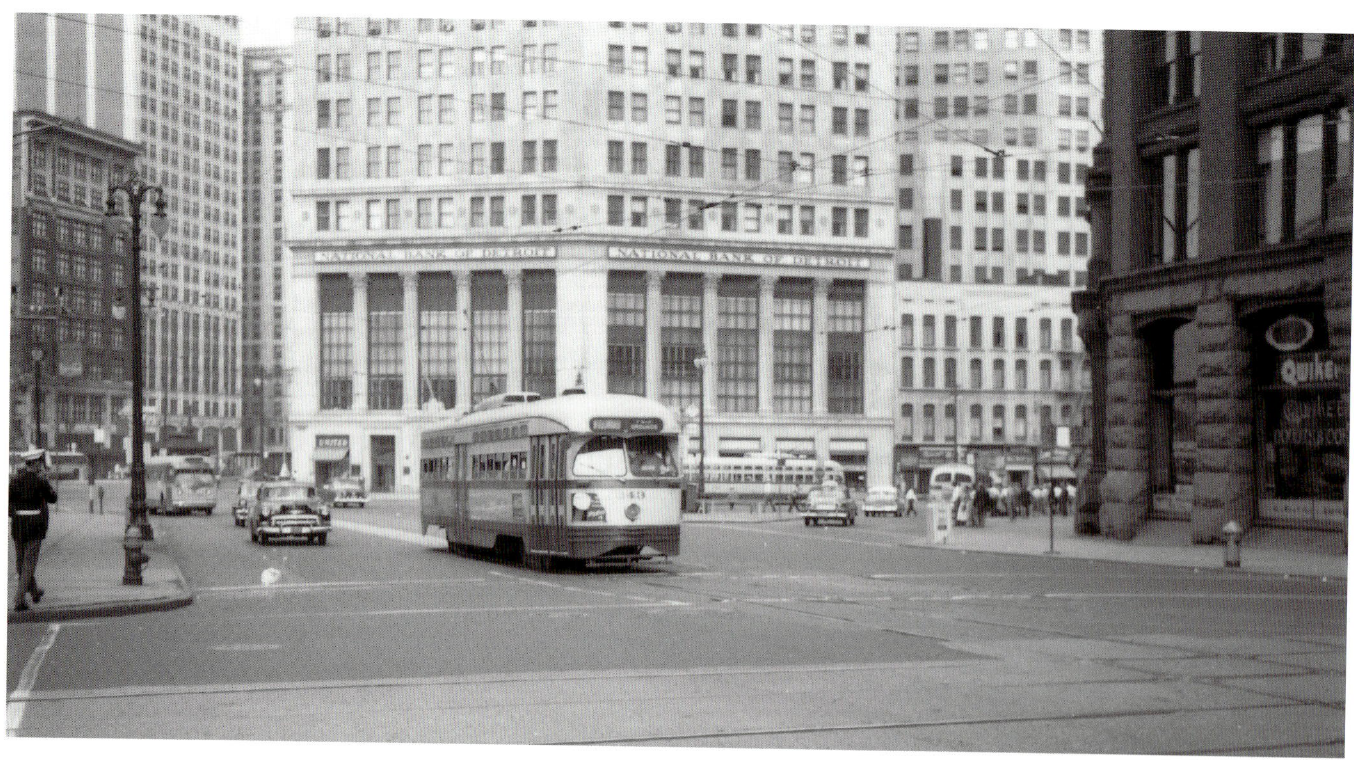

On September 5, 1955, PCC car No. 243 is on Woodward Avenue. Behind the streetcar is the twenty-five-story First National Bank Building, which was designed by Albert Kahn and completed in March 1922. The 106 St. Louis Car Company-built PCC cars (Nos. 181–233, with General Electric type 1220 motors, and Nos. 234–286, with Westinghouse type 1432 motors) were delivered between August and October 1949. These were the longest (50.5 feet long) PCC cars and last new streetcars purchased for Detroit. (*Clifford R. Scholes collection*)

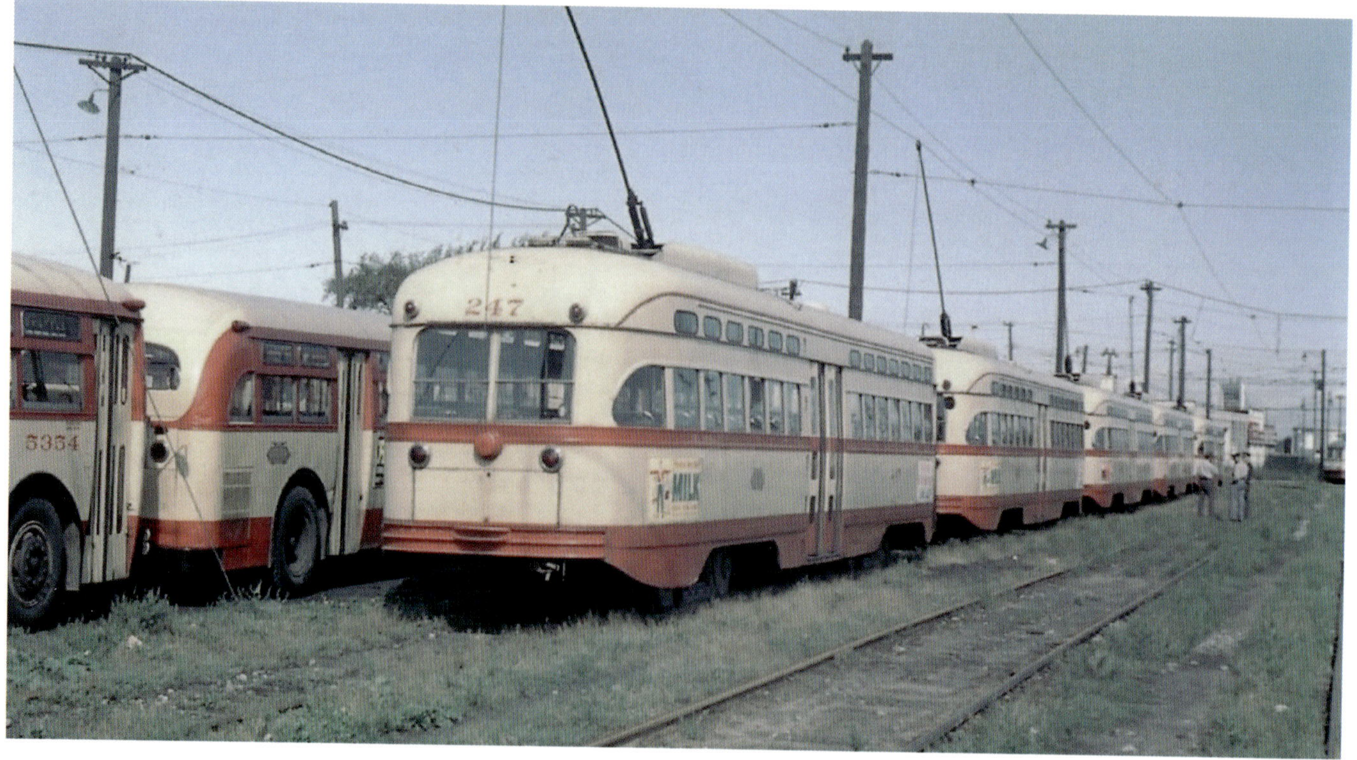

PCC car No. 247 is at the end of a row of operating PCC cars at the Wyoming car house ready for duty on November 11, 1955. On June 20, 1948, remaining streetcar lines were transferred to Baker car house. Streetcars returned to Warren car house on October 2, 1949, and trackless trolleys, which began operating December 15, 1949 for the Crosstown line, were housed at the Warren car house. On September 7, 1955, streetcars were transferred from Warren to Highland Park to service the two remaining streetcar lines: Woodward and Gratiot. (*Clifford R. Scholes collection*)

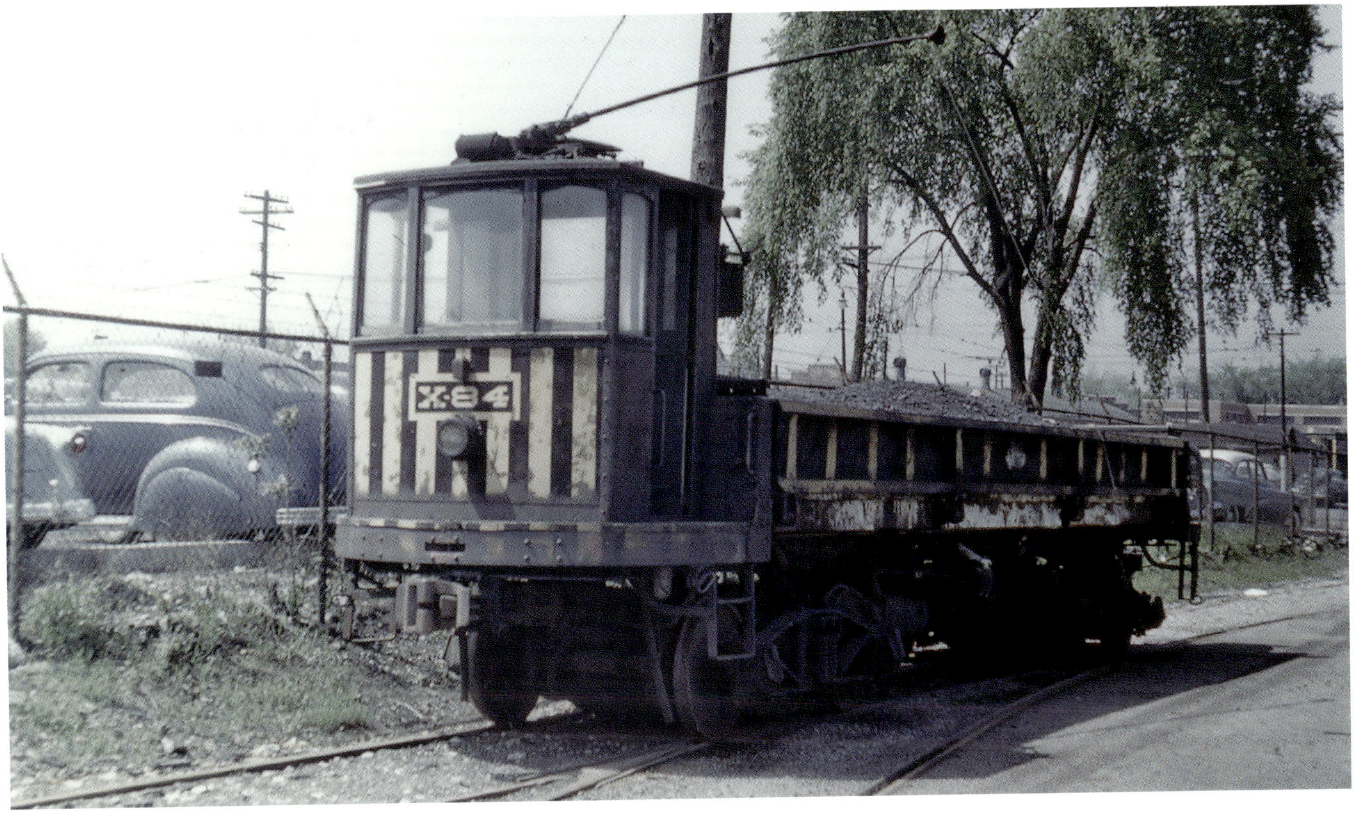

Single end side dump car No. X-84 was at the St. Jean car house in 1950 and was used to haul ballast and dirt. Powered by four Westinghouse type 93 motors and weighing 61,040 pounds, this car was built by Differential Steel Car Company in 1925. (*Clifford R. Scholes collection*)

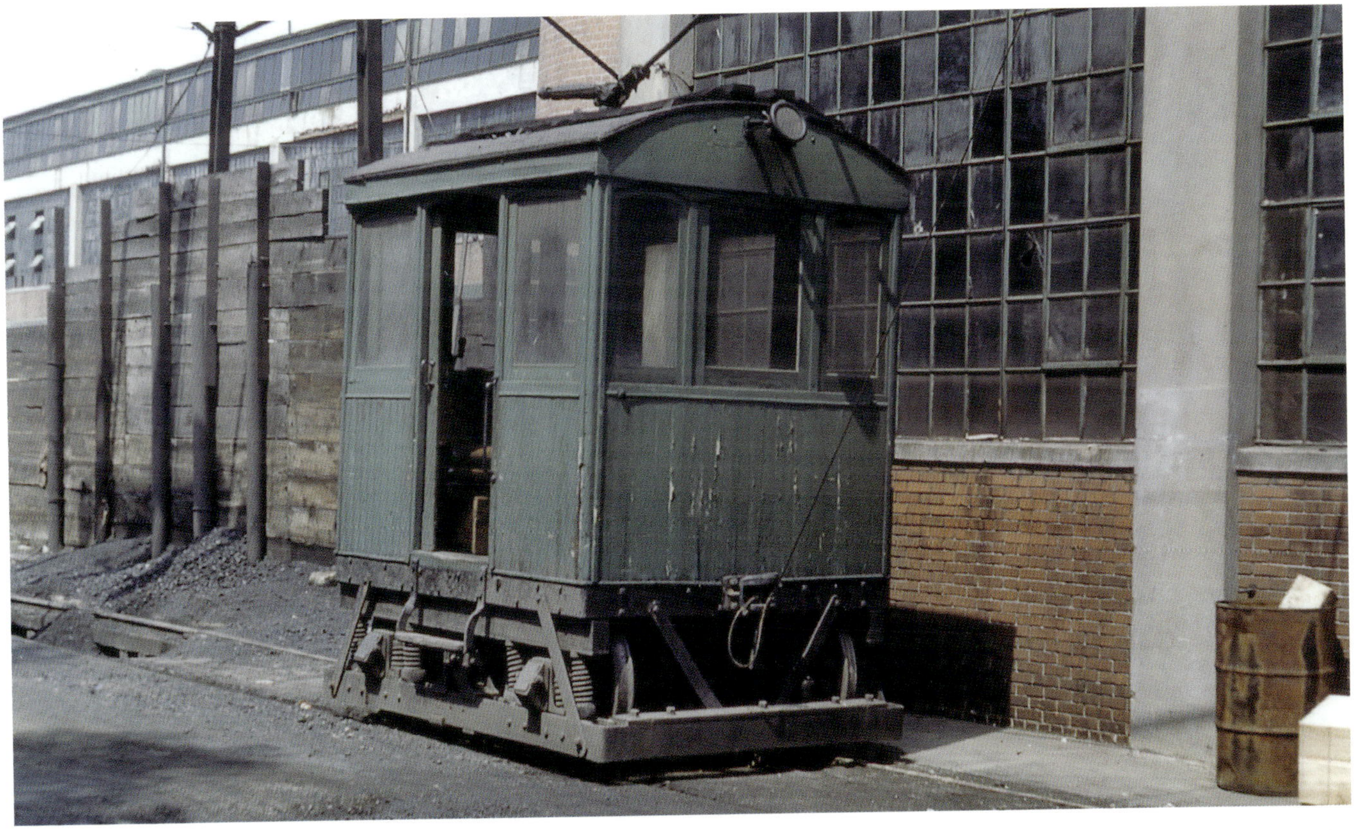

Shop shifter No. X-76 is at the Woodward Avenue shops on March 14, 1955. Weighing 14,000 pounds and powered by two General Electric type 203 motors, the shifter was built by DUR in 1902. (*Bob Crockett photograph—Clifford R. Scholes collection*)

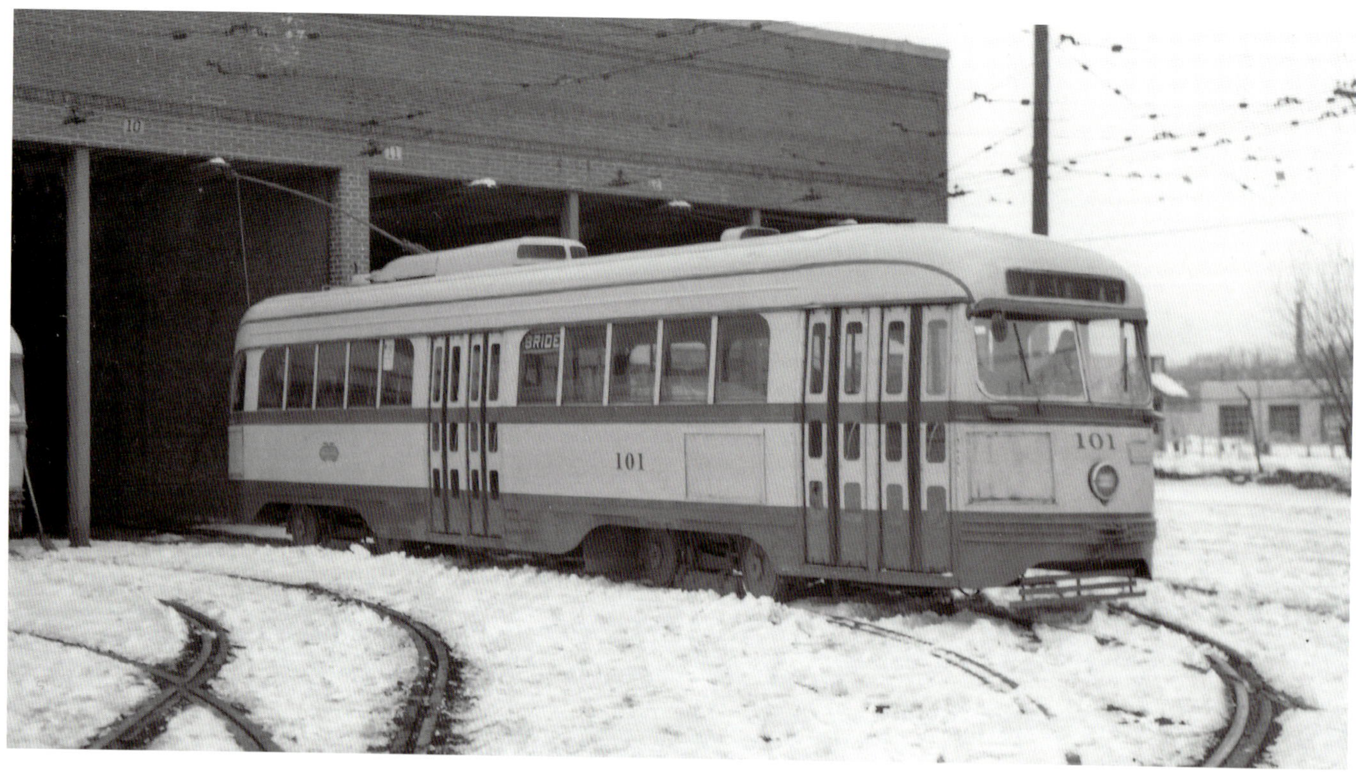

In April 1956, with a blanket of snow on the ground, PCC car No. 101 is at the Highland Park-Woodward Avenue car barn. Powered by four General Electric type 1198 motors, this car had been diverted from a Pittsburgh Railways Company 1600 series order and was delivered from St. Louis Car Company in September 1945. The 46.5-foot-long car weighed 33,000 pounds, seated fifty-four passengers, and was scrapped in July 1956. (*Bob Crockett photograph—Clifford R. Scholes collection*)

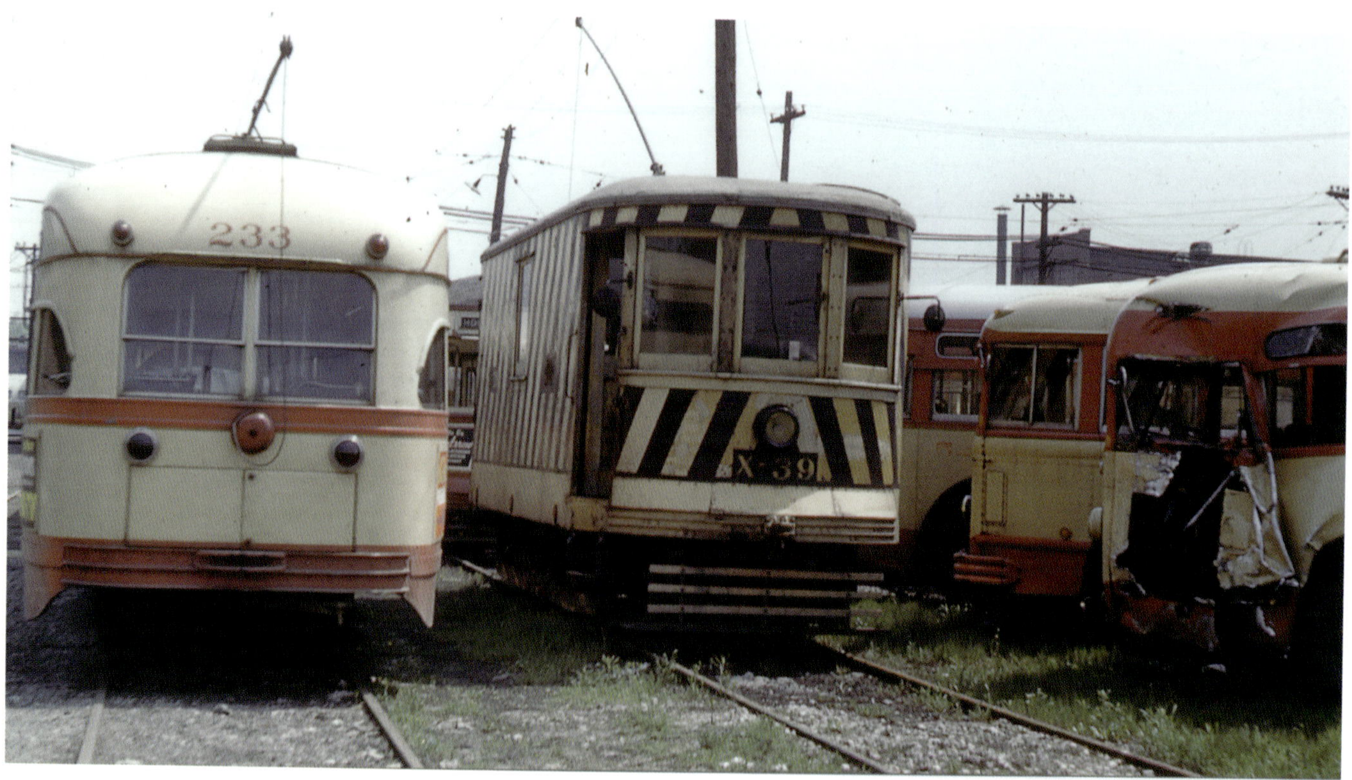

On March 14, 1956, Woodward Avenue shops is the location of PCC car No. 233 (one of fifty-three cars, Nos. 181–233, delivered by St. Louis Car Company during August–October 1949) and rail grinder No. X-39, built by American Car Company in 1912, with rebuilding by DSR in 1926 and again in 1945. (*Clifford R. Scholes collection*)

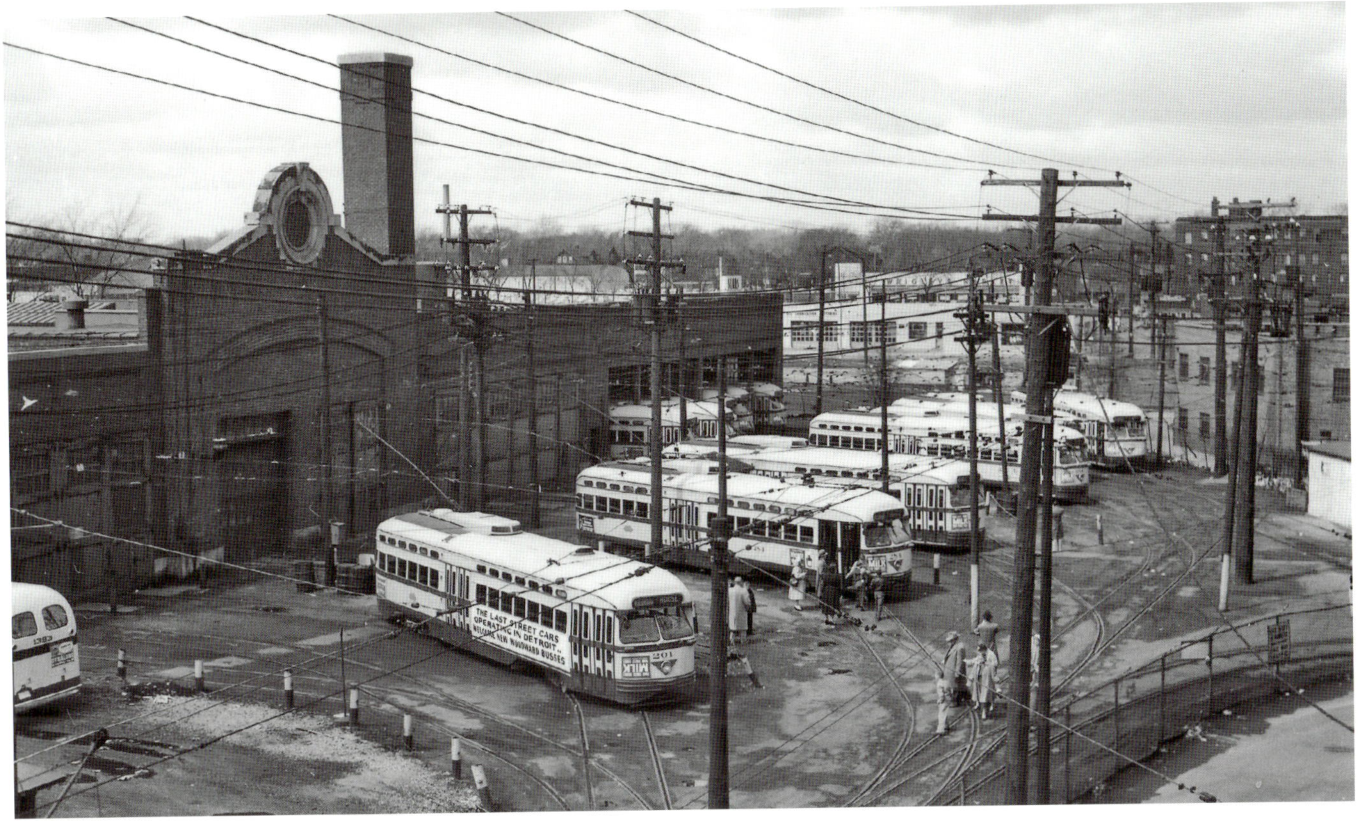

The Highland Park–Woodland Avenue car house is the location of numerous PCC cars, including car No. 201 with the sign "The last streetcars operating in Detroit. Welcome new Woodward buses" on April 7, 1956. (*Bob Crockett photograph—Clifford R. Scholes collection*)

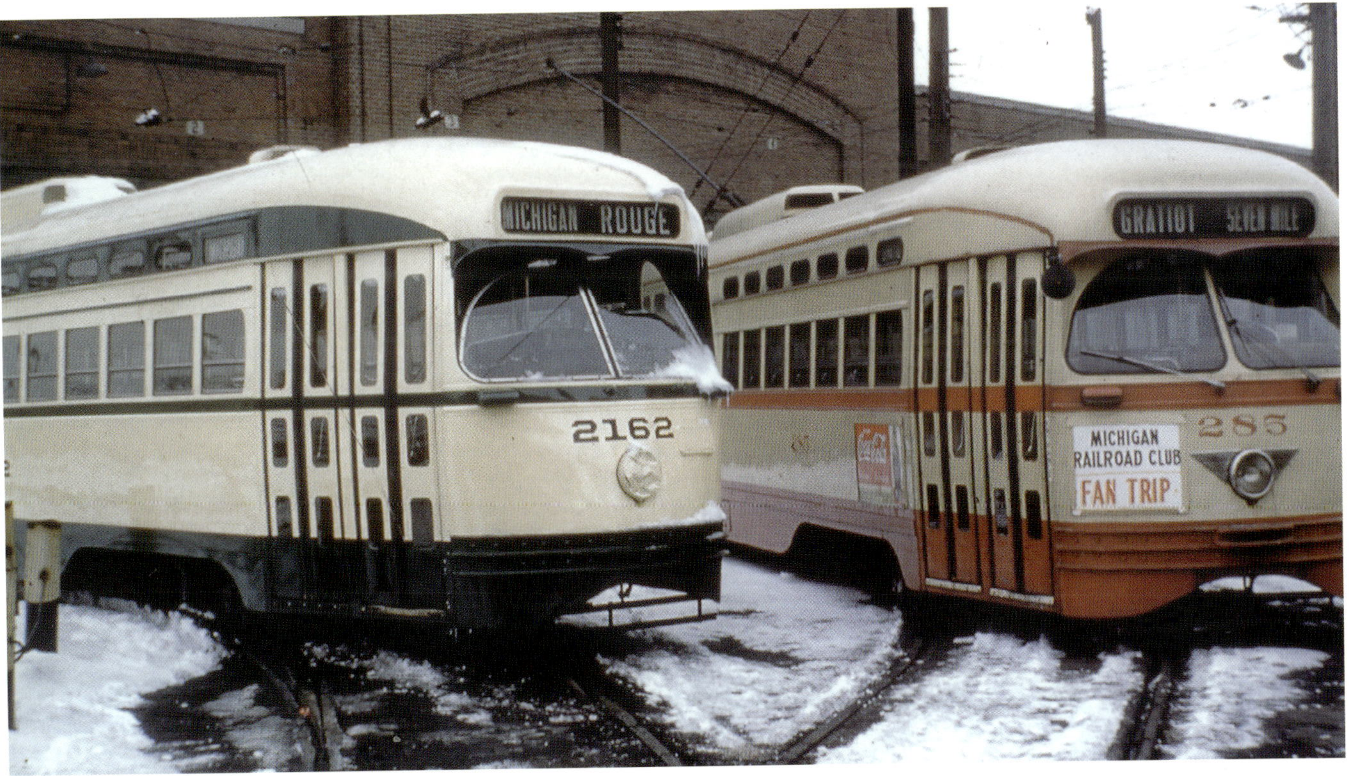

In 1956, former DSR PCC car No. 162 is at the Woodward Avenue shops, now repainted in cream with green trim, renumbered No. 2162, and heading for Mexico City. PCC car No. 285 is on the right in the Detroit cream with red trim paint scheme and with a sign on the lower left front announcing "Michigan Railroad Club Fan Trip." (*Bob Crockett photograph—Clifford R. Scholes collection*)

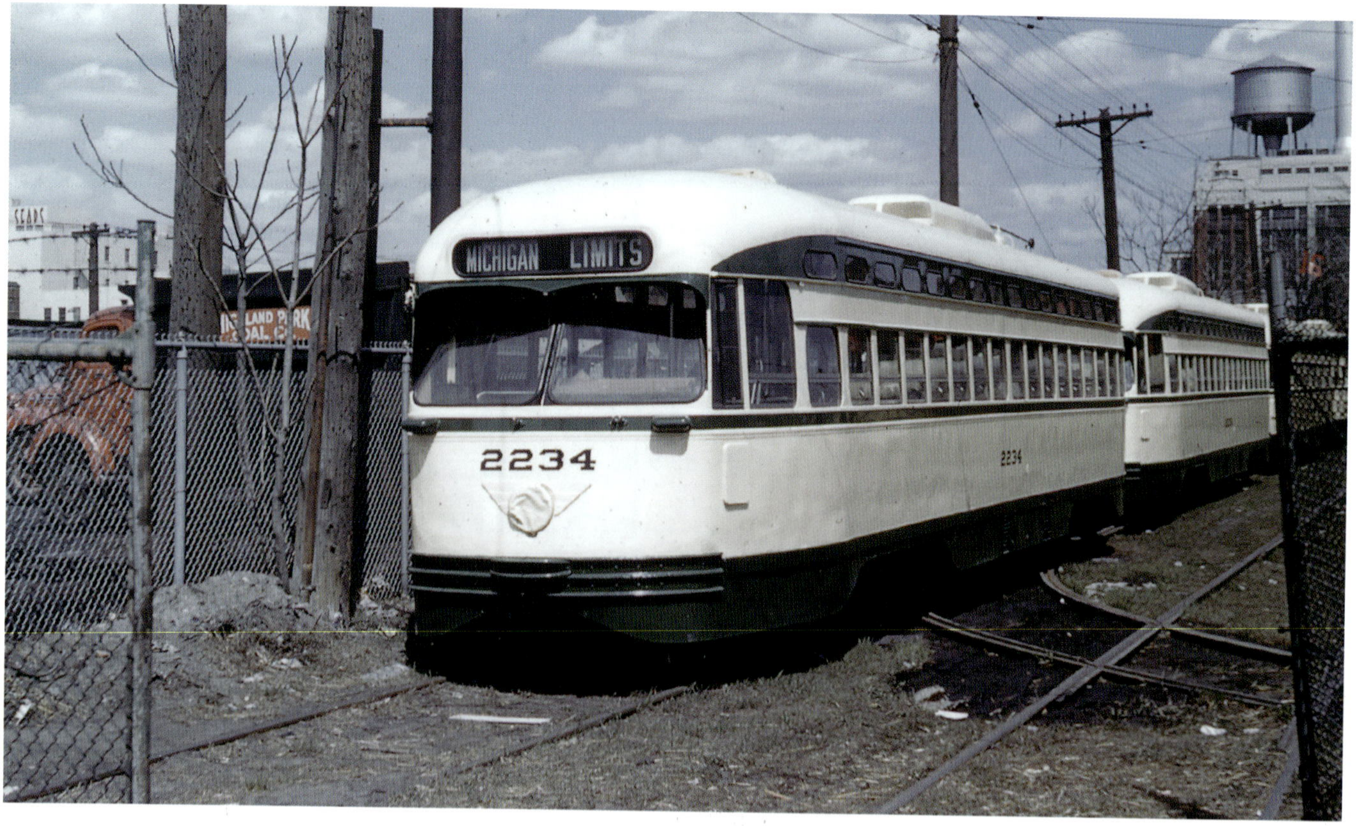

On April 23, 1956, PCC car No. 2234 (originally DSR No. 234) is heading the lineup of PCC cars at the Highland Park shops that have been repaired, repainted, and renumbered for Mexico City. (*Bob Crockett photograph—Clifford R. Scholes collection*)

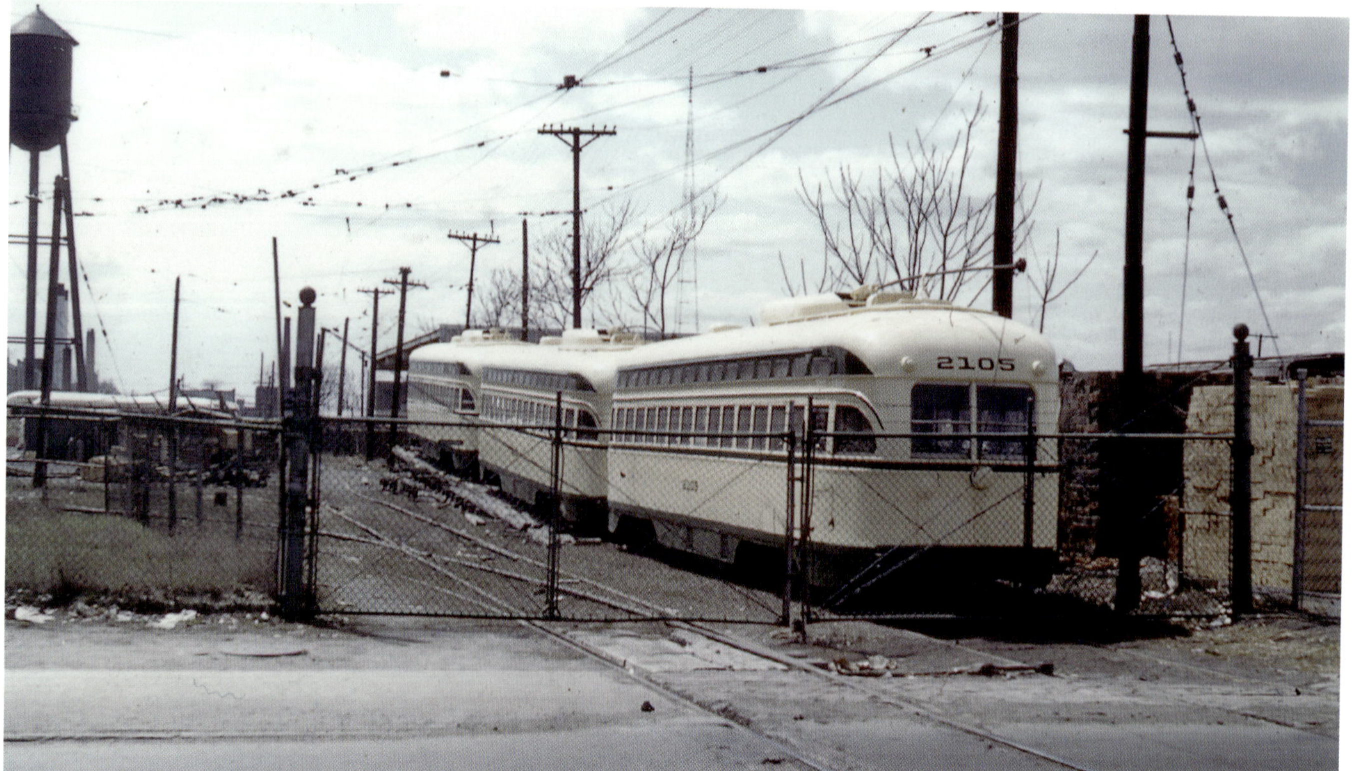

Refurbished PCC car No. 2105 (originally DSR No. 105) and with two other PCC cars are on the loading ramp at the Highland Park shops on March 29, 1956, ready for shipment to Mexico. (*Bob Crockett photograph—Clifford R. Scholes collection*)

2

Routes Baker, Clairmount, Crosstown, and Grand River

The Baker line, with its large ridership, connected the Ford Rouge plant in the City of Dearborn through downtown Detroit to the City of Hamtramck and east end of Detroit. Although Baker Street in Detroit was changed to Bagley Avenue, the streetcar line continued to be called Baker. In 1948, route Baker streetcars operated westbound from Van Dyke via Nevada, Mt. Elliott, Davison, Jos. Campau, Chene, Gratiot, Randolph, Monroe, Michigan, Porter, Brooklyn, Bagley, 23rd, Vernor Highway, Ferndale, private right of way, and Eagle to the Ford Motor Rouge Plant. Eastbound route Baker streetcars operated from the Ford Motor Rouge Plant via Eagle, private right of way, Ferndale, Vernor Highway, 24th, Bagley, Trumbull, Abbott, Michigan, Monroe, Randolph, Gratiot, Grandy, Chene, Jos. Campau, Davison, Mt Elliott, and Nevada to Van Dyke. DSR's only two direction single track line was on the Baker line on Nevada Avenue. The Baker line was converted to bus operation on April 6, 1952.

Clairmount was like an upside down "U" that crossed the other eleven surviving streetcar lines in 1948 and operated westbound from St. Jean and Jefferson via St. Jean, Shoemaker, Montclair, Harper, Mt. Elliott, E. Milwaukee, Russell, Owen, Clairmount, Linwood, Joy Road, Epworth, Warren, Junction, Devereaux, 35th, Michigan, Junction, Fort, Scotten, Spring, and Clark to Fort. Eastbound Clairmount streetcars operated from Clark via Fort, Junction, Warren, Epworth, Joy Road, Linwood, Clairmount, Owen, Russell, E. Milwaukee, Mt. Elliott, Harper, Montclair, Shoemaker, St. Jean, Kercheval, Hart, and Jefferson to St. Jean. The Clairmount line was converted to bus operation July 29, 1951.

Crosstown was an east-west line about 1.5 miles north of downtown Detroit. It operated westbound from Warren and St. Jean, west on Warren to Cadillac, south to Forest, west to Gratiot, southwest to Mt. Elliott, north to Forest, west to 14th, north to Warren, and west to Pierson. Eastbound was the same route to Warren and 14th and continuing east on Warren to Beaubien, south to Forest, and then via the same route. This line was converted to bus operation on October 26, 1947, converted to trackless trolley operation on December 15, 1949, and went back to bus operation on March 31, 1961.

Grand River was a heavy 14-mile line westbound from Capitol Park in downtown Detroit north on Griswold, to Grand River heading northwest on Grand River to Seven Mile Road. Eastbound, the line went the same route to Grand River and Cass, south to Shelby, and east to Capitol Park. It was converted to bus operation on May 5, 1947, became a trackless trolley line on September 5, 1951, and went back to bus operation on November 16, 1962.

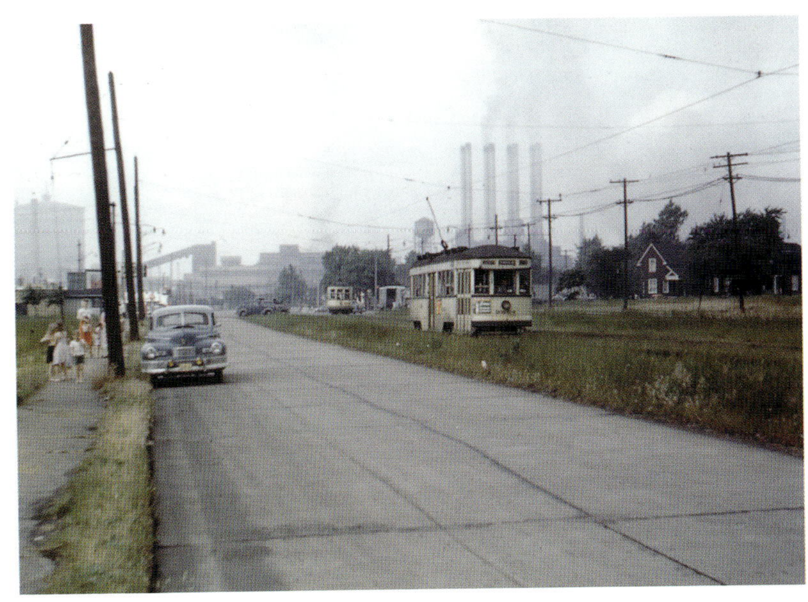

On June 27, 1950, Peter Witt-type car No. 3723 is on the private right of way alongside Vernor Highway of the Baker line. This was one of fifty cars (Nos. 3700–3749) delivered by St. Louis Car Company in 1927. Powered by four General Electric type 265 motors, each car weighed 37,140 pounds and seated fifty-two passengers. (*Bob Crockett photograph—Clifford R. Scholes collection*)

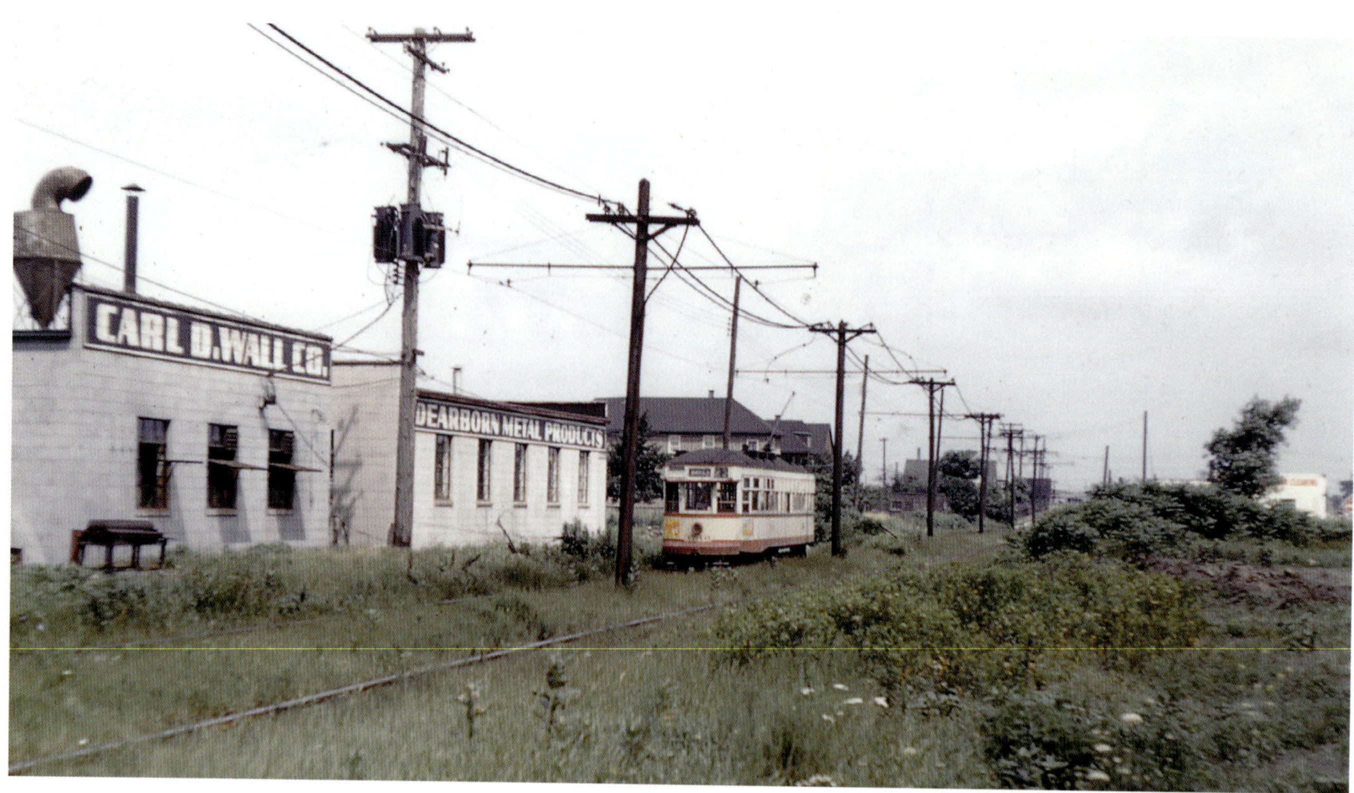

The Vernor Highway private right of way of the Baker line near the Ford Rouge plant is the location of Peter Witt type car No. 3810 on June 27, 1951. This was one of 100 cars (Nos. 3750–3849) built by Perley A. Thomas Car Company in 1929. Powered by four General Electric type 265 motors, each 48.5-foot-long car weighed 36,060 pounds and seated fifty-two passengers. (*Bob Crockett photograph—Clifford R. Scholes collection*)

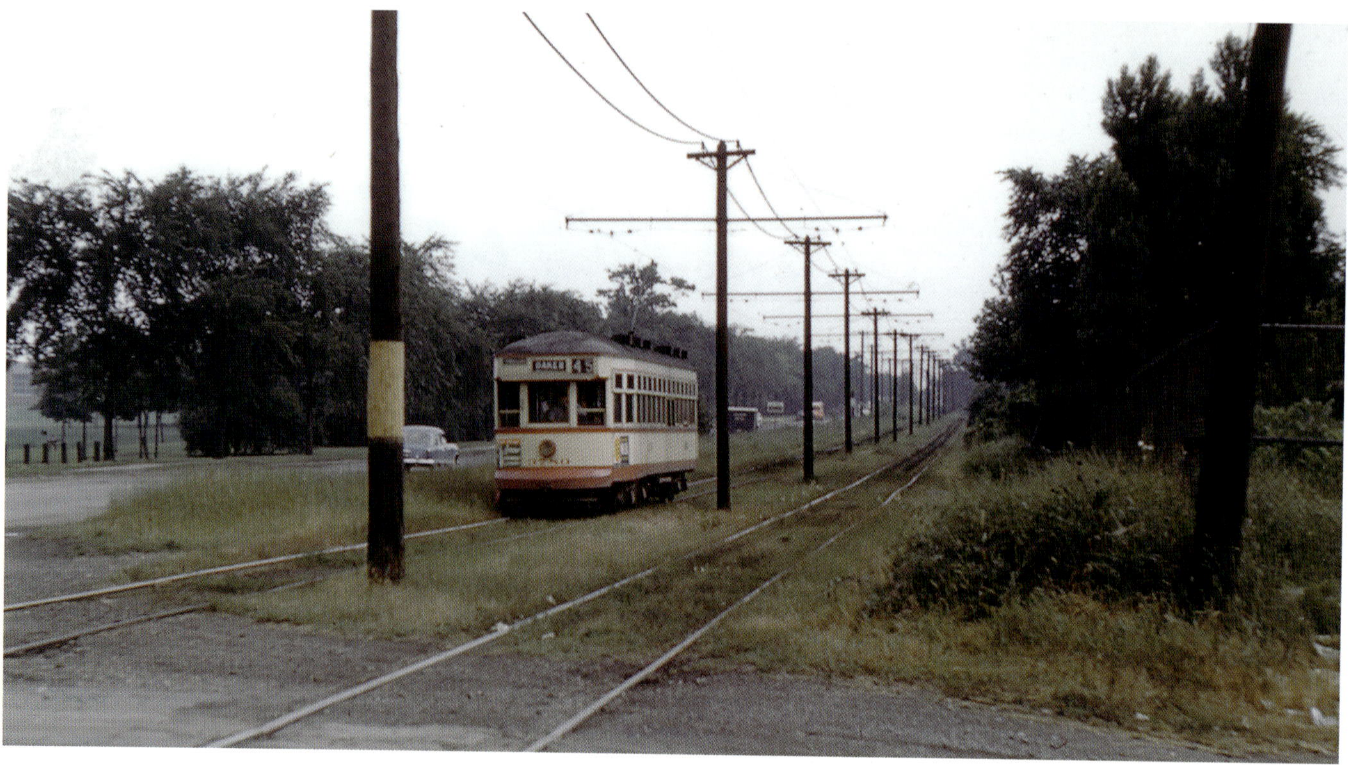

On June 27, 1951, Peter Witt-type car No. 3780 is on the Baker line private right of way paralleling the Vernon Highway. The well patronized Baker line connected the Ford Rouge plant west of Detroit in Dearborn, Michigan, with downtown Detroit and passed through the city of Hamtramck, a municipality completely surrounded by Detroit, and ended back in Detroit at Nevada and Van Dyke Avenues. (*Bob Crockett photograph—Clifford R. Scholes collection*)

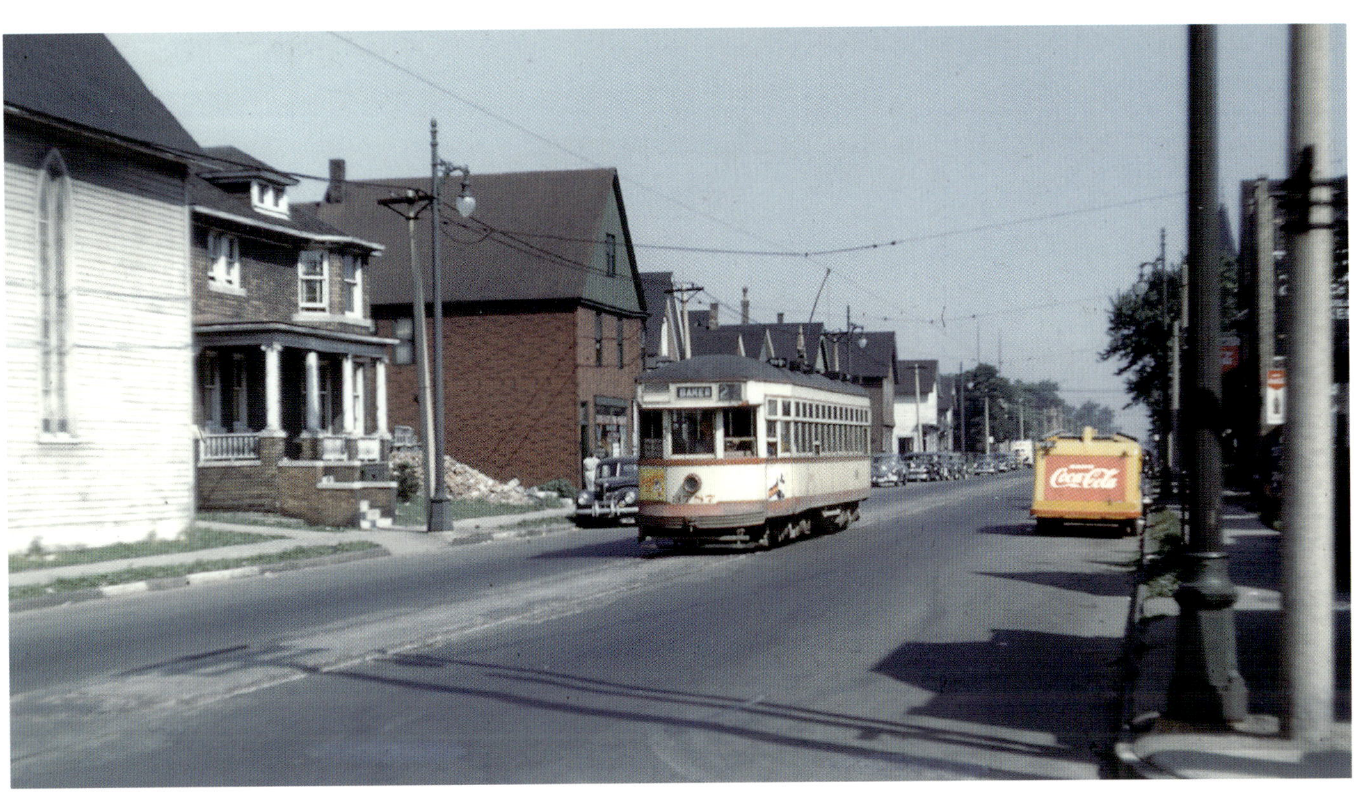

Chene at Pierce Streets is the location of Peter Witt type car No. 3787, making a trip on the Baker line on June 27, 1951. Baker Street was changed to Bagley Avenue around the 1900s, but the line name was not changed. (*Bob Crockett photograph—Clifford R. Scholes collection*)

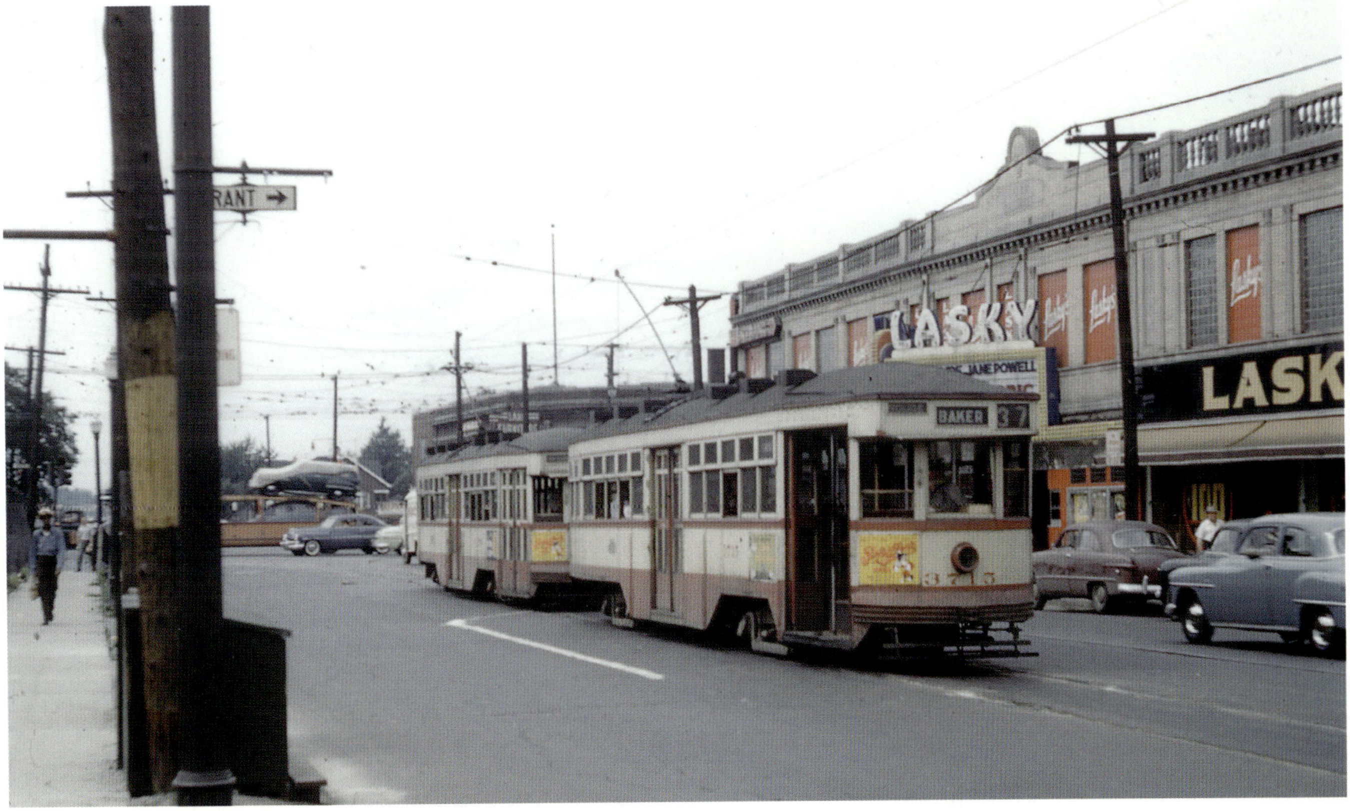

On June 27, 1951, Peter Witt-type car No. 3715 is along the Baker line on Joseph Campau Street at Grant Street with another Peter Witt-type car behind it. (*Bob Crockett photograph—Clifford R. Scholes collection*)

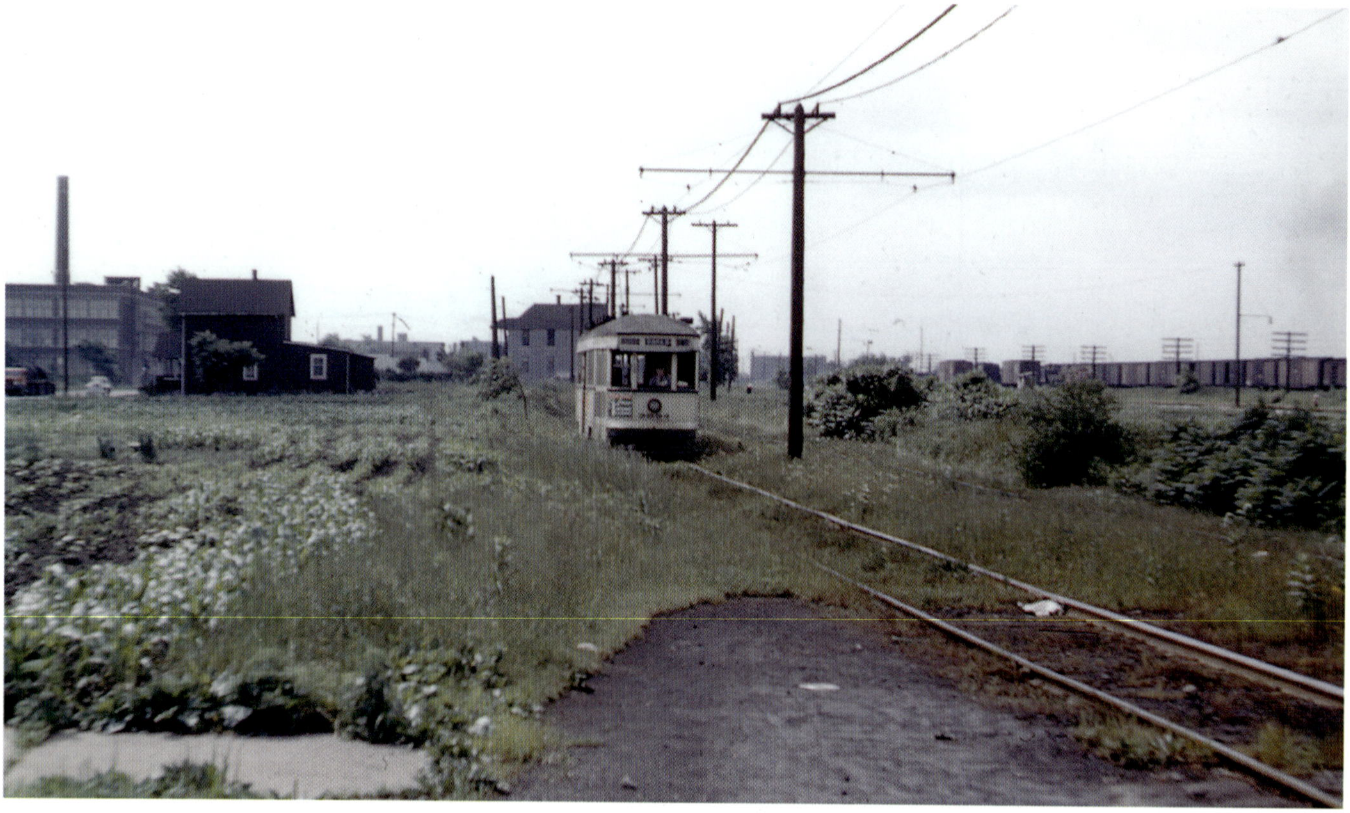

The Baker line right of way near the Ford Rouge plant is the location of Peter Witt-type car No. 3894 on June 27, 1951. A significant portion of the west side of the Baker line was on private right of way. (*Clifford R. Scholes collection*)

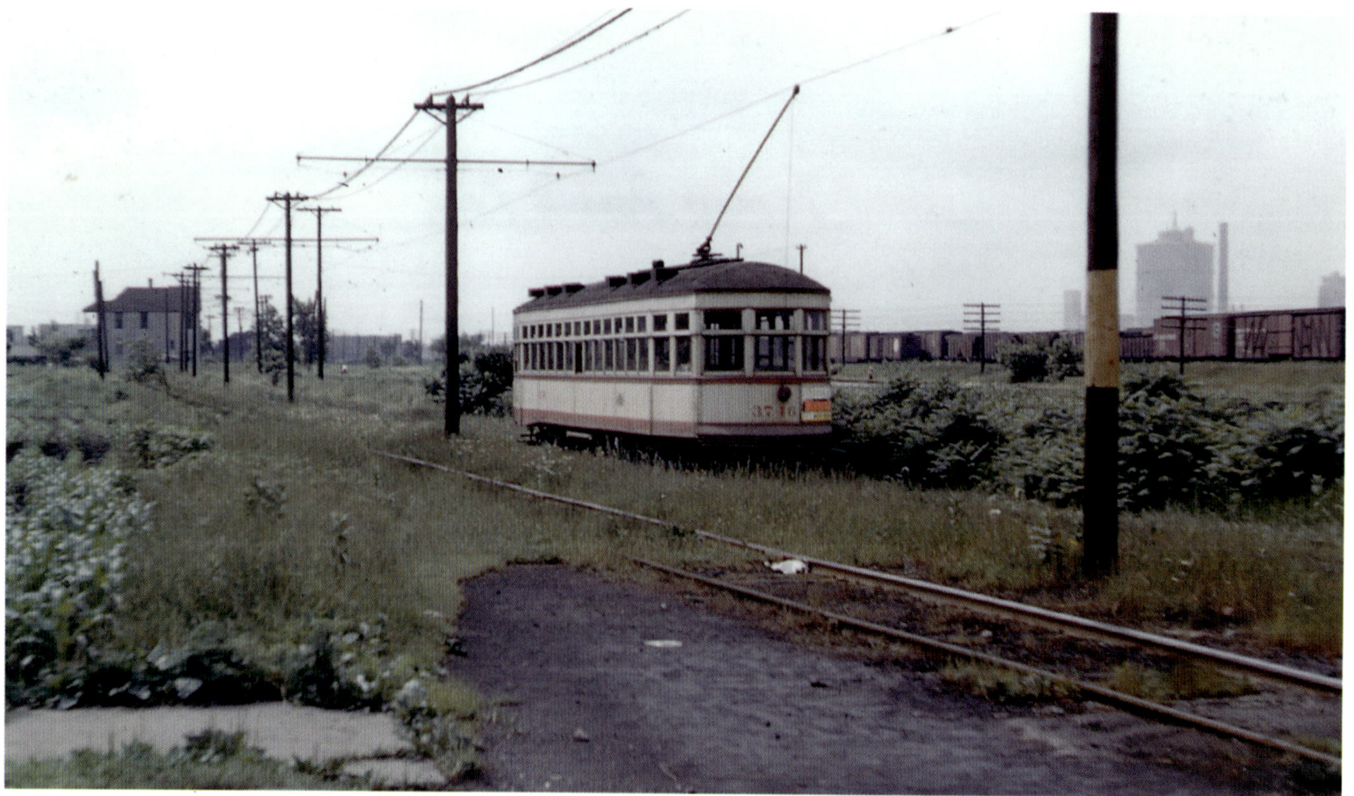

On June 21, 1957, Peter Witt type car No. 3746 is on the private right of way near the River Rouge Ford plant. (*Bob Crockett photograph—Clifford R. Scholes collection*)

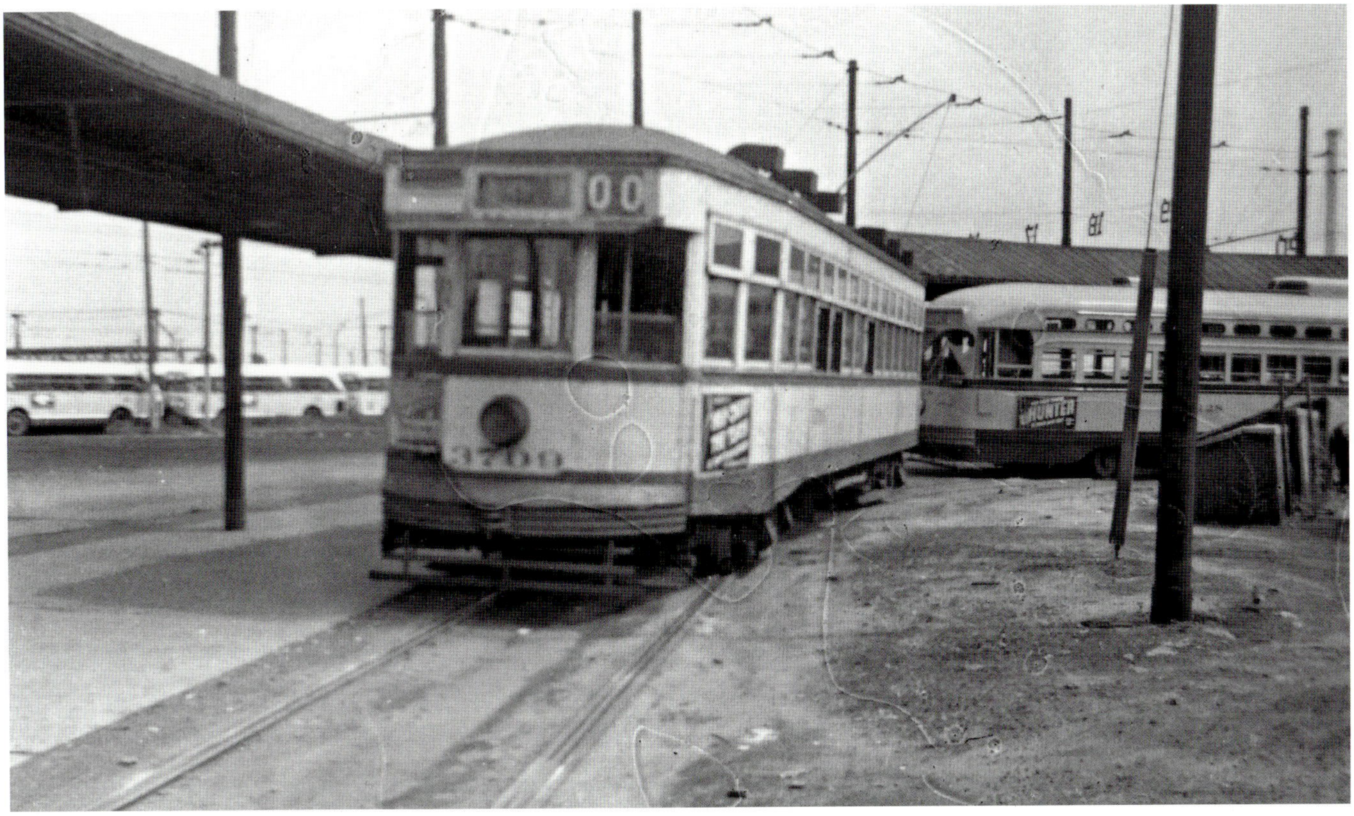

Peter Witt-type car No. 3709 and PCC car No. 128 are at the Miller Road loop serving the Ford Rouge plant in 1953. (*Clifford R. Scholes collection*)

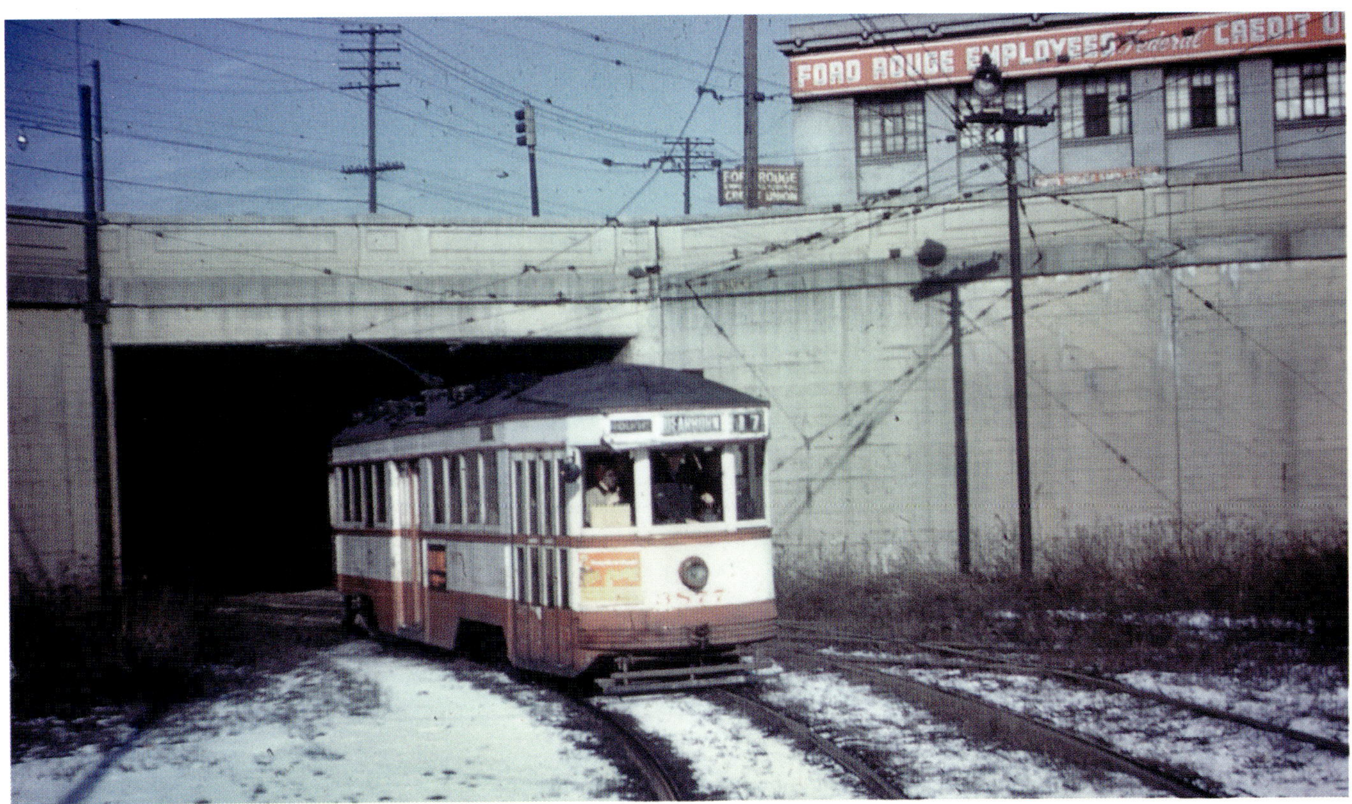

On February 6, 1954, Peter Witt-type car No. 3877 is crossing under the Pere Marquette Railway to serve the Miller Road terminal of the Ford Rouge plant. (*R. F. Glaze—Clifford R. Scholes collection*)

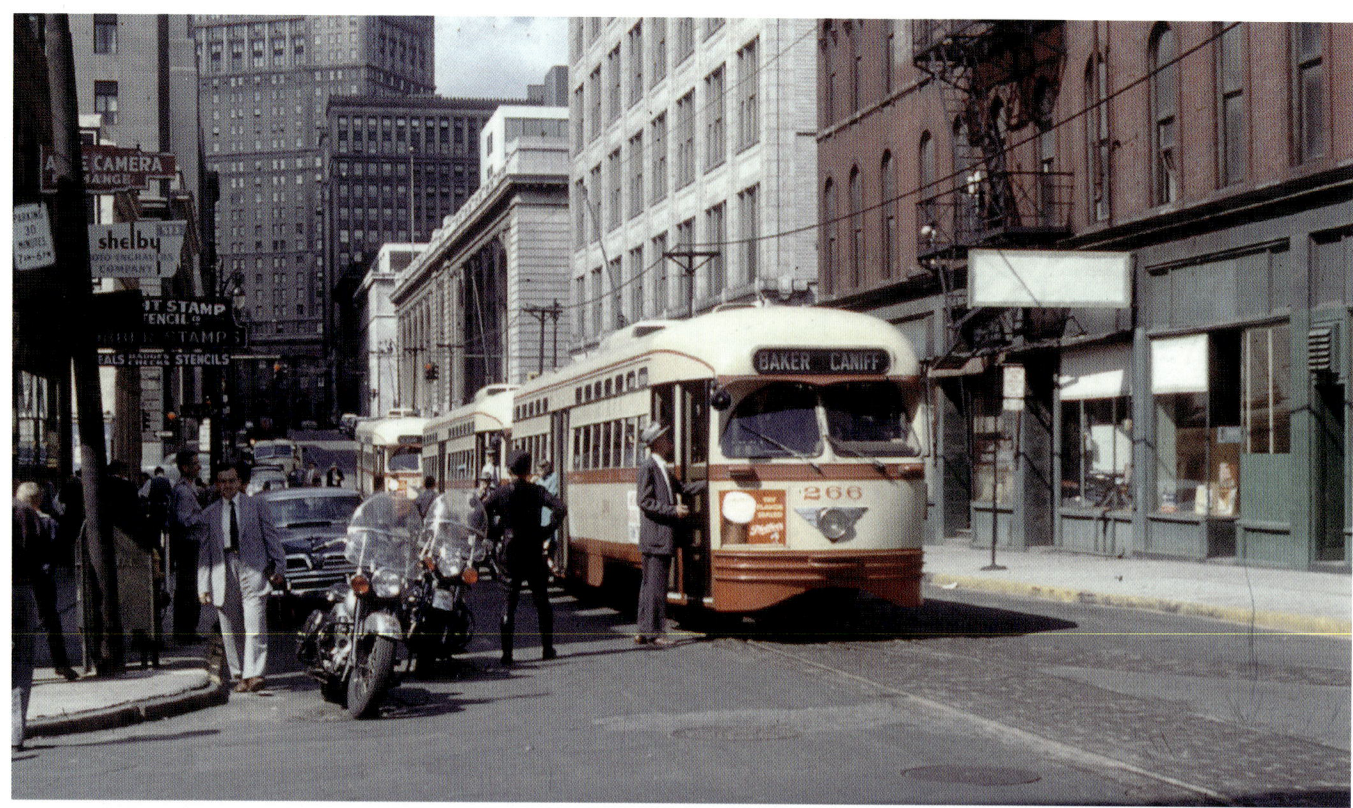

PCC car No. 266 is at a passenger stop in downtown Detroit on a route Baker car bound for Caniff Street in the City of Hamtramck, followed by PCC cars Nos. 269 and 273, in 1950. DSR management used passenger safety to try selling the idea that buses were better by stating that streetcar passengers had to board within the center of the roadway while buses offered curb service. (*Bob Crockett photograph—Clifford R. Scholes collection*)

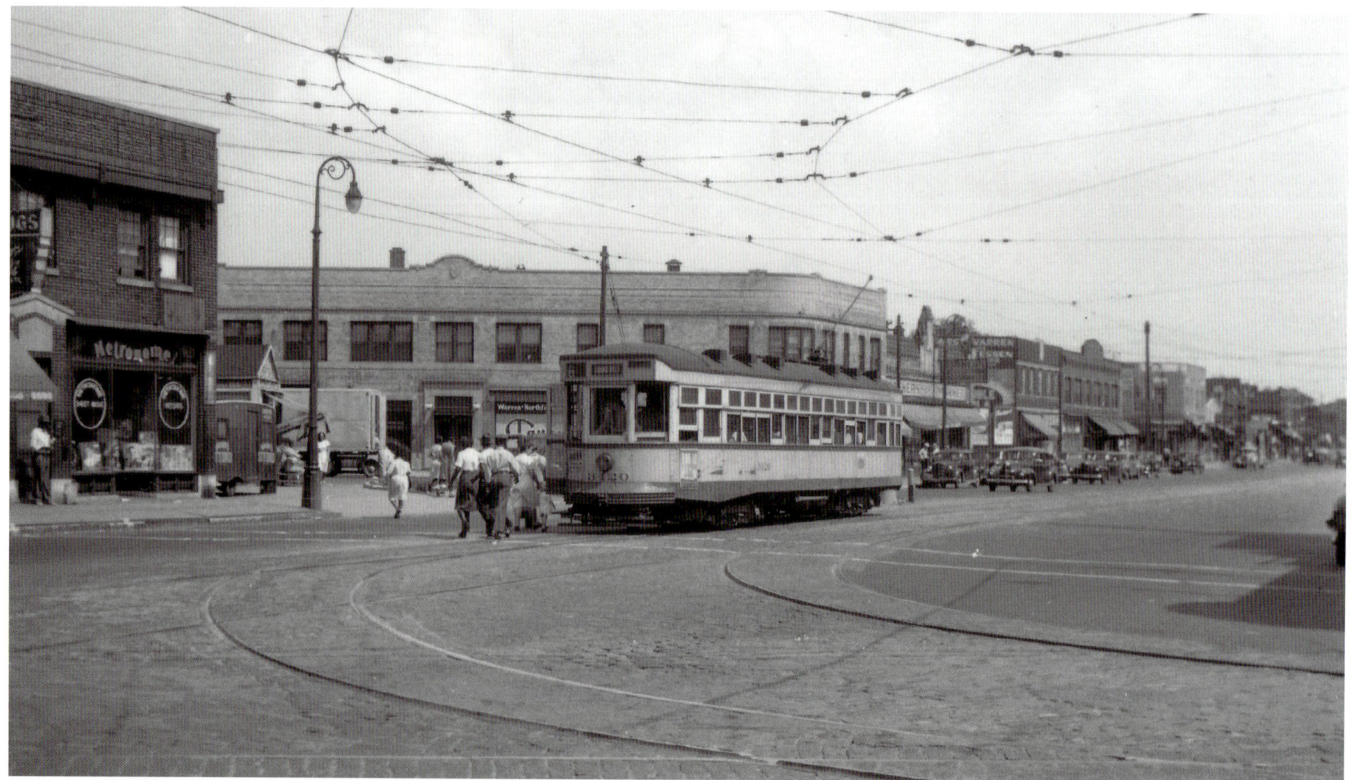

On August 27, 1947, Peter Witt-type car No. 3420 is on the Clairmount line at Warren Avenue and Junction Street. This was one of seventy-five cars (Nos. 3350–3424) built by St. Louis Car Company in 1922. (*Bob Crockett photograph—Clifford R. Scholes collection*)

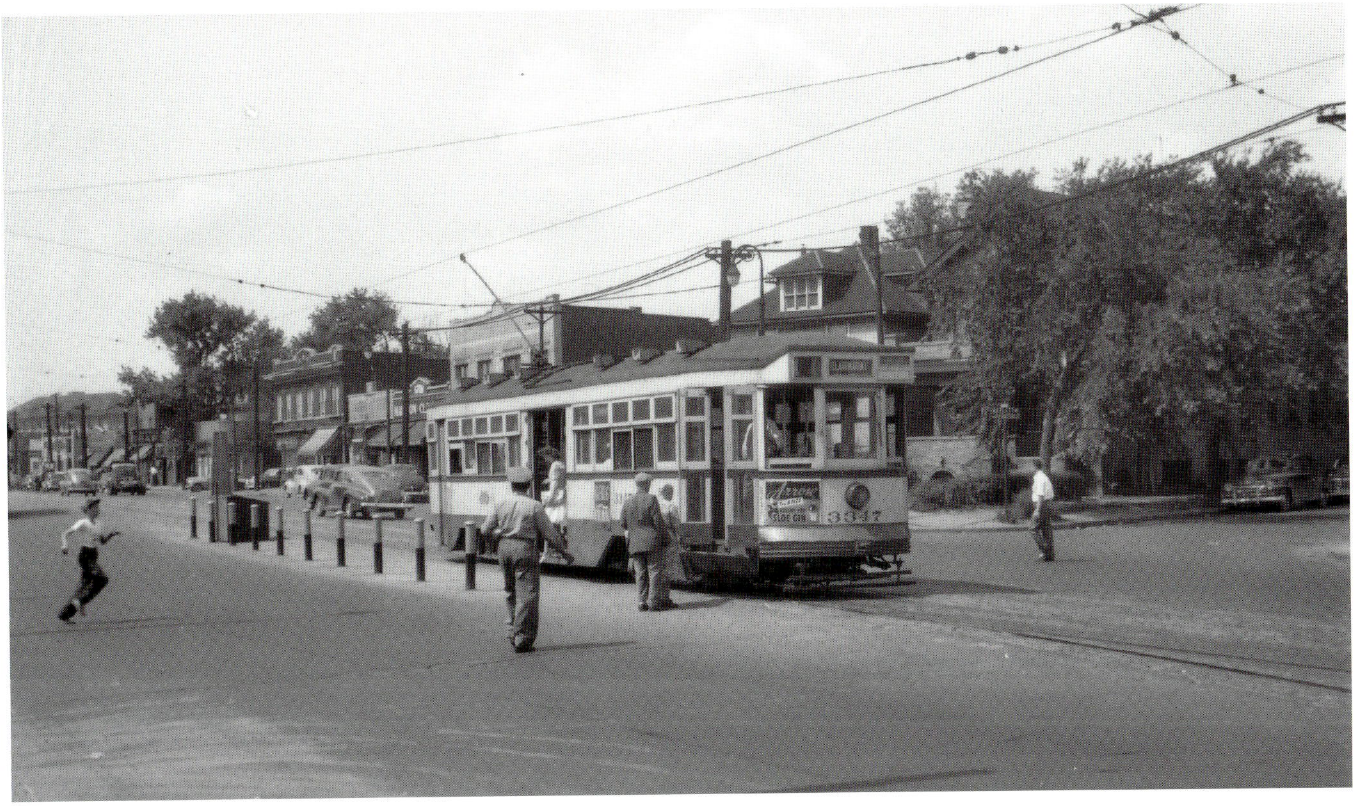

Warren Avenue and Hazlett Street is the location of route Clairmount car No. 3347 on August 27, 1947. Out of the fleet of 781 Peter Witt cars, car No. 3347 was one of thirty-eight Peter Witt cars modified with rear doors to speed up passenger unloading. This was funded as part of a United States Government program to create jobs for the unemployed during the Depression. (*Bob Crockett photograph—Clifford R. Scholes collection*)

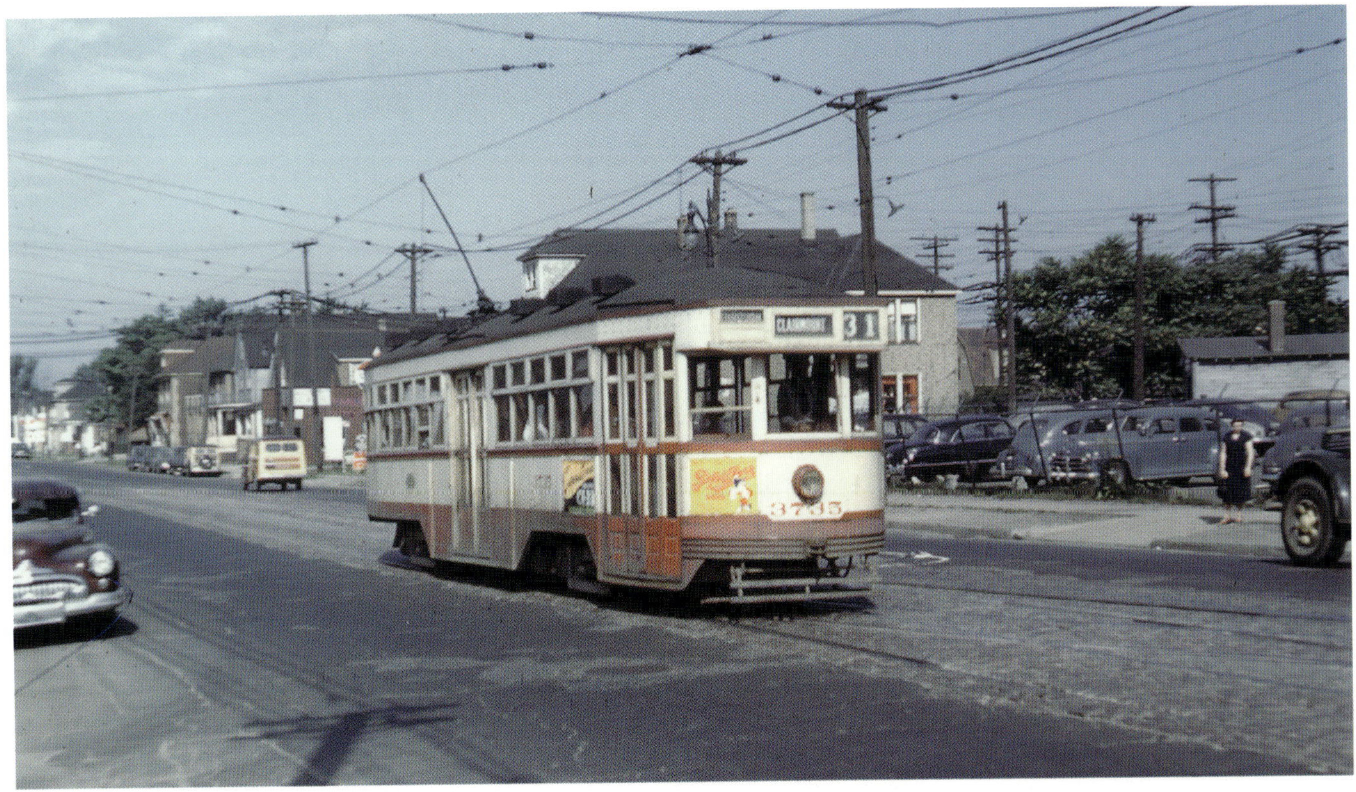

On June 27, 1951, Peter Witt-type car No. 3735 is operating on the Clairmount line on Harper Avenue between Montclair Street and Mt. Elliott Street. The Clairmount line was a long upside down U-shaped belt line with a large ridership. (*Bob Crockett photograph—Clifford R. Scholes collection*)

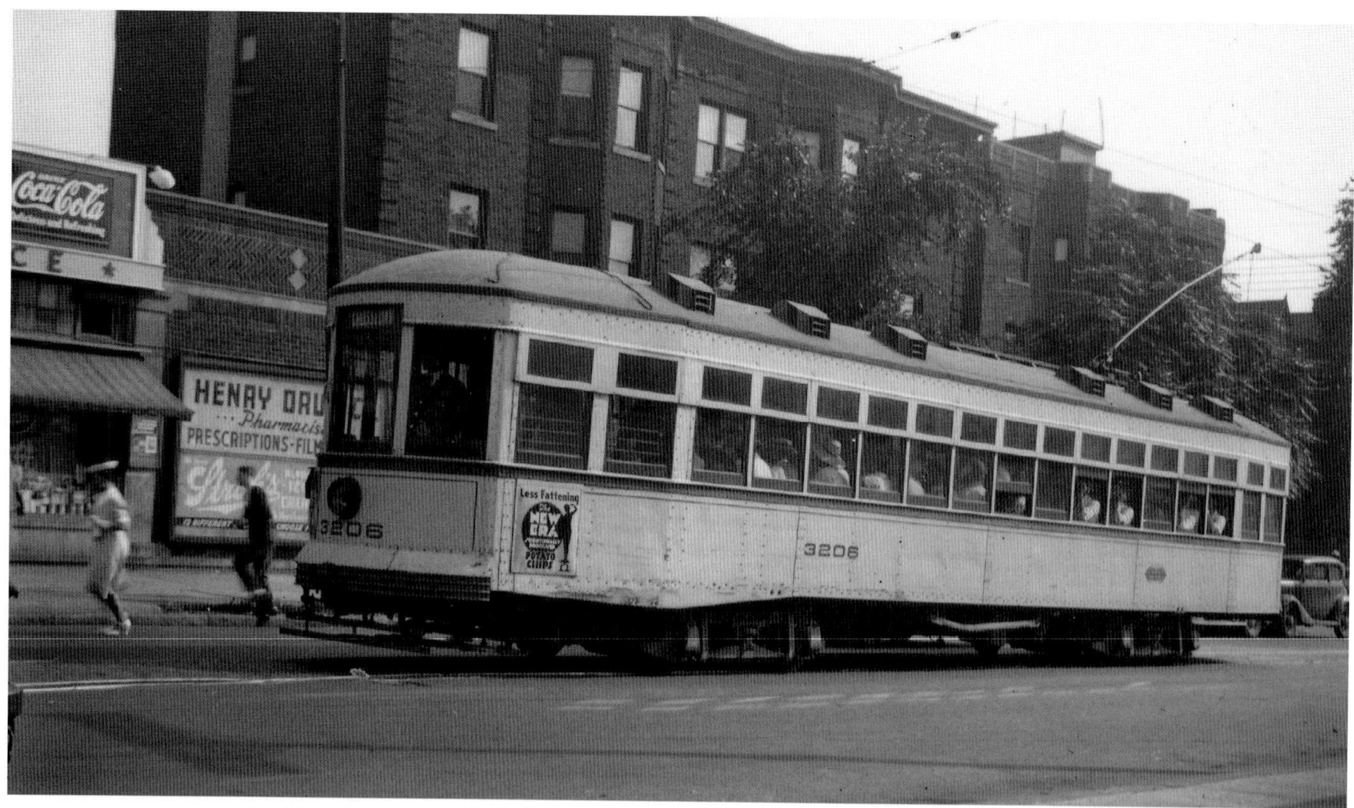

On July 1, 1940, car No. 3206 is on the Crosstown line on Forest Avenue at Third Street. The Crosstown line was an east-west line running about 1.5 miles north of downtown Detroit. (*Bob Crockett photograph—Clifford R. Scholes collection*)

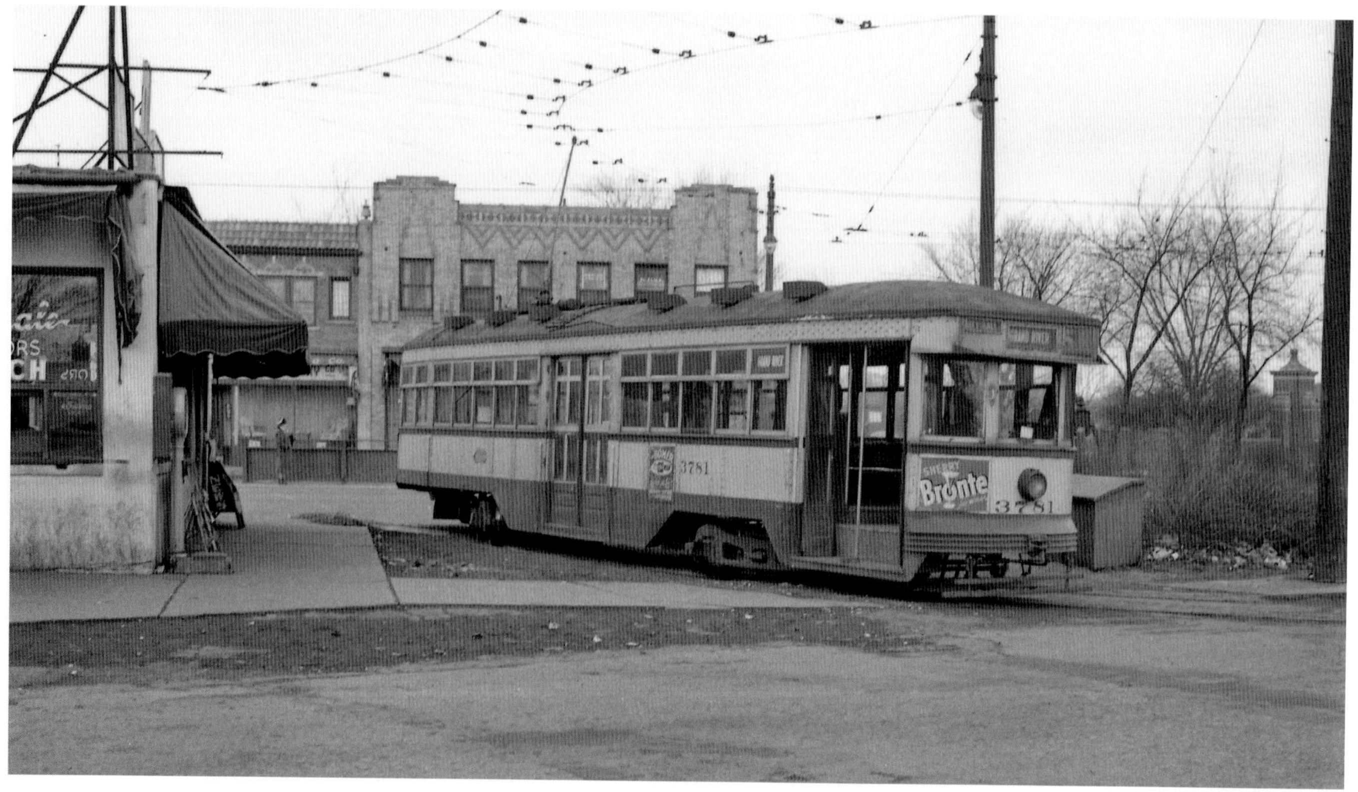

The Grand River Avenue and Fenkell Street terminal loop of the Grand River line is the location of Peter Witt-type car No. 3781 on March 8, 1947. Heavy ridership characterized the Grand River line, which operated in a straight line from the western city limits on Grand River Avenue to downtown Detroit. (*Bob Crockett photograph—Clifford R. Scholes collection*)

3

Routes Fort-Kercheval, Gratiot, and Hamilton Park

Fort-Kercheval was an east-west route that operated through downtown Detroit. East of Woodward Avenue, the line had a zigzag routing that had single track for east and west routing to avoid the Elmwood Cemetery. In 1948, route Fort-Kercheval streetcars operated westbound from Hart and Jefferson west on Jefferson to Lycaste, Kercheval, Mt. Elliott, Hendricks, Jos. Campau, Sherman, Hastings, Clinton, Gratiot, Randolph, Monroe, Michigan, Griswold, Fort, Stocker, private right of way, and Electric Boulevard to Gleason. Eastbound Fort-Kercheval streetcars operated from Gleason and Electric Boulevard via Electric Boulevard east to private right of way, Stocker, Fort, east on Fort to Cadillac Square, Bates, Farmer, Gratiot, Macomb, Russell, Madison, Jos. Campau, Waterloo, Mt. Elliott, Kercheval, and Hart to Jefferson. Shift change trippers operated to the Ford Rouge plant from Fort and Dearborn northwest on Dearborn to Industrial and private right of way north to Ford Rouge. The Fort (west side portion of the Fort-Kercheval line) was converted to bus operation on June 23, 1949 followed by the Kercheval (east side portion the line) on December 15, 1949.

On May 15, 1922, route Gratiot operated from downtown Detroit to Harper with rush hour trippers extended to French Road. By July 5, 1922, streetcar service was extended to a new wye at Seven Mile Road. When the city limits were extended to Eight Mile Road, a shuttle bus service was established to that area on October 1, 1925. A Birney streetcar shuttle service replaced the bus line between Seven and Eight Mile Roads on April 22, 1928, and that shuttle was replaced by regular Gratiot streetcar service on December 9, 1928 to Hauss Road (Ten Mile Road). In 1948, route Gratiot streetcars operated southbound from Eight Mile Road and Gratiot, southwest on Gratiot to Randolph, and Monroe, to the south side of Cadillac Square. Northbound route Gratiot streetcars operated from Cadillac Square, east to Randolph, and northeast on Gratiot to Seven Mile Road. Streetcars displaying "Limits" sign ran to Eight Mile Road. The Gratiot and Michigan lines were consolidated on November 13, 1950. Buses took over the Michigan portion of the line on September 7, 1955 followed by the Gratiot portion on March 25, 1956.

Hamilton Park connected downtown Detroit with Highland Park. It operated northbound from Woodward and Atwater on Woodward to Grand River, west to Hamilton, and north to McNichols. Southbound cars operated from Hamilton and McNichols south on Hamilton to Holden, southeast to 3rd, south to Grand River, west to Woodward, south to Woodbridge, west to Griswold, south to Atwater, and west to Woodward. The line was converted to bus operation on April 28, 1947.

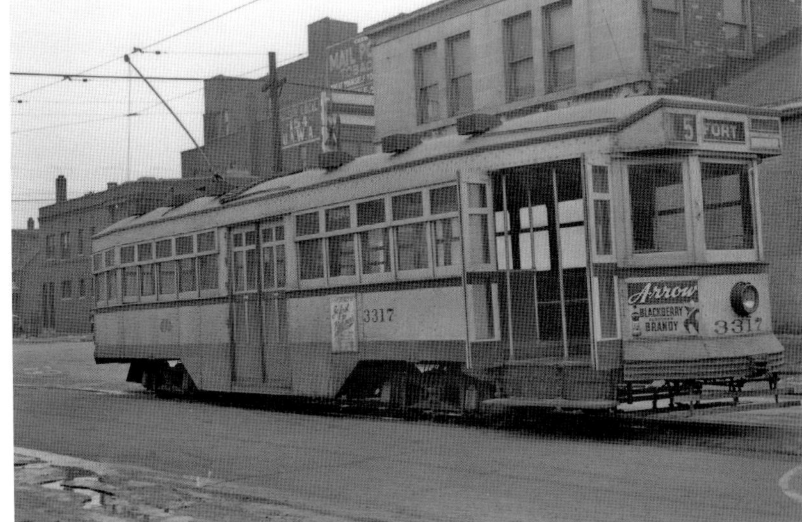

On February 15, 1947, Peter Witt-type car No. 3317 is at the route Fort-Kercheval terminal loop on Lycaste Street at Jefferson Avenue. The Fort Kercheval route was an east-west line that operated through downtown Detroit. East of downtown, the line operated with single track on separate streets to avoid the Elmwood Cemetery. (*Bob Crockett photograph—Clifford R. Scholes collection*)

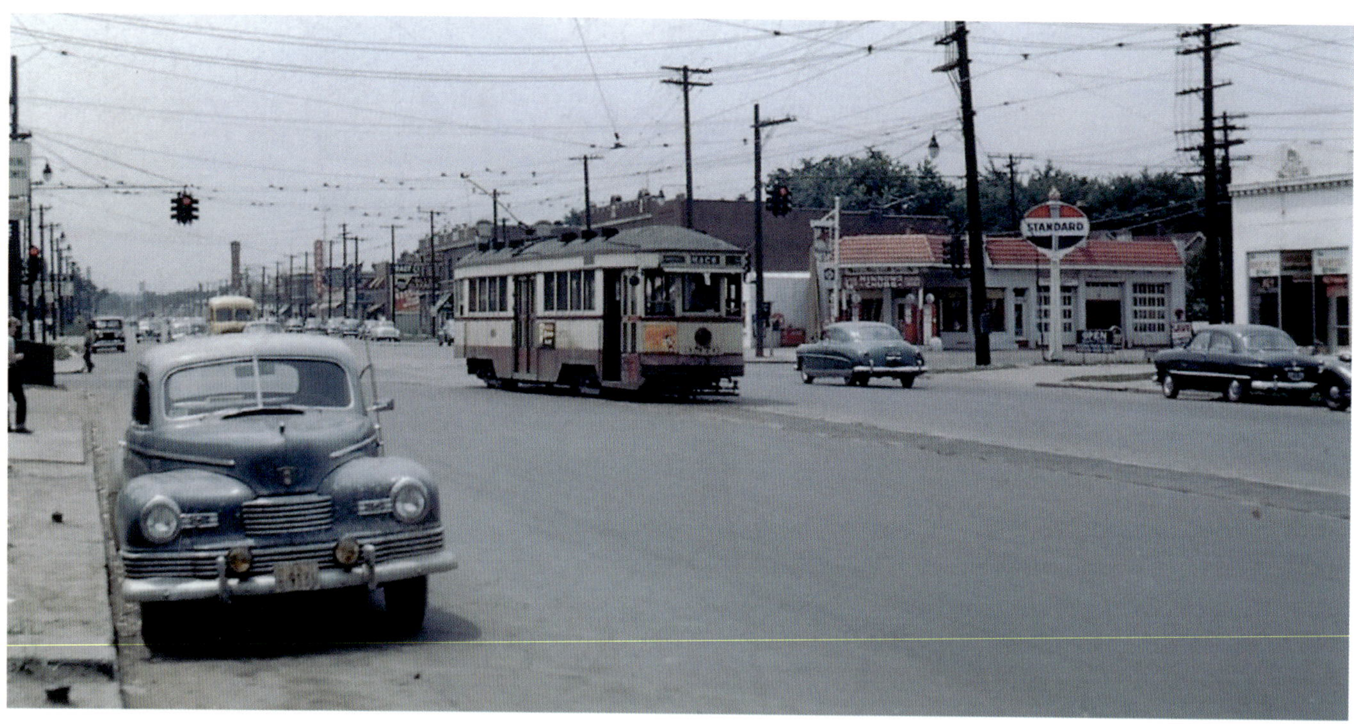

On June 19, 1949, Peter Witt-type car No. 3855 is on Fort at Third Streets. West of downtown Detroit, the line operated on Fort Street mainly through commercial and industrial areas. (*Bob Crockett photograph—Clifford R. Scholes collection*)

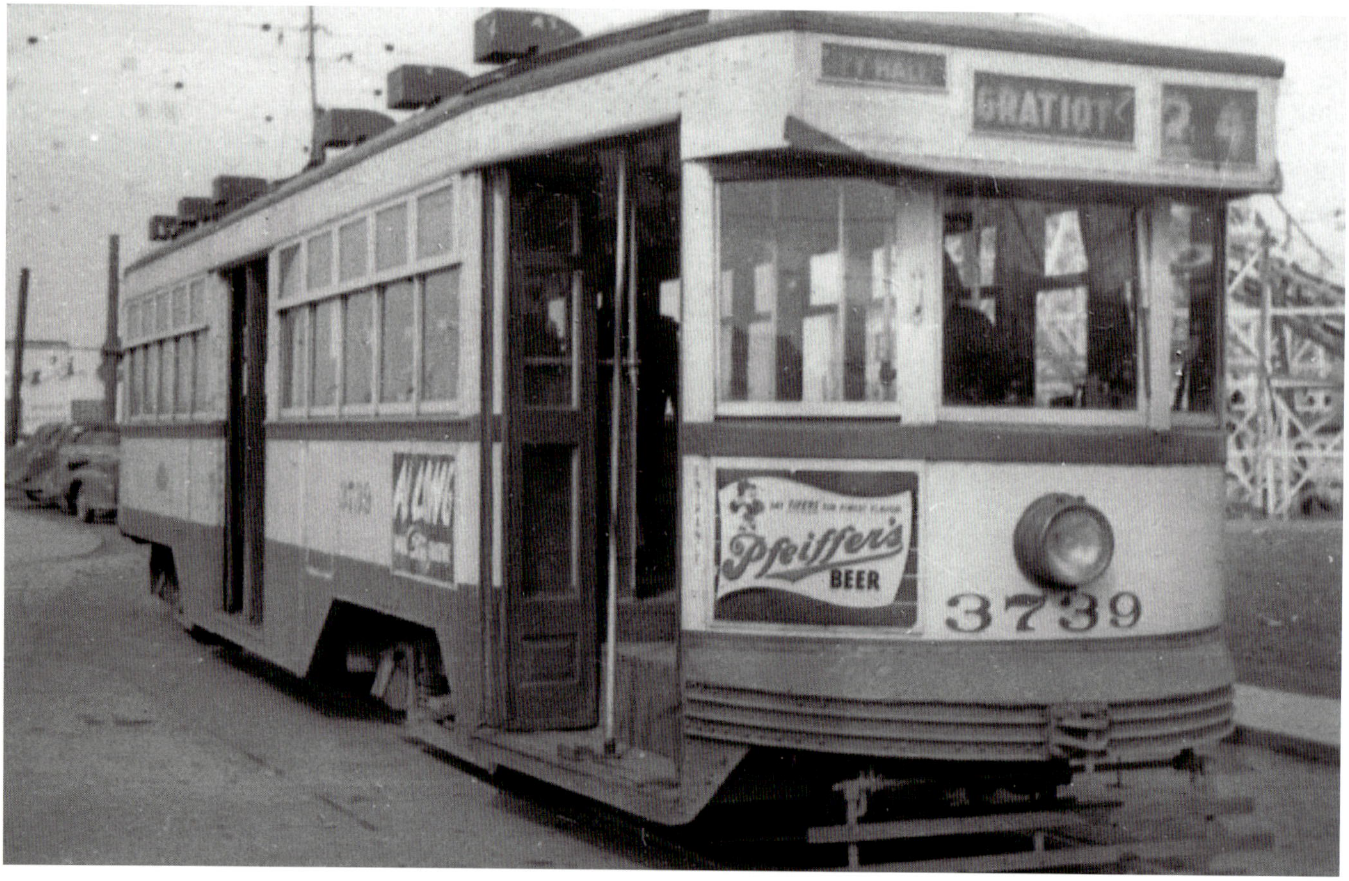

Eastwood Park loop, located off Gratiot Avenue, just north of Eight Mile Road on the Gratiot line, is the location of Peter Witt type car No. 3739 in 1939. The Gratiot line, with its heavy ridership, operated from downtown Detroit in a northeasterly direction to the Eastwood Amusement Park. (*Clifford R. Scholes collection*)

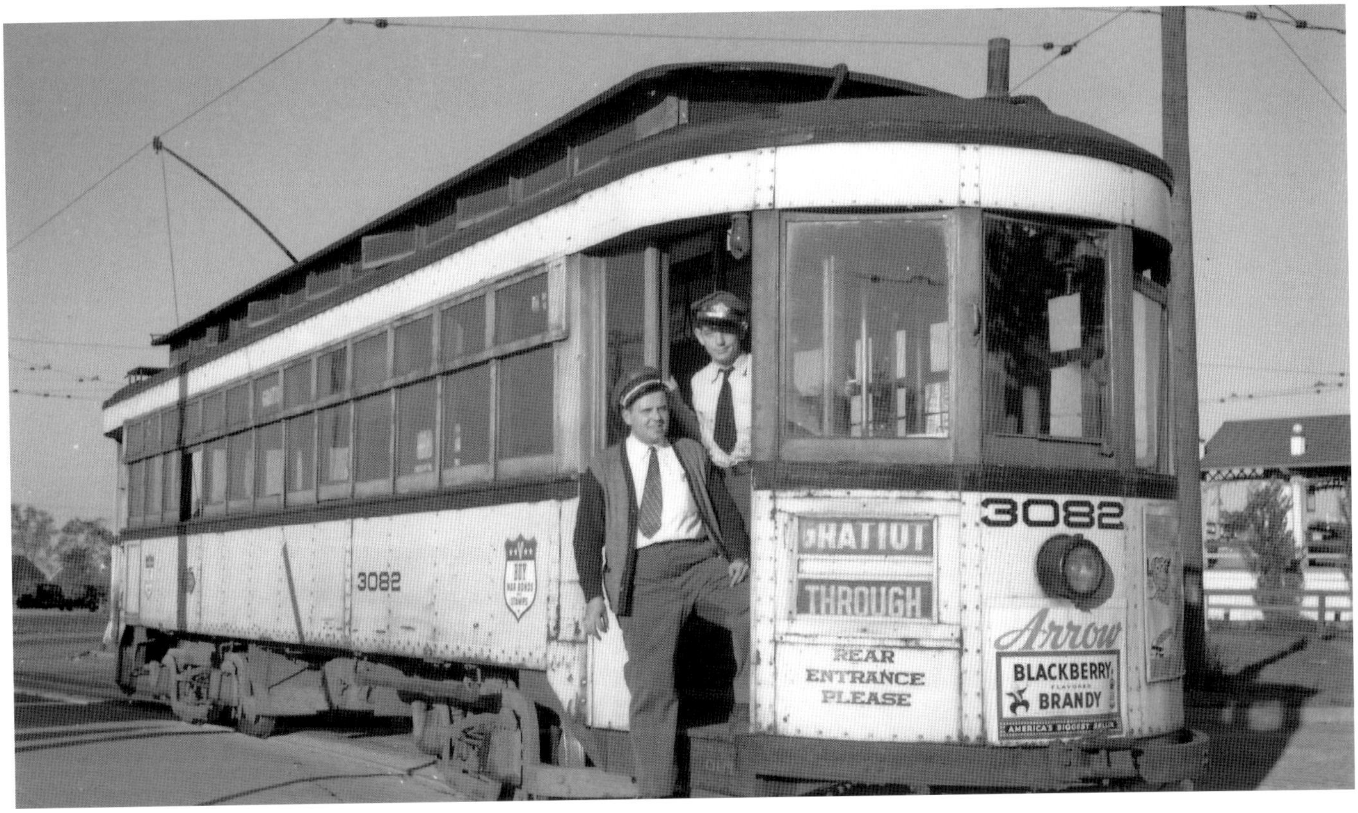

In 1939, route Gratiot car No. 3082 is at the Eastwood Park terminal loop, with the crew waiting for departure time. This was one of twenty-five cars (Nos. 3075–3099 built) by G. C. Kuhlman Car Company and delivered in 1917. Powered by four General Electric type 203L motors, each 33.5-foot-long car weighed 48,000 pounds and seated forty-six passengers. (*Bob Crockett photograph—Clifford R. Scholes collection*)

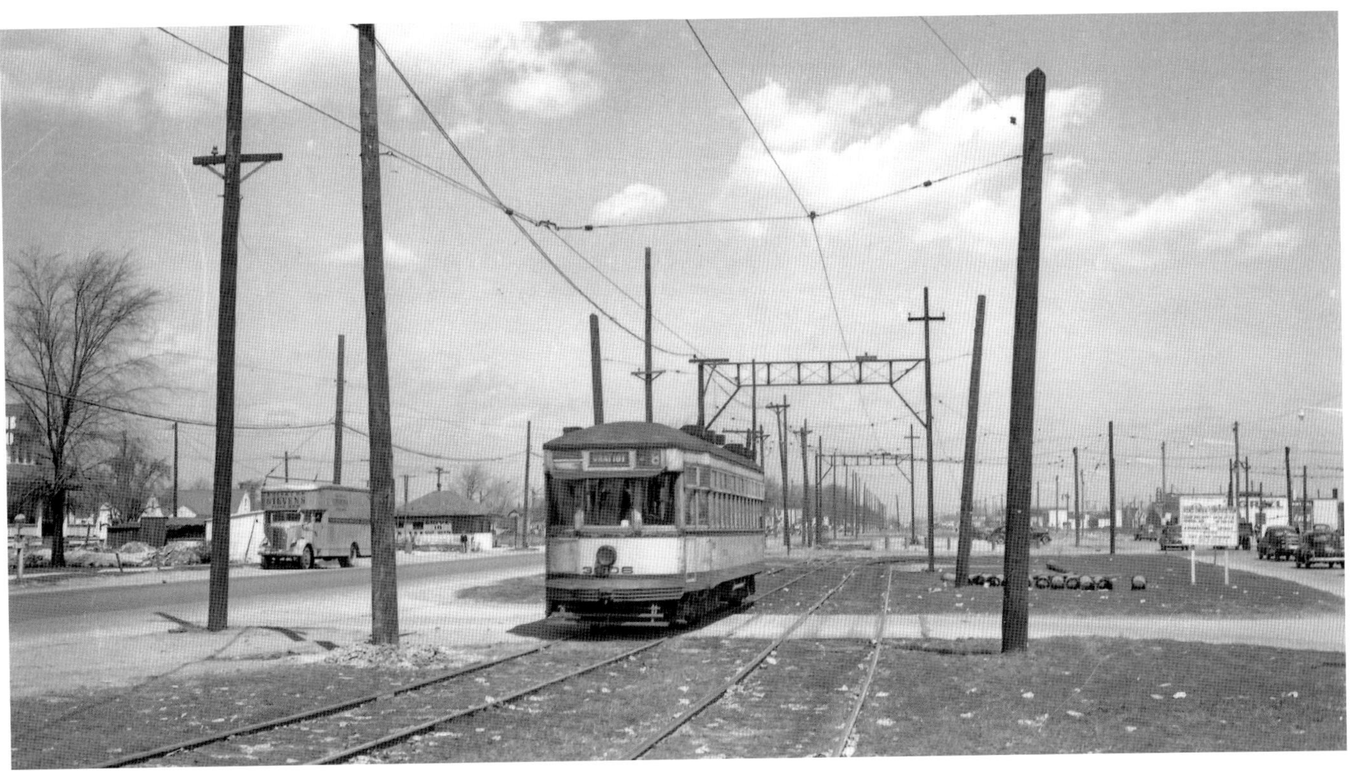

Peter Witt-type car No. 3806 is handling a route Gratiot run on private right of way paralleling Gratiot Avenue near Eight Mile Road on April 26, 1947. (*Bob Crockett photograph—Clifford R. Scholes collection*)

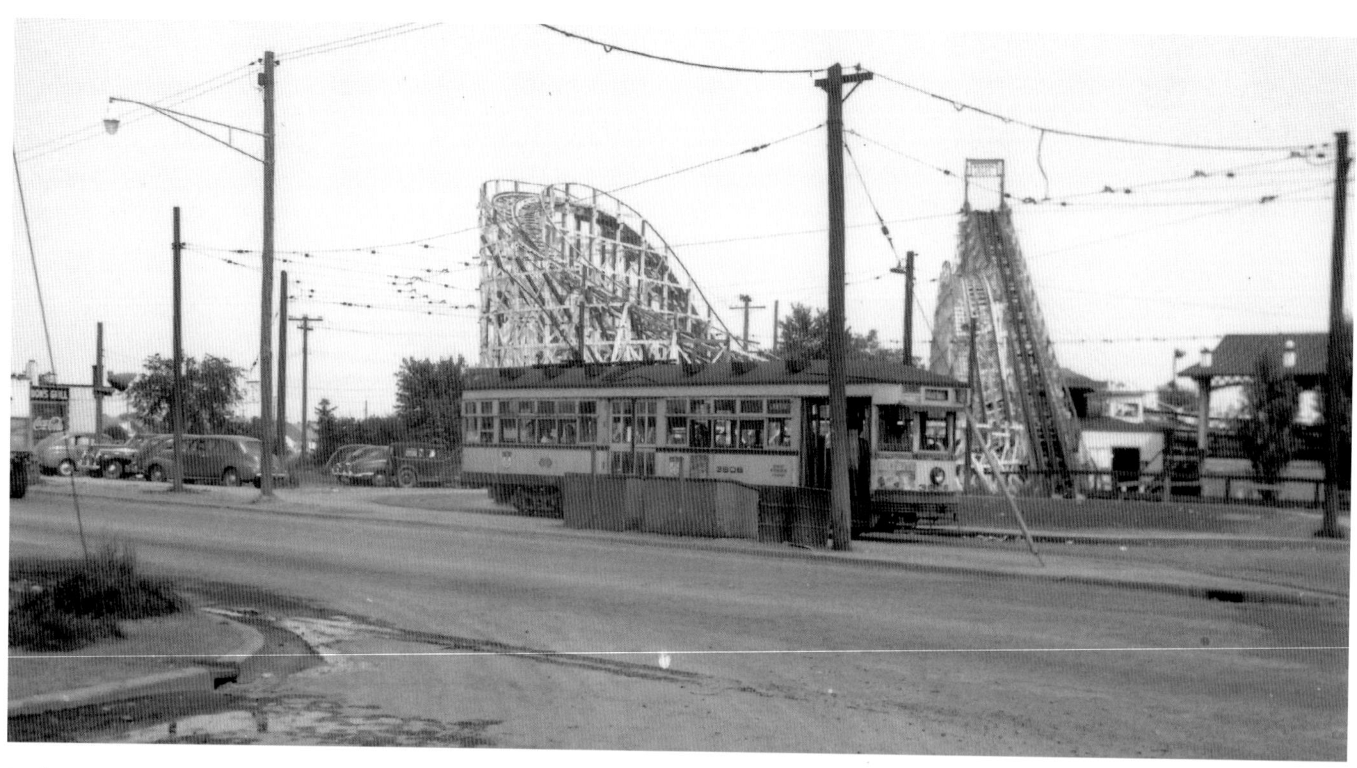

In this August 27, 1947 view of the Eastwood Amusement Park, Peter Witt-type car No. 3806 is on the Gratiot line at the Gratiot Avenue terminal loop. The park, located on the northeast corner of Eight Mile Road and Gratiot Avenue, opened in 1926 and closed in 1952. (*Bob Crockett photograph—Clifford R. Scholes collection*)

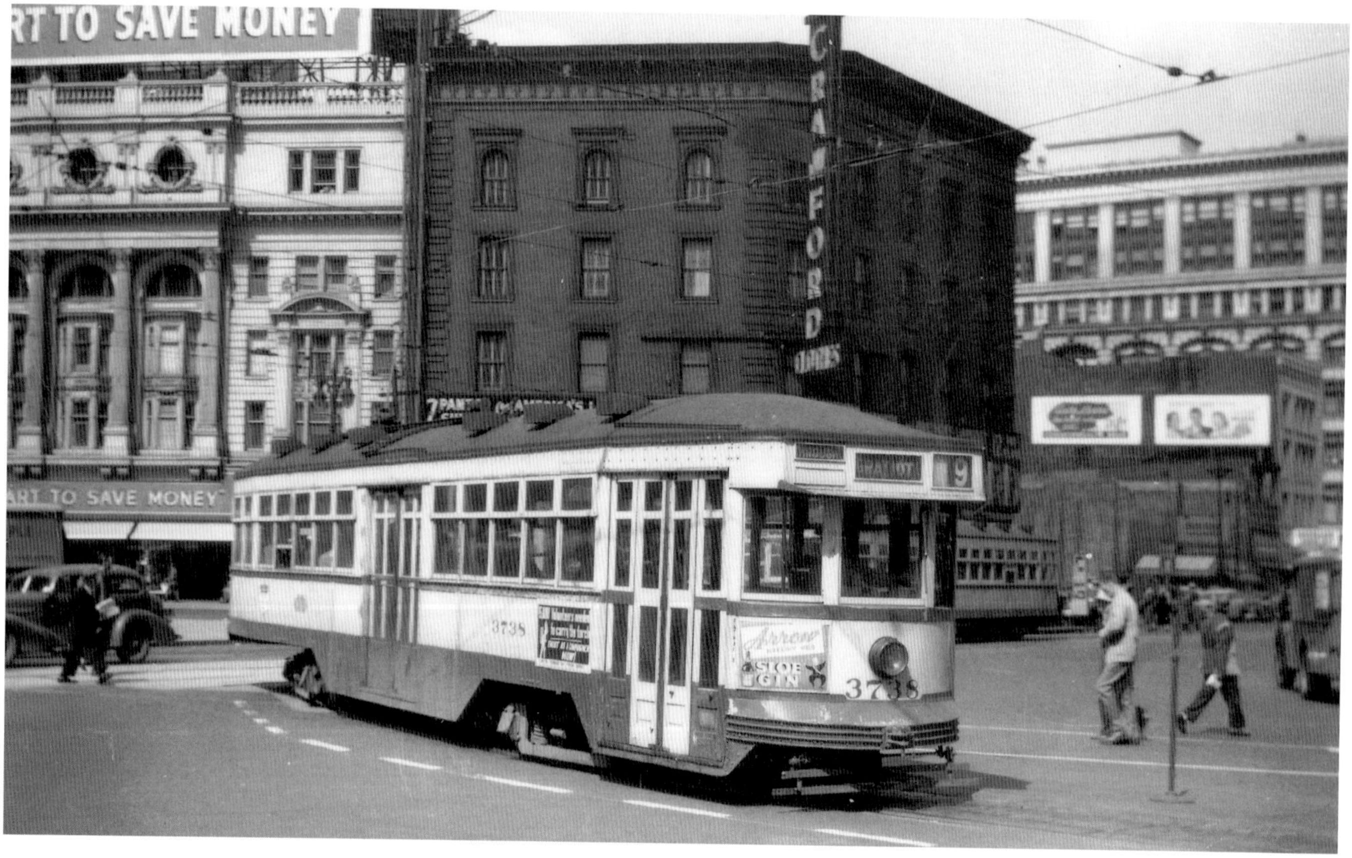

Route Gratiot car No. 3738 is on Monroe Street at Cadillac Square in downtown Detroit on September 15, 1949. (*Bob Crockett photograph—Clifford R. Scholes collection*)

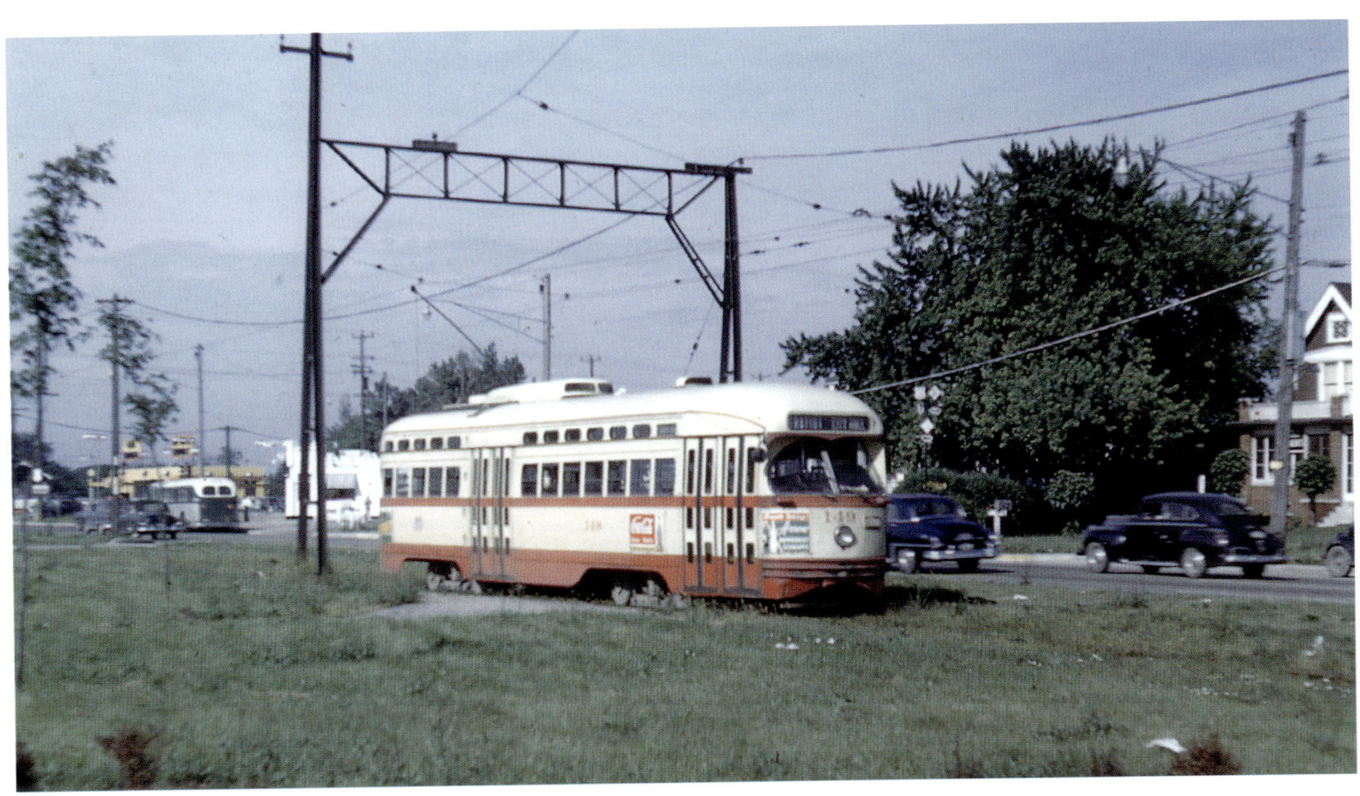

Route Gratiot PCC car No. 149 is on Gratiot Avenue near the Eastwood Park terminal loop on June 27, 1951. The Gratiot schedule that was effective September 6, 1950 required thirty-one cars for a three-minute headway in the morning rush hour, sixteen cars for a six-minute headway in the off peak period, and thirty cars for a three-minute headway in the evening rush hour. Gratiot cars were assigned to the Gratiot car house. (*Bob Crockett photograph—Clifford R. Scholes collection*)

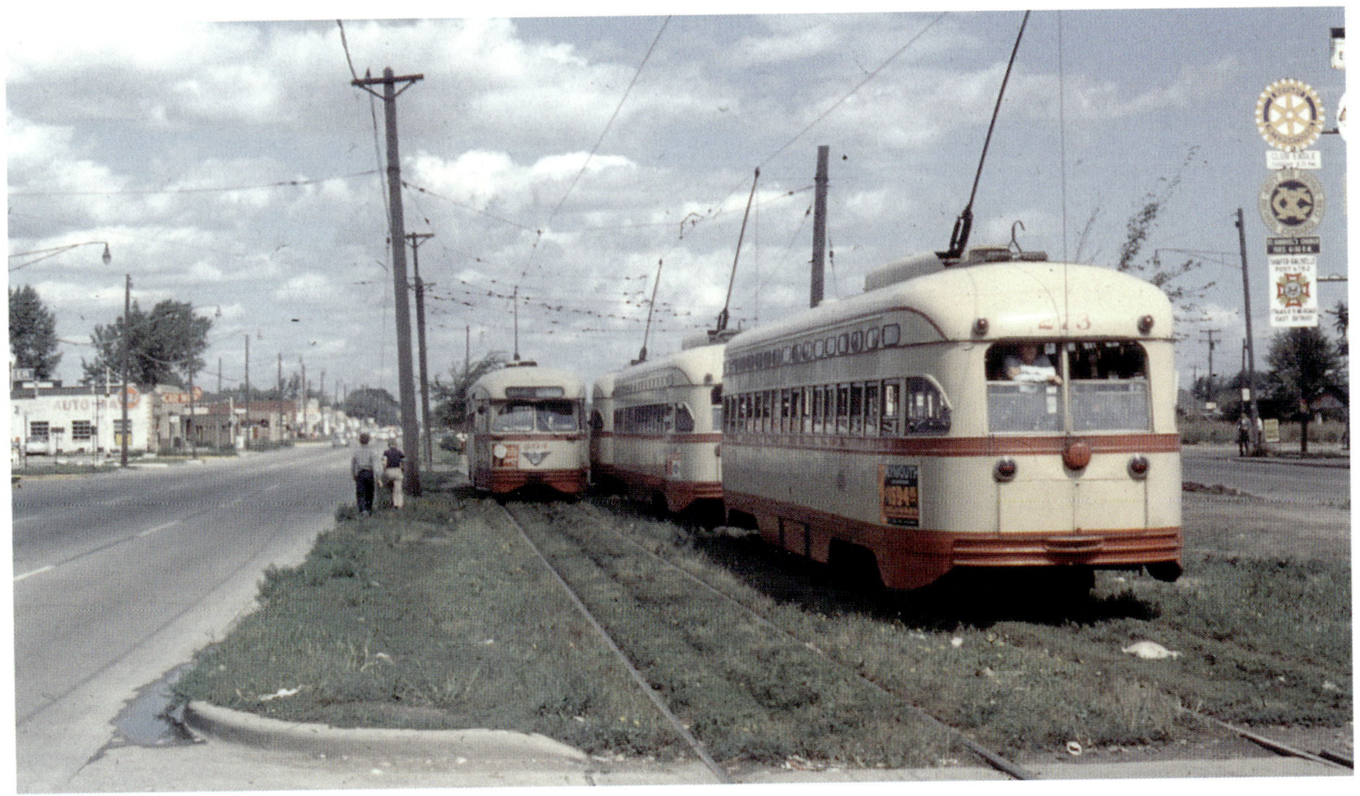

On September 11, 1955, Gratiot line PCC cars Nos. 266, 269, and 273 are on Gratiot Avenue near Eight Mile Road. (*Bob Crockett photograph—Clifford R. Scholes collection*)

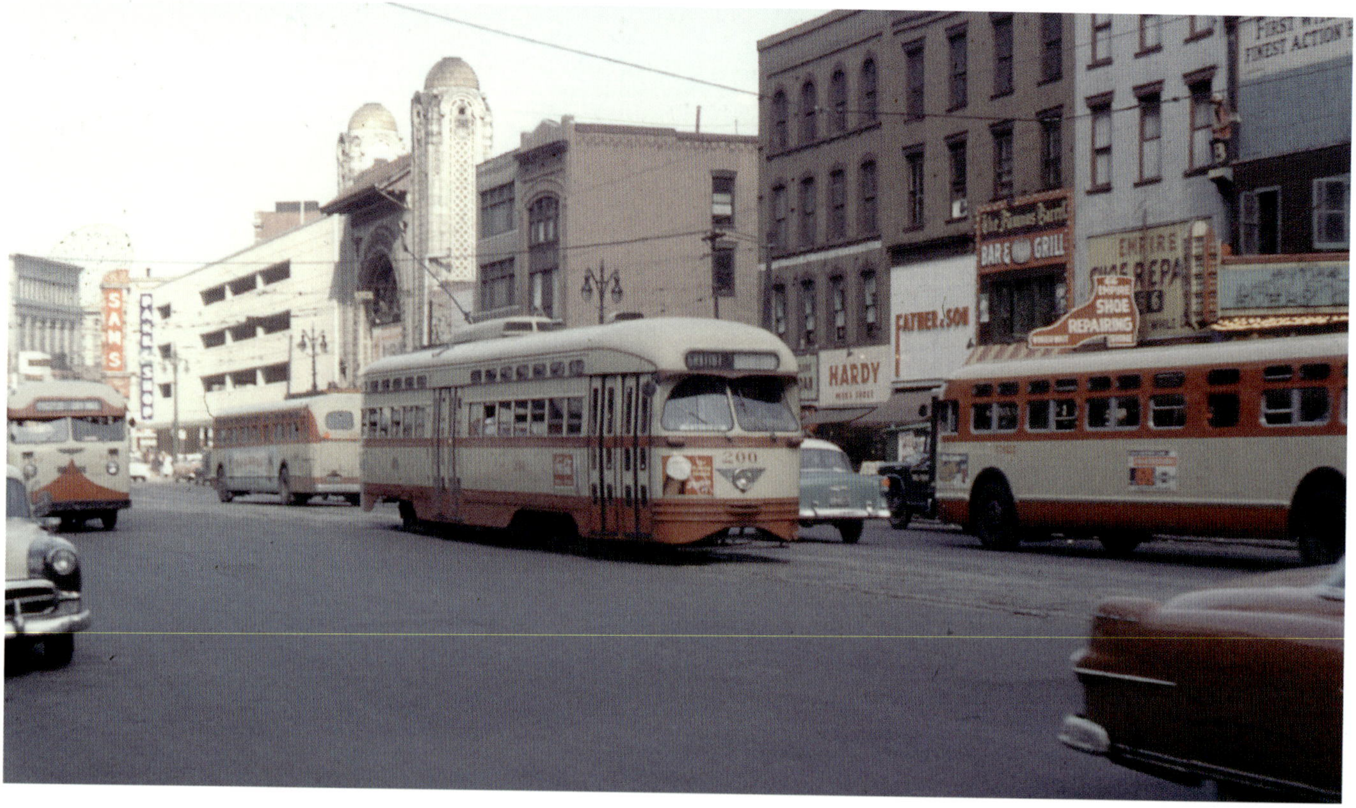

Route Gratiot PCC car No. 200 is on Monroe Avenue near City Hall on September 12, 1955. Two buses manufactured by General Motors Corporation buses are in the opposite lane and a bus manufactured by Ford Motor Company is shown on the left. (*Clifford R. Scholes collection*)

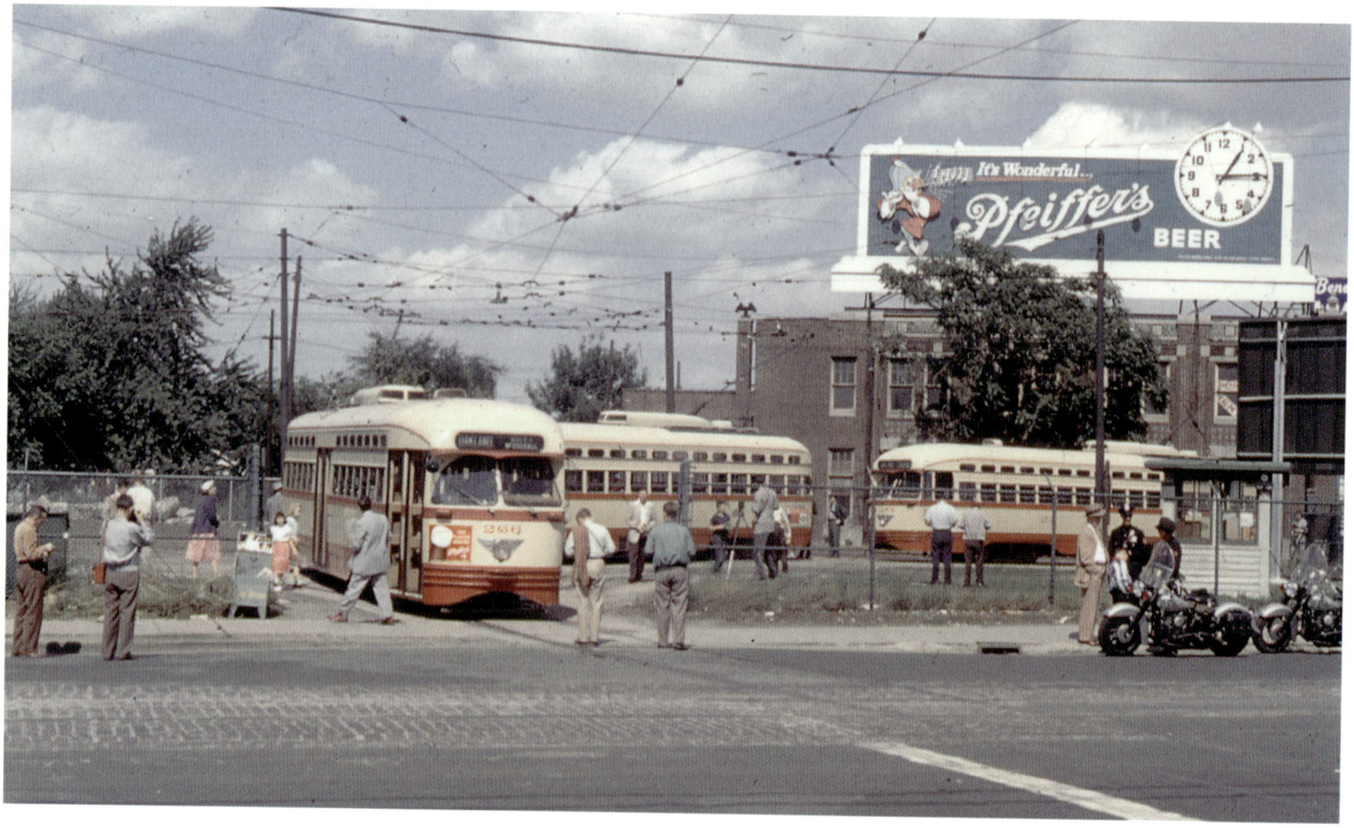

On a sunny September 11, 1955, route Gratiot PCC cars Nos. 266, 269, and 273 are at the Gratiot Avenue loop at the car house. (*Bob Crockett photograph—Clifford R. Scholes collection*)

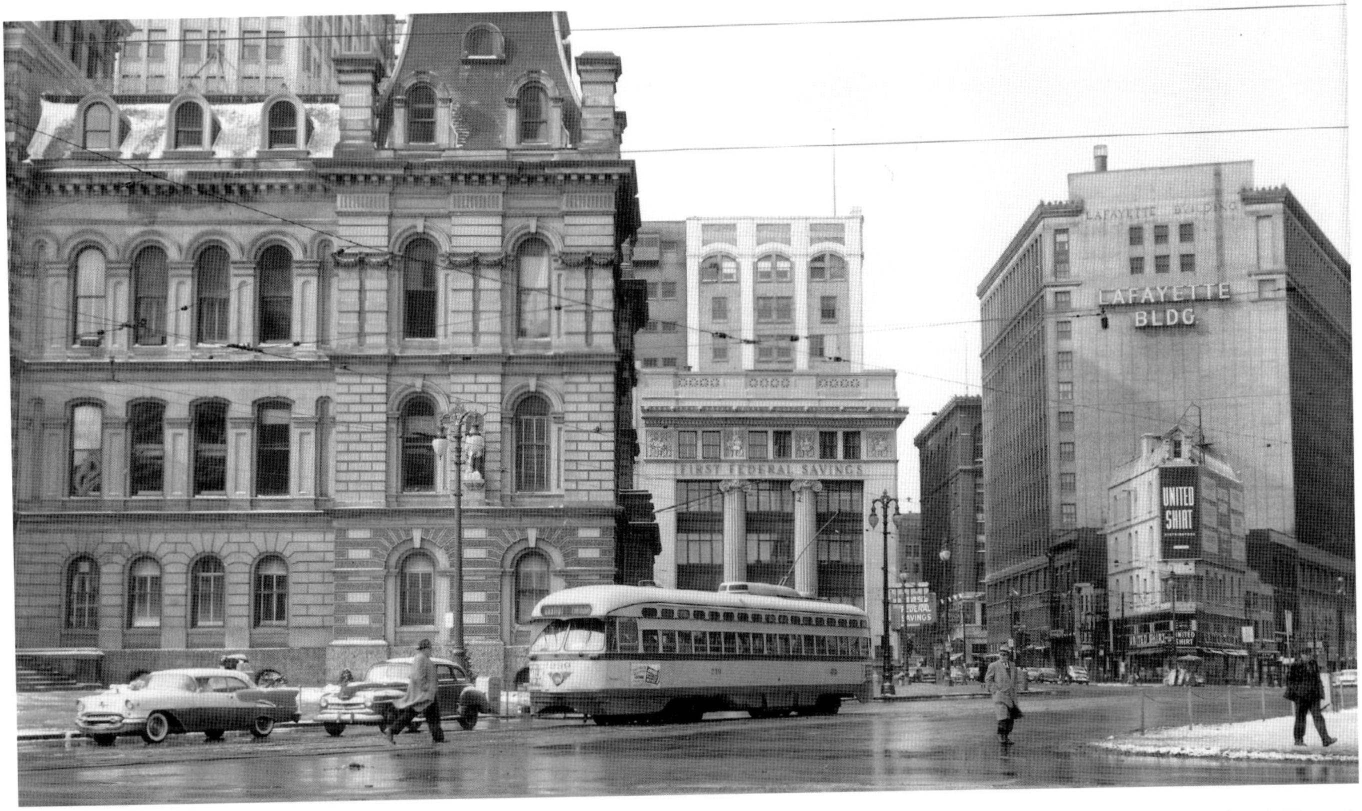

On March 18, 1955, Gratiot–Michigan through PCC car No. 239 is eastbound on Michigan Avenue at Woodward Avenue, with the old Detroit City Hall on the left. On the right is the triangular-shaped (United Shirt sign on the front) building with the Lafayette Building behind it. The fourteen-story Lafayette Building (V-shaped, which allowed more offices to have windows and natural sunlight) was completed in September 1923 and featured marble drinking fountains. Falling into disrepair, demolishing the building was completed on March 6, 2009. The Michigan section of the Gratiot–Michigan line made its last streetcar run on September 7, 1955. Early morning on March 25, 1956, PCC car No. 210 completed the final regular service run on the Gratiot line. (*Birdsall H. Nichols photograph*)

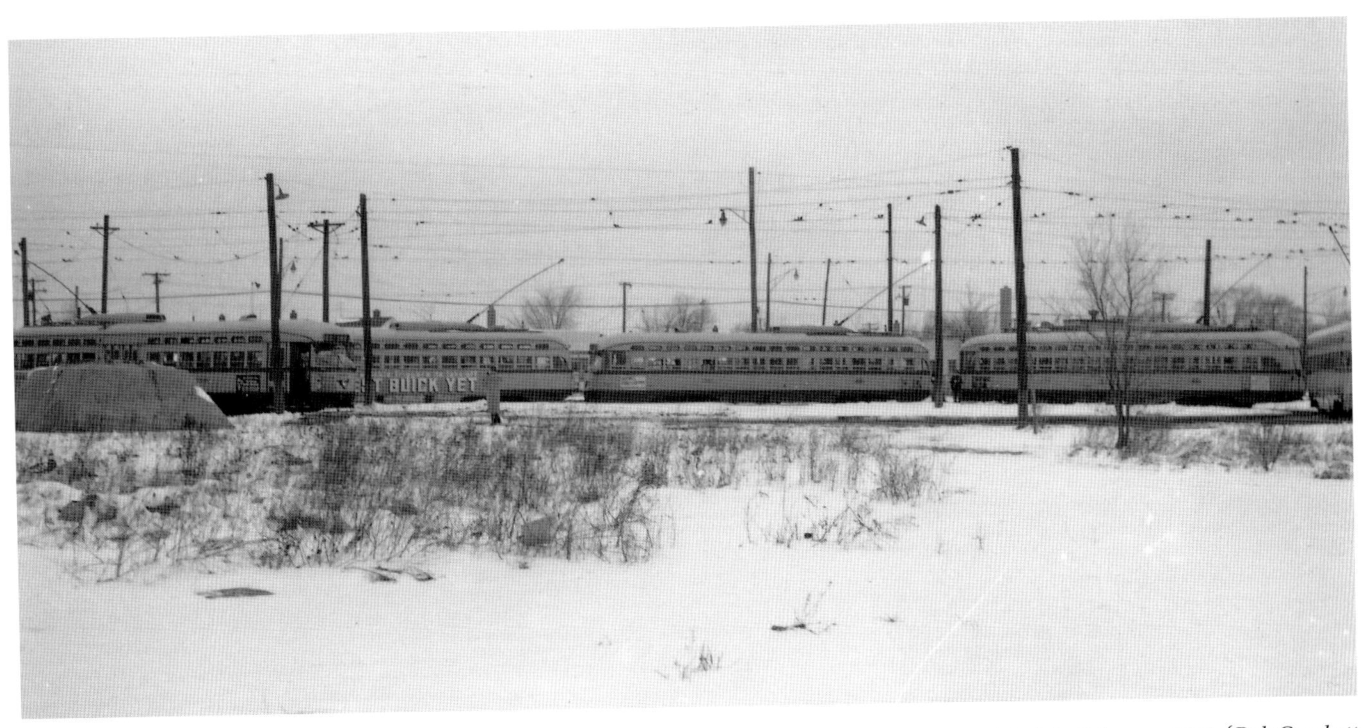

PCC cars Nos. 269, 201, 274, and 283 are at the snow covered route Gratiot terminal loop at Eastwood Park in February 1956. (*Bob Crockett photograph—Clifford R. Scholes collection*)

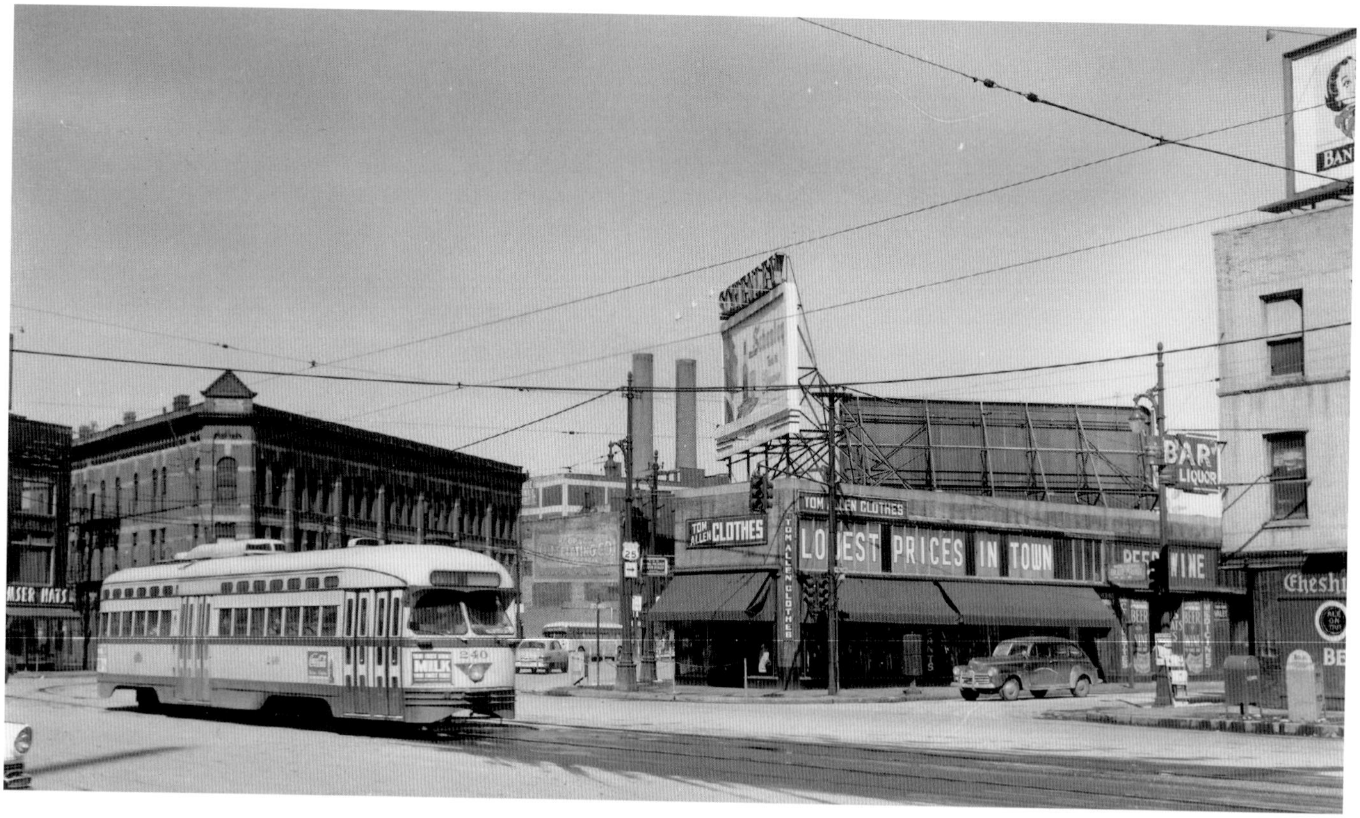

On March 18, 1956, route Gratiot PCC car No. 240 is on Randolph Street in downtown Detroit. Gratiot cars came into downtown from Gratiot, south on Randolph, and west on Monroe to the south side of Cadillac Square. They left downtown going east on Cadillac Square, north on Randolph, and turned east on Gratiot. (*Birdsall H. Nichols photograph*)

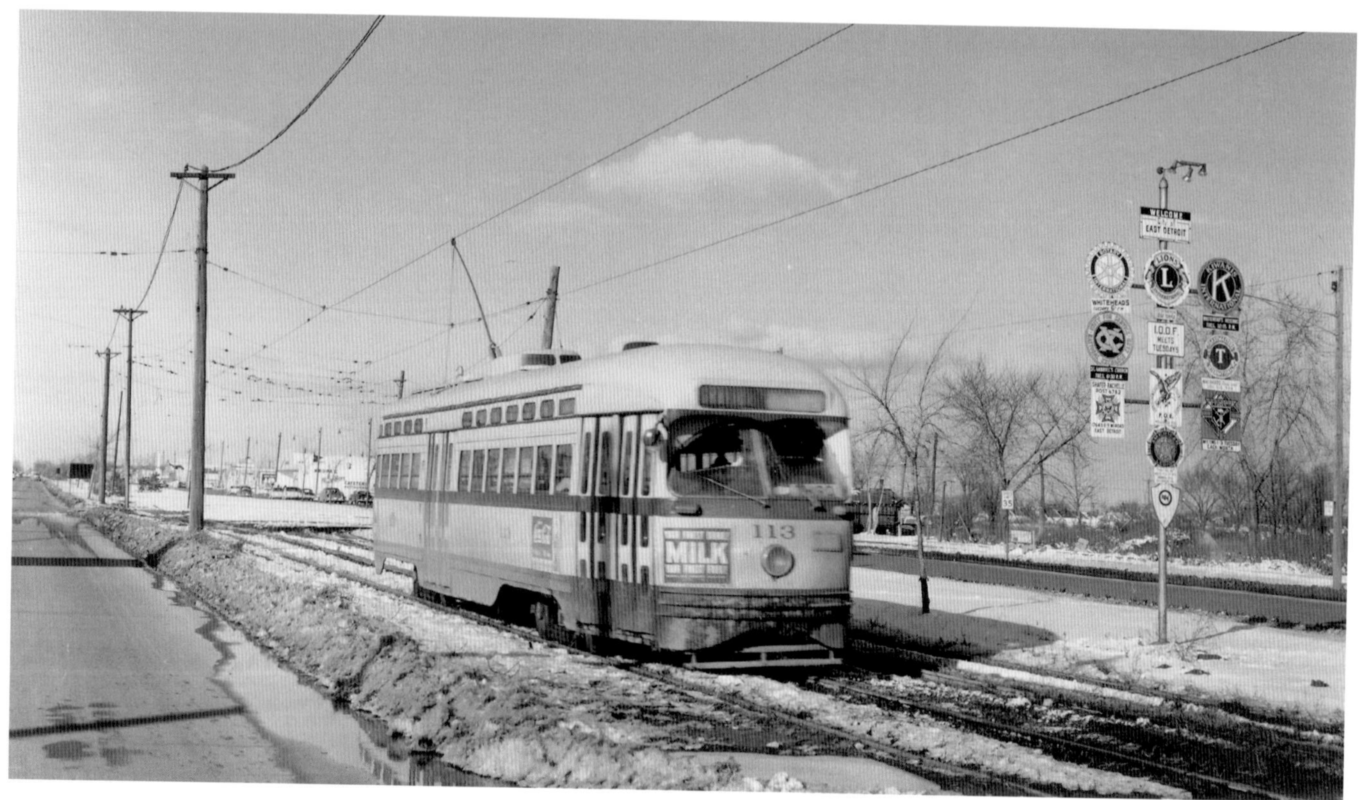

PCC car No. 113 had left the Eight Mile Road terminal and is on the center median of Gratiot Avenue for a route Gratiot trip back to downtown Detroit on March 24, 1956. (*Birdsall H. Nichols photograph*)

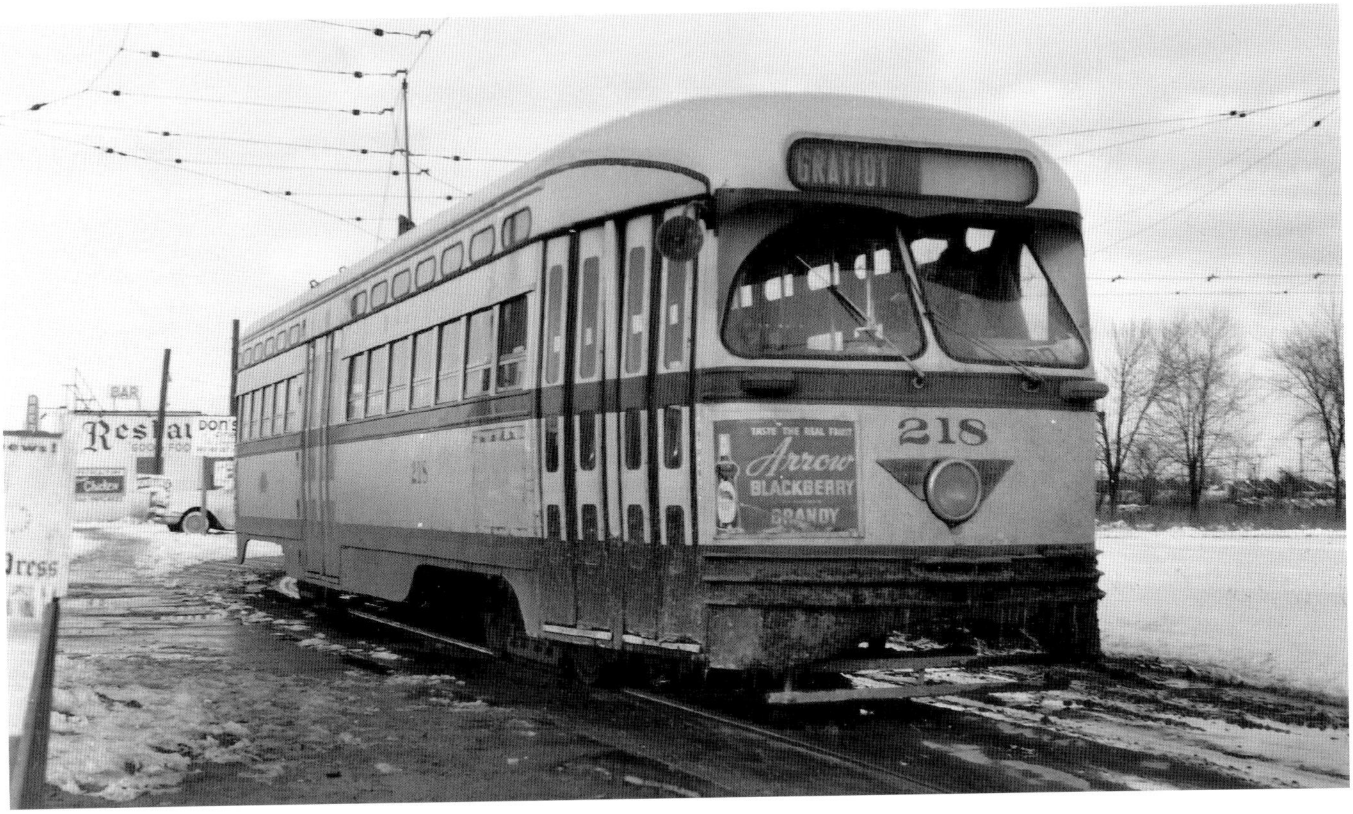

On a cold day in February 1956, PCC car No. 218 is at the Eight Mile Road terminus (about ¼ mile beyond the Detroit city limits in the City of Eastpointe, Macomb County, Michigan) preparing for another trip on the Gratiot line to downtown Detroit. (*Birdsall H. Nichols photograph*)

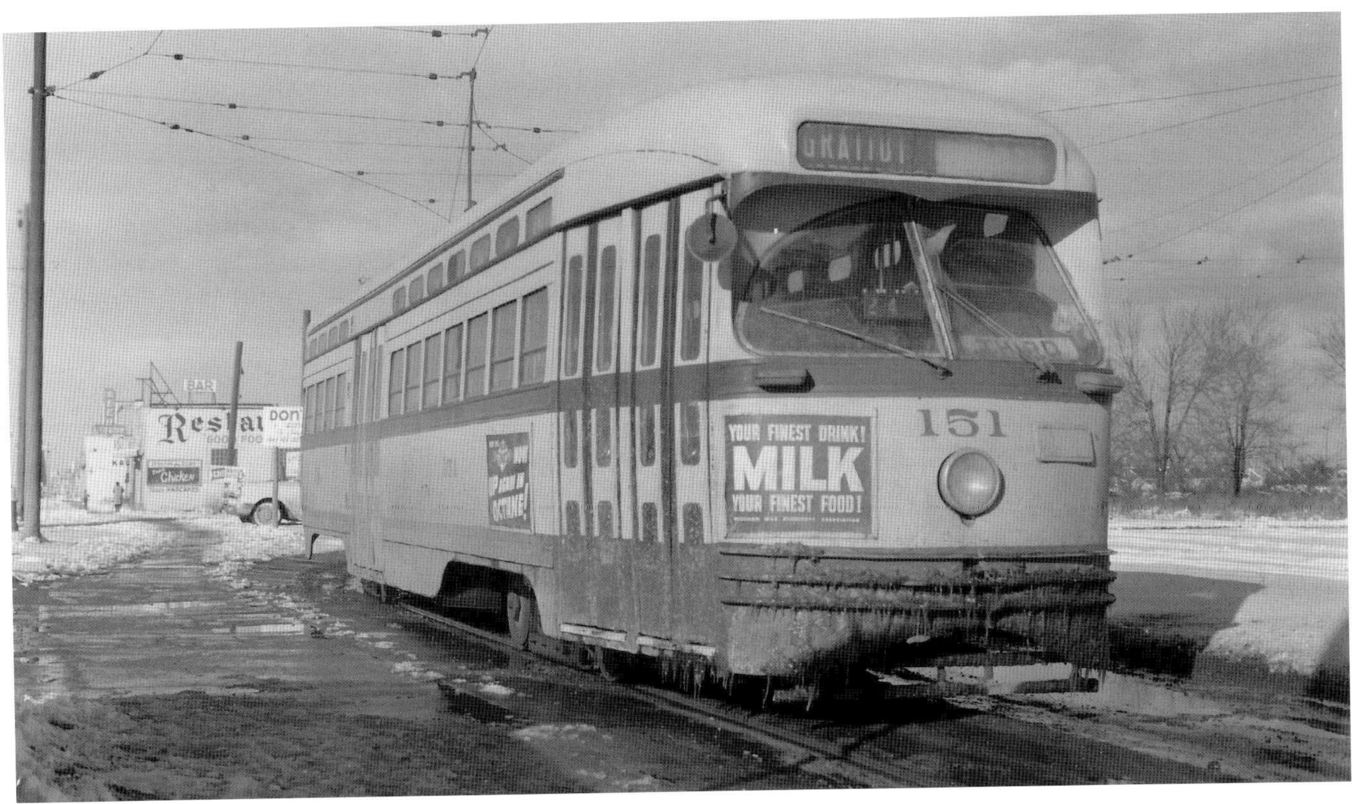

PCC car No. 151, displaying the residue of slush and grime of a harsh winter, is at the terminus of the Gratiot line at Eight Mile Road in February 1956. (*Birdsall H. Nichols photograph*)

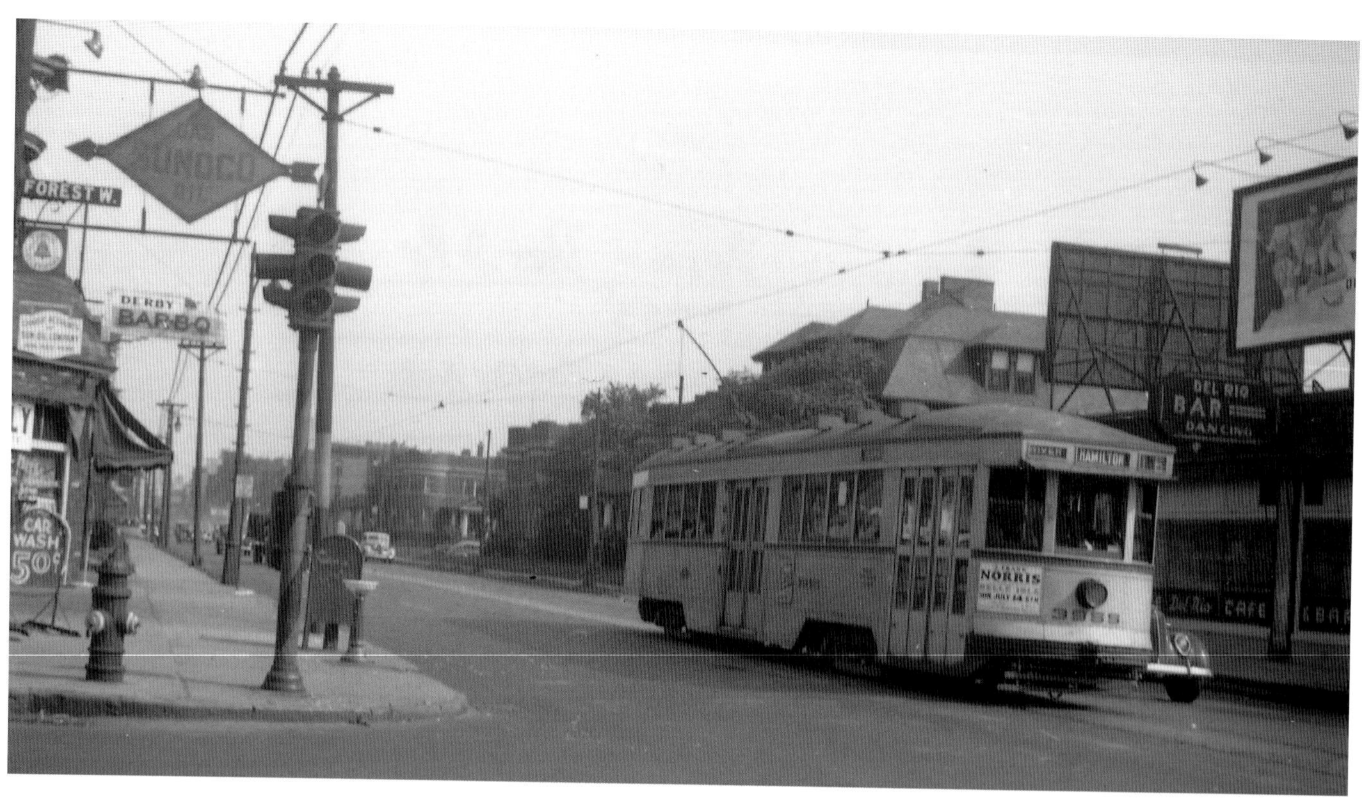

In July 1940, Peter Witt-type car No. 3955 is on the Hamilton line on Hamilton Avenue at Forest Avenue. This was one of forty-four cars (Nos. 3915–3958) built by St. Louis Car Company in 1930. Powered by four Westinghouse type 510 motors, the 48.5-foot-long car weighed 37,200 pounds and seated fifty-two passengers. (*Bob Crockett photograph—Clifford R. Scholes collection*)

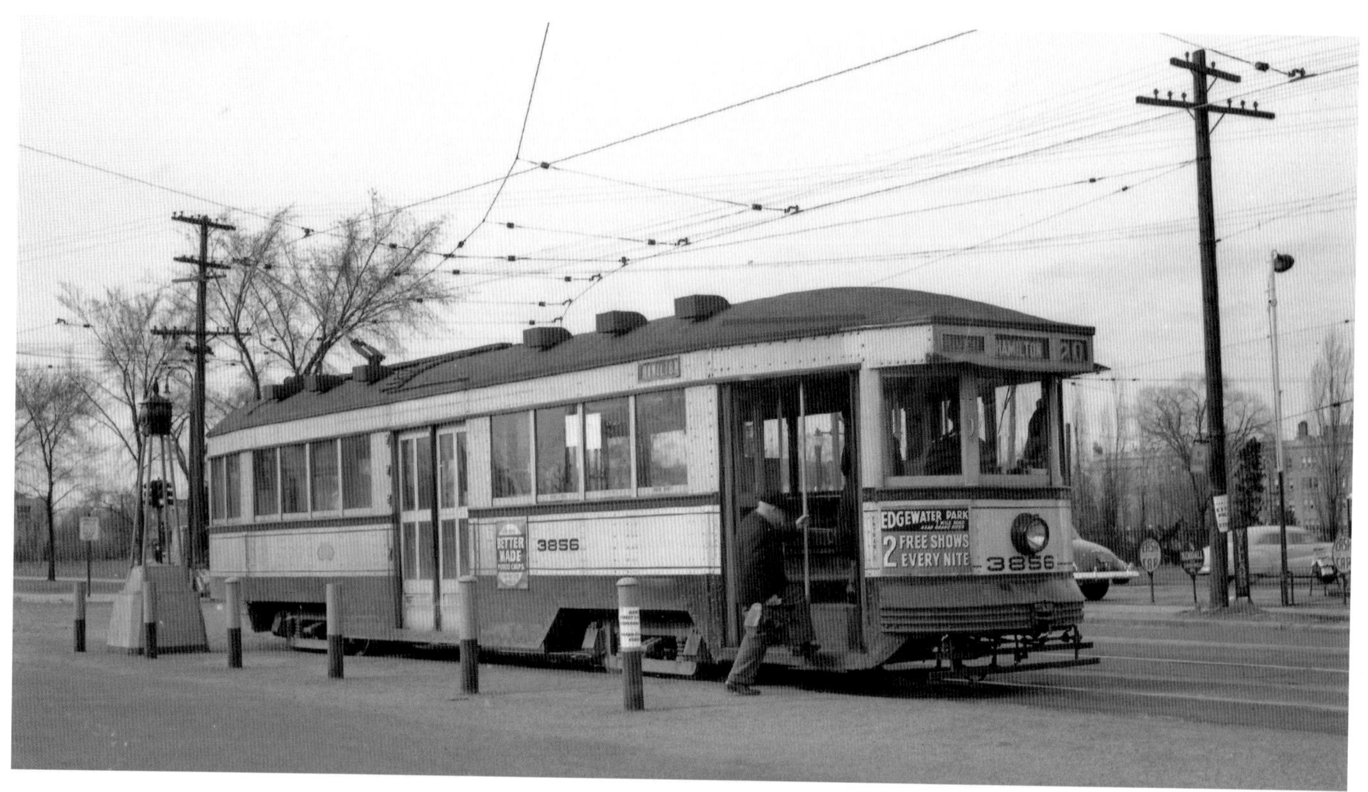

On April 26, 1947, Peter Witt-type car No. 3856 is at the Hamilton Avenue and McNichols Road terminus of the Hamilton line loading a passenger for a southbound trip to Atwater Street on the Detroit riverfront. Buses took over the line on April 28, 1947. (*Bob Crockett photograph—Clifford R. Scholes collection*)

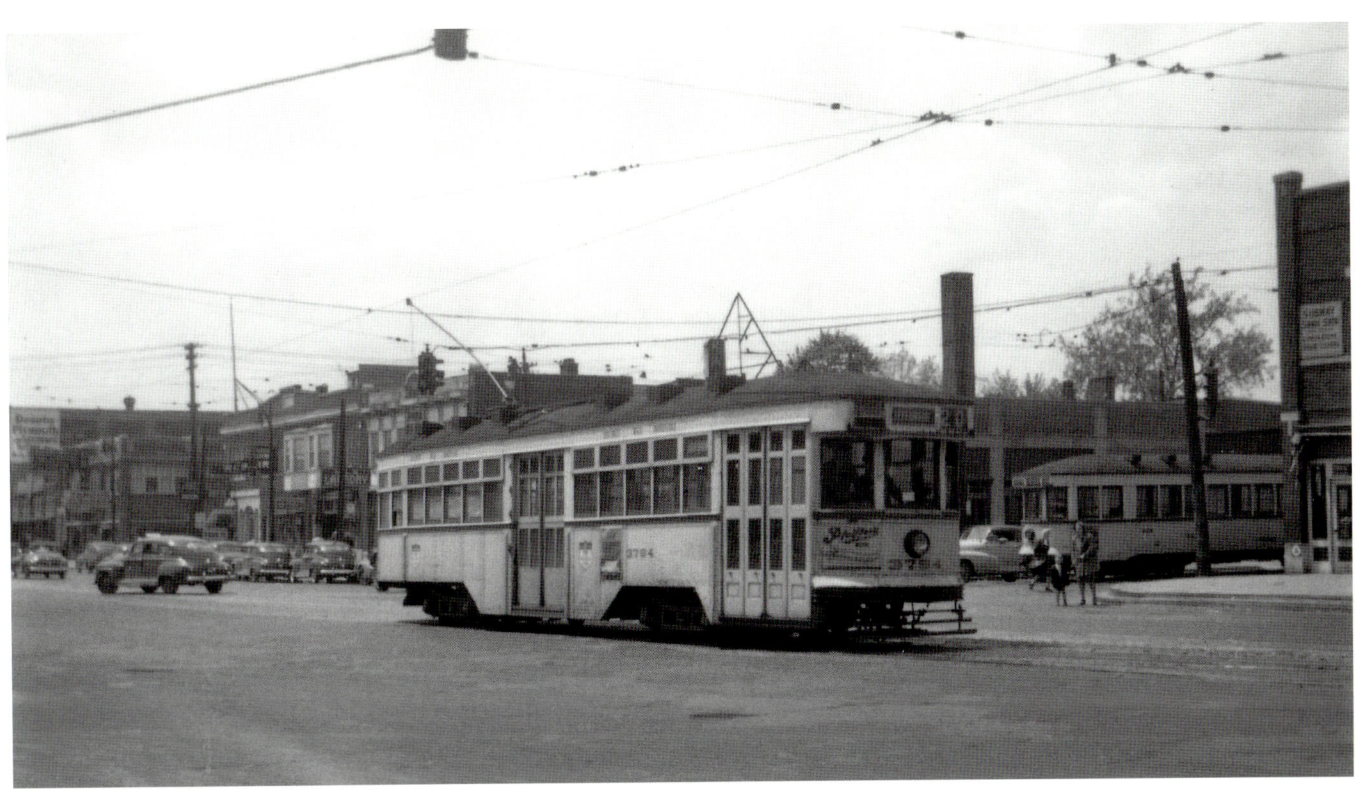

Peter Witt-type car No. 3474 is on Jefferson Avenue at the Wayburn Street terminal loop of the Jefferson line on May 31, 1947. (*Bob Crockett photograph—Clifford R. Scholes collection*)

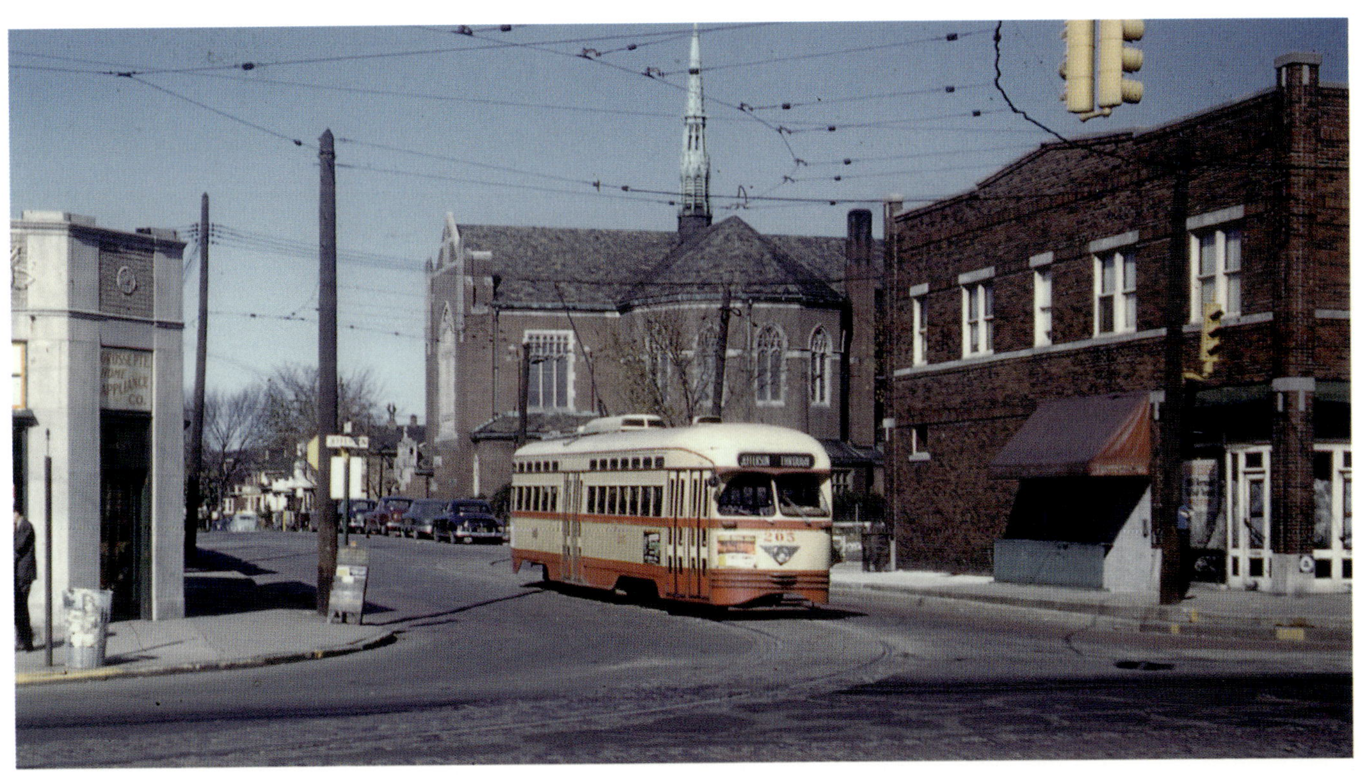

In 1950, PCC car No. 205 is on Wayburn Street at Jefferson Avenue—the Jefferson line terminal. The Jefferson schedule that was effective September 6, 1950 required thirty-three cars for a one-and-a-half-minute headway in the morning rush hour, sixteen cars for a five-minute headway in the off peak period, and thirty-eight cars for a one-minute headway in the evening rush hour. Jefferson cars were assigned to the Jefferson car house. (*Clifford R. Scholes collection*)

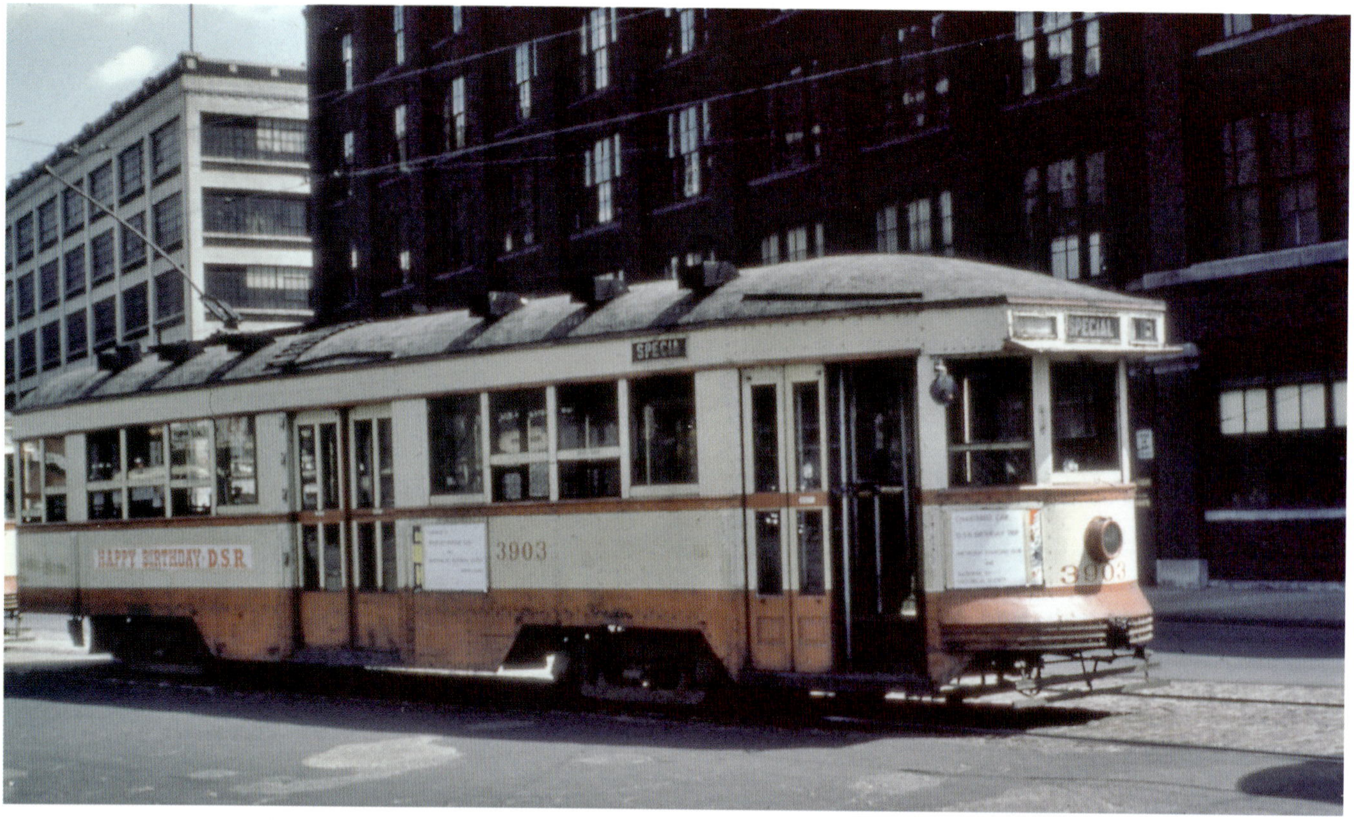

On August 16, 1953, Peter Witt car No. 3903 is on West Jefferson Avenue east of Woodward Avenue. (*Bob Crockett photograph—Clifford R. Scholes collection*)

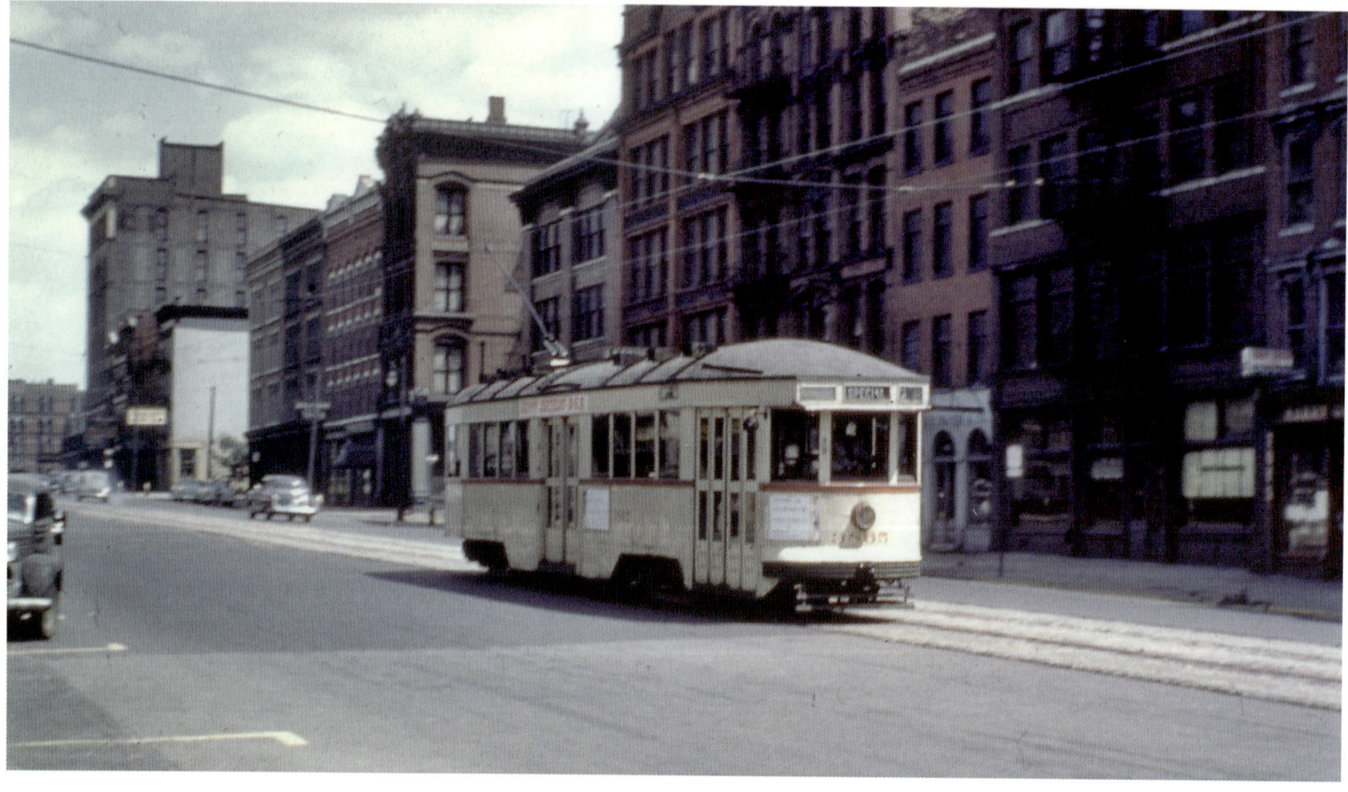

Peter Witt-type car No. 3865 is traveling along Jefferson Avenue in August 1953. (*Bob Crockett photograph—Clifford R. Scholes collection*)

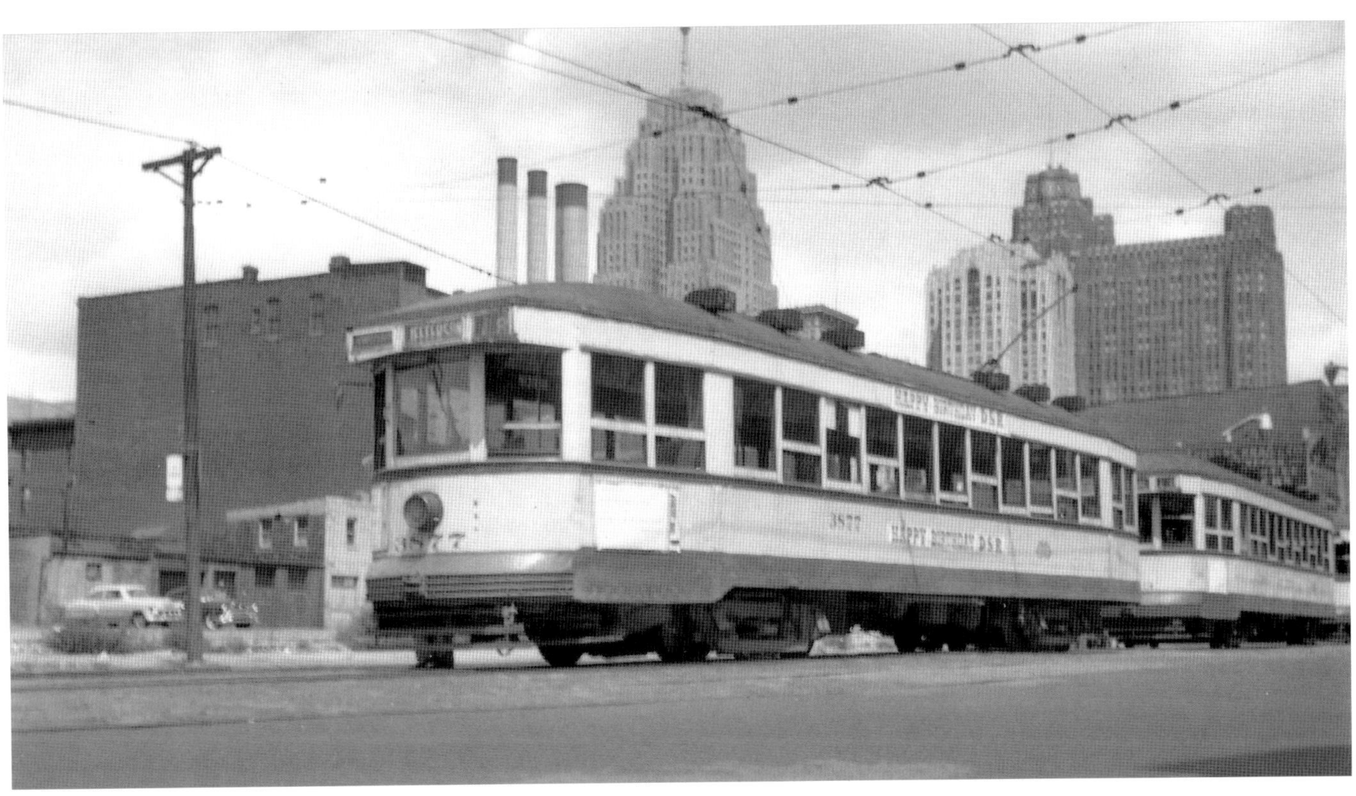

On August 16, 1953, three Peter Witt-type cars, headed by car No. 3877, with the sign "Happy Birthday DSR," are on Jefferson Avenue west of Woodward Avenue on a special trip. Jefferson, the first horsecar line in Detroit, opened on August 4, 1863 on Jefferson Avenue from Third Street to Mt. Elliott Street. On August 22, 1892, Detroit's first electric streetcar line opened on Jefferson Avenue from St. Antoine Street to Baldwin Street. (*Clifford R. Scholes collection*)

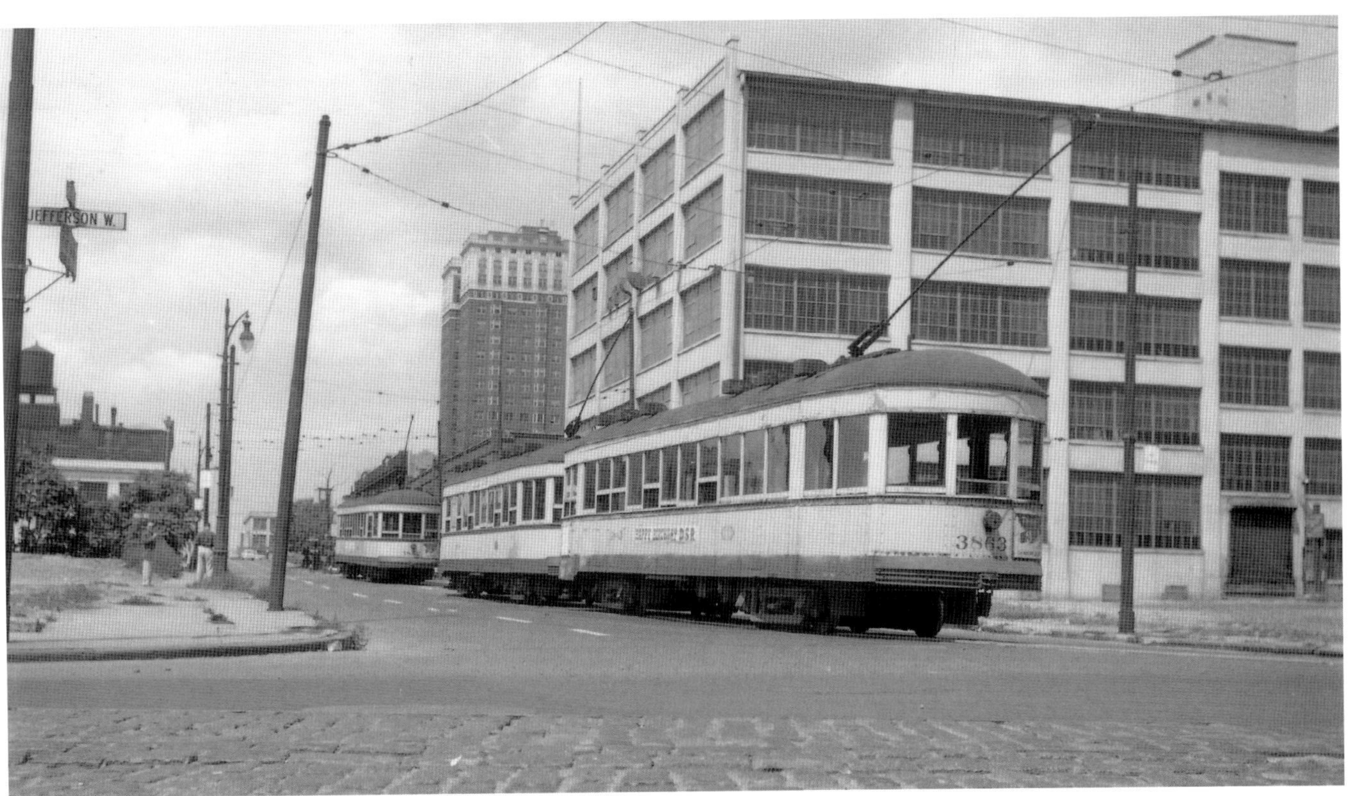

Peter Witt streetcars Nos. 3877, 3852, and 3863 are on a special trip on August 16, 1953 commemorating the ninetieth anniversary of the first horse-drawn streetcar operation in Detroit, which occurred on August 4, 1863. (*Clifford R. Scholes collection*)

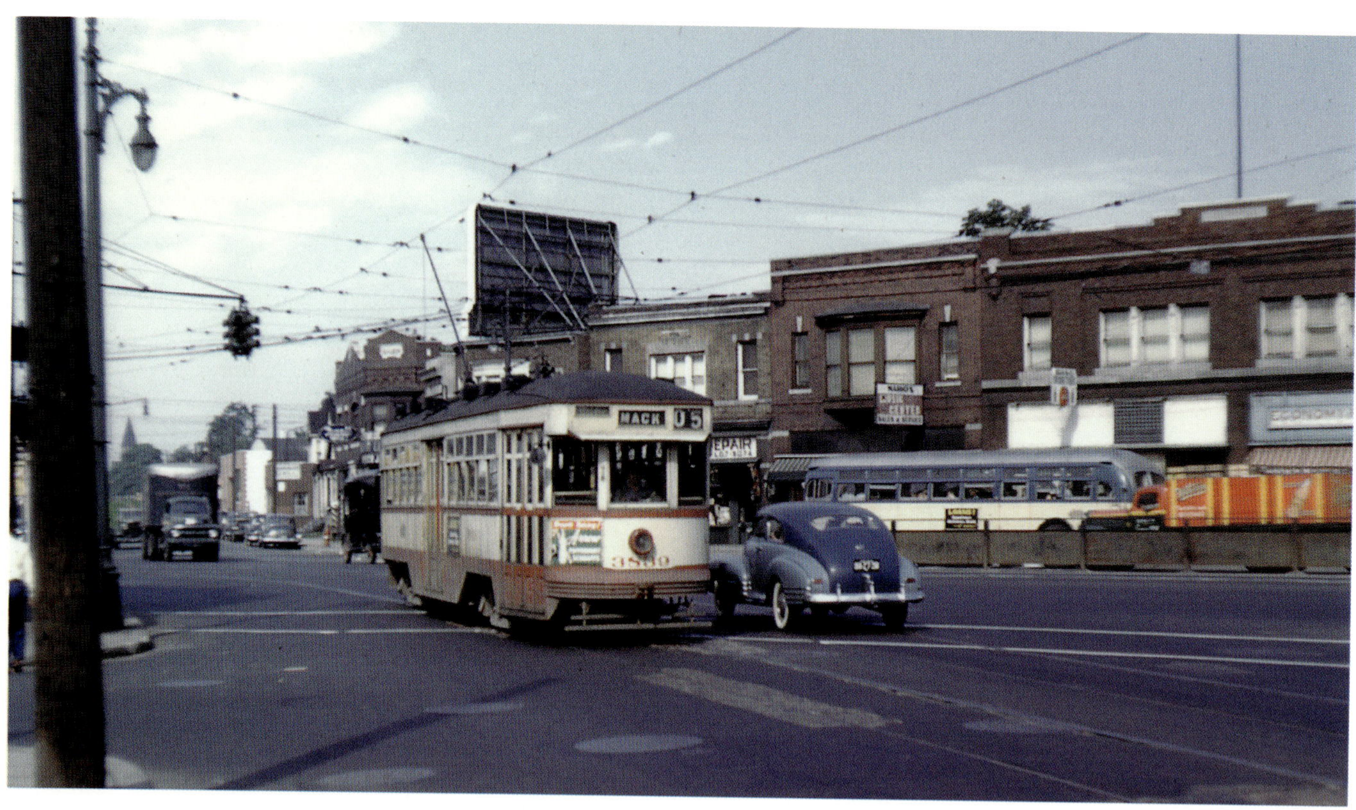

On June 21, 1951, Peter Witt-type car No. 3839 turns from Gratiot Avenue onto Mack Avenue and is crossing Elmwood Street for an eastbound trip on the Mack line. The Mack streetcar line operated from Cadillac Square via Gratiot Avenue and Mack Avenue to the Alter Road city limits. (*Bob Crockett photograph—Clifford R. Scholes collection*)

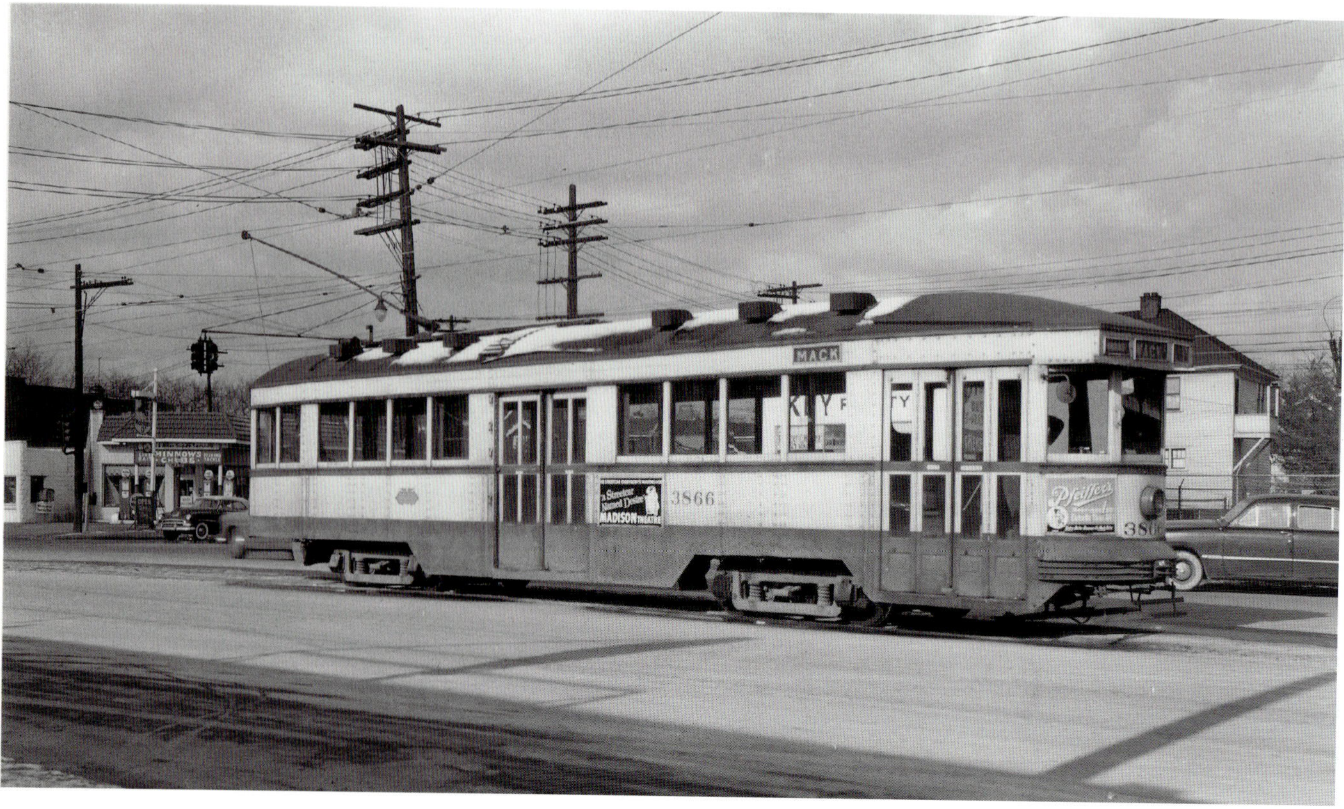

The Mack line eastern terminus on Mack Avenue and Alter Road is the location of Peter Witt type car No. 3866 on November 3, 1951. (*Birdsall H. Nichols photograph*)

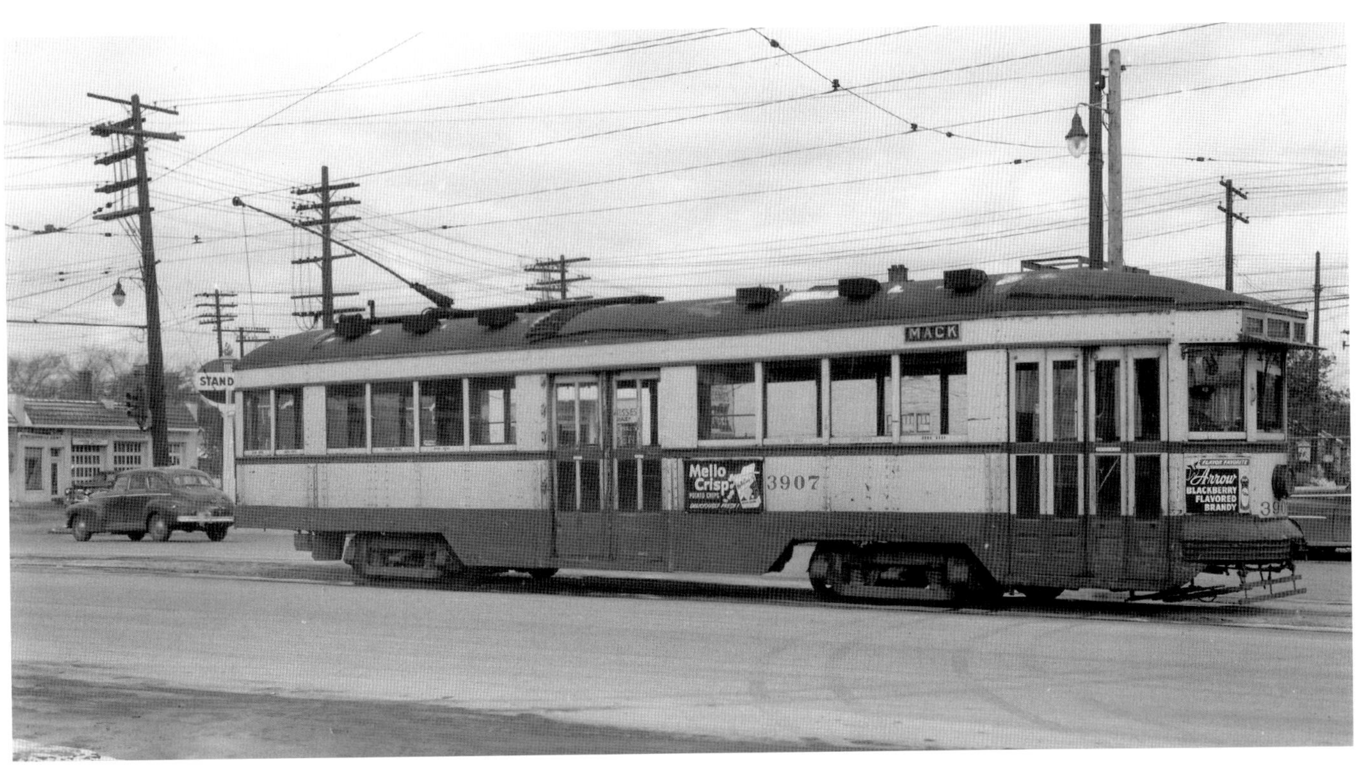

On November 3, 1951, Peter Witt-type car No. 3907 is waiting for departure time at the eastern terminus of the Mack line on Mack Avenue at Alter Road. The Mack line was part of the Gratiot line until it became a separate line on December 3, 1922. A bus line began operation from the Hart Street terminus to Cadieux Road on December 1, 1928. The bus route was partially replaced when the Mack streetcar line was extended from Hart Street to the Alter Road wye on December 1, 1928. (*Birdsall H. Nichols photograph*)

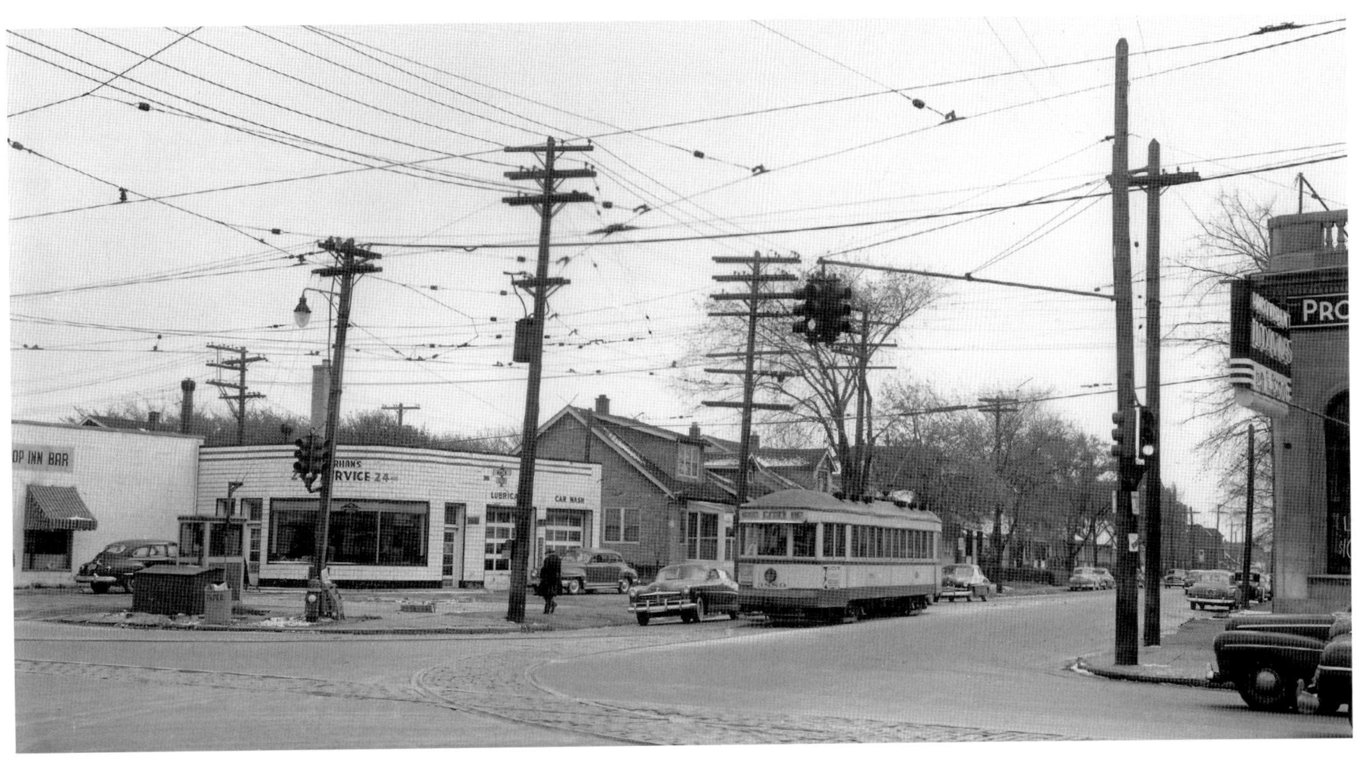

Peter Witt-type car No. 3889 is on the Alter Road portion of the wye at the eastern end of the Mack line on November 3, 1951. On December 1, 1929, a streetcar extension opened on Anderdon from Mack to Warren and east on Warren to a wye at Barham. Sunday and night service was discontinued on this extension on July 12, 1931, and it became rush hour only by November 1, 1932. Warren extension streetcar service ended on August 16, 1946. (*Birdsall H. Nichols photograph*)

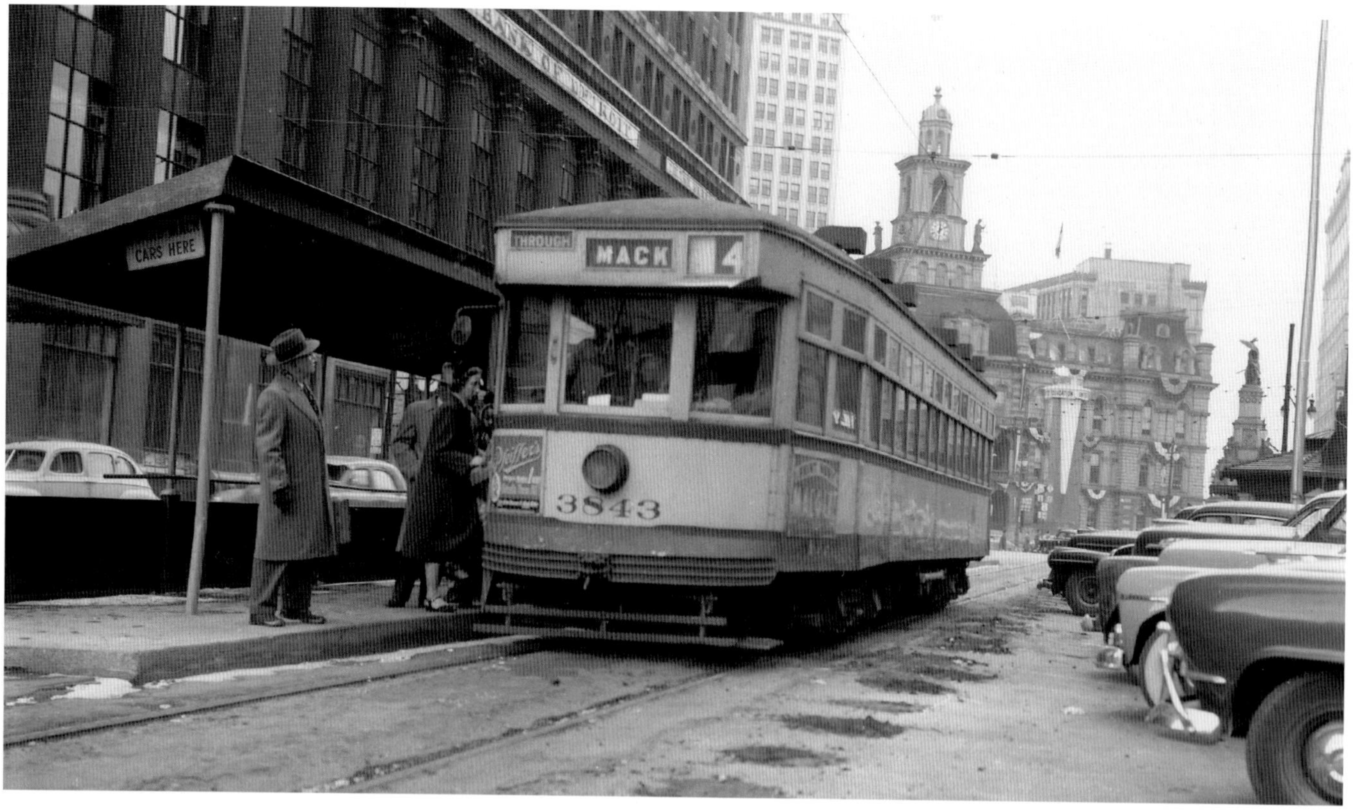

With the old City Hall in the background, on November 3, 1951, Peter Witt-type car No. 3843 is at the Cadillac Square stop loading passengers for a trip on the Mack line. (*Birdsall H. Nichols photograph*)

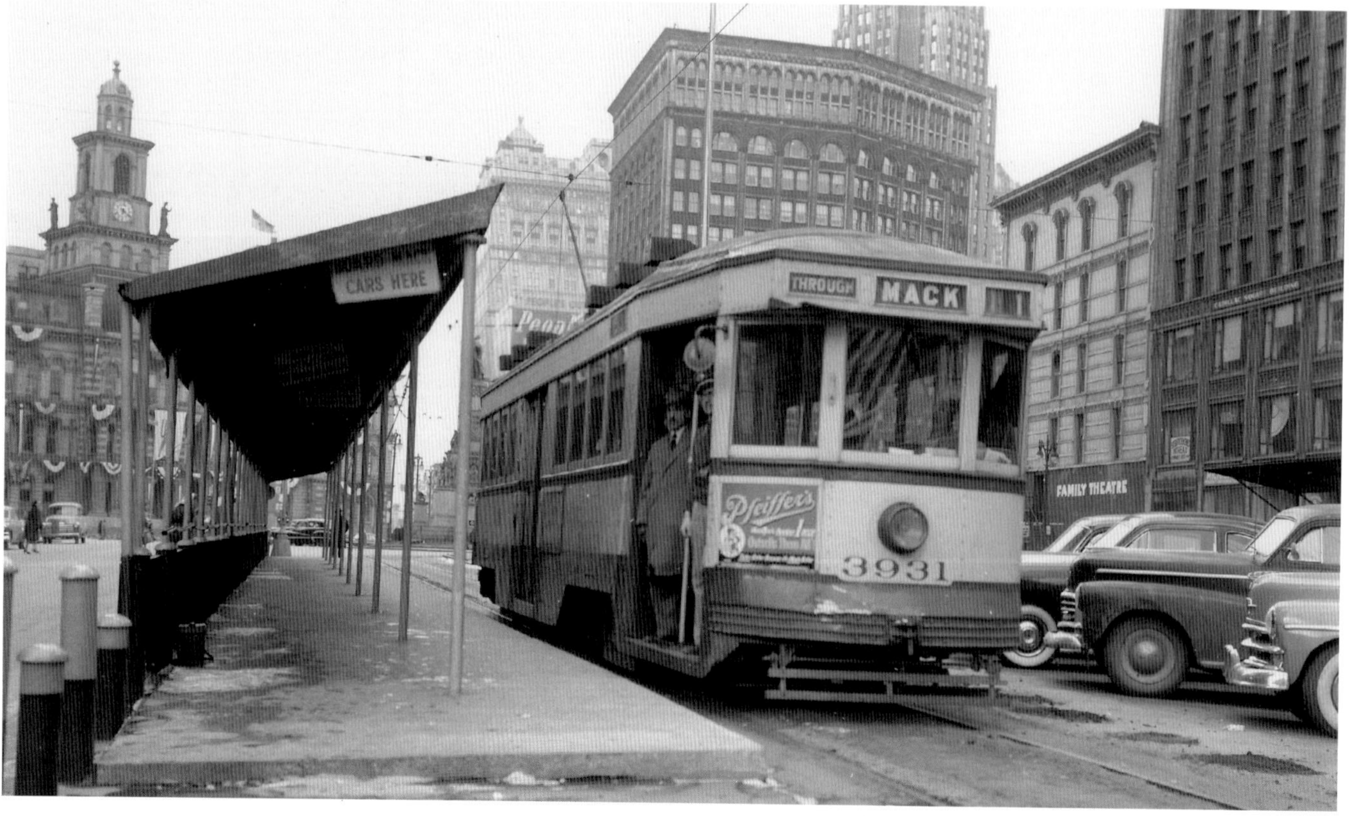

Downtown Detroit is quiet as Peter Witt car No. 3931 pauses at the Cadillac Square passenger stop on November 3, 1951. It would soon make another trip on the Mack line. (*Birdsall H. Nichols photograph*)

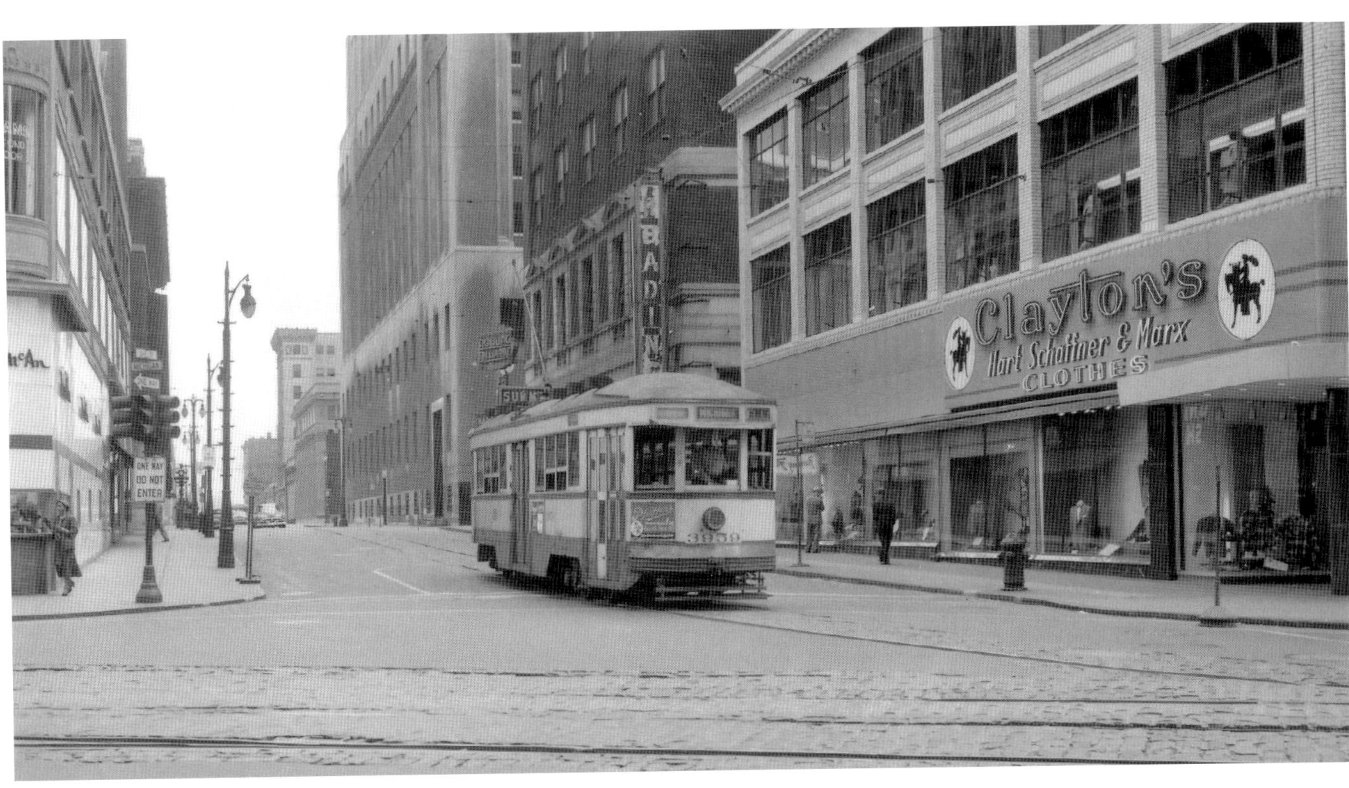

Free of traffic and pedestrians in downtown Detroit, on Sunday August 16, 1953, Peter Witt-type car No. 3959 is on Shelby Street, ready to turn onto Michigan Avenue for a trip on the Michigan line. This was one of two cars Nos. 3959-3960 built by St. Louis Car Company in 1930. Powered by four General Electric type 1192 motors, each car weighed 35,500 pounds and seated fifty-two passengers. (*Clifford R. Scholes collection*)

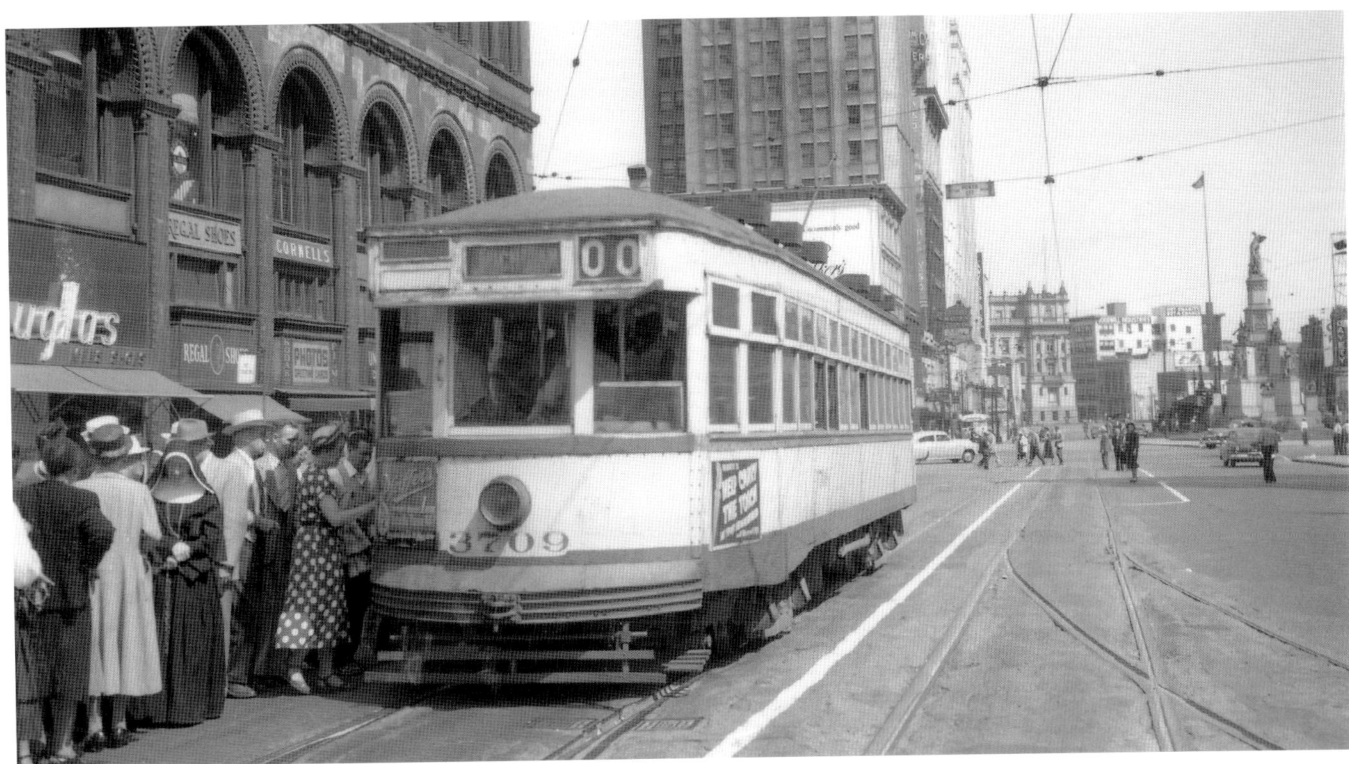

A crowd of well-dressed passengers boarding Peter Witt-type car No. 3709, which is operating on route Michigan on Michigan Avenue at Griswold Street on August 16, 1953. The Michigan schedule that was effective from September 6, 1950 required twenty-seven cars for a three-minute headway in the morning rush hour, seven cars for an eleven-minute headway in the off-peak period, and twenty-seven cars for a three-minute headway in the evening rush hour. Michigan cars were assigned to the Wyoming car house. (*Clifford R. Scholes collection*)

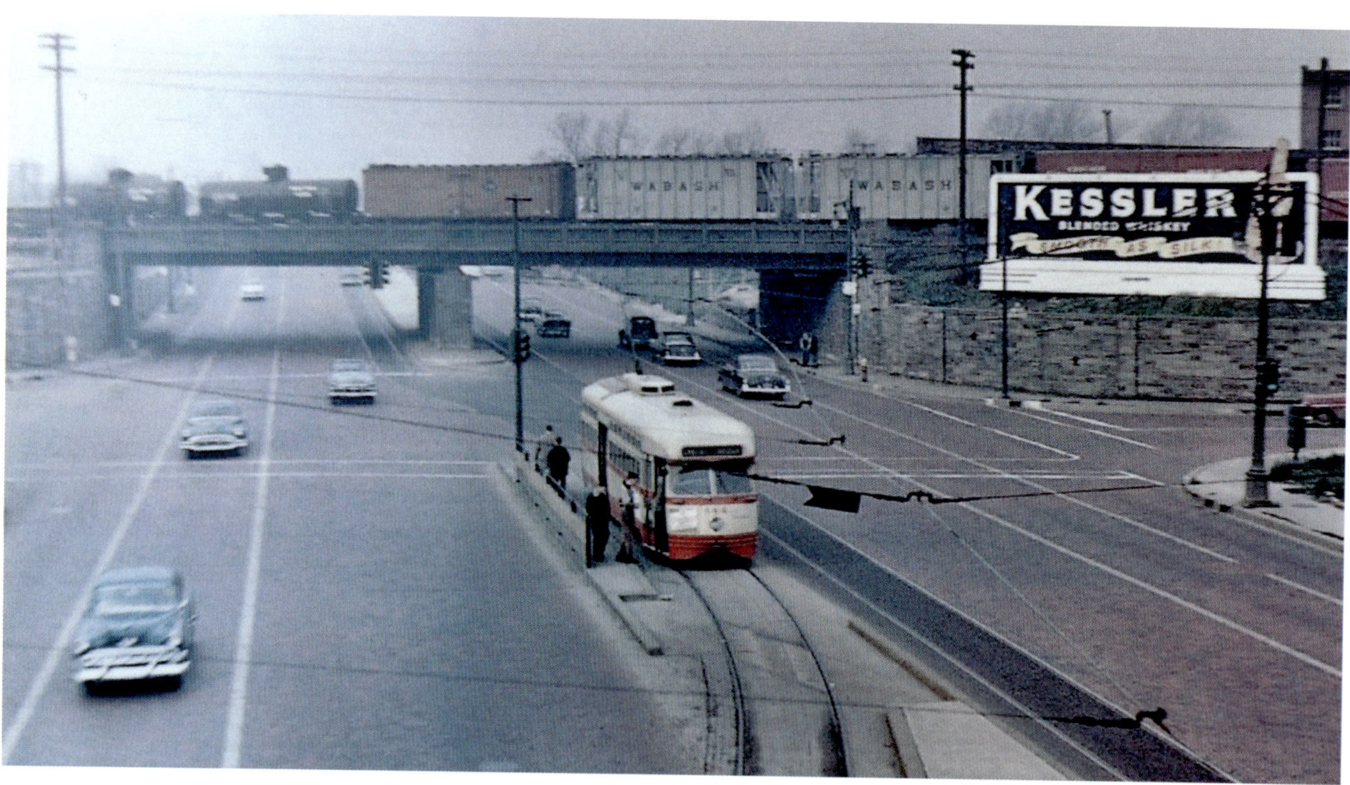

Michigan Avenue and Clark Street in southwest Detroit is the location of Michigan line PCC car No. 144 on November 16, 1954. Michigan Avenue is part of east-west U.S. Highway 12 that runs from Aberdeen, Washington, to Detroit, Michigan. It is known as Michigan Avenue in Detroit. (*Bob Crockett photograph—Clifford R. Scholes collection*)

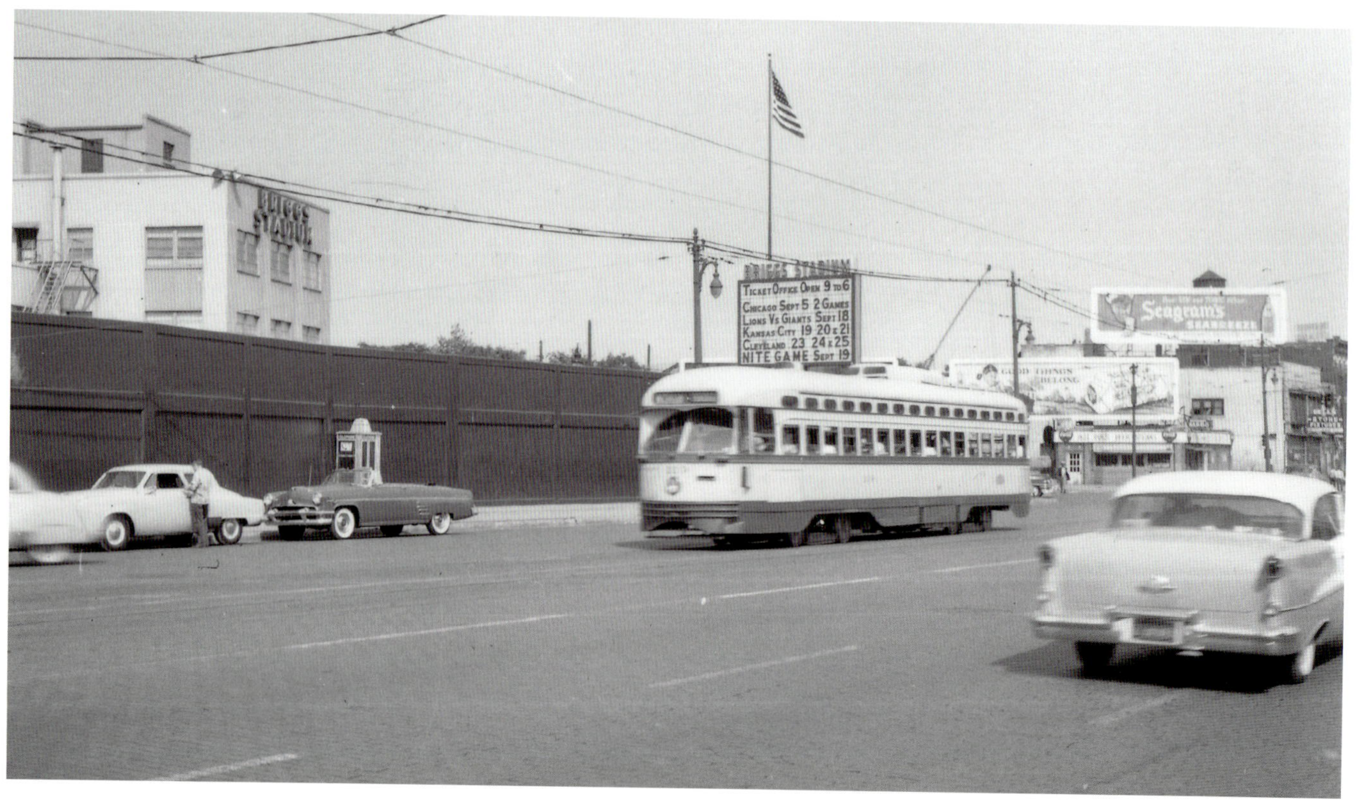

PCC car No. 119 is handling a route Michigan trip on Michigan Avenue passing Briggs Stadium on September 5, 1955. This stadium, designed by Osborn Engineering Company, under Tigers' owner Frank Navin, opened as Navin Field; it seated 23,000 on April 20, 1912. After Navin's death in 1935, new owner, Walter Briggs, expanded the stadium to seat 36,000, and it became known as Briggs Stadium. (*Clifford R. Scholes collection*)

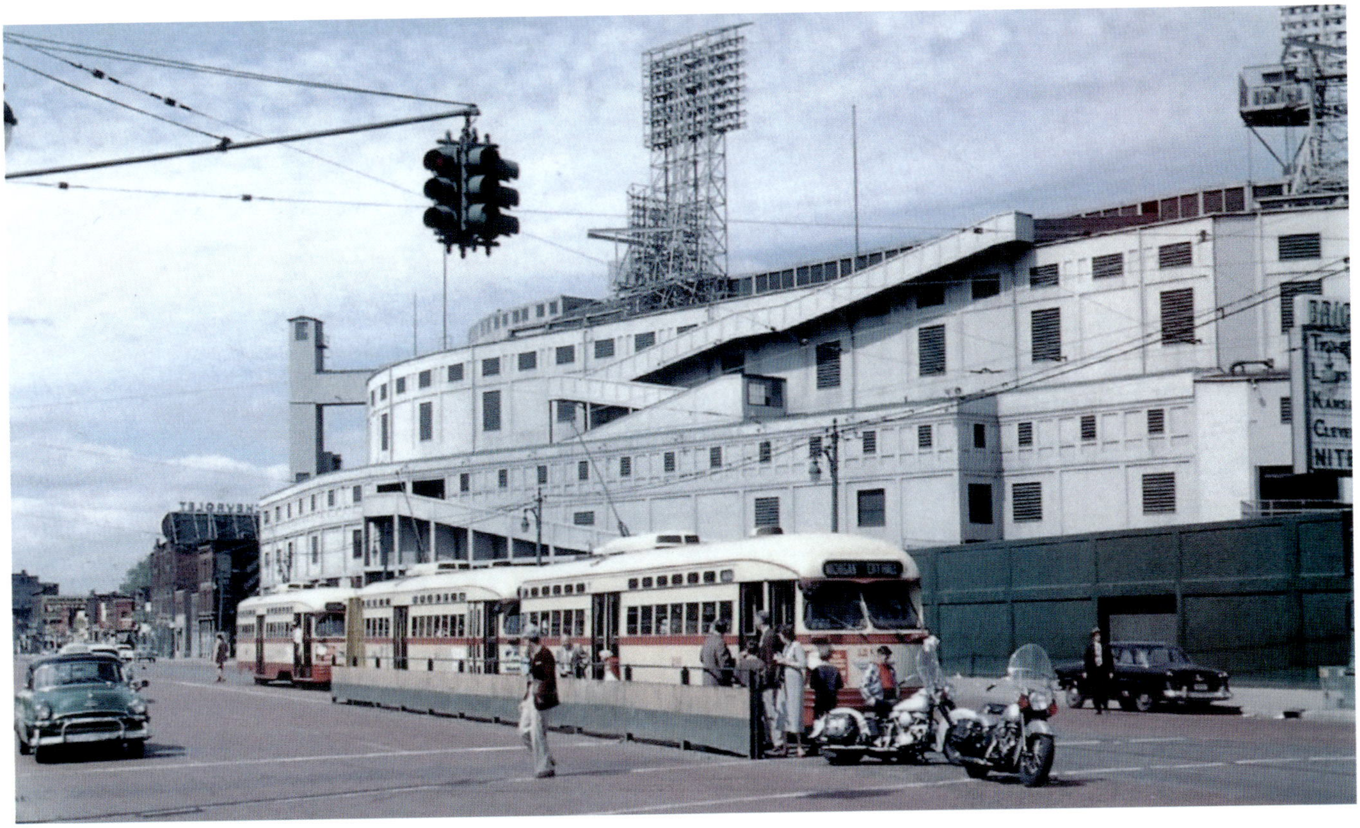

On September 11, 1955, three PCC cars, Nos. 266, 269, and 272, are on Michigan Avenue at Trumbull Street in the Corktown neighborhood west of downtown Detroit at the passenger stop for Briggs Stadium (later known as Tiger Stadium), seen behind the streetcars. Major League Baseball was played here from 1912 until 1999. National Football League games were played here from 1938 to 1974. Demolition of the stadium was completed on September 21, 2009. (*Bob Crockett photograph—Clifford R. Scholes collection*)

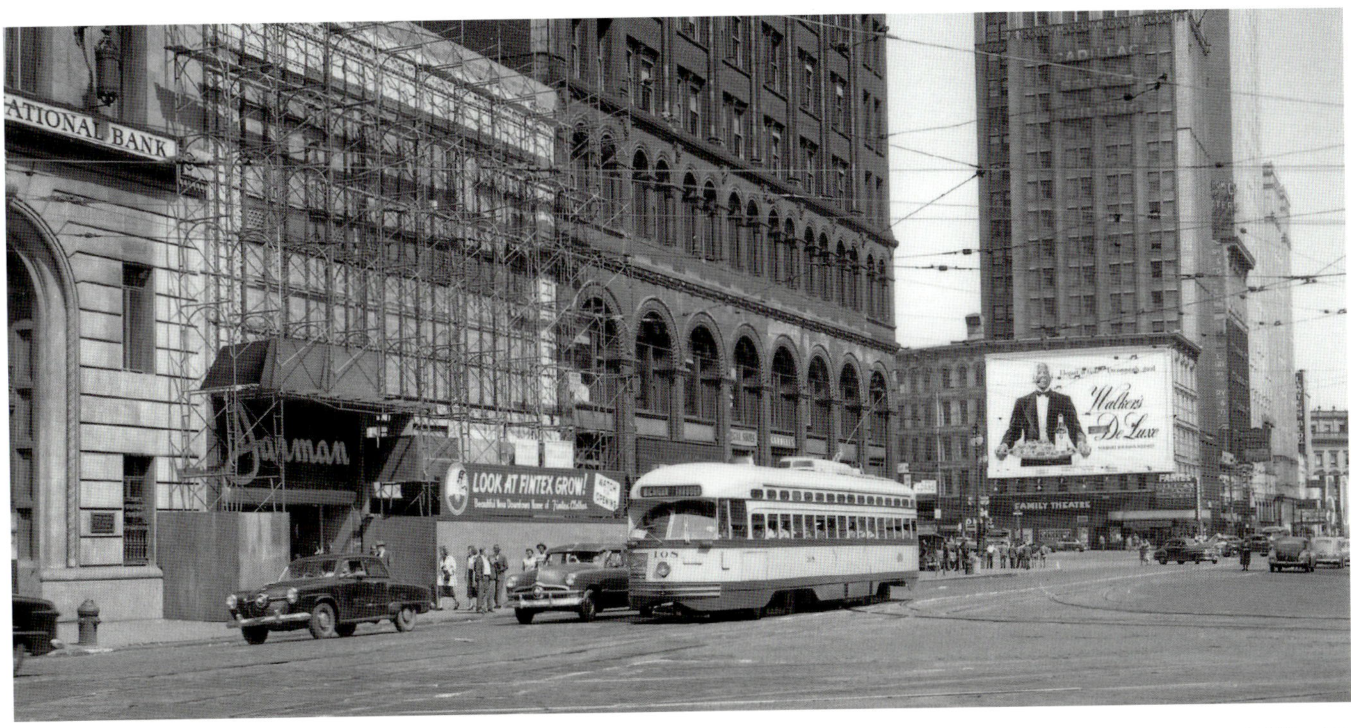

Michigan Avenue at Griswold Street is the location of PCC car No. 108 operating on the Michigan line on September 5, 1955. (*Clifford R. Scholes collection*)

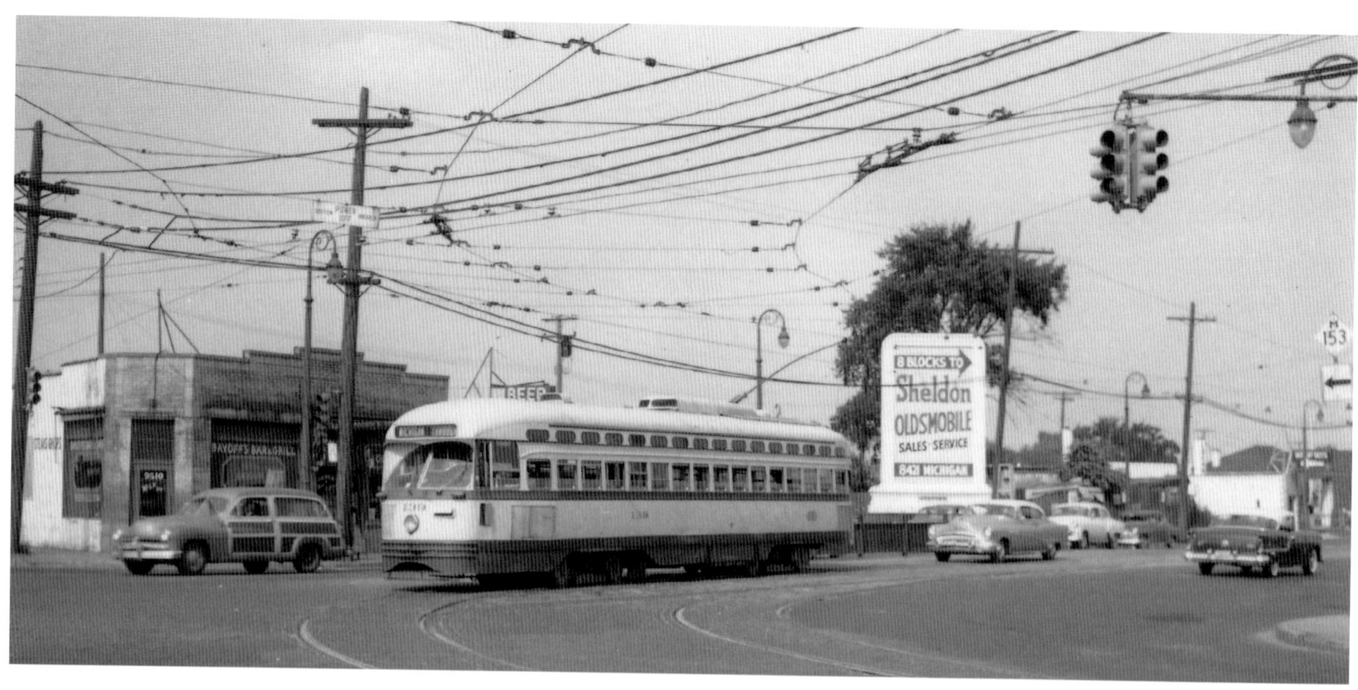

PCC car No. 159 is on Michigan Avenue, ready to turn onto Wyoming Avenue in the City of Dearborn, Michigan, on September 5, 1955. In the morning, afternoon, and at midnight, certain route Michigan cars operated to the Ford Rouge plant. (*Clifford R. Scholes collection*)

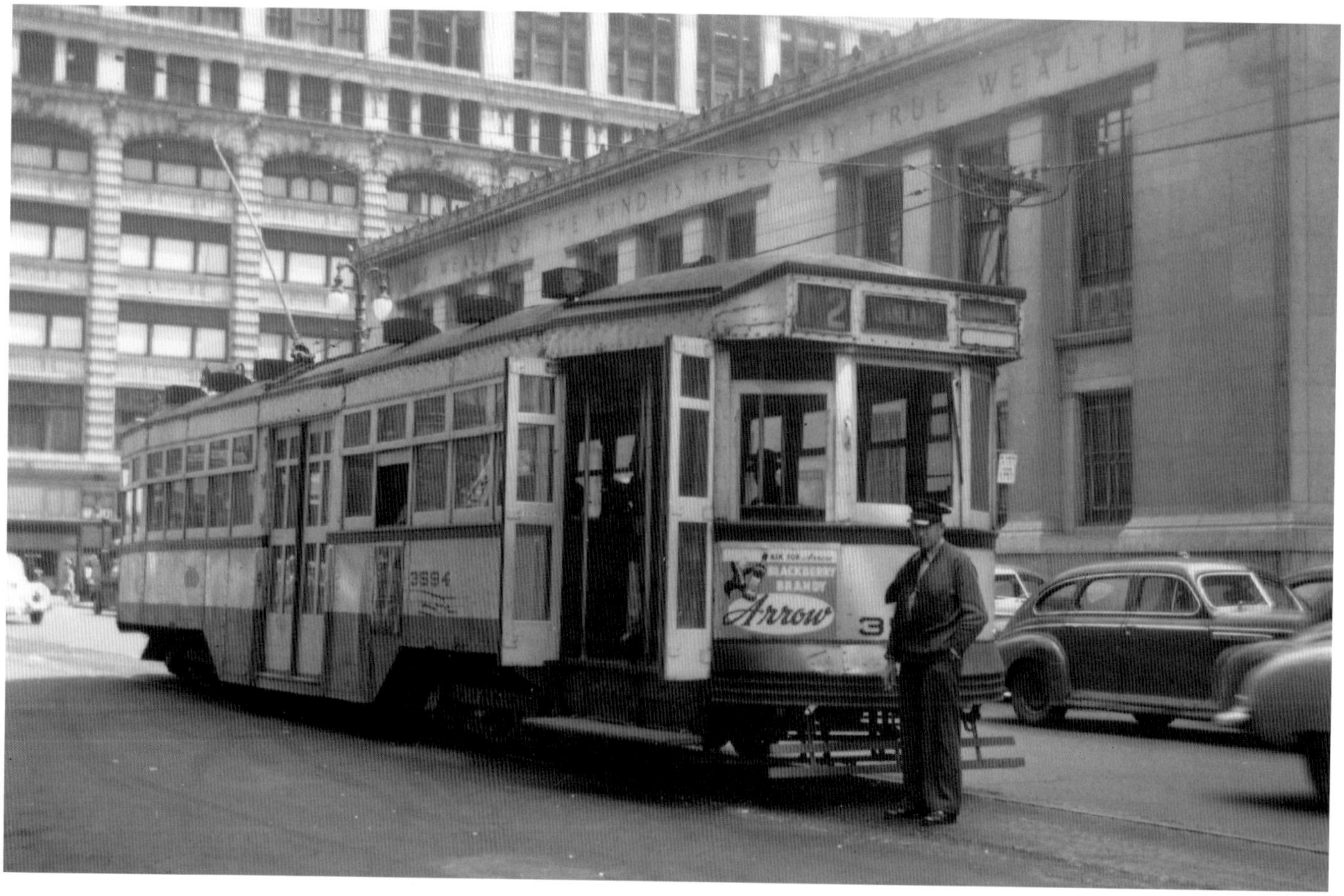

On May 31, 1997, the motorman for route Oakland car No. 3594 is waiting for departure time on Library Street north of Gratiot Avenue. This was one of fifty Peter Witt-type cars (Nos. 3550–3599) built by McGuire Cummings Manufacturing Company in 1924. This heavy ridership line connected a densely populated area north and east of downtown with the Ford Highland plant and the Fisher Body plant. (*Bob Crockett photograph—Clifford R. Scholes collection*)

5

Route Woodward

Woodward was Detroit's best line. It carried the most passengers, had the most frequent service, operated the newest cars, and was the most profitable line. On April 17, 1931, when the Flint interurban line through Royal Oak, Michigan, was abandoned, the City of Royal Oak purchased the track and overhead north of Eight Mile Road and made an agreement with the DSR for streetcar service, which began with the first car, No. 3940, on May 30, 1931 on the extension of the Woodward line from Eight mile loop, about 4.5 miles to Royal Oak. Passengers travelling on the Royal Oak line paid an extra fare. About 2.5 miles of that extension was in the center median of Woodward Avenue, and the remainder was street operation in Royal Oak. This line was replaced by a shuttle bus from the Fairgrounds on May 3, 1947. Woodward was the only line to have two branches. Streetcars displaying "River" on the destination sign operated from Woodward to Woodbridge, Griswold, Atwater, to Woodward. Streetcars displaying "Boat-Piers" on the destination sign operated from Woodward west on Jefferson to Second, Larned, Third, Jefferson to Woodward. Northbound Woodward streetcars from the "River" (Woodbridge, Griswold, Atwater loop) operated north on Woodward Avenue to the Fairgrounds. Northbound Woodward streetcars from the "Boat-Piers" (Second, Larned, Third loop) operated east on Jefferson and north on Woodward to the Fairgrounds. On October 21, 1949, streetcar service was discontinued on the Boat Piers branch. The Woodward line was completely converted to bus operation on April 8, 1956.

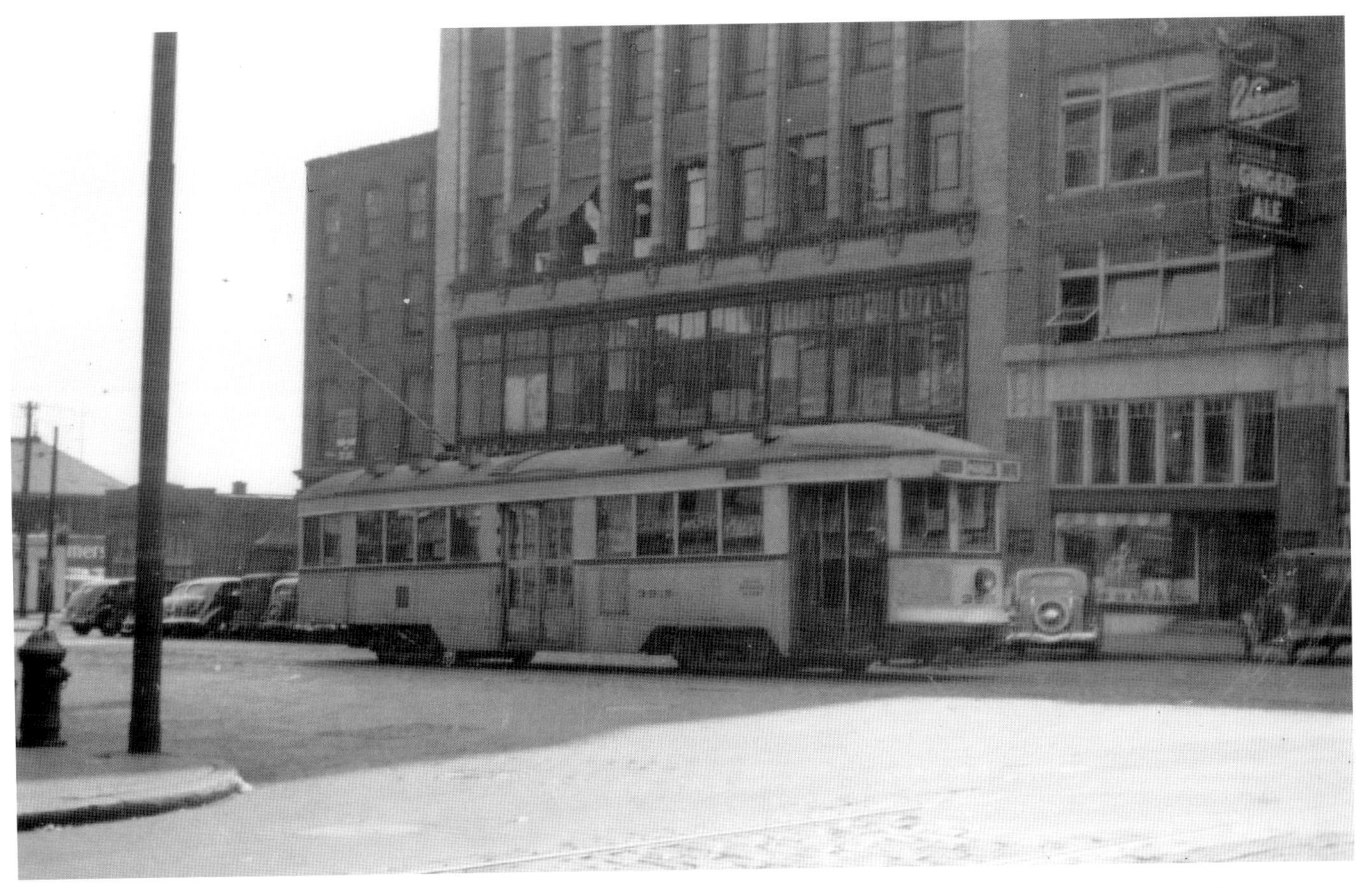

On September 8, 1937, Peter Witt-type car No. 3915 is on Woodward Avenue (State Highway M-1) at Woodbridge Street. Highway M-1 is a north-south state highway running from Detroit (where it is known as Woodward Avenue) northwesterly to Pontiac, Michigan. (*Bob Crockett photograph—Clifford R. Scholes collection*)

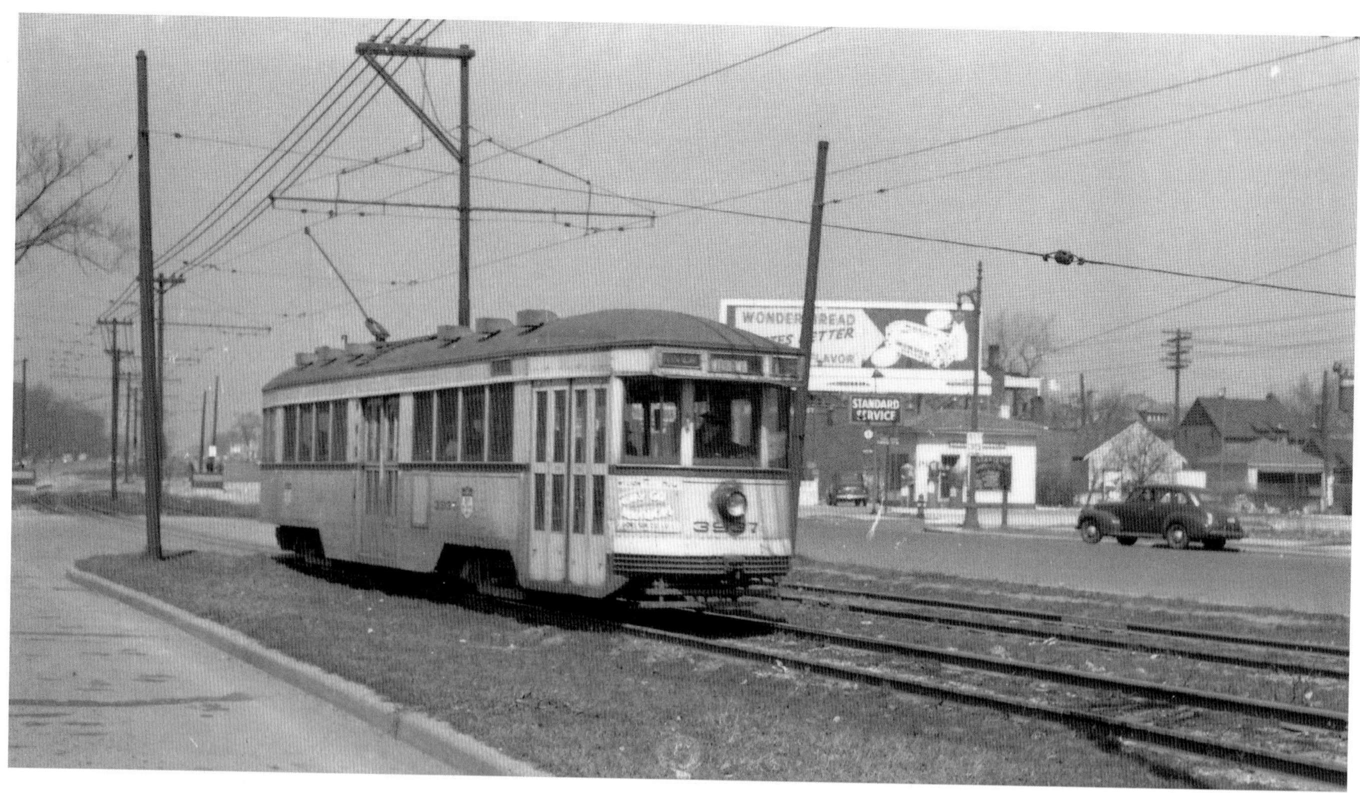

Woodward Avenue north of Six Mile Road is the location of Peter Witt-type car No. 3937 operating on the Woodward line in April 1943. (*Clifford R. Scholes collection*)

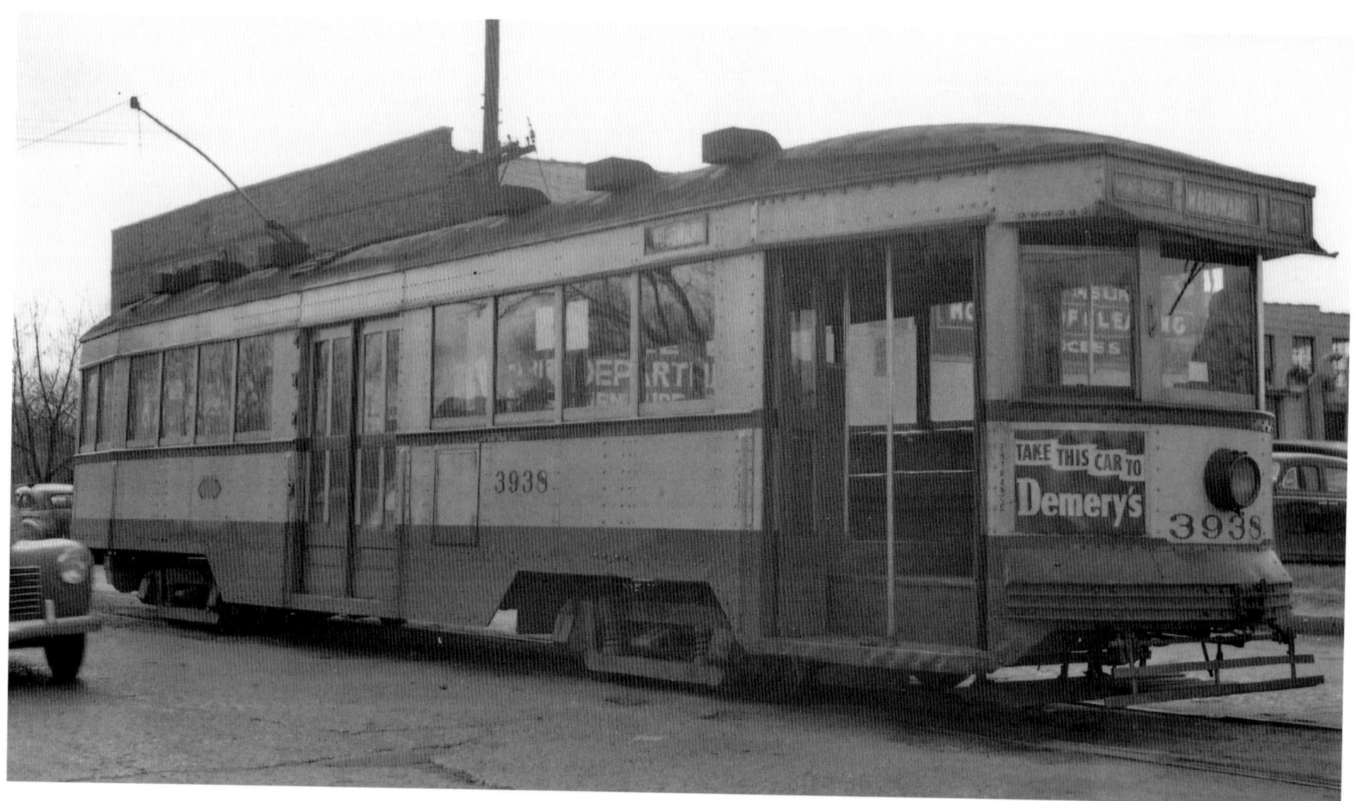

In the City of Royal Oak, Peter Witt-type car No. 3938 is on the Catalpa Drive and Main Street terminal wye on May 3, 1947. This was the last day of streetcar operation on Woodward Avenue north of the Fairgrounds. The Woodward Avenue line north to Royal Oak was the only DSR line that charged a second fare. (*Bob Crockett photograph—Clifford R. Scholes collection*)

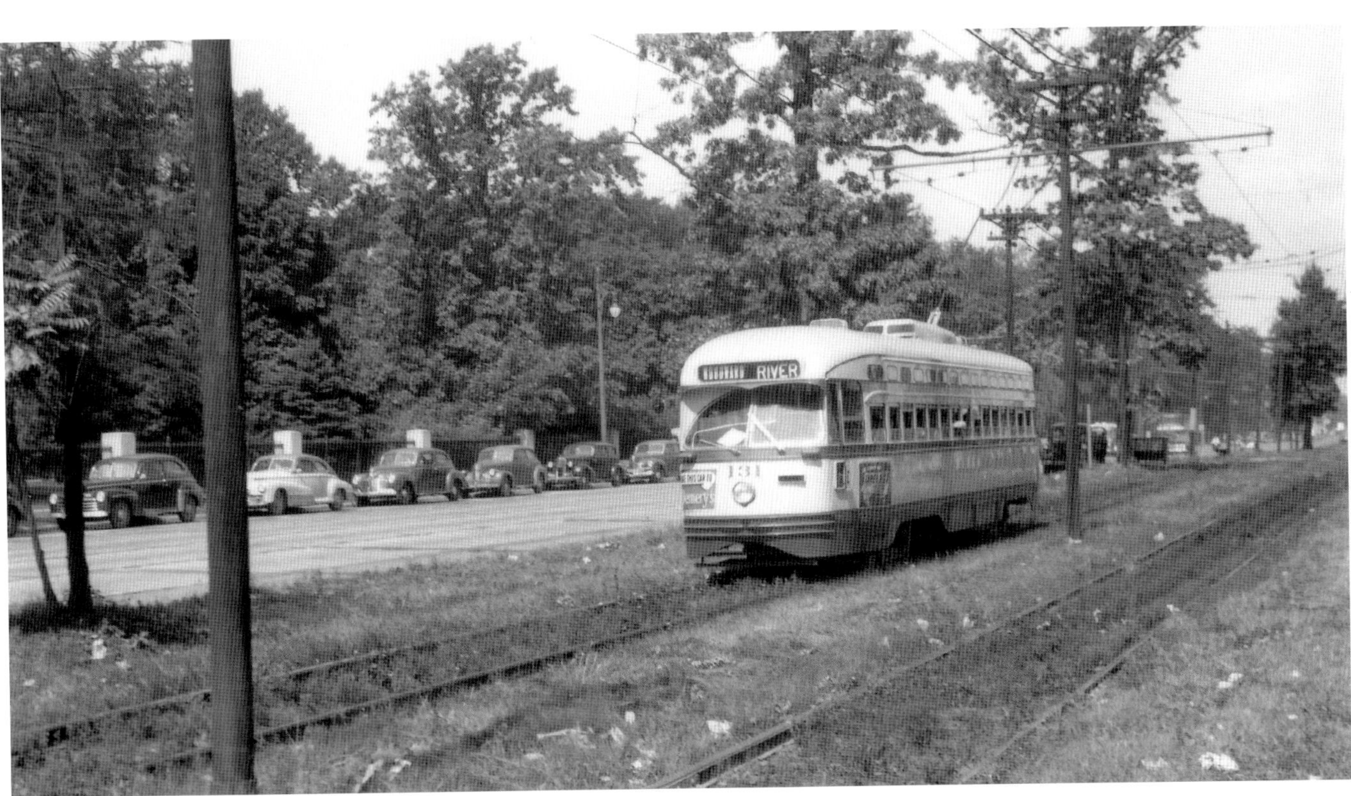

On the center of the median of Woodward Avenue, PCC car No. 131 is near the Fairgrounds terminal loop of the Woodward line on August 27, 1947. Between the Fairgrounds loop and Six Mile Road, Woodward line streetcars operated in that center median. (*Bob Crockett photograph—Clifford R. Scholes collection*)

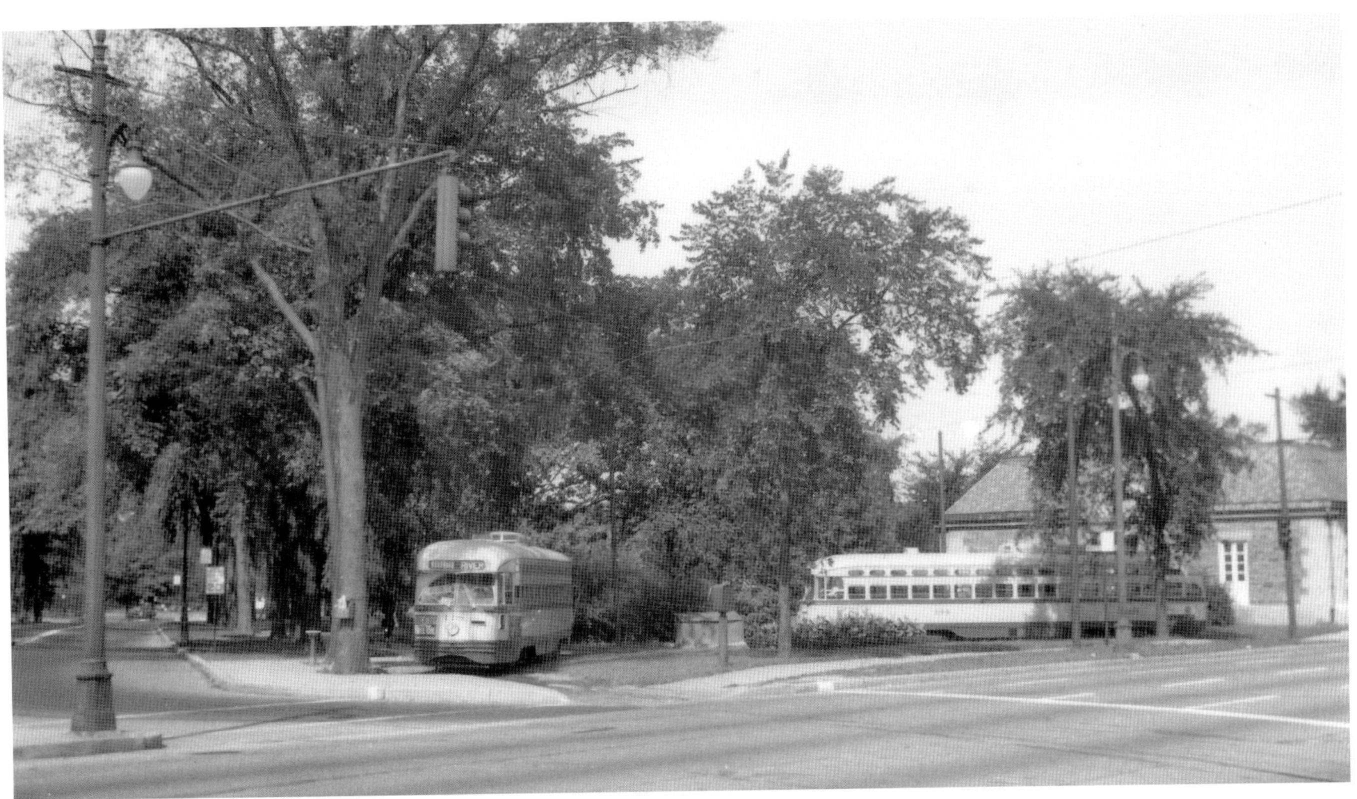

On August 27, 1947, PCC cars Nos. 144 and 118 are at the Palmer Park Loop. By 1955, about two out of every three streetcars turned at Palmer Park Loop with the remainder continuing to the Fairgrounds Loop. (*Bob Crockett photograph—Clifford R. Scholes collection*)

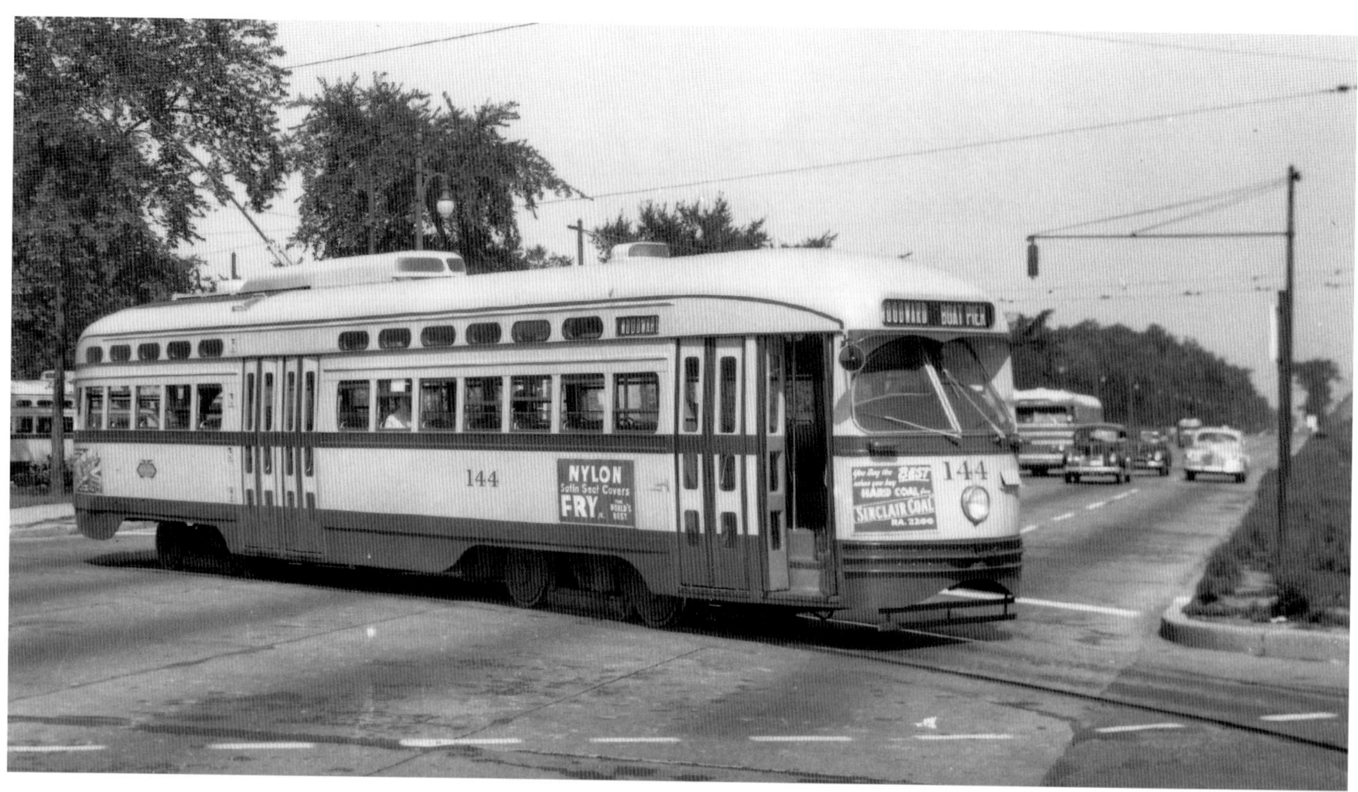

PCC car No. 144 is leaving the Palmer Park Loop, crossing the busy Woodward Avenue on August 27, 1947 for a southbound trip on the Woodward line to the Boat Pier close to the Detroit River in downtown Detroit. (*Bob Crockett photograph—Clifford R. Scholes collection*)

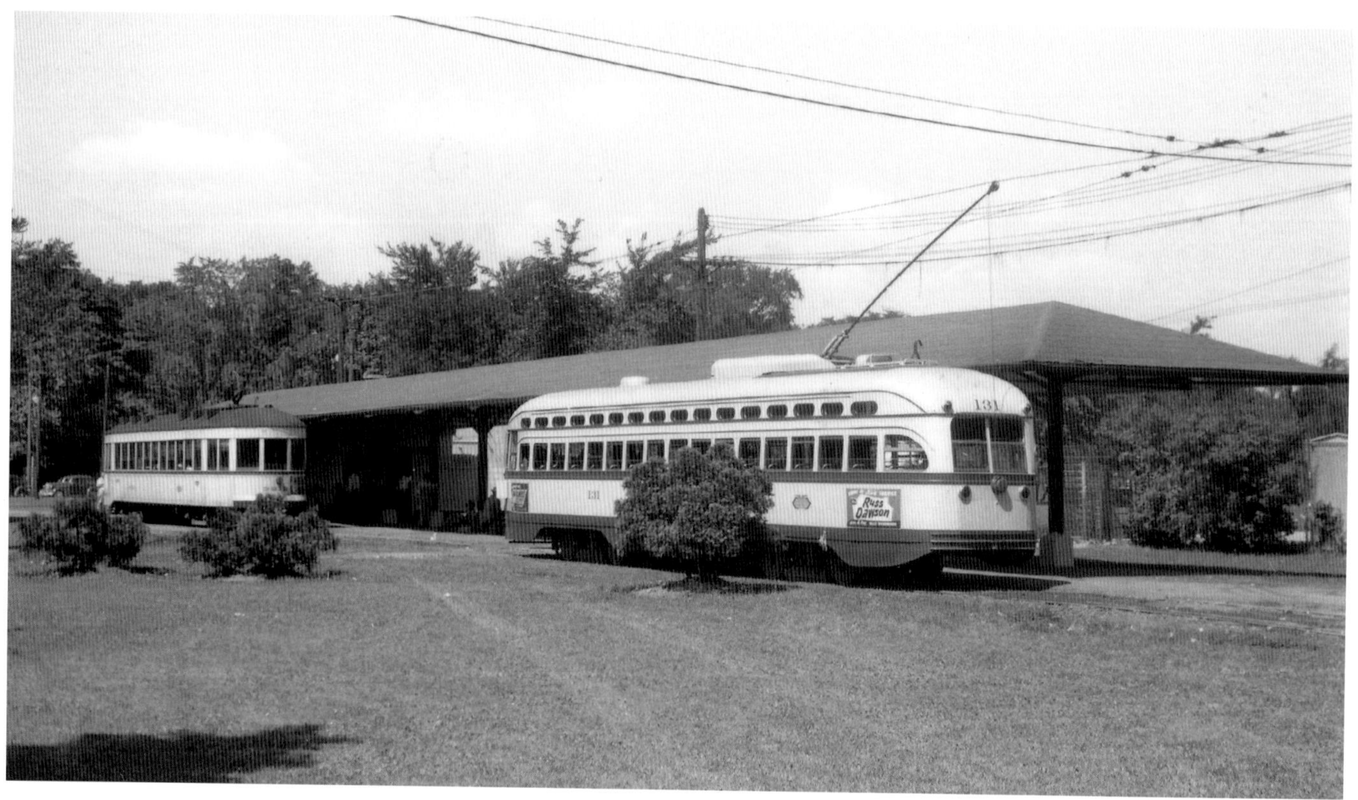

The Woodward line Fairgrounds Terminal Loop station is the location of Peter Witt-type car No. 3913 and PCC car No. 131 on August 27, 1947. (*Bob Crockett photograph—Clifford R. Scholes collection*)

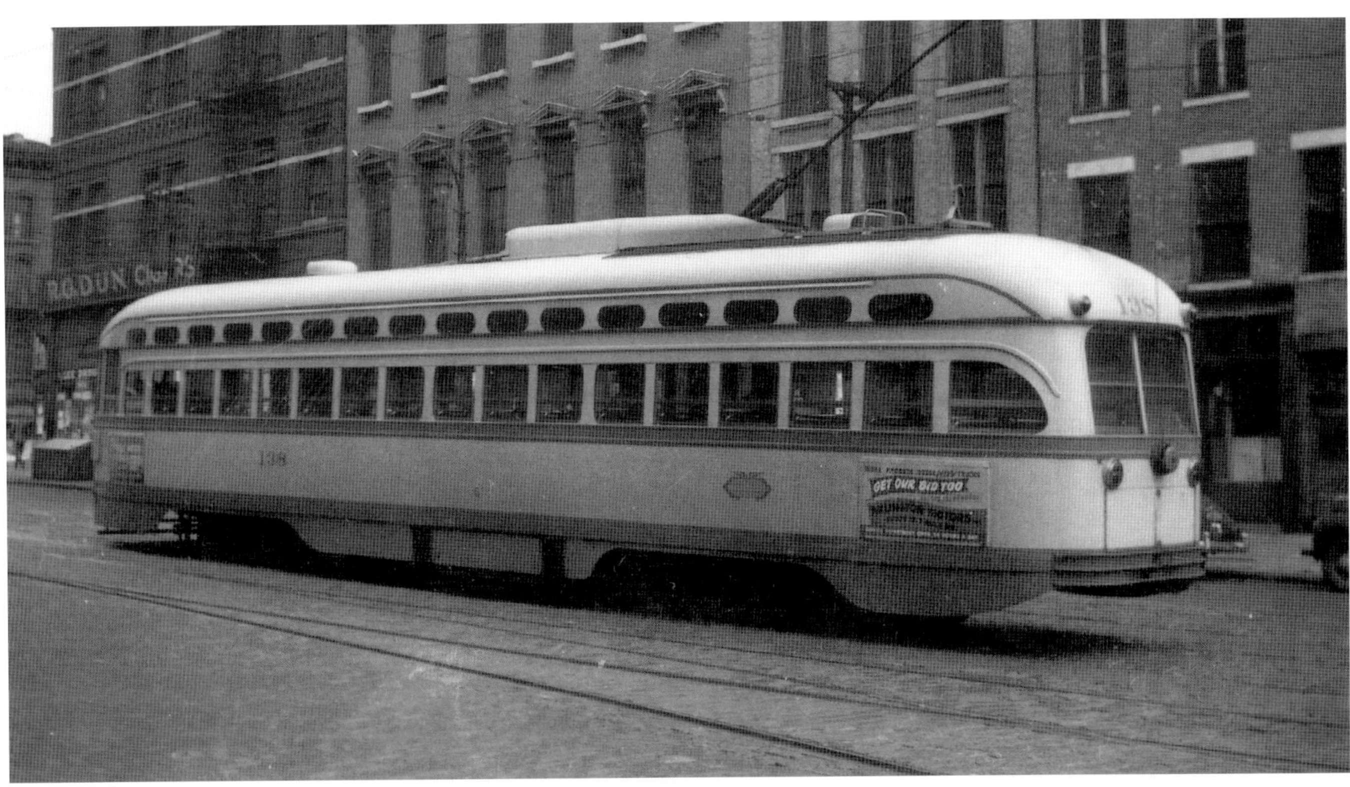

On September 15, 1949, PCC car No. 138 is on Woodward Avenue and Woodbridge Street in downtown Detroit. The Woodward schedule that was effective from September 6, 1950 required sixty-eight cars for a one-minute headway in the morning rush hour, forty-three cars for a two-and-a-half-minute headway in the off-peak period, and sixty-five cars for a one-minute headway in the evening rush hour. Woodward cars were assigned to the Woodward car house. (*Bob Crockett photograph—Clifford R. Scholes collection*)

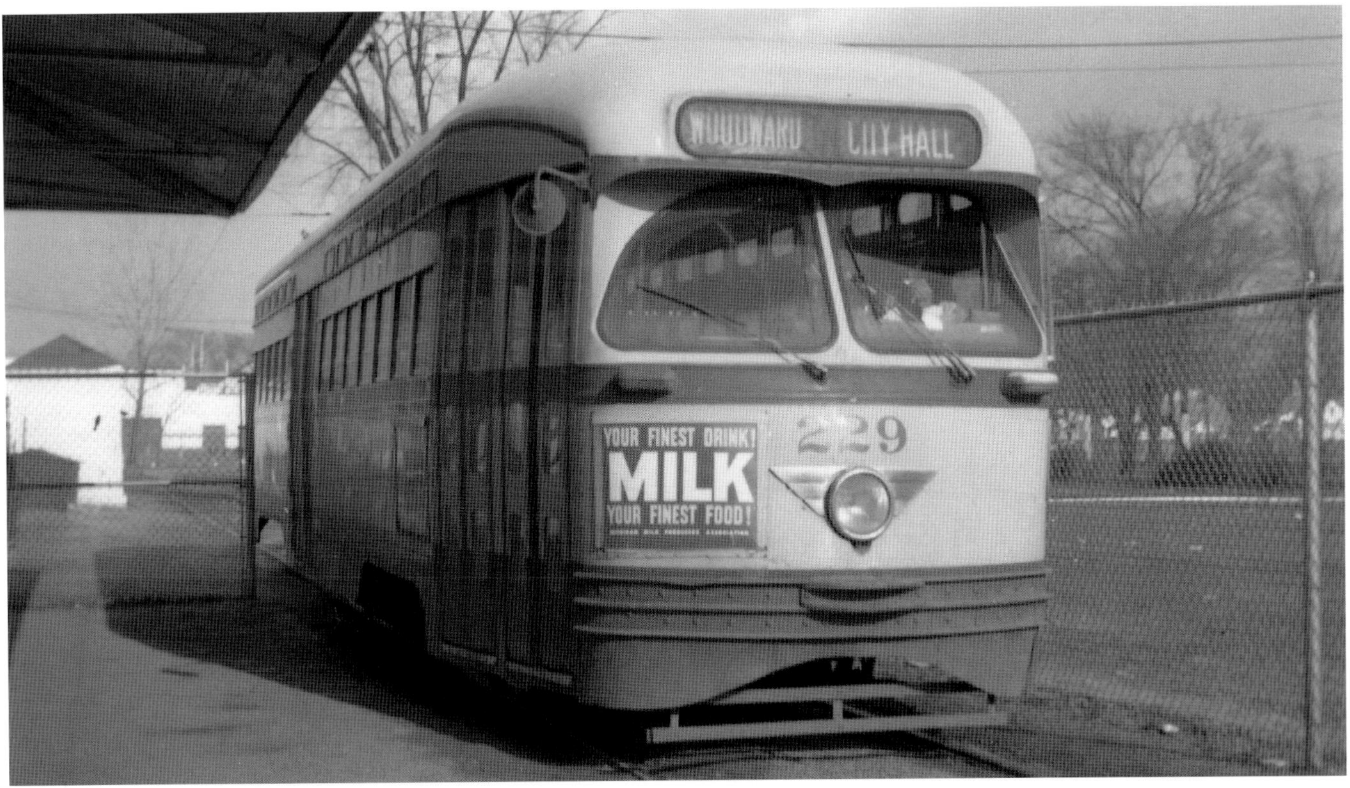

In 1953, PCC car No. 229 is at the Woodward Avenue Fairgrounds terminal loop station, waiting for departure time for a southbound trip on the Woodward line to downtown Detroit. (*Clifford R. Scholes collection*)

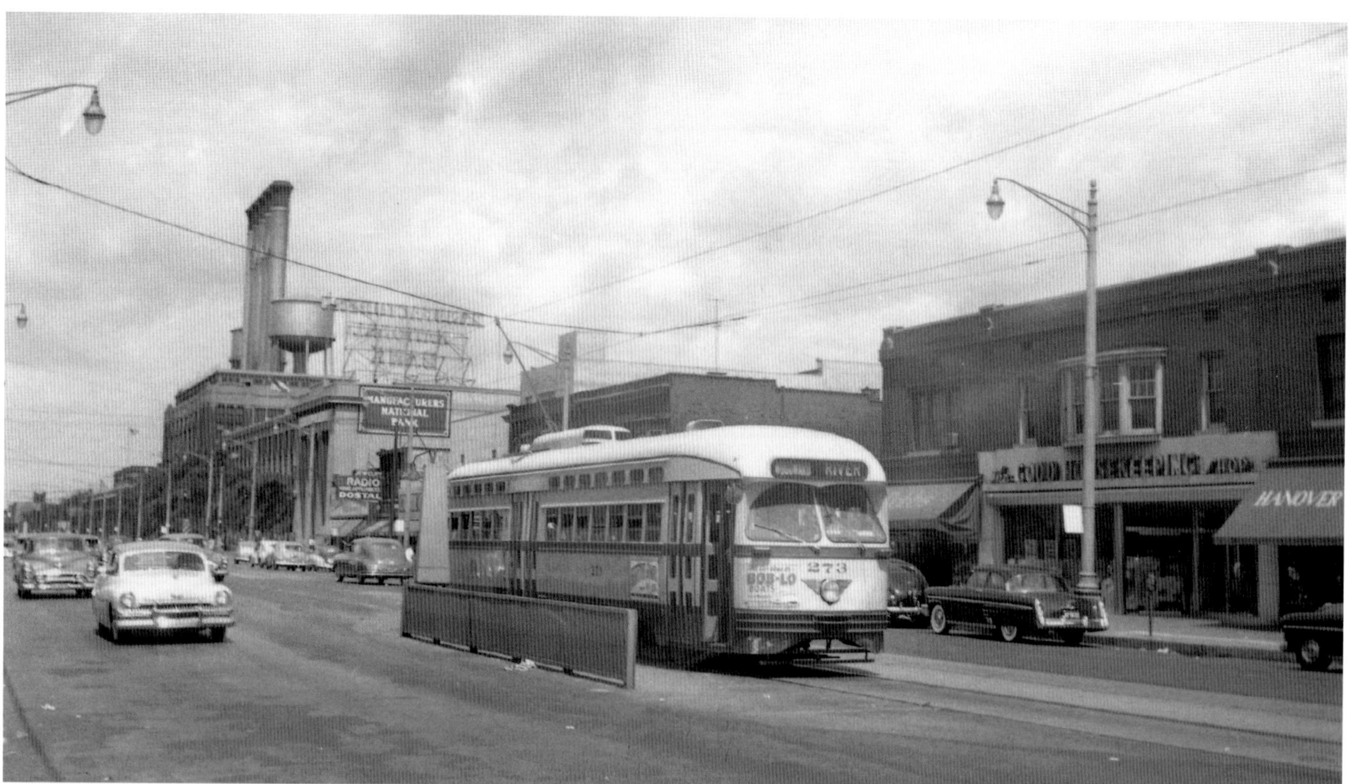

Woodward Avenue at Victor Street is the location of PCC car No. 273, handling a southbound Woodward line run to just north of the Detroit River on August 16, 1953. All of the automobiles in this scene were made in the United States. (*Clifford R. Scholes collection*)

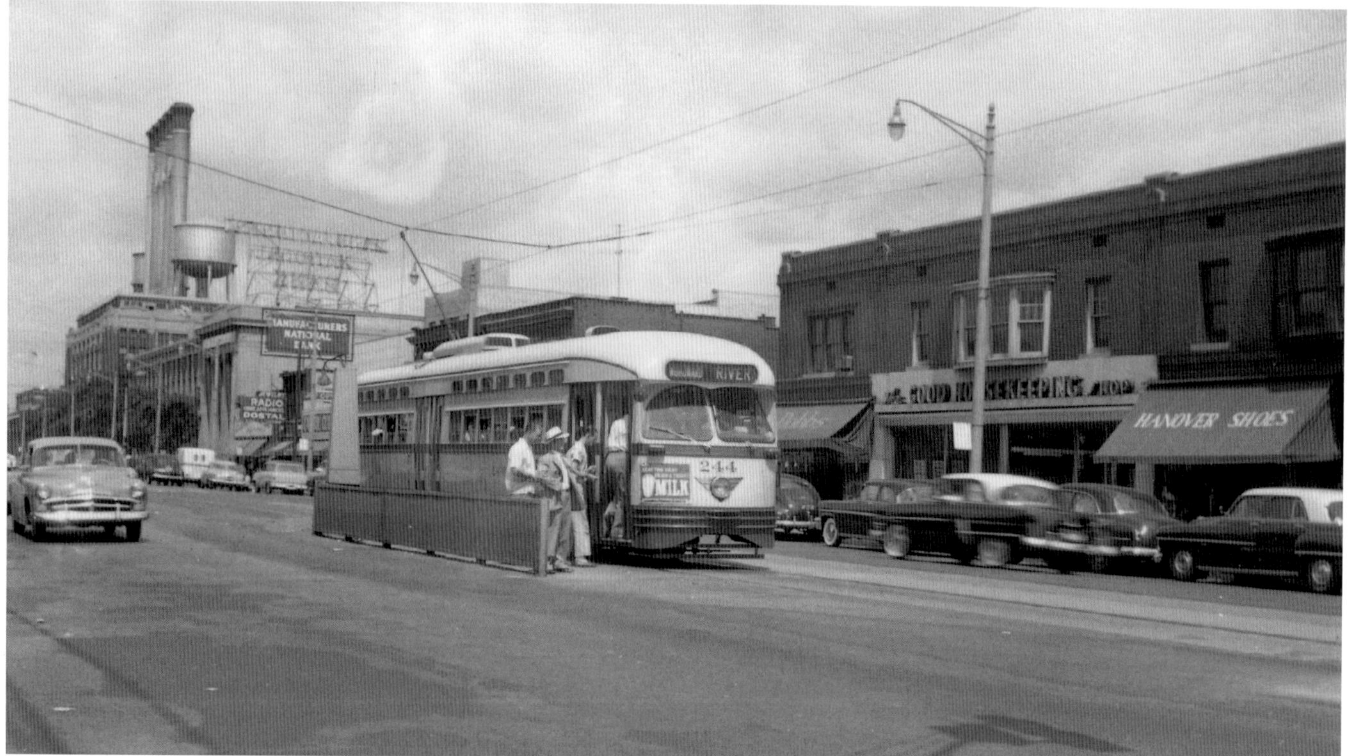

Passengers are boarding PCC car No. 244 on Woodward Avenue at Victor Street for a southbound trip to downtown Detroit with the route Woodward destination sign showing "River" on August 16, 1953. Woodward Avenue had very frequent service, as this picture was taken just a short time after the above picture was taken. Of the transit systems in United States and Canada in 2018, only the King Street streetcar line of the Toronto Transit Commission in Toronto, Canada, has a service frequency that approaches the Woodward line of 1953. (*Clifford R. Scholes collection*)

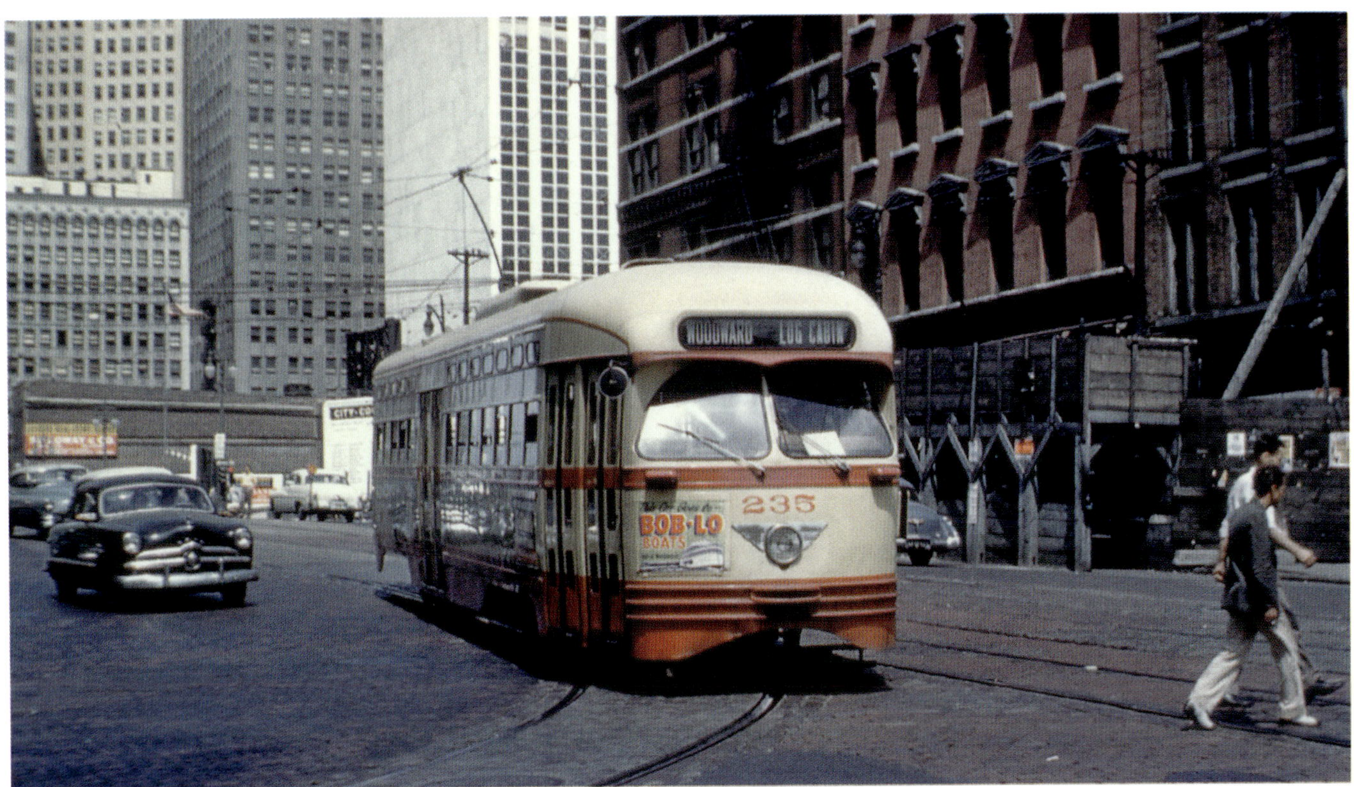

On August 16, 1953, PCC car No. 235 is on Woodward Avenue, turning onto Woodbridge Street in downtown Detroit; it would shortly loop south on Griswold, east on Atwater, and north on Woodward to complete a Woodward line trip to Log Cabin, which is noted on the front destination sign. (*Bob Crockett photograph—Clifford R. Scholes collection*)

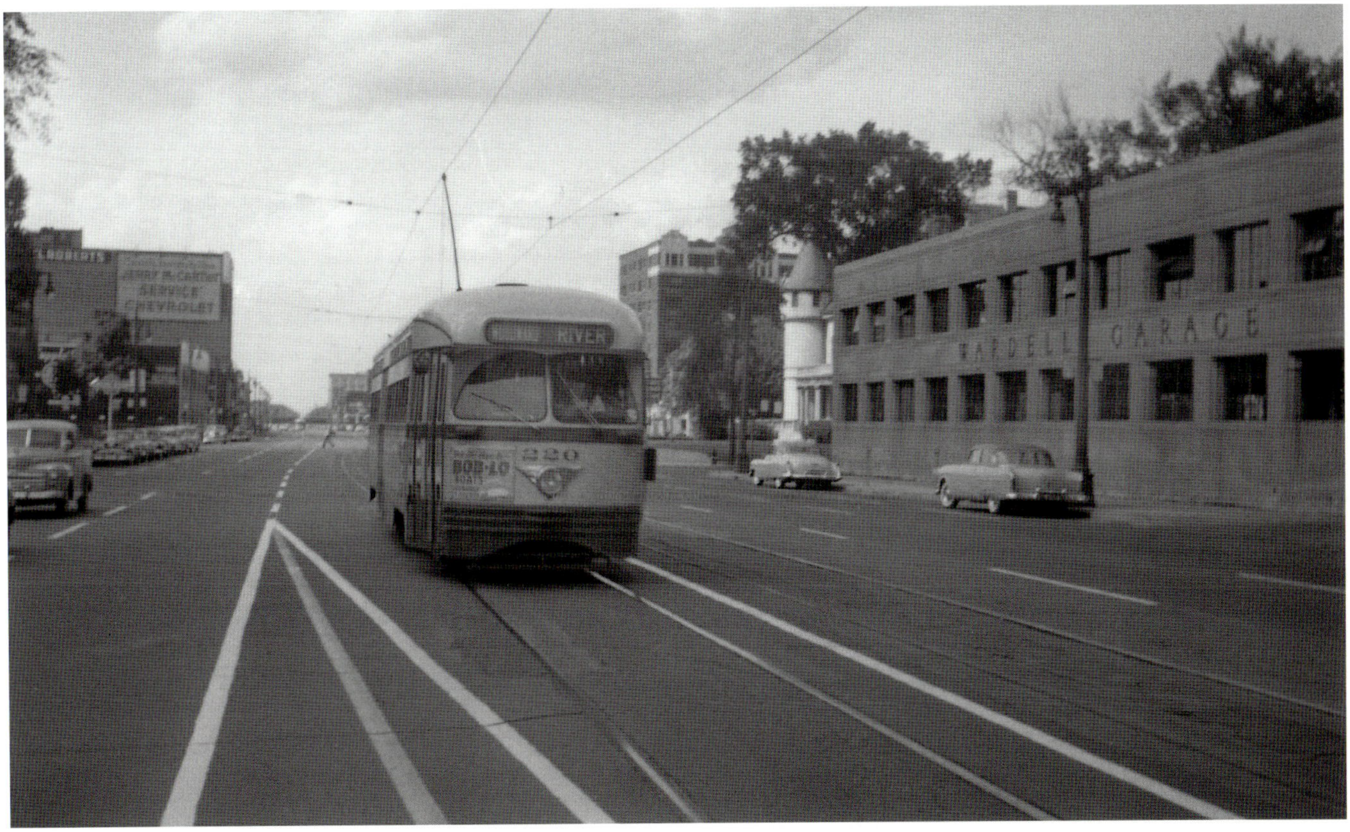

On a quiet August 16, 1953, PCC car No. 220 is on Woodward Avenue at Ferry Street. (*Clifford R. Scholes collection*)

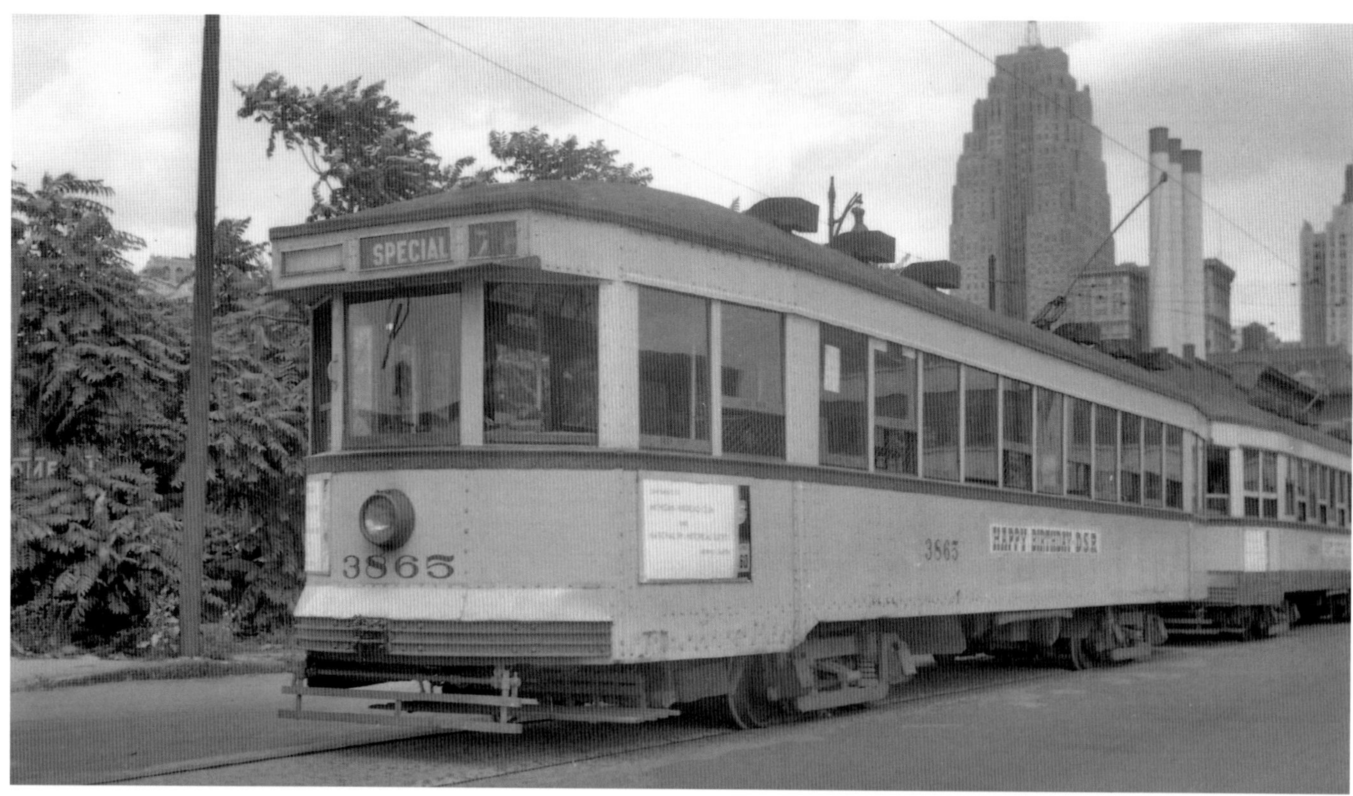

The Larned and Third Streets "Boat Pier Loop" trackage, normally used by route Woodward cars, is a photo stop on August 16, 1953 for a special excursion of Peter Witt-type cars, with No. 3865 in the lead to celebrate the ninetieth anniversary of the Detroit Street Railway with the special side sign "Happy Birthday DSR." (*Clifford R. Scholes collection*)

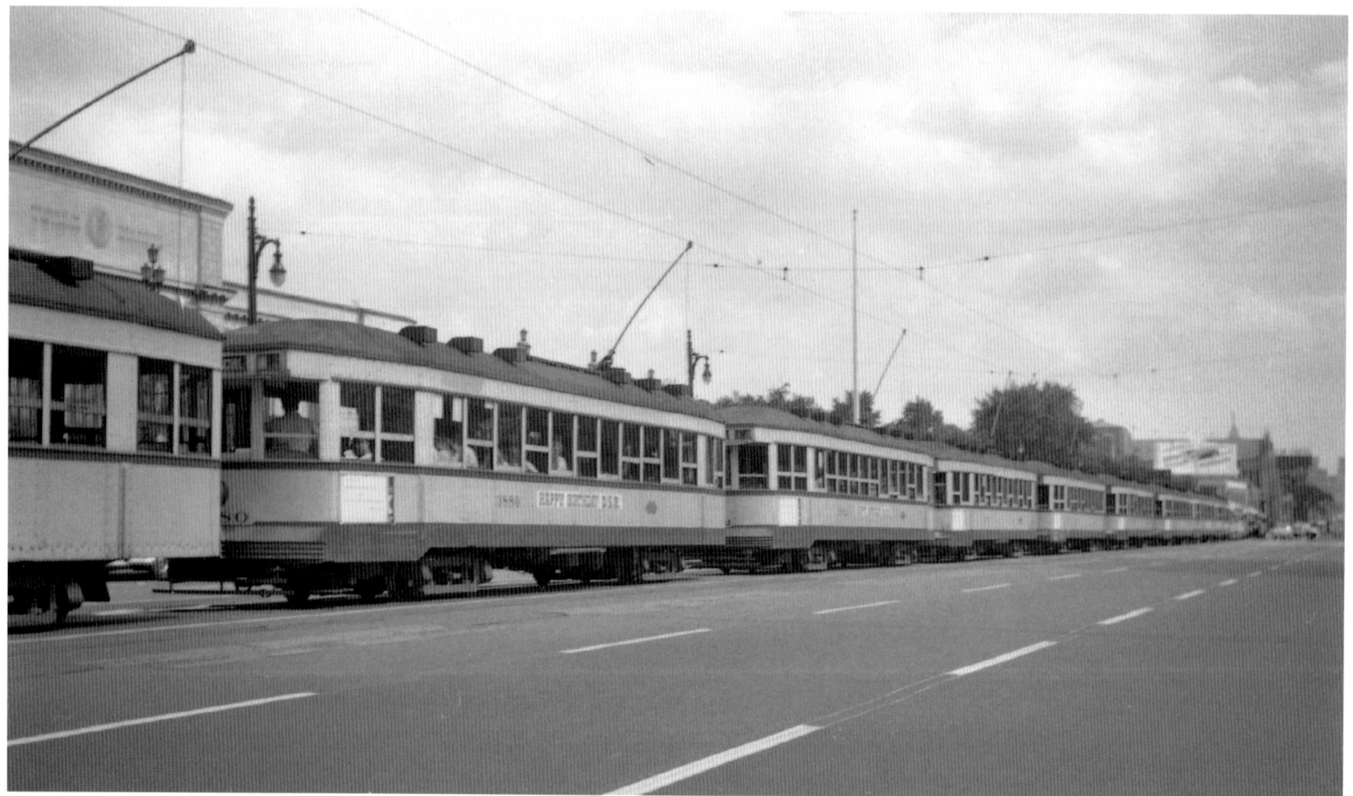

On August 16, 1953, a parade of Peter Witt cars is posing for a photo stop on Woodward Avenue at Kirby Street to commemorate the ninetieth anniversary of the DSR. Car No. 3880 has the most visible number in this picture. (*Clifford R. Scholes collection*)

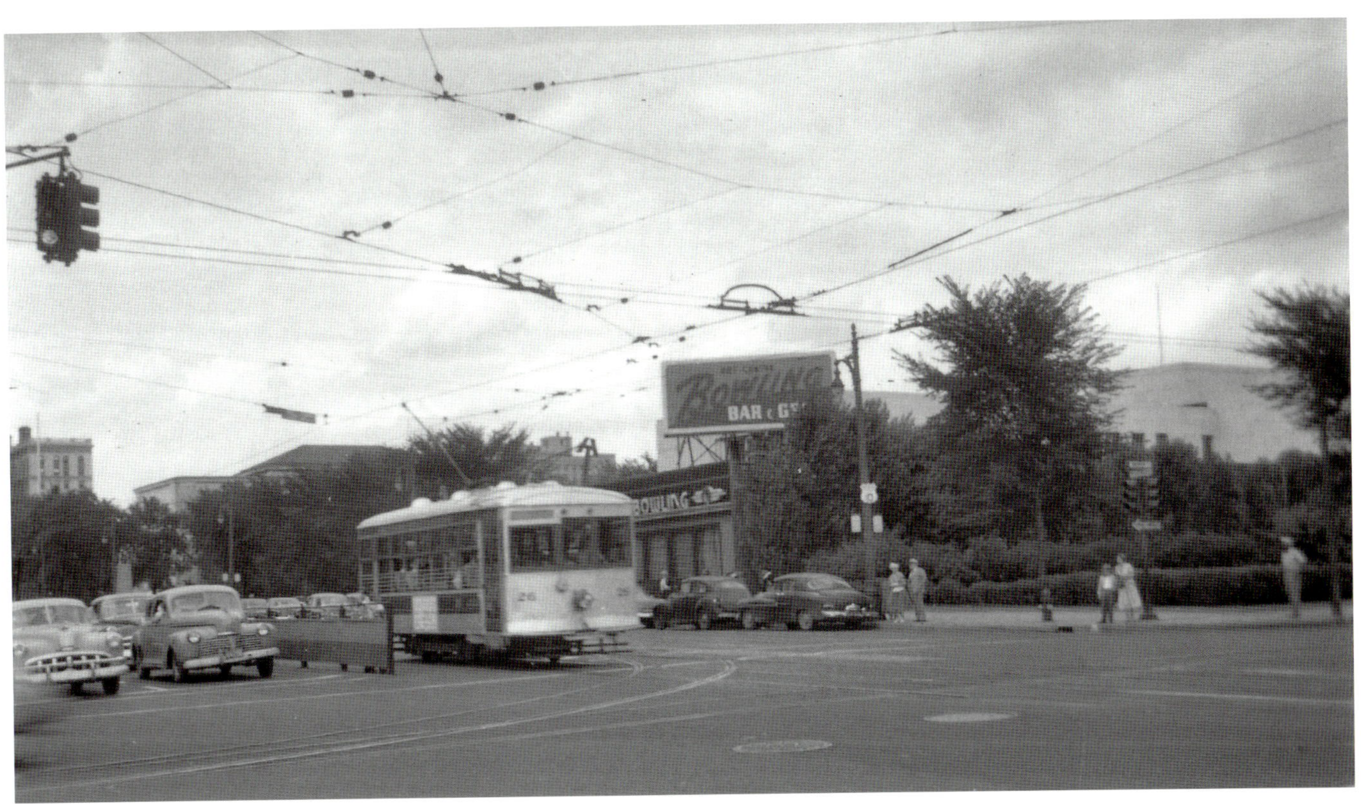

Former Birney car No. 26 (originally No. 7, built in 1922 by the American Car Company for the Cheyenne Electric Railway, later becoming No. 26 at the Fort Collins Municipal Railway from 1924 to 1951) is on an excursion on the Woodward line on Woodward Avenue at Warren Avenue before heading to the Henry Ford Museum in Dearborn, Michigan. (*Clifford R. Scholes collection*)

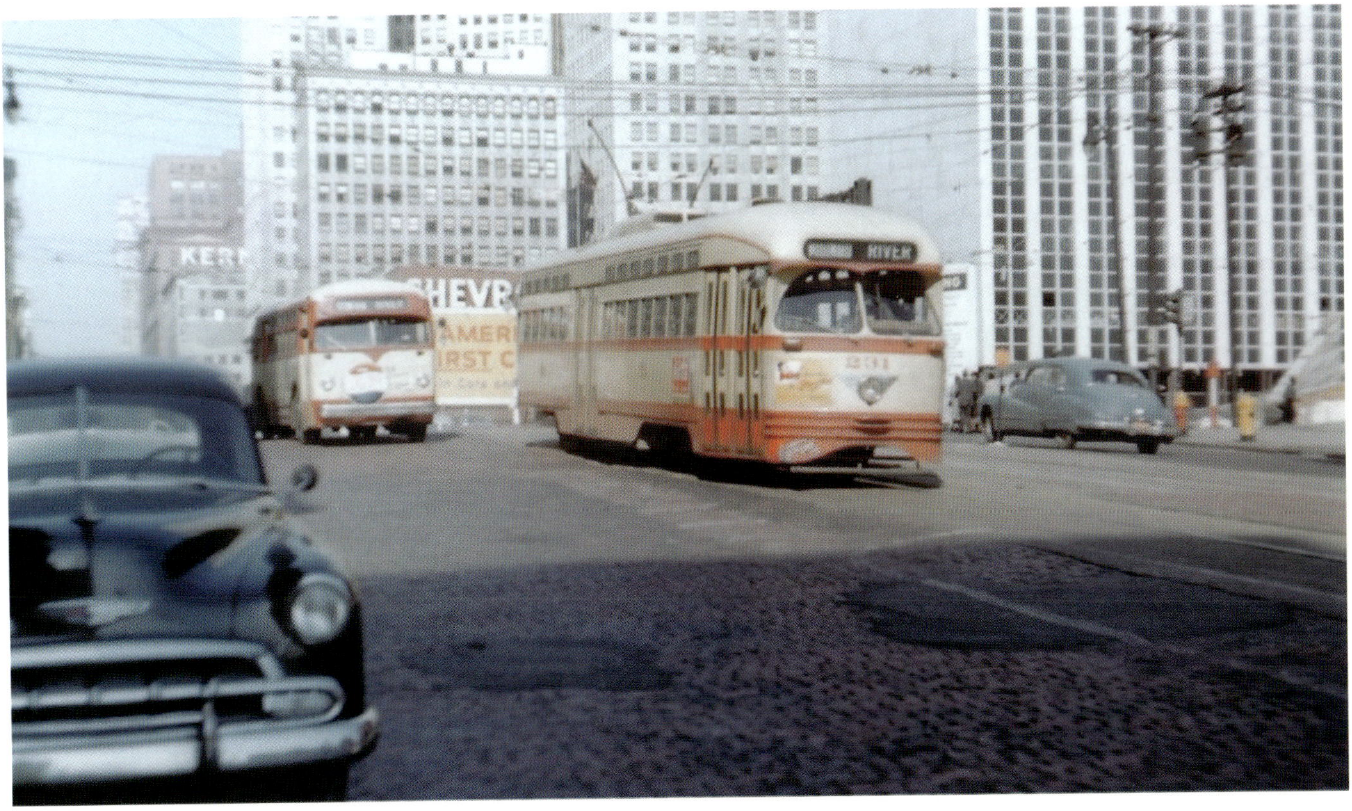

On October 29, 1954, PCC car No. 231 is on Woodward at Jefferson Avenues. On this portion of the Woodward line, there were three tracks at the southern end of the line. (*Bob Crockett photograph—Clifford R. Scholes collection*)

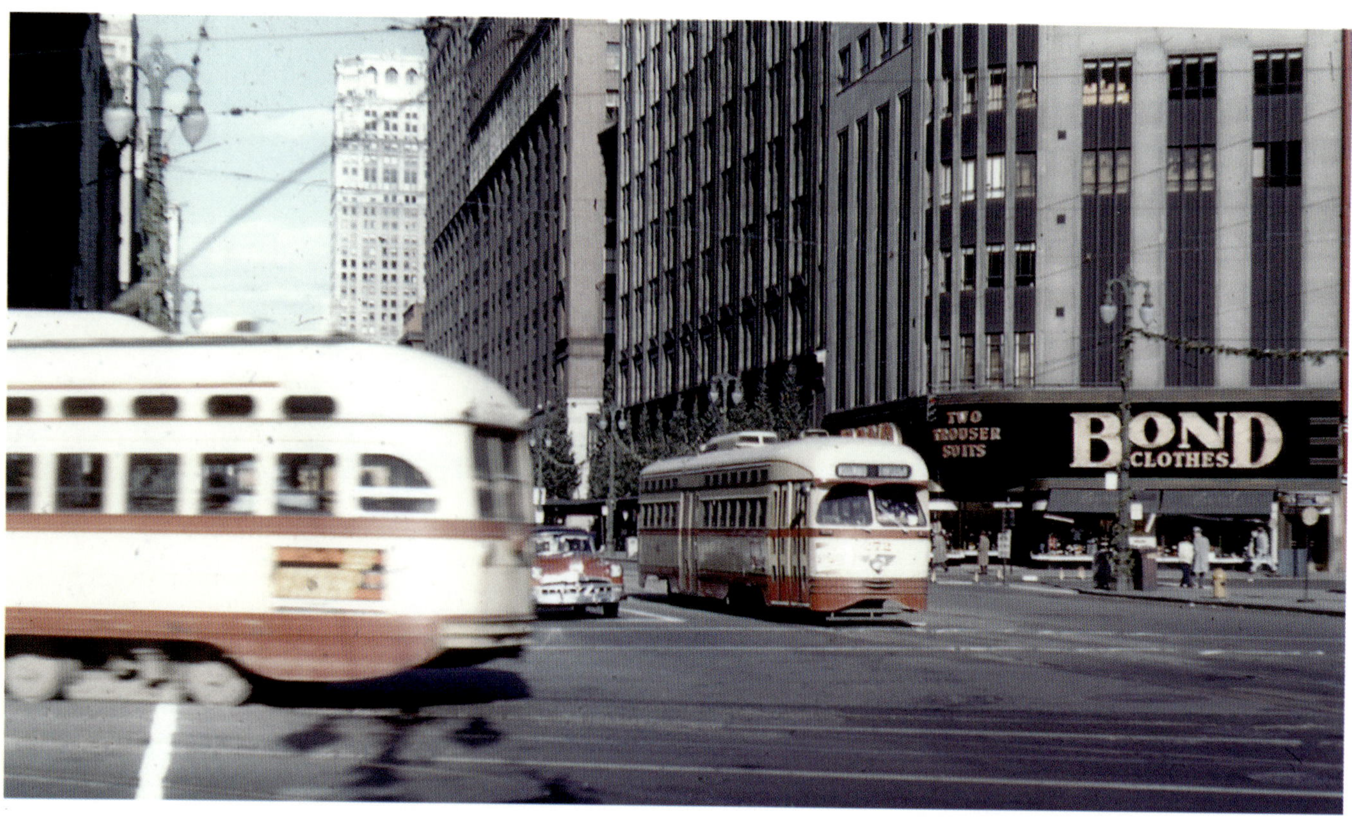

PCC car No. 271 was southbound on Woodward Avenue, crossing Michigan Avenue after a PCC car on Michigan Avenue dashed by on November 14, 1954. (*Bob Crockett photograph—Clifford R. Scholes collection*)

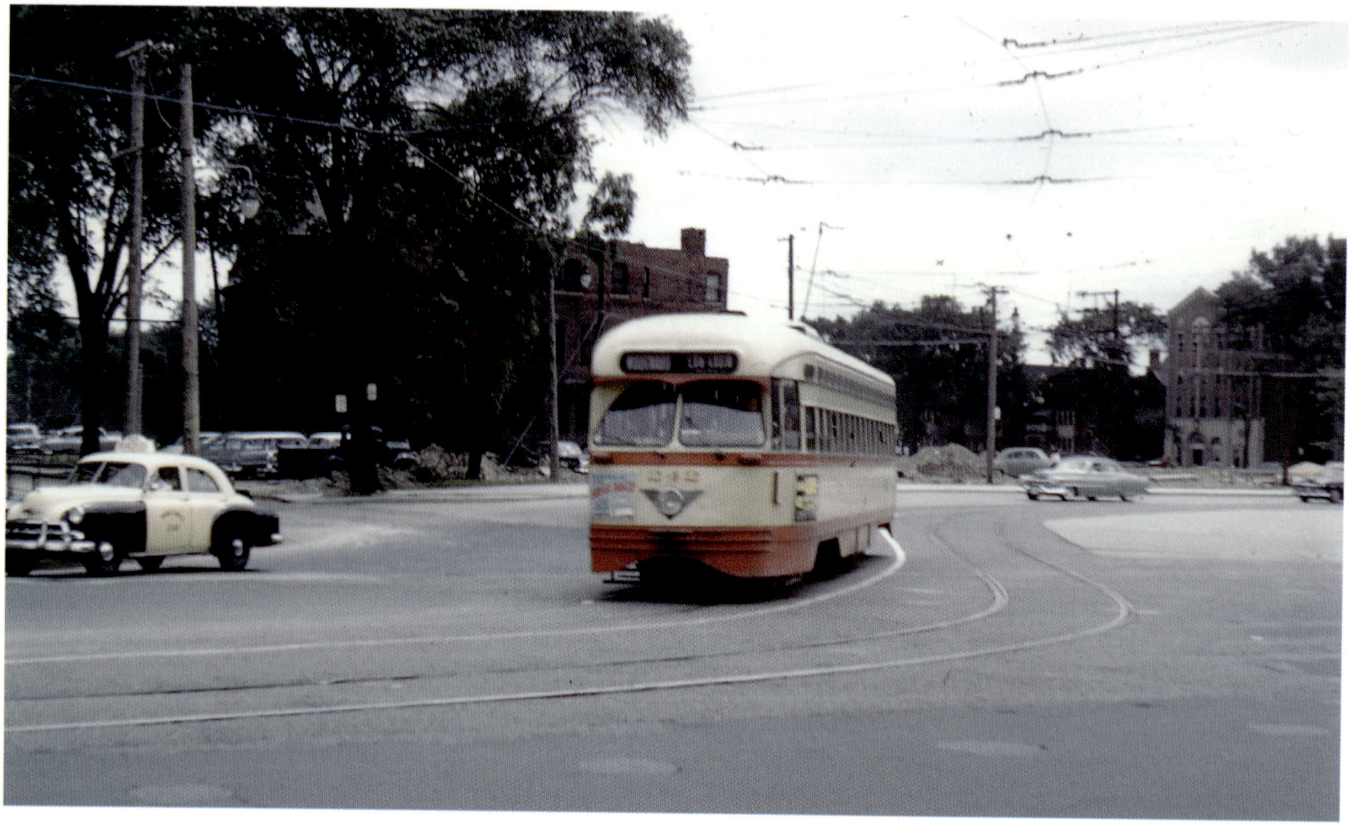

On November 16, 1954, PCC car No. 242 is on Woodward Avenue near the Ford Expressway on November 16, 1954. (*Bob Crockett photograph—Clifford R. Scholes collection*)

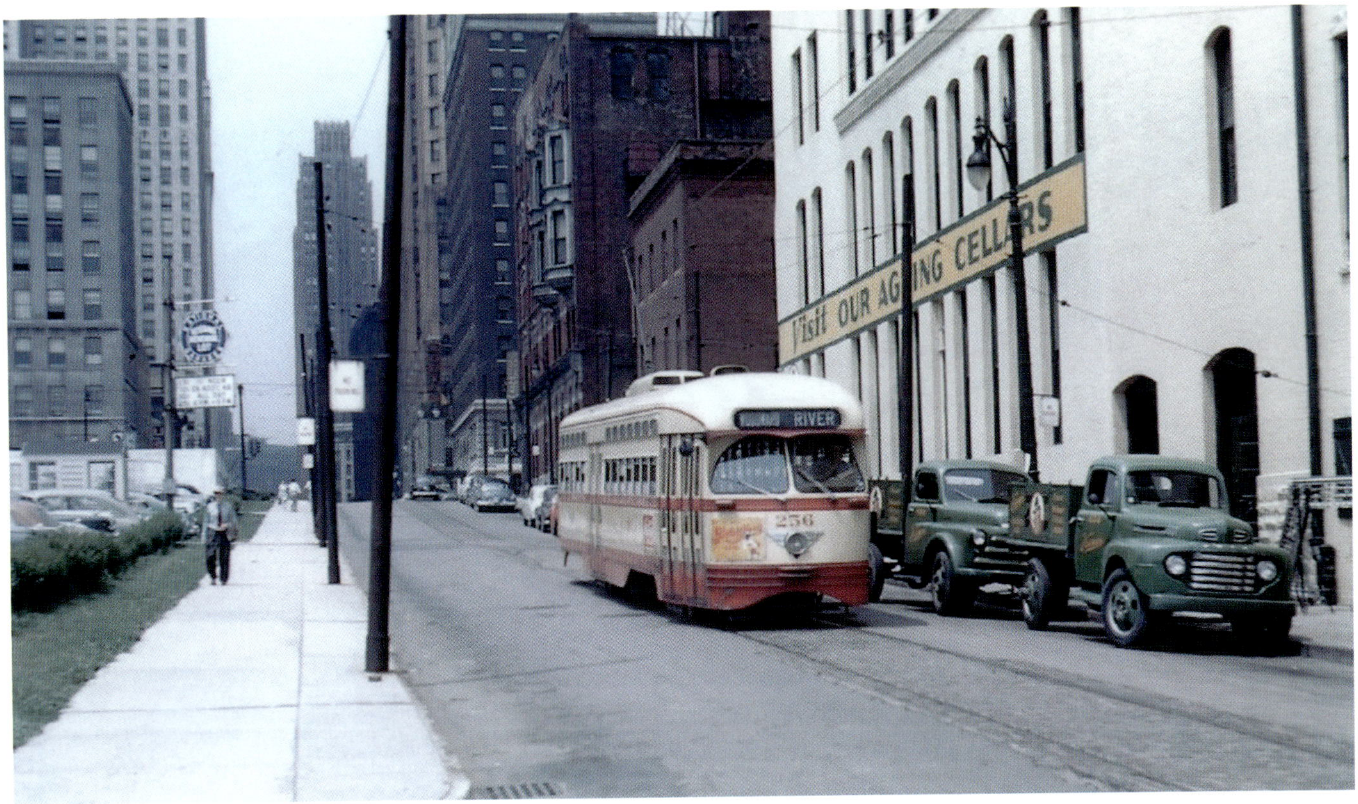

PCC car No. 256 is on Larned Street near Third Street on a southern loop of the Woodward line on June 27, 1955. (*Clifford R. Scholes collection*)

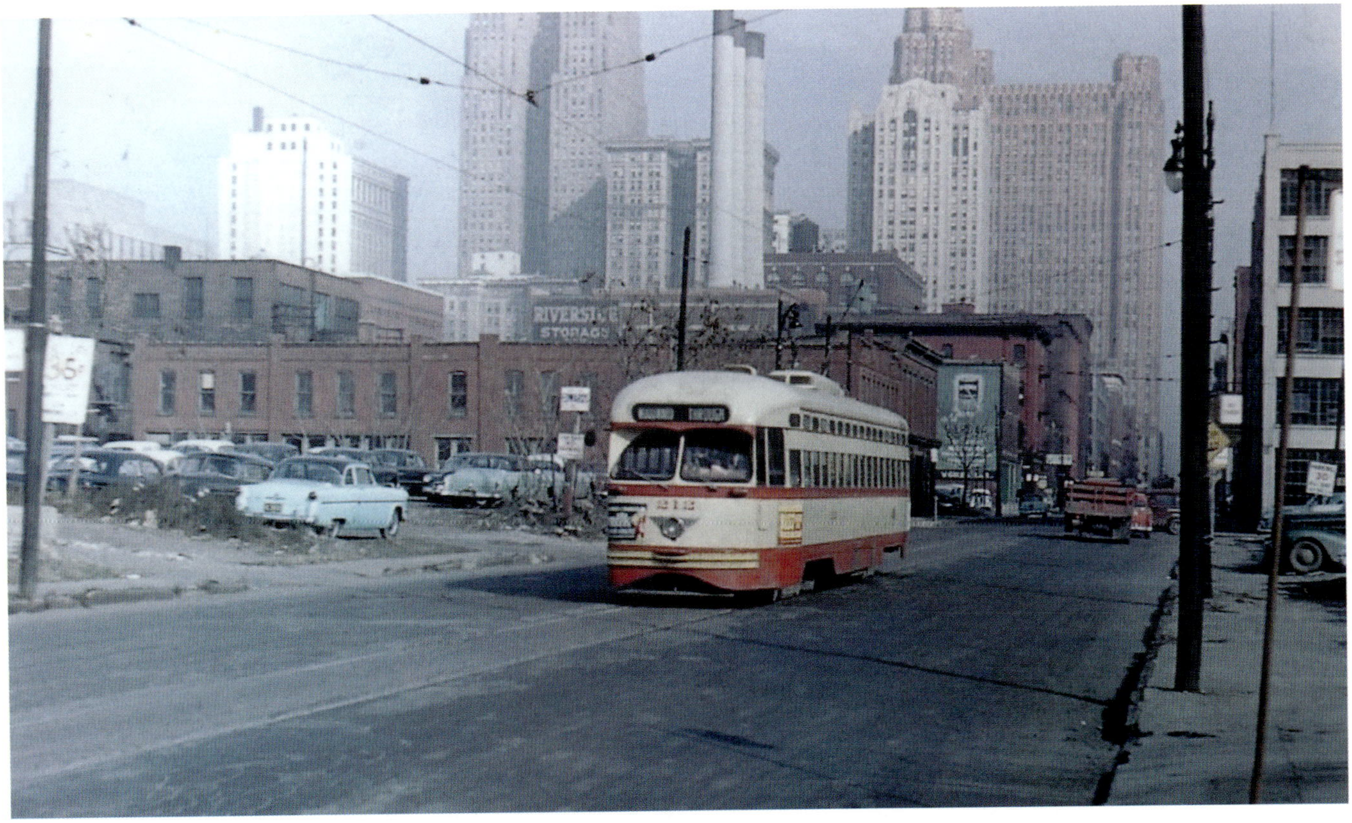

With the downtown Detroit skyscrapers in the background, PCC car No. 212 is on Larned Street and used Third Street and Jefferson Avenue to get back to Woodward Avenue on November 16, 1954. (*Clifford R. Scholes collection*)

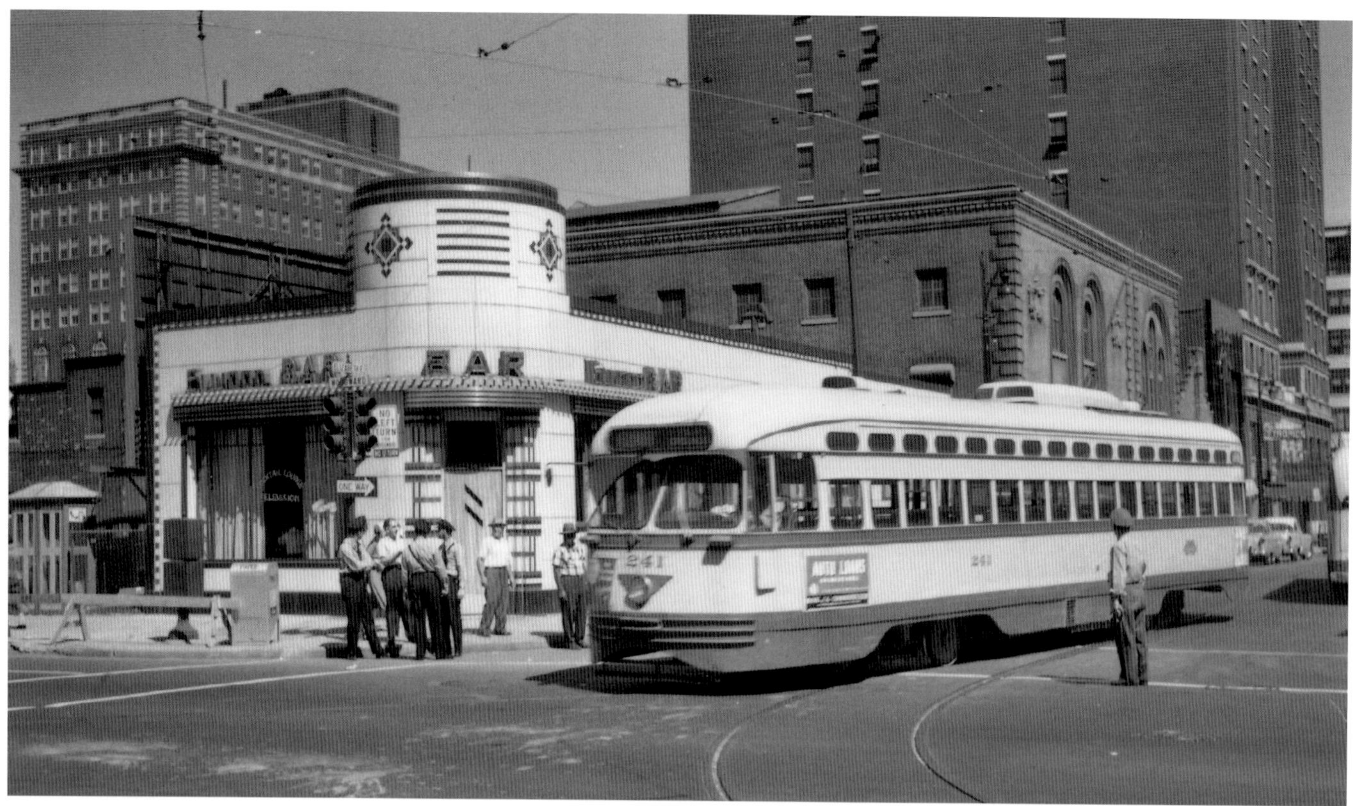

PCC car No. 241 is using the Elizabeth Street wye to head north on Woodward Avenue on September 5, 1955. (*Clifford R. Scholes collection*)

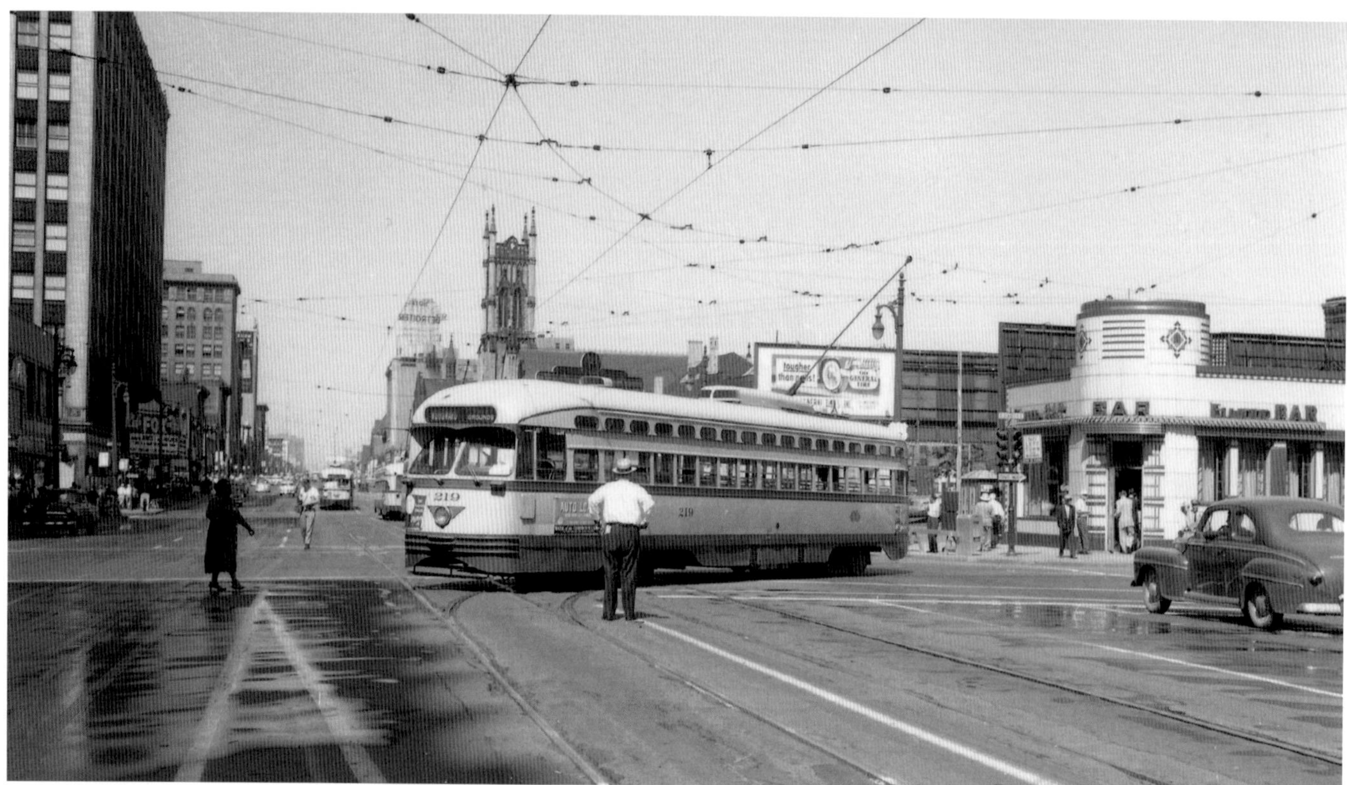

On September 5, 1955, PCC car No. 219 is carefully backing onto the Elizabeth Street wye to head back north on Woodward Avenue. This would save almost a mile of running through congested downtown Detroit and help get a late streetcar run back on schedule. (*Clifford R. Scholes collection*)

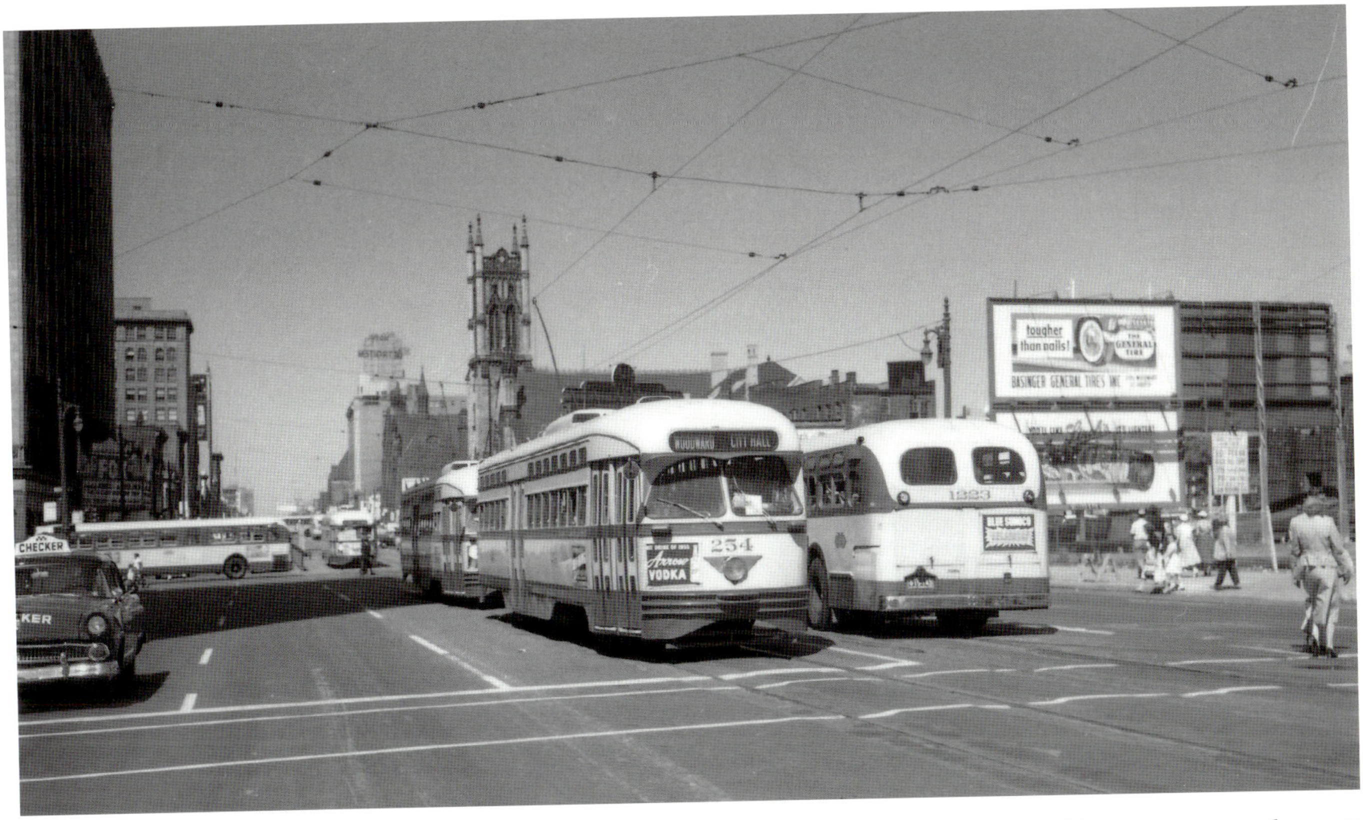

PCC car No. 254 is passing bus No. 1223 (one of twenty-five model TDH-5105 buses, Nos. 1201–1225, seating fifty-one passengers; they were built by General Motors Corporation in 1953) on Woodward Avenue at Elizabeth Street on September 5, 1955. (*Clifford R. Scholes collection*)

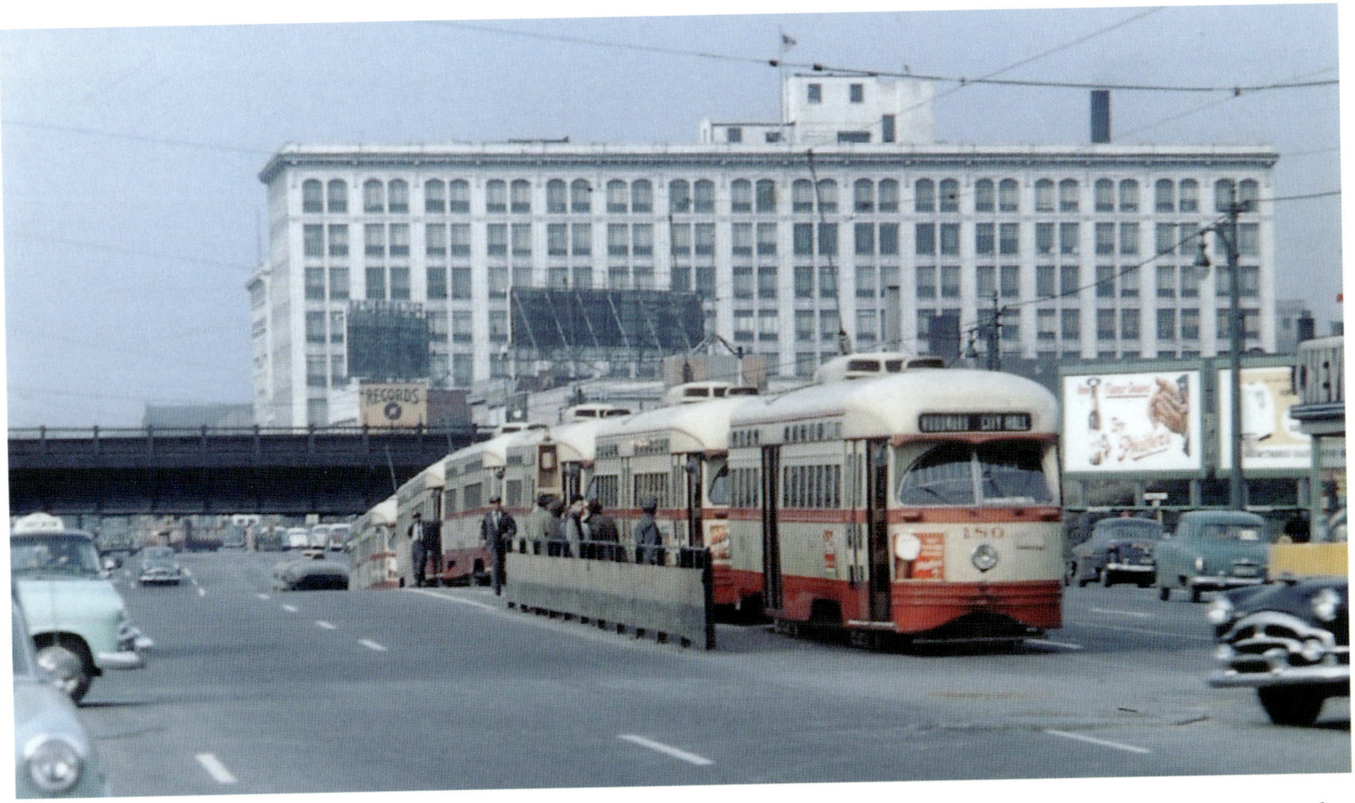

On November 9, 1955, PCC car No. 180 is heading a lineup of PCC cars on Woodward Avenue at Endicott Street. (*Bob Crockett photograph—Clifford R. Scholes collection*)

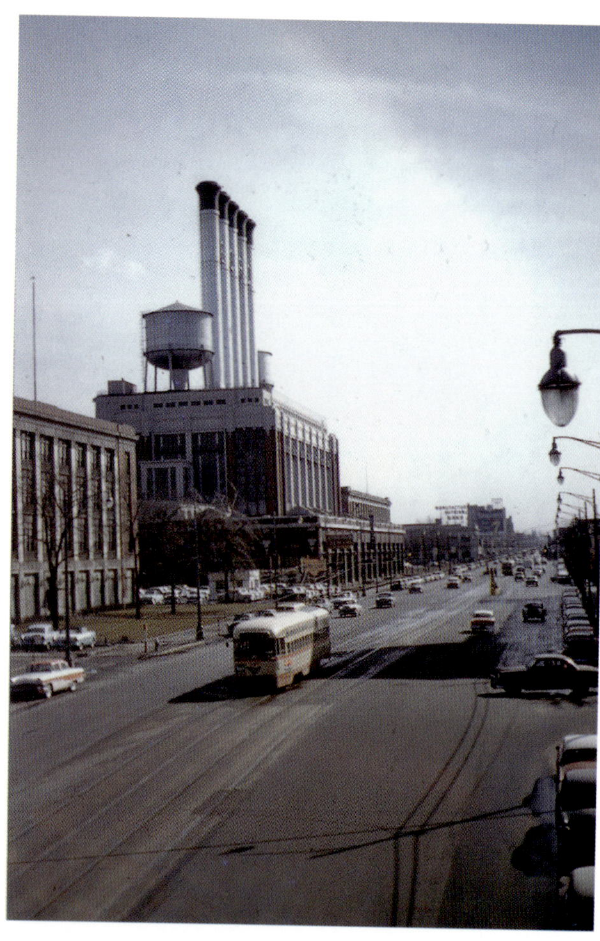

Left: PCC car No. 241 on a northbound route Woodward trip is dwarfed by the power house with the five tall stacks for the Ford Motor Company's Highland Park plant on Woodward Avenue in February 1956. On January 1, 1910, Ford shifted operations to the Highland Park plant. In 1913, this became the first production facility to manufacture a complete car by using an assembly line. (*Clifford R. Scholes collection*)

Below: In February 1956, PCC car No. 250 is on Woodward Avenue in the City of Highland Park, which is surrounded by Detroit except for a small part that borders the City of Hamtramck. (*Clifford R. Scholes collection*)

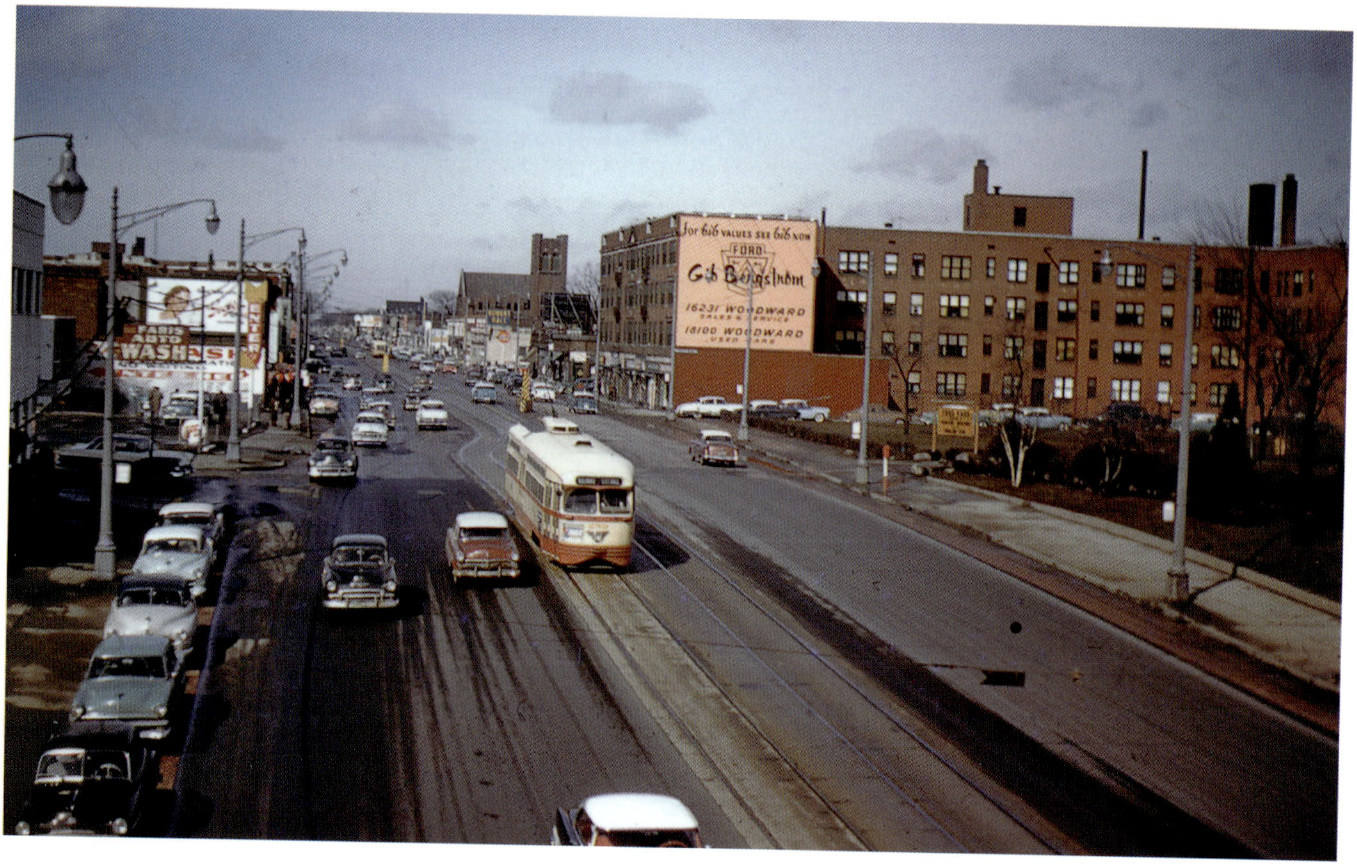

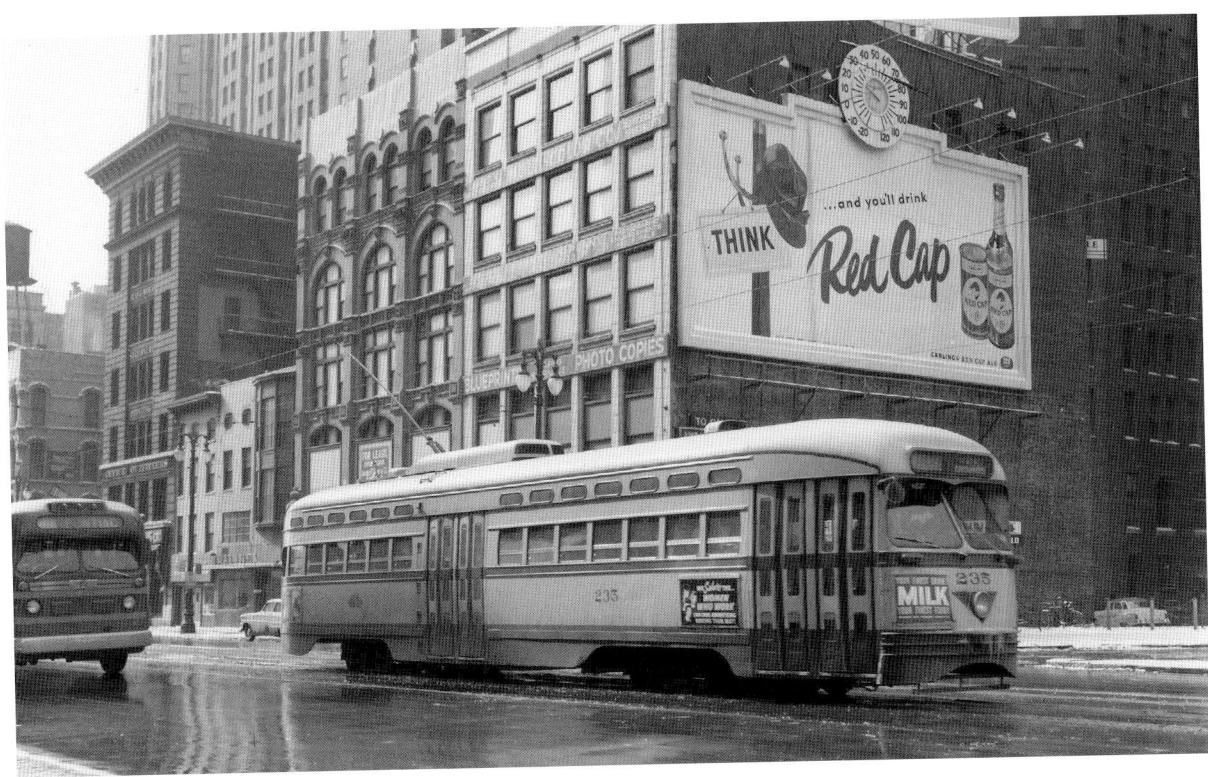

On March 18, 1956, PCC car No. 235 is northbound on Woodward south of Fort Street in downtown Detroit. In less than a month, Woodward line streetcars would be replaced by buses. Before the end of 1956, all the buildings seen in the picture of this block were demolished and were replaced by a new fourteen-story headquarters building for the National Bank of Detroit, which opened in 1959. This is Detroit's Financial District, which is bounded by Woodward, Jefferson, Lafayette, and Washington Boulevard. (*Birdsall H. Nichols photograph*)

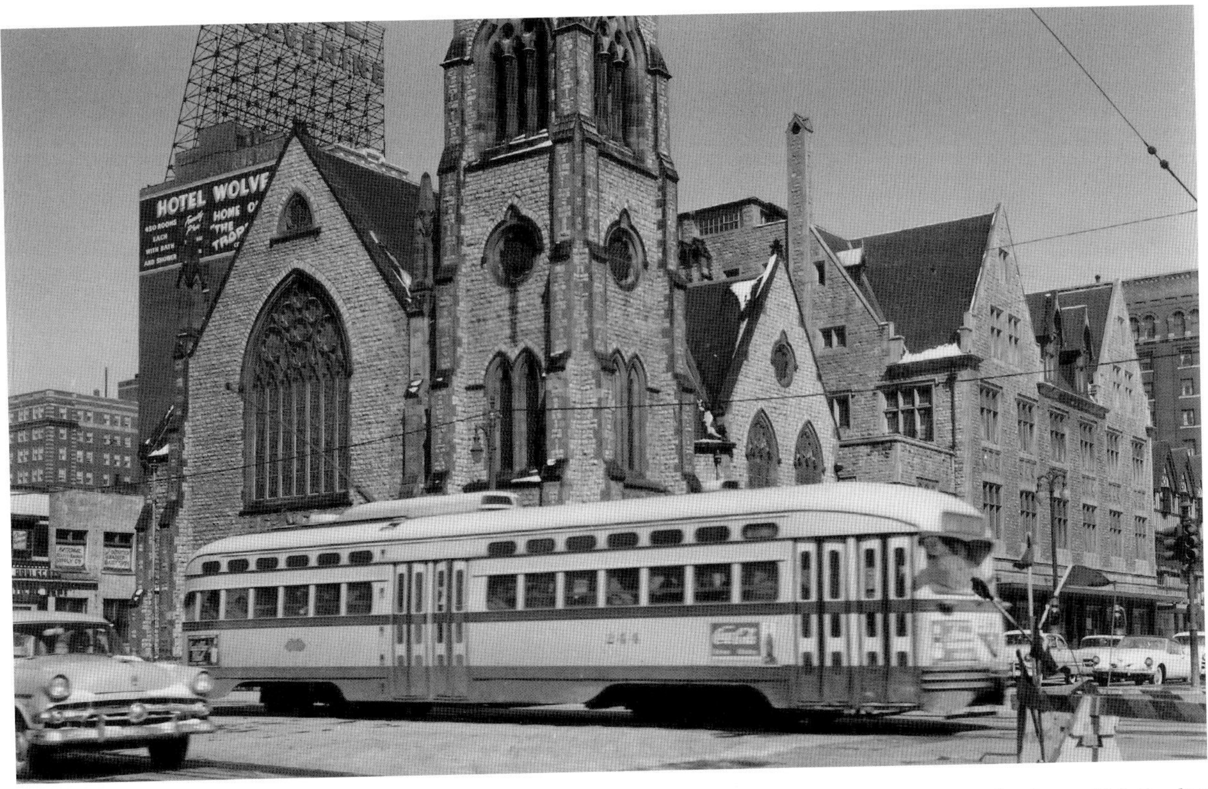

Southbound Woodward line PCC car No. 244 is on Woodward Avenue at Adams Avenue, passing the Central Methodist Church on March 18, 1956. (*Birdsall H. Nichols photograph*)

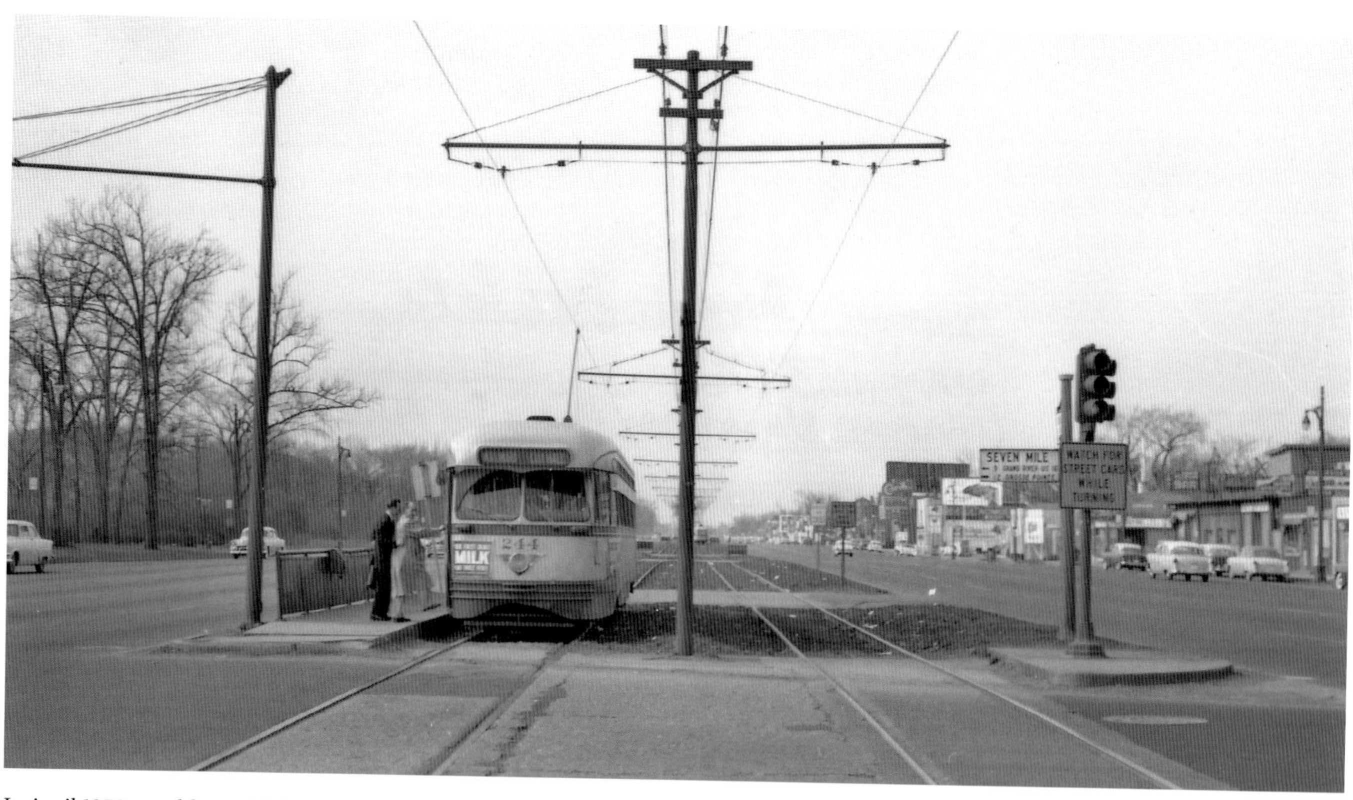

In April 1956, southbound PCC car No. 244 with "City Hall" showing on the front destination sign is making a passenger stop on Woodward Avenue at Six Mile Road. (*Bob Crockett photograph—Clifford R. Scholes collection*)

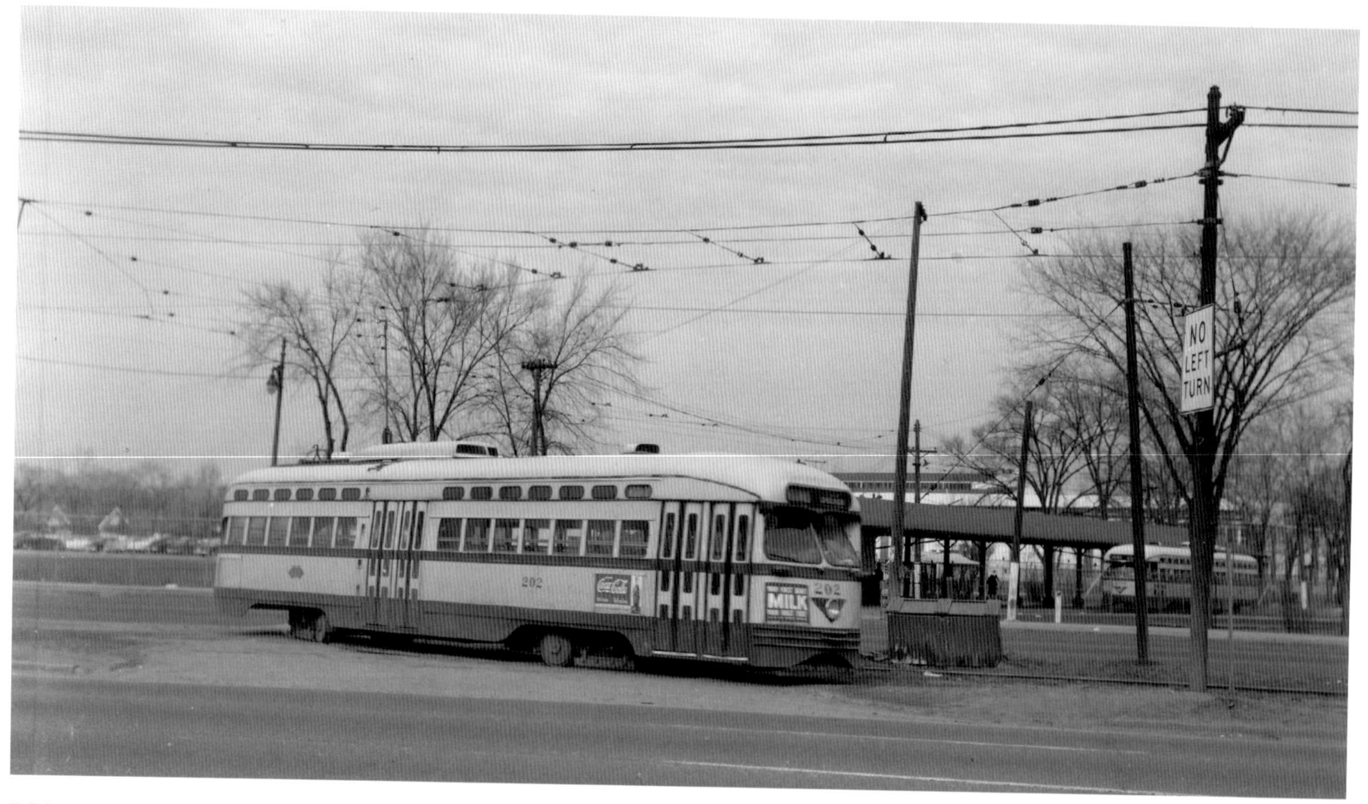

PCC car No. 201 was pulling out of the roof-covered Fairgrounds loop shelter for a southbound route Woodward trip to downtown Detroit on April 1, 1956. (*Birdsall H. Nichols photograph*)

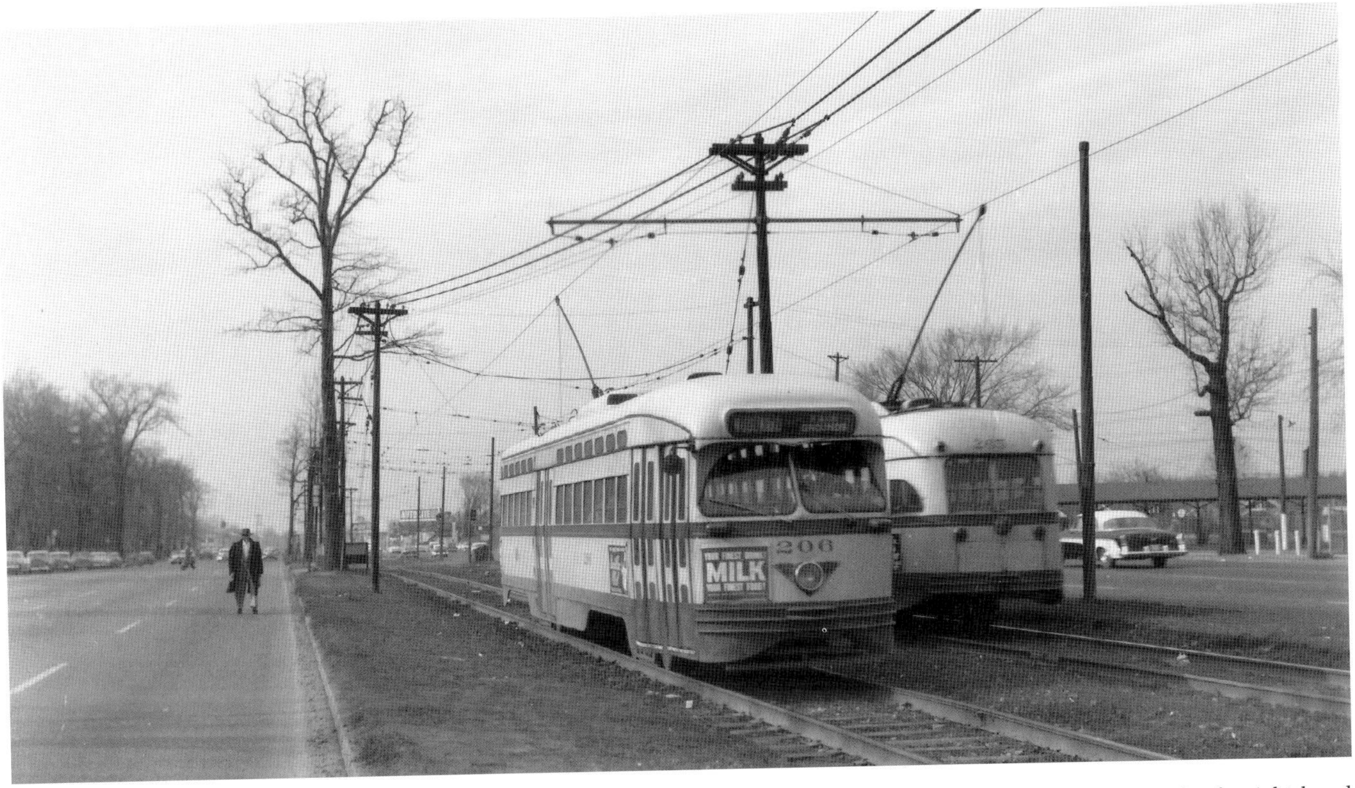

Southbound PCC car No. 206 is passing northbound PCC car No. 265 just south of the Fairgrounds loop on April 1, 1956. On the right-hand side of the picture, the Fairgrounds Loop can be viewed. The destination sign on car No. 206 should read City Hall instead of State Fairgrounds. From the Fairgrounds loop to Six Mile Road, the Woodward car line operated in the center median private right of way of Woodward Avenue, which provided faster service on that portion of the line. (*Birdsall H. Nichols photograph*)

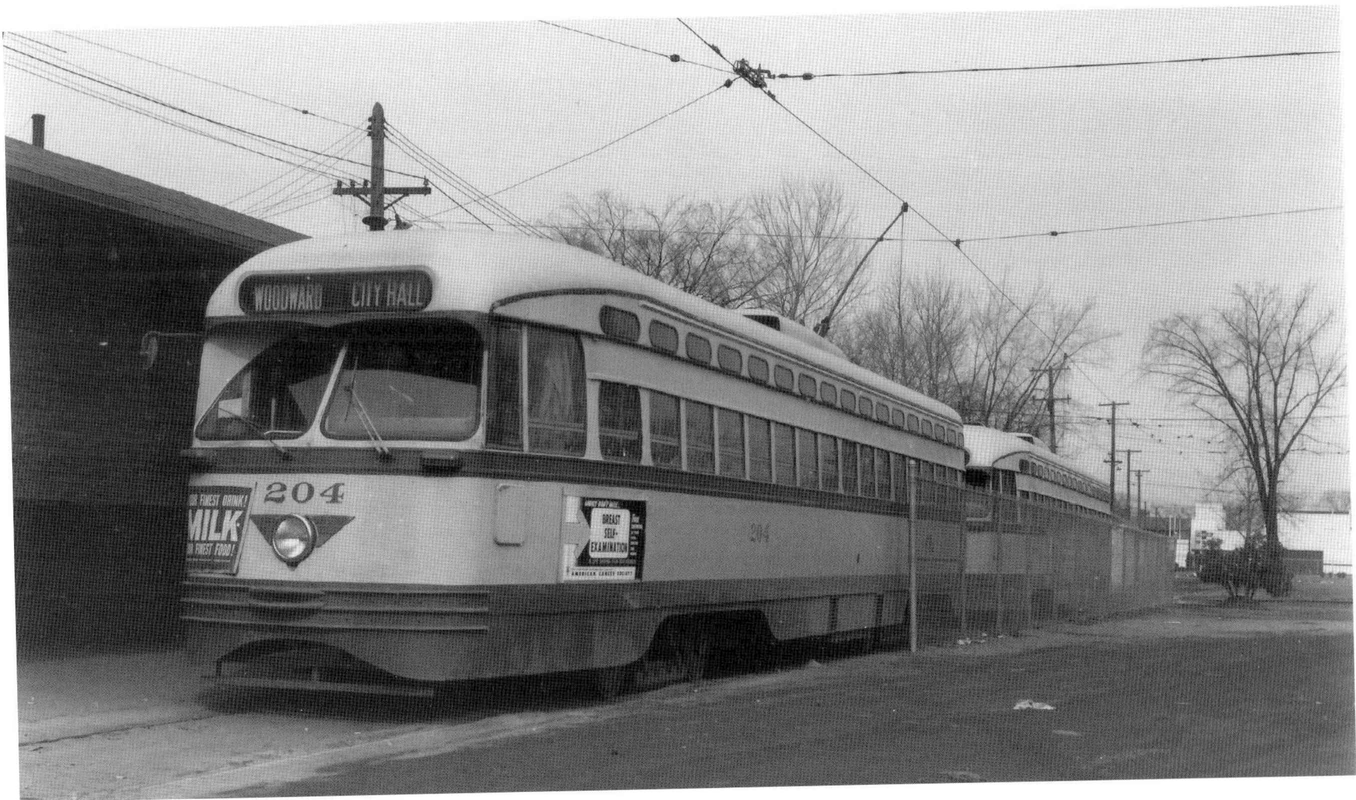

Two PCC cars led by No. 204 are at the Fairgrounds Loop northern terminus of the Woodward line on April 1, 1956. (*Birdsall H. Nichols photograph*)

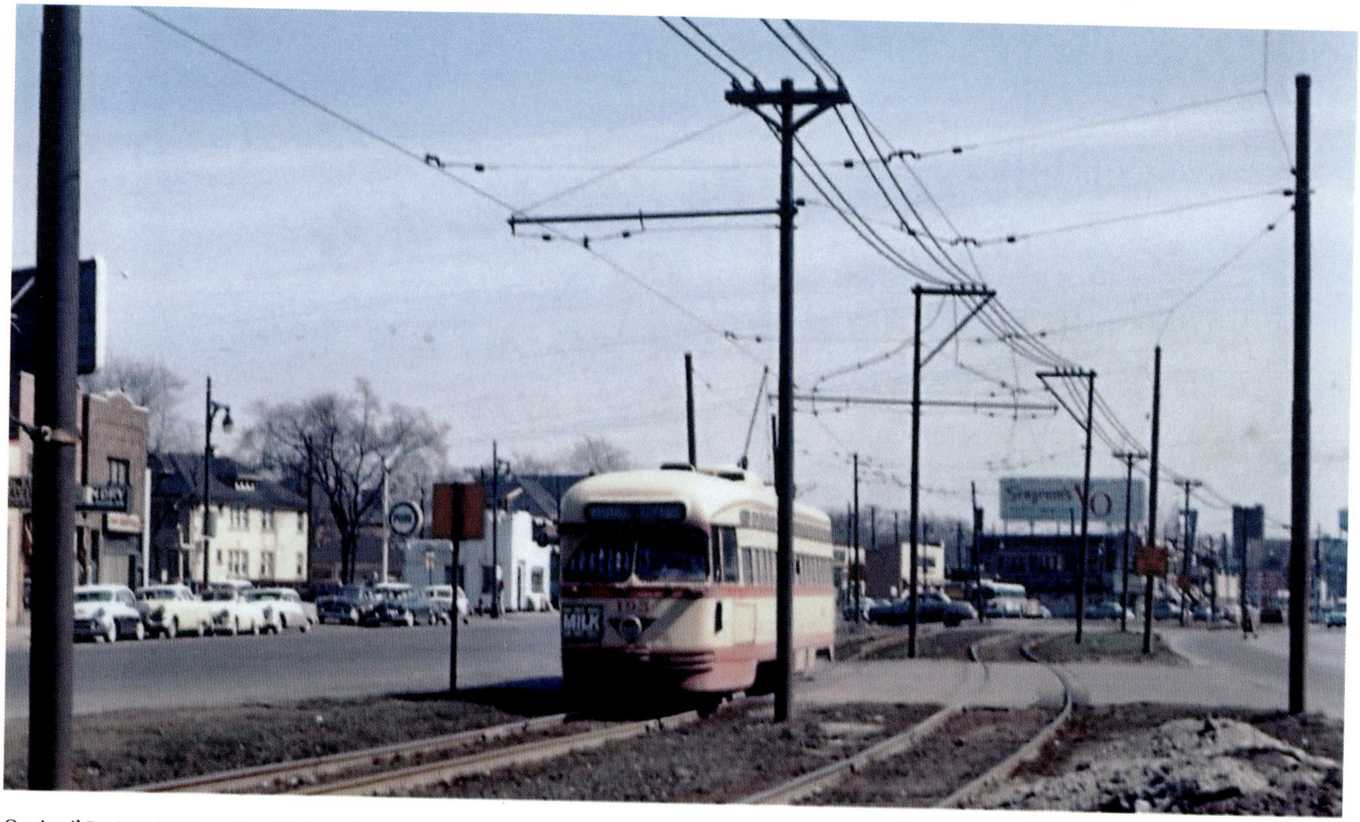

On April 5, 1956, PCC car No. 195 is on the center of the road median strip of Woodward Avenue north of Six Mile Road. (*Clifford R. Scholes collection*)

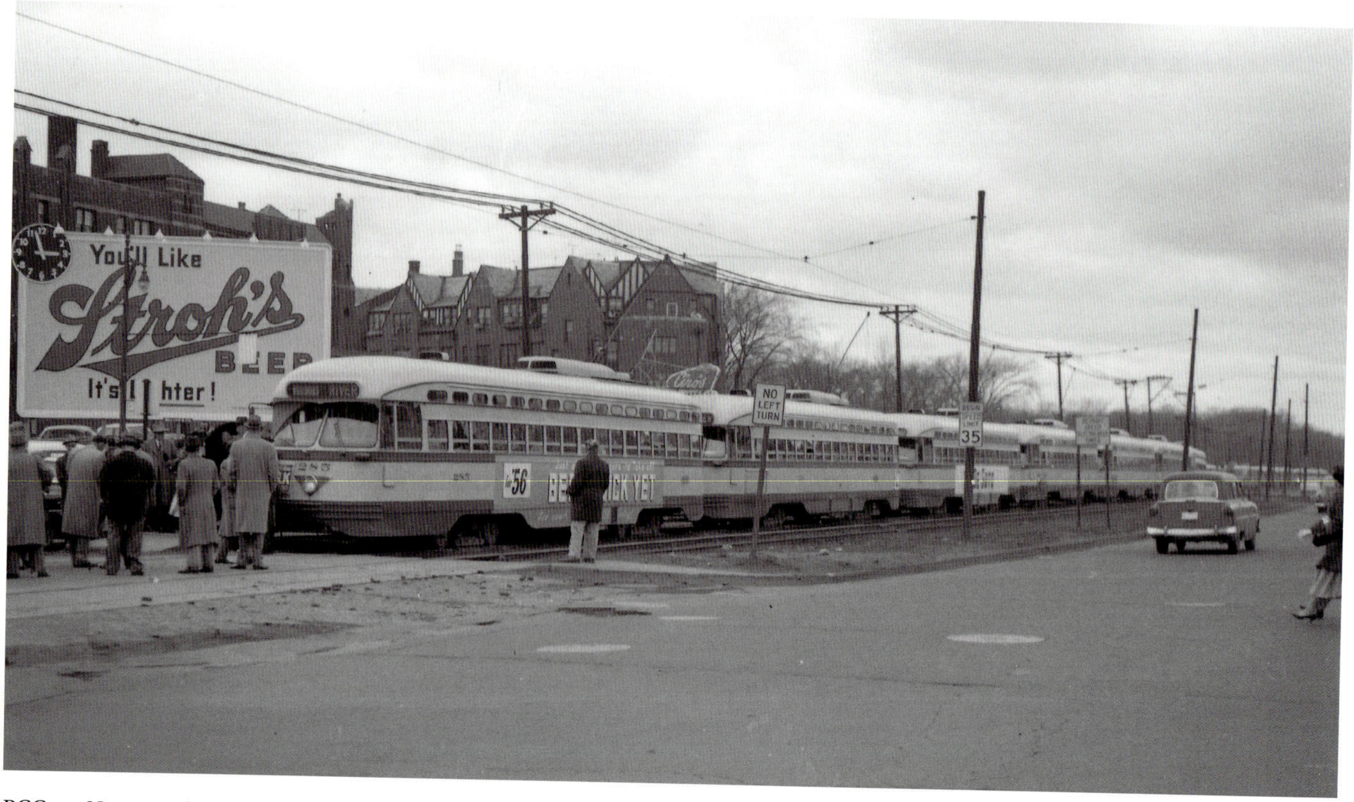

PCC car No. 285 is leading a number of PCC cars on Woodward Avenue at Six Mile Road on April 7, 1956, the last day of regular scheduled streetcar operation on the Woodward Avenue line. (*Bob Crockett photograph—Clifford R. Scholes collection*)

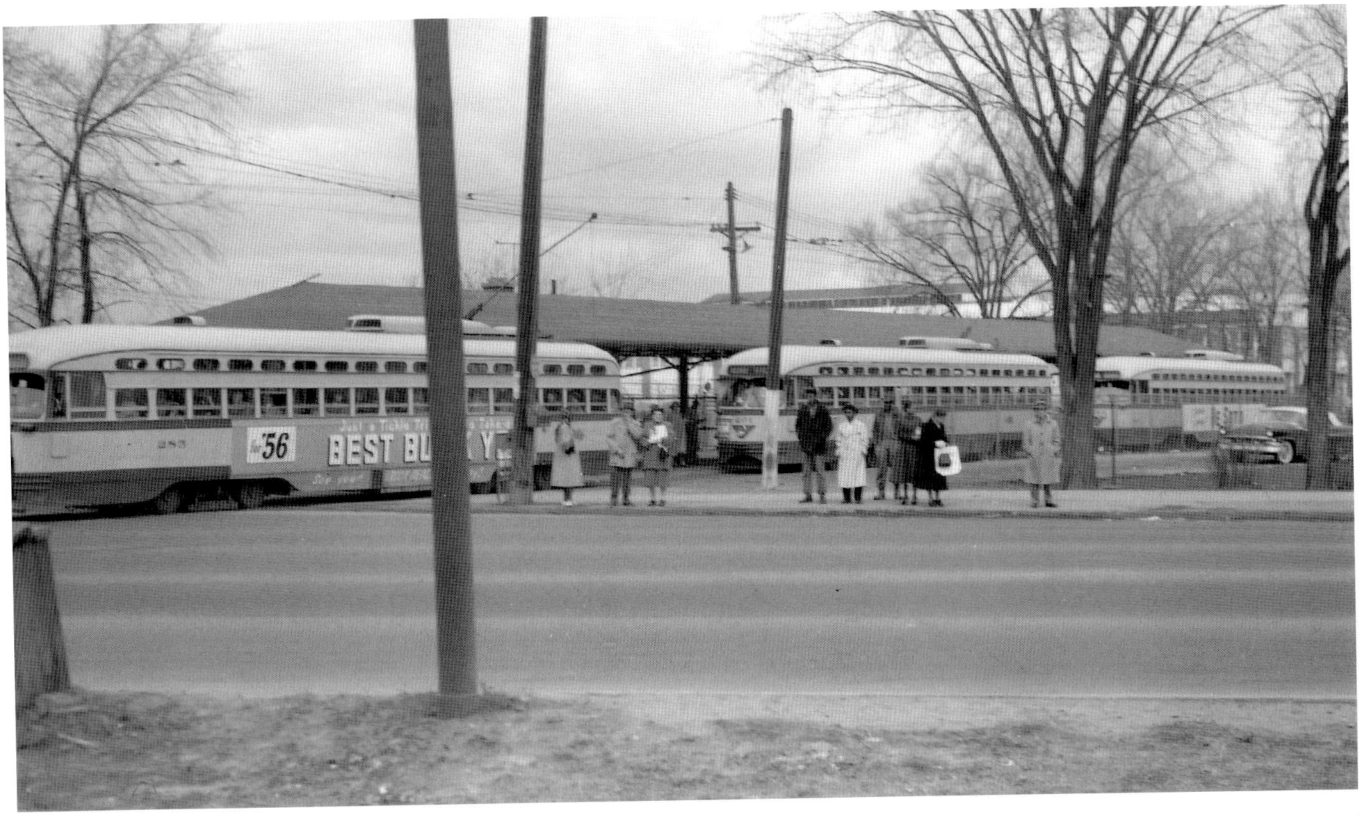

The Woodward Avenue Fairgrounds terminal loop is the location of PCC cars Nos. 285, 201, and 284 on April 7, 1956, which was the last day of Woodward Avenue regular scheduled streetcar service. Buses took over on April 8, 1956. (*Bob Crockett photograph—Clifford R. Scholes collection*)

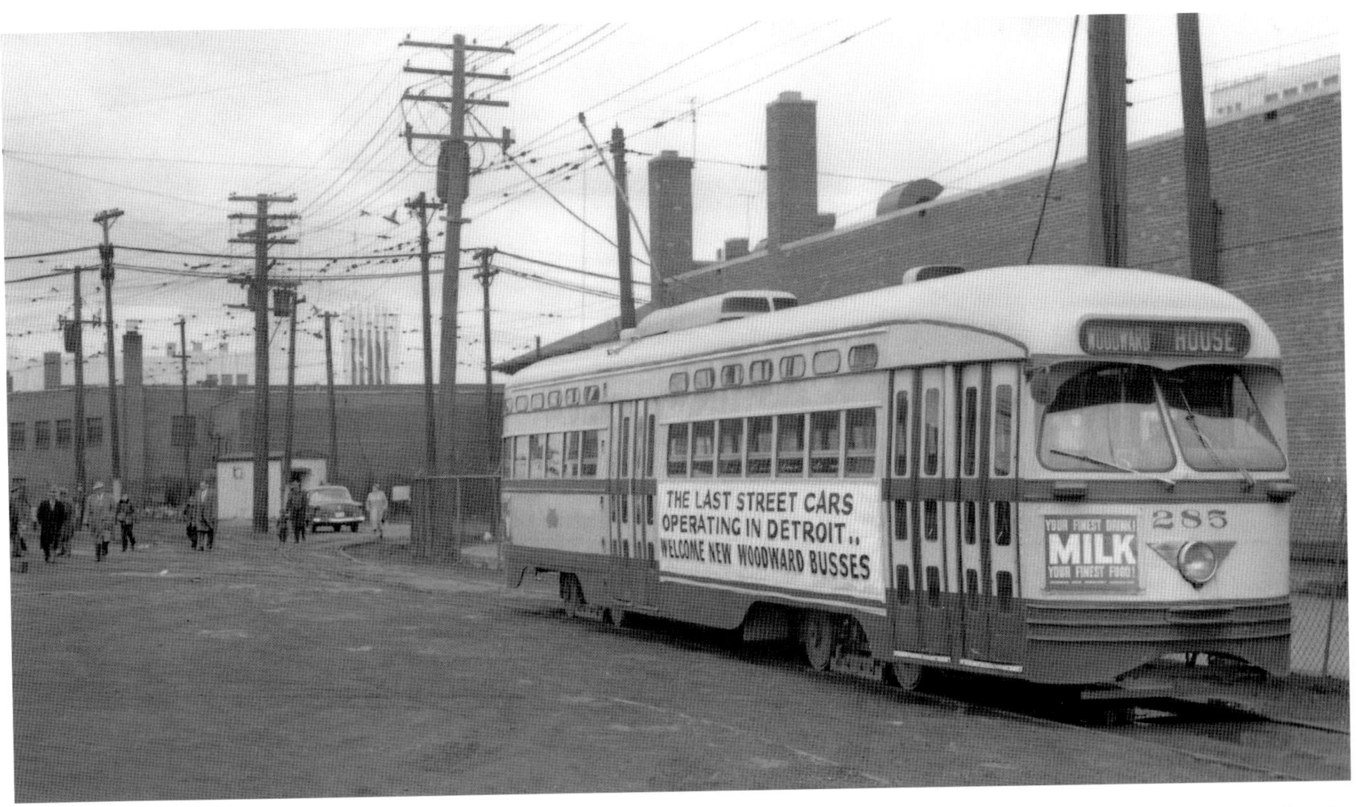

PCC car No. 285 with the side sign "The last streetcars operating in Detroit. Welcome new Woodward buses" is at the Highland Park–Woodland Avenue car house on the last day of Woodward Avenue's regular operation on April 7, 1956. (*Bob Crockett photograph—Clifford R. Scholes collection*)

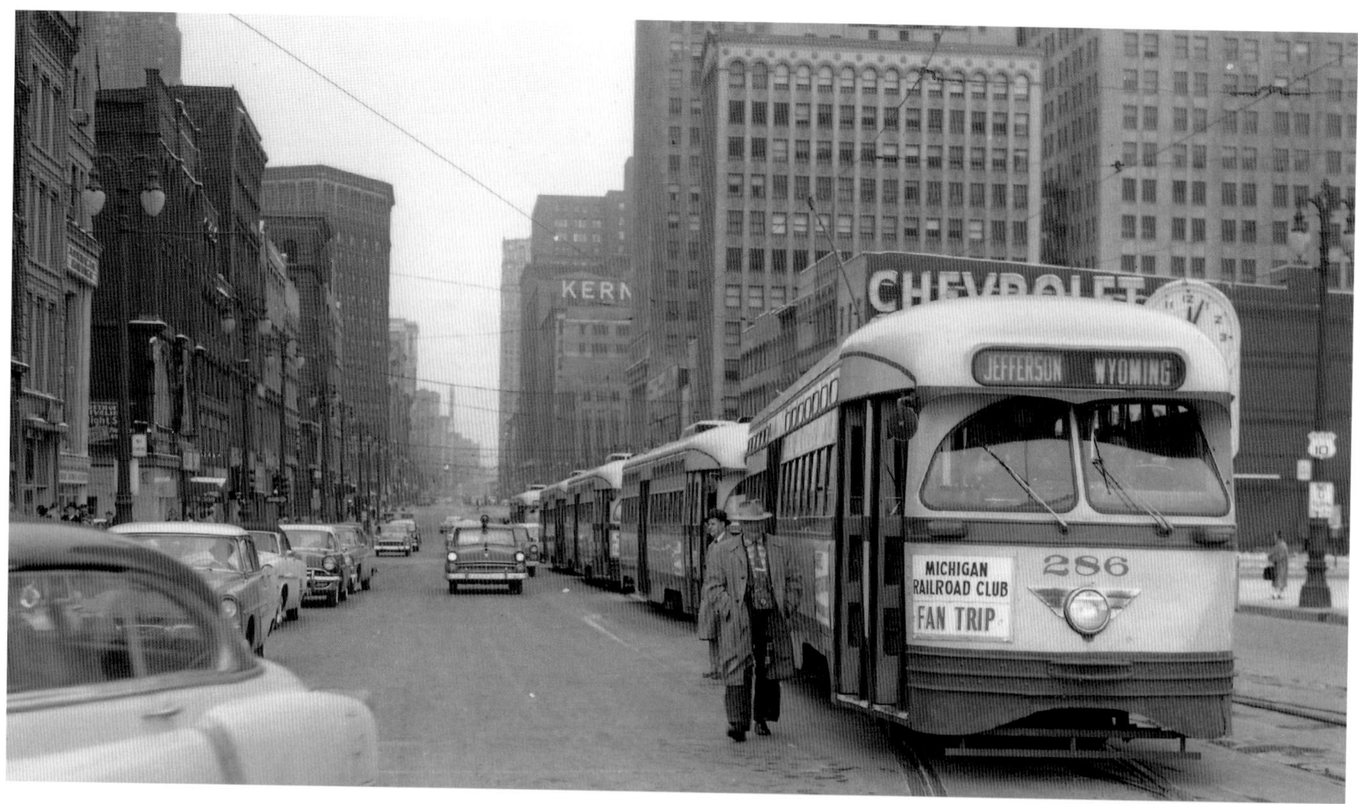

Woodward and Jefferson Avenues is the location of five PCC cars, headed by car No. 286, on a Michigan Railroad Fan Trip for the last day of regular scheduled streetcar operation on Woodward Avenue on April 7, 1956. (*Bob Crockett photograph—Clifford R. Scholes collection*)

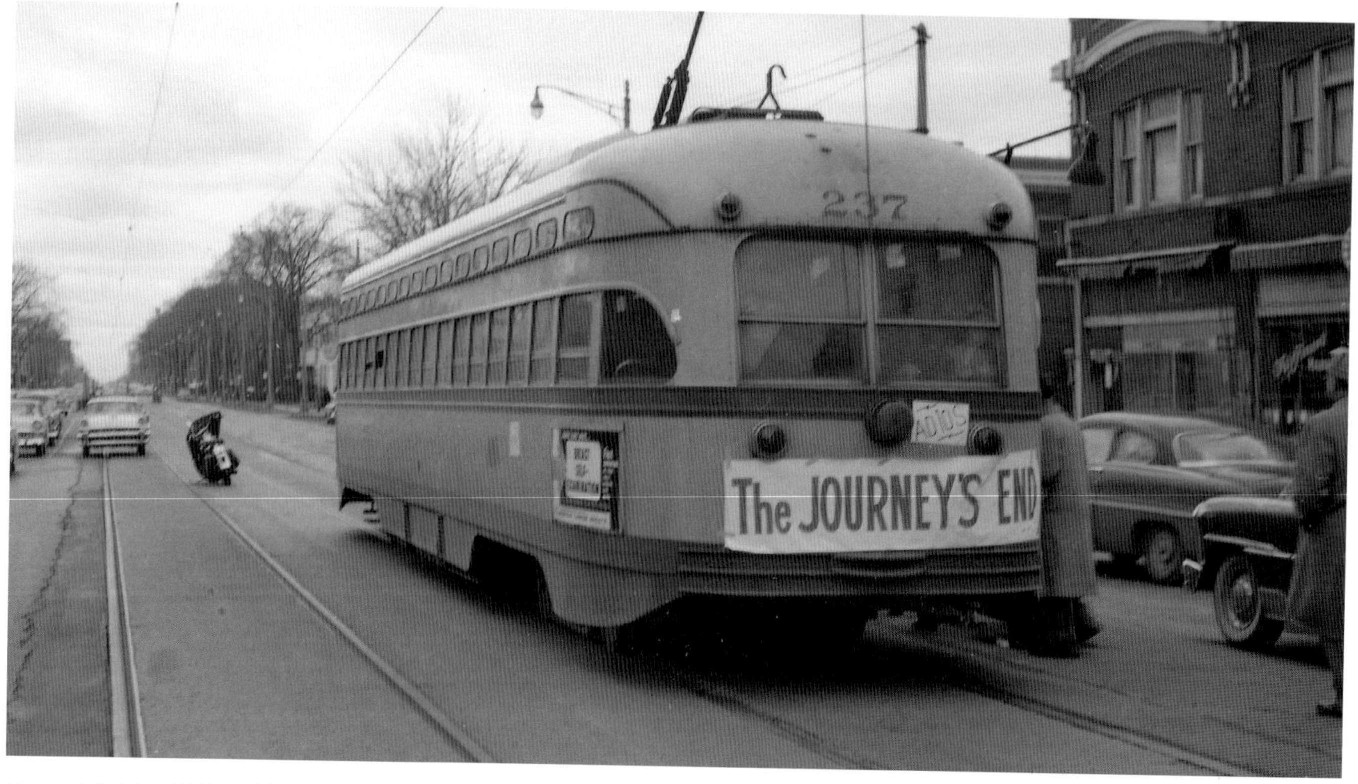

On April 8, 1956, PCC car No. 237 is on Woodward Avenue at Webb Street with a fitting sign, "The Journeys End." On the afternoon of April 8, 1956, the DSR sponsored a parade of twenty-four PCC cars, and car No. 237 was the last regular service car and the last car in the parade. Around 5:30 p.m., this car, carrying members of the Michigan Railroad Club, entered the Woodward car house, ending almost ninety-three years of street railway service in Detroit. (*Bob Crockett photograph—Clifford R. Scholes collection*)

6

Detroit's Trackless Trolleys

The Municipal Operation (MO) built an experimental trackless trolley line in September 1921, with a single ground wire added to the existing streetcar overhead on Monclair and west on Harper and double wires strung on Harper east of Monclair and south on Lemay. A demonstration vehicle was built by St. Louis Car Company, one by the Trackless Transportation Company, and two by the Packard Motor Company for the line. During a demonstration ride for Detroit Mayor Couzens, the ride was so rough on newly paved streets that he vetoed plans for trackless trolley operation. A second trackless trolley demonstration was conducted on East Warren Avenue between Cadillac and St. Jean Avenues on May 28, 1924, using one Brill Rail-less vehicle. That demonstration ended with the vehicle sold to the Philadelphia Rapid Transit Company, where it was used on the Oregon Avenue trackless trolley line. A successful trackless trolley operation began on June 14, 1930 on Plymouth Road. A 1936 merger of the Plymouth trackless trolley line and Caniff bus line required a 3-mile gap to be filled between the two lines that would have required an expensive erection of overhead wire. The merged line became a bus line with six Twin Coach trackless trolleys sold to the Cincinnati Street Railway Company.

On December 15, 1949, Detroit Department of Street Railways (DSR) began trackless trolley service on the Crosstown line, which operated on Warren Avenue using sixty new trackless trolleys purchased from the Twin Coach Company in 1949. Cold weather froze trolley retrievers, resulting in the poles not rising to contact the overhead wire at high points. The retriever problems were solved, and the trackless trolleys provided excellent service. In 1955, the Crosstown line was extended west on W. Warren Avenue from Pierson Street to Edward Heinz drive. On September 5, 1951, the Grand River bus line was converted to trackless trolley operation. In 1957, the extension of the Crosstown line was abandoned and the rest of the line was converted to bus operation on March 31, 1961. Regular trackless trolley service on the Grand River line ended on November 16, 1962, with the final run made by the Omnibus Society of America on November 18, 1962.

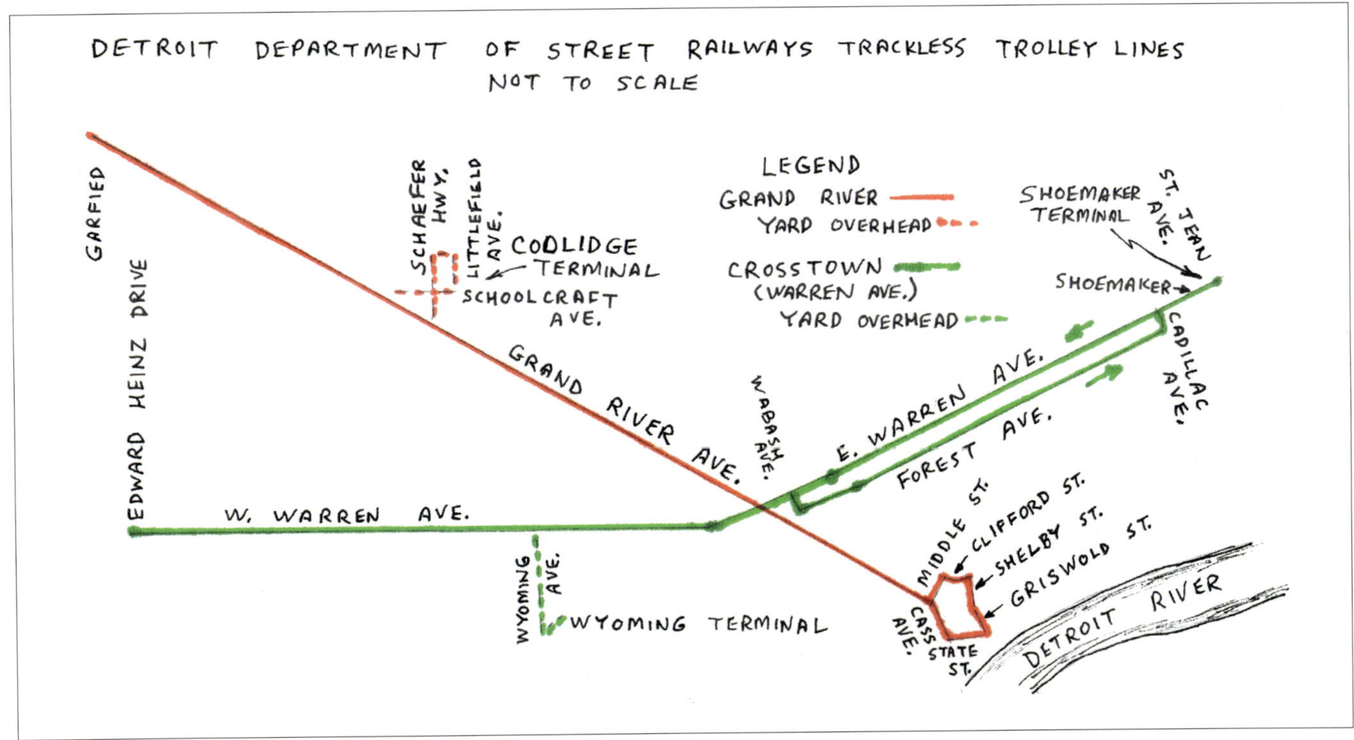

This is a map of the Detroit, Department of Street Railways (DSR) trackless trolley lines in 1956. At the end of 1956, there were 1,753 buses and 140 trackless trolleys. By the end of 1978, the system declined to 886 buses.

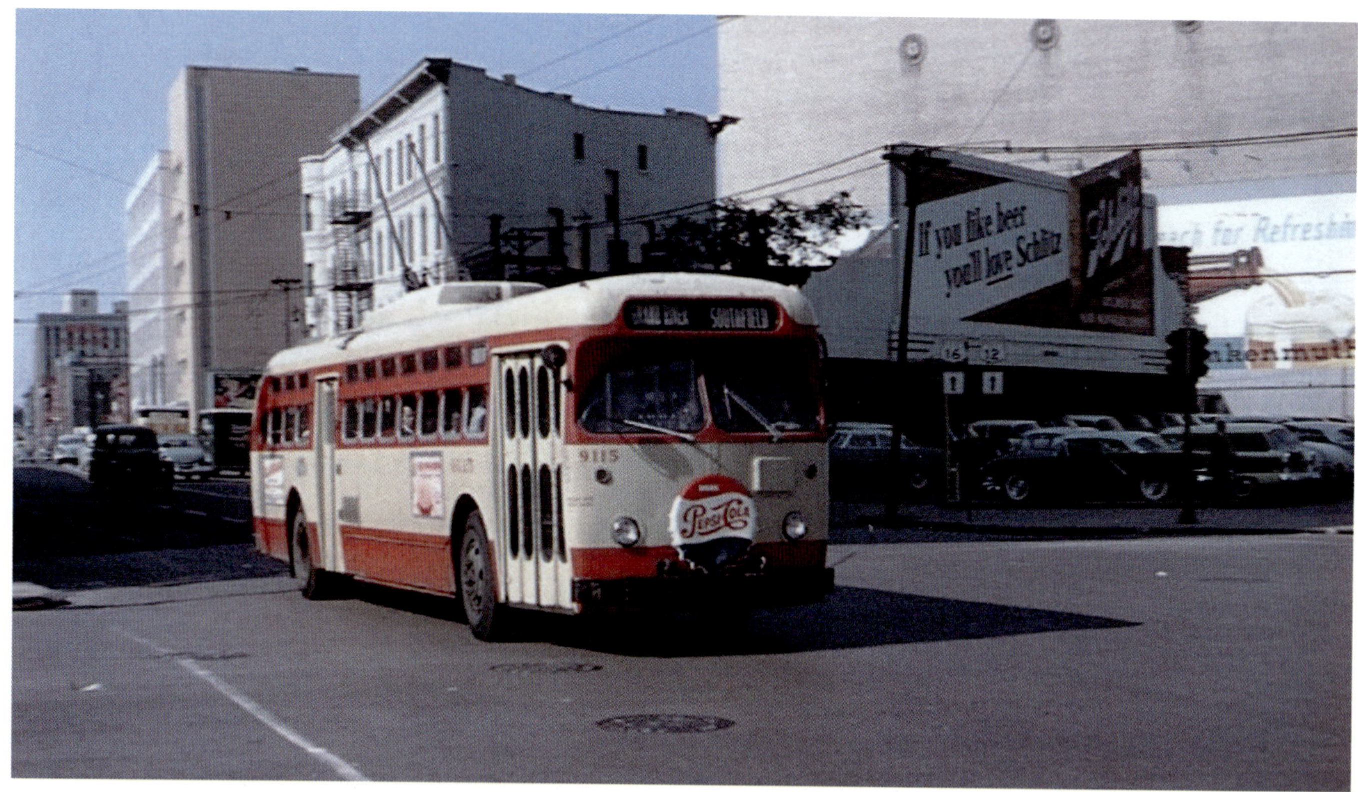

On September 12, 1955, trackless trolley No. 9115 is at Cass Avenue and Grand River Avenue. This was one of sixty model 48TT2 trackless trolleys (Nos. 9001–9060) built by Twin Coach Company in 1949. Powered by two General Electric type 1213 motors, each 38.25-foot-long coach weighed 19,000 pounds and seated forty-eight passengers. (*Bob Crockett photograph—Clifford R. Scholes collection*)

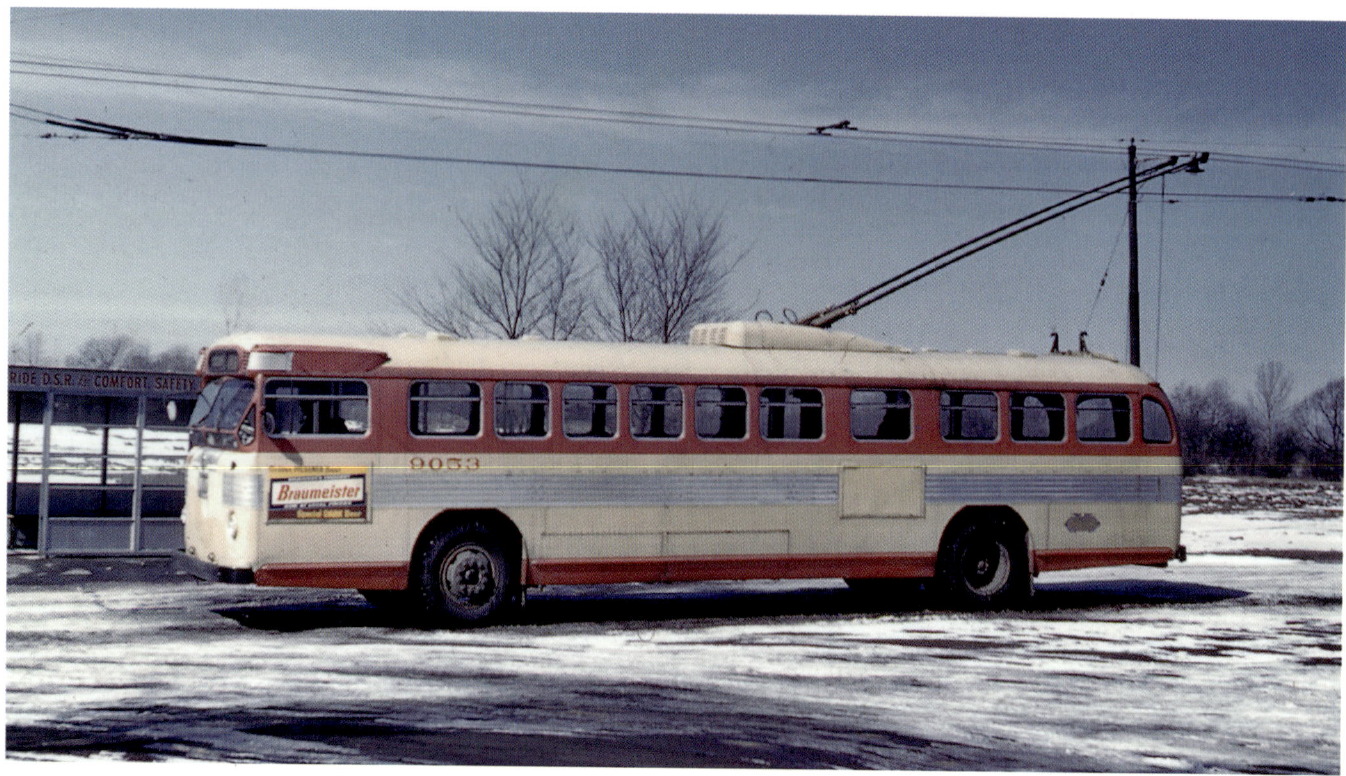

The Warren, Michigan, terminal is the location of trackless trolley No. 9053 on March 16, 1959. A new city charter, approved by the voters in 1973, took effect on July 1, 1974 and changed the Department of Street Railways to Department of Transportation. (*Chas. Able photograph—Clifford R. Scholes collection*)

7

Detroit's Streetcars to Mexico City

Detroit's streetcars were sold to Servicio de Transportes Eléctricos del Distrito Federal (STE), which in English is Federal District Electric Transport Service, the municipal street railway system of Mexico City. The history of Mexico City's electric streetcar system began on June 1, 1906 with the creation of the Mexico Tramways Company under foreign ownership. System mileage declined from 216.5 miles in 1926 to 198.1 miles by 1935. In February 1945, the system went from private to public operation. STE ordered its first Presidents' Conference Committee (PCC) car No. 2000 in June 1946 from St. Louis Car Company. STE purchased ninety-one PCC cars from Twin City Rapid Transit Company of Minneapolis in August 1953 and were renumbered by prefixing "2" to the original number resulting in car Nos. 2299–2319, 2365–2414, and 2420–2439. In the spring of 1956, 183 PCC cars were purchased from the City of Detroit, Department of Street Railways, and were renumbered by prefixing "2" to the original number, resulting in car Nos. 2102–2140, 2142–2149, and 2151–2286. In the older part of the city, many streets were two lanes wide, and one-way track was sometimes on the left side of the street. This permitted curb loading and prevented parked automobiles from blocking the streetcar. To allow curb loading in those locations, doors were cut into the left side of all cars. The line to Xochimilco past Churubusco had a rock-ballasted right of way. At Huipulco, there was a private right of way junction with the Tlalpan line. In 1970, a Metro opened along the Calzada de Tlalpan and replaced the northern portion of the Xochimilco and Tlalpan streetcar lines making the southern portion of both lines isolated from the rest of the streetcar system. PCC cars were now serviced at a small facility at Huipulco and operated from the Tasqueña metro station to serve the floating gardens of Xochimilco. STE renovated one of its vintage 1899 Brill cars and began a tourist line over a portion of the Valle streetcar line in December 1971. By 1979, only the Xochimilco and Tlalpan lines remained, and both lines closed in 1984.

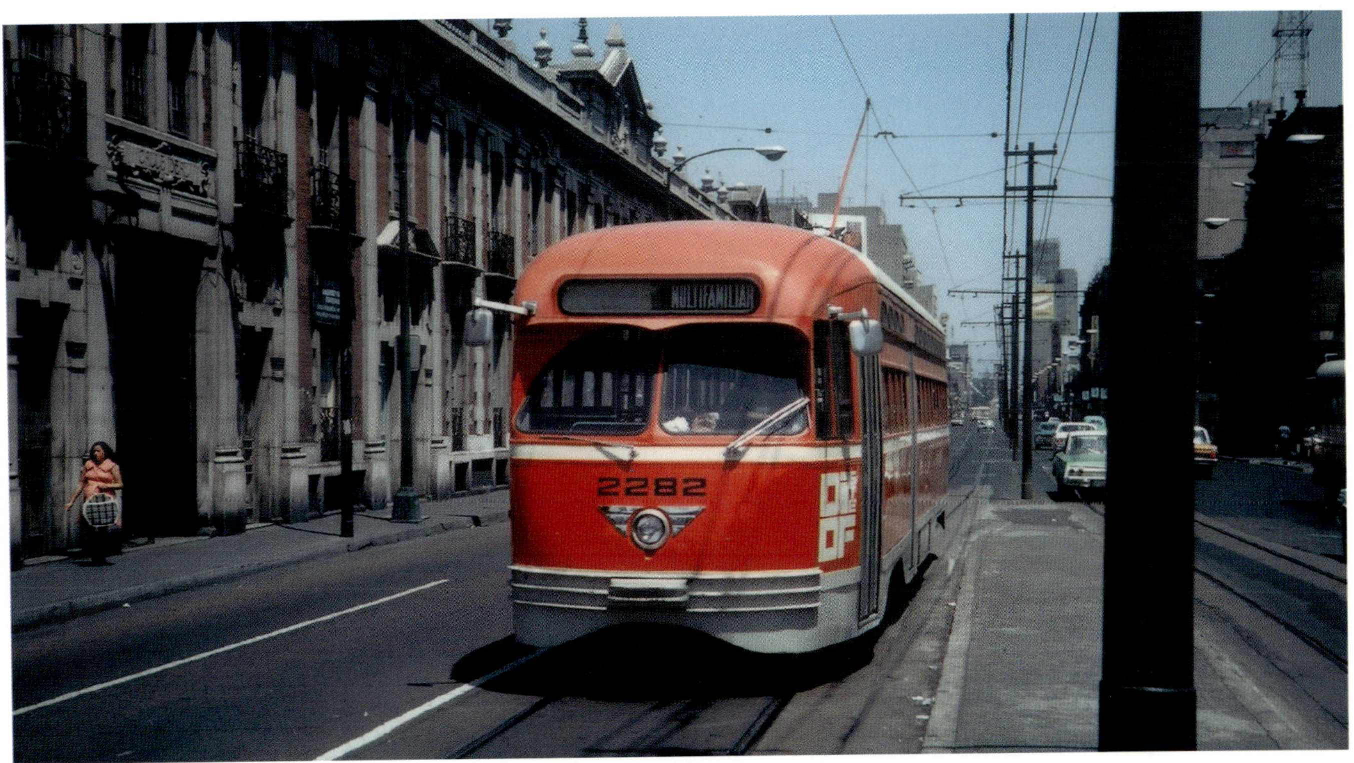

Mexico City refurbished PCC car No. 2282, formerly Detroit, DSR, No. 282, with Multifamiliar on the front destination sign, is gliding along a downtown Mexico City street. The left-hand doors were installed by STE to make it easier to load passengers on left hand platforms. (*Kenneth C. Springirth photograph*)

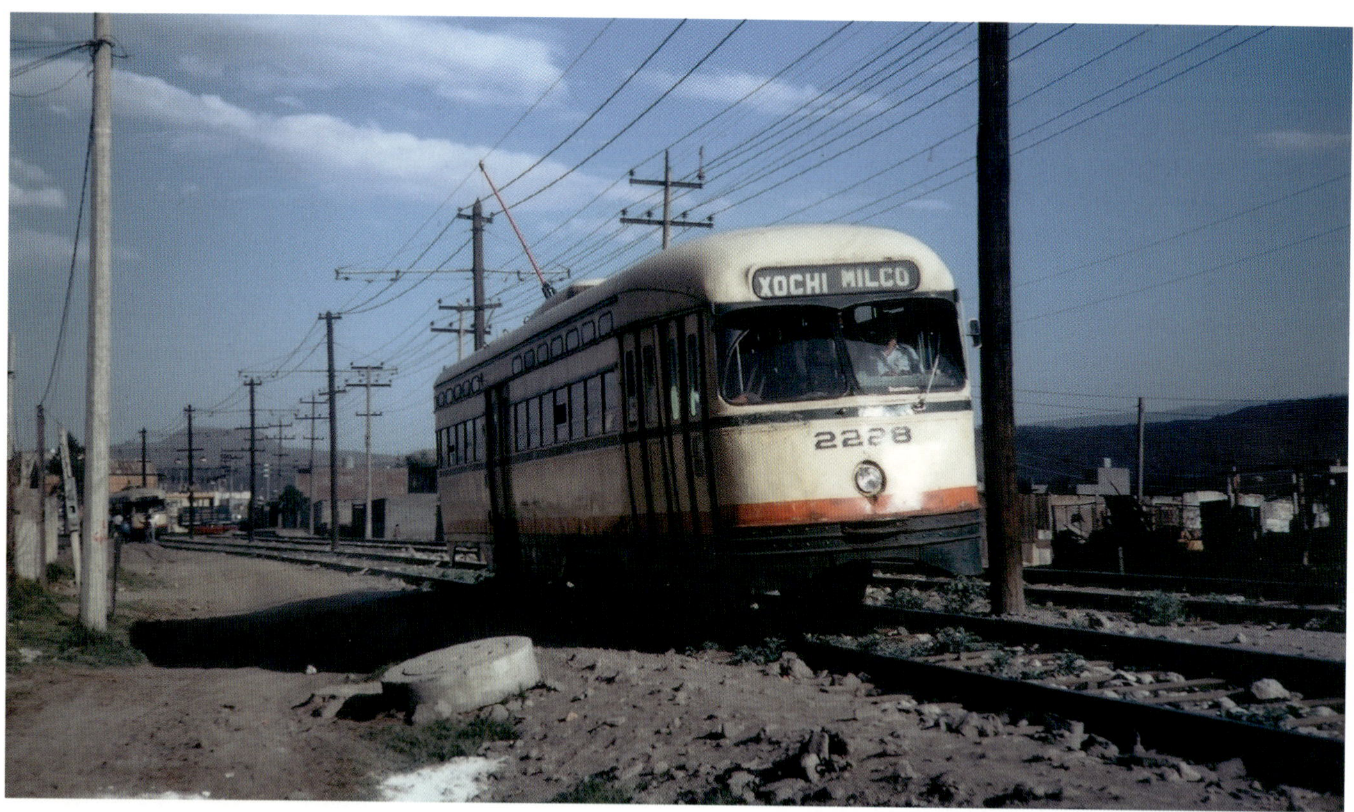

The rock-ballasted private right of way provided a traffic-free ride on the Xochimilco line for PCC car No. 2228, formerly DSR No. 228, on March 19, 1972. (*Kenneth C. Springirth photograph*)

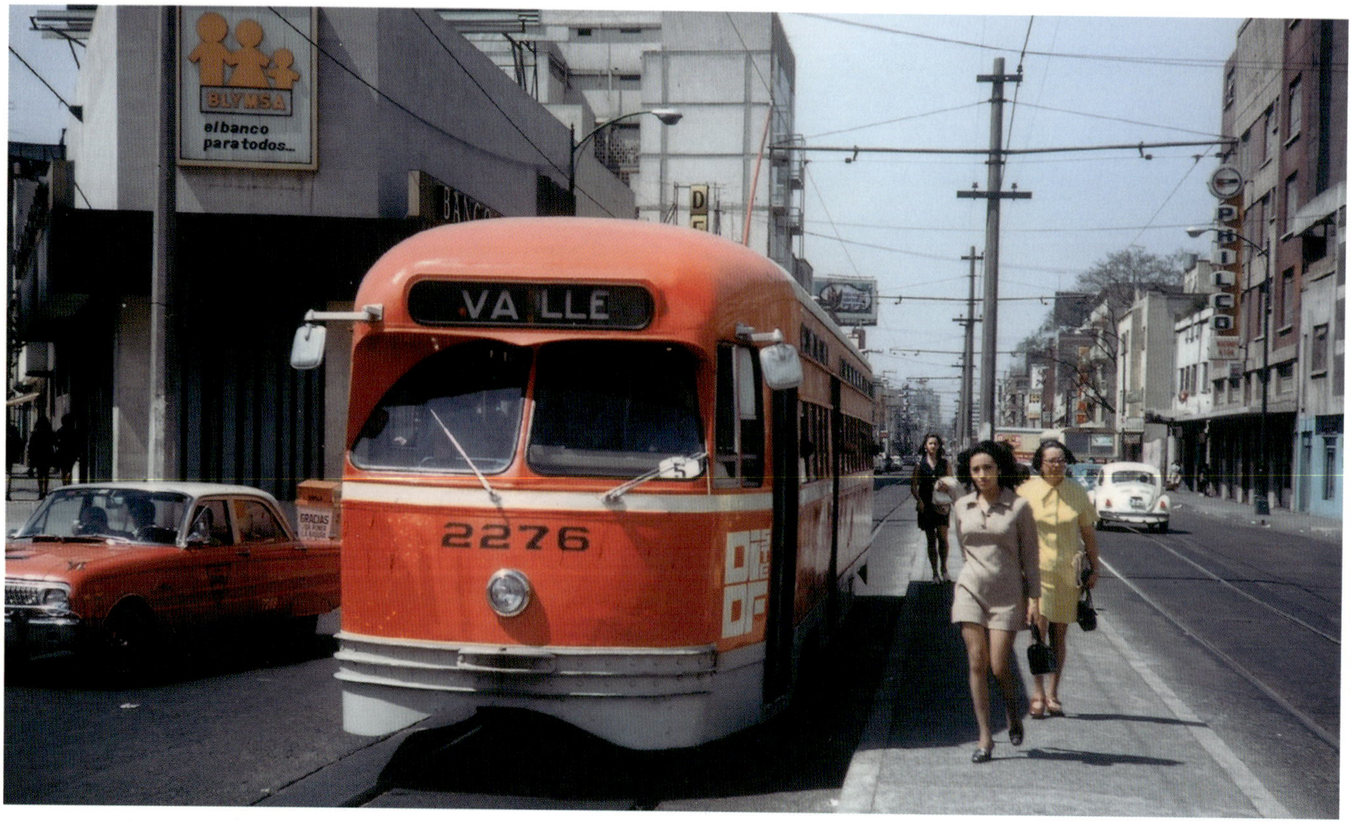

On March 20, 1972, the left-hand side doors on refurbished PCC car No. 2276, formerly DSR No. 276, improves safety for boarding and exiting the streetcars on Mexico City's sometimes crowded streets. (*Kenneth C. Springirth photograph*)

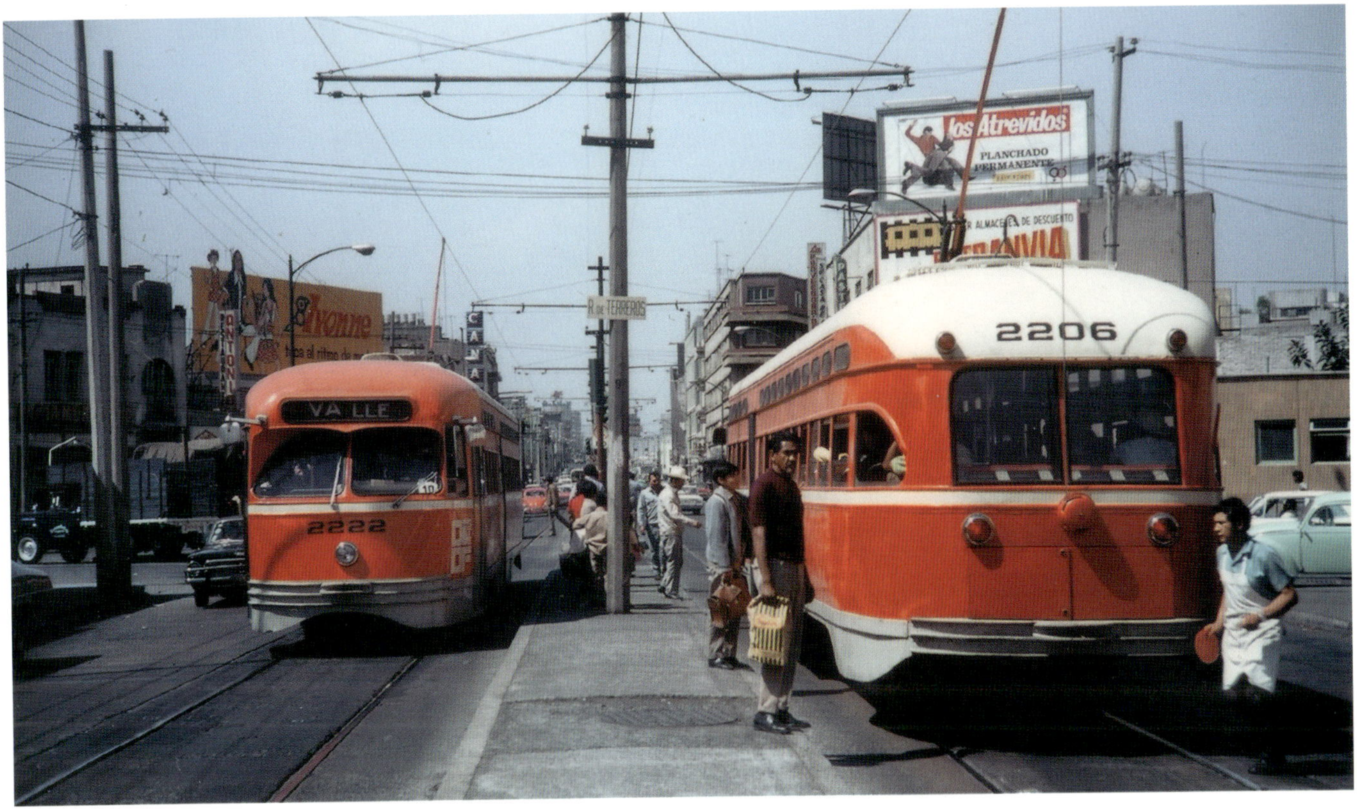

Refurbished PCC car No. 2222, formerly DSR No. 222 with Valle on the front destination sign, is about to pass refurbished PCC car No. 2206, formerly DSR 206, along the center of the road passenger loading and unloading island on March 20, 1972. (*Kenneth C. Springirth photograph*)

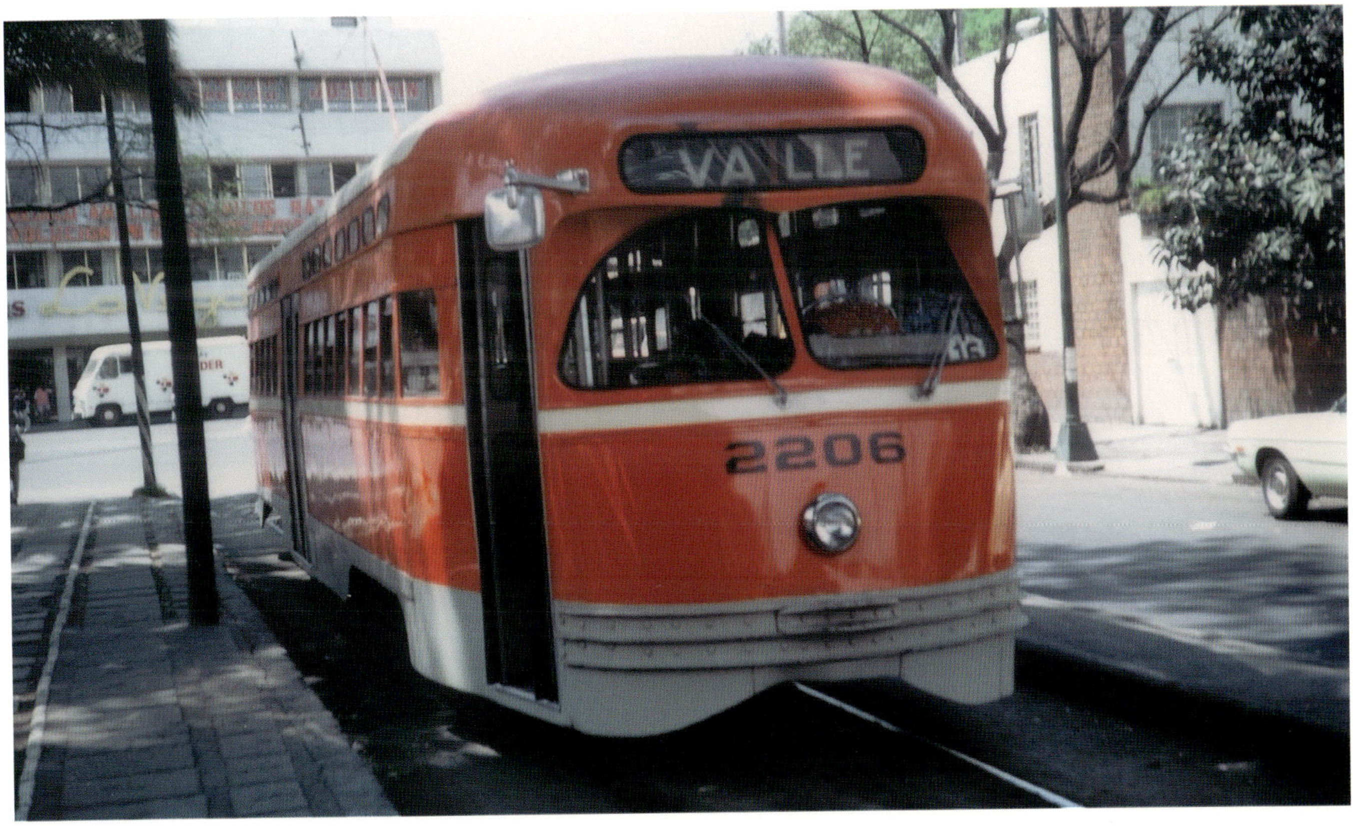

PCC car No. 2206, formerly DSR No. 206, is waiting for departure time on the Valle line on March 20, 1972. The front entranceway door width has been reduced on this refurbished car. (*Kenneth C. Springirth photograph*)

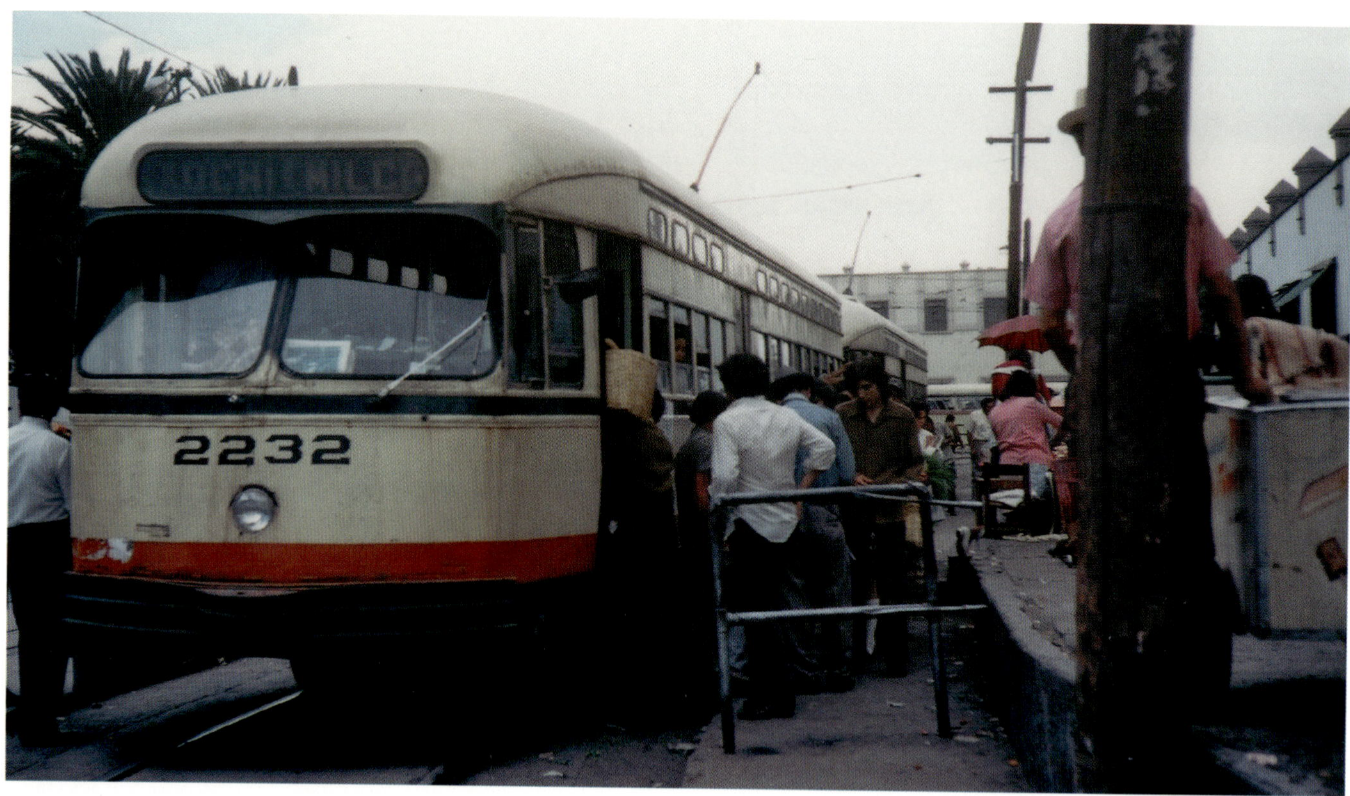

The Xochimilco line had a heavy ridership as evidenced by the number of passengers boarding car No. 2232, formerly DSR No. 232, on March 20, 1972. (*Kenneth C. Springirth photograph*)

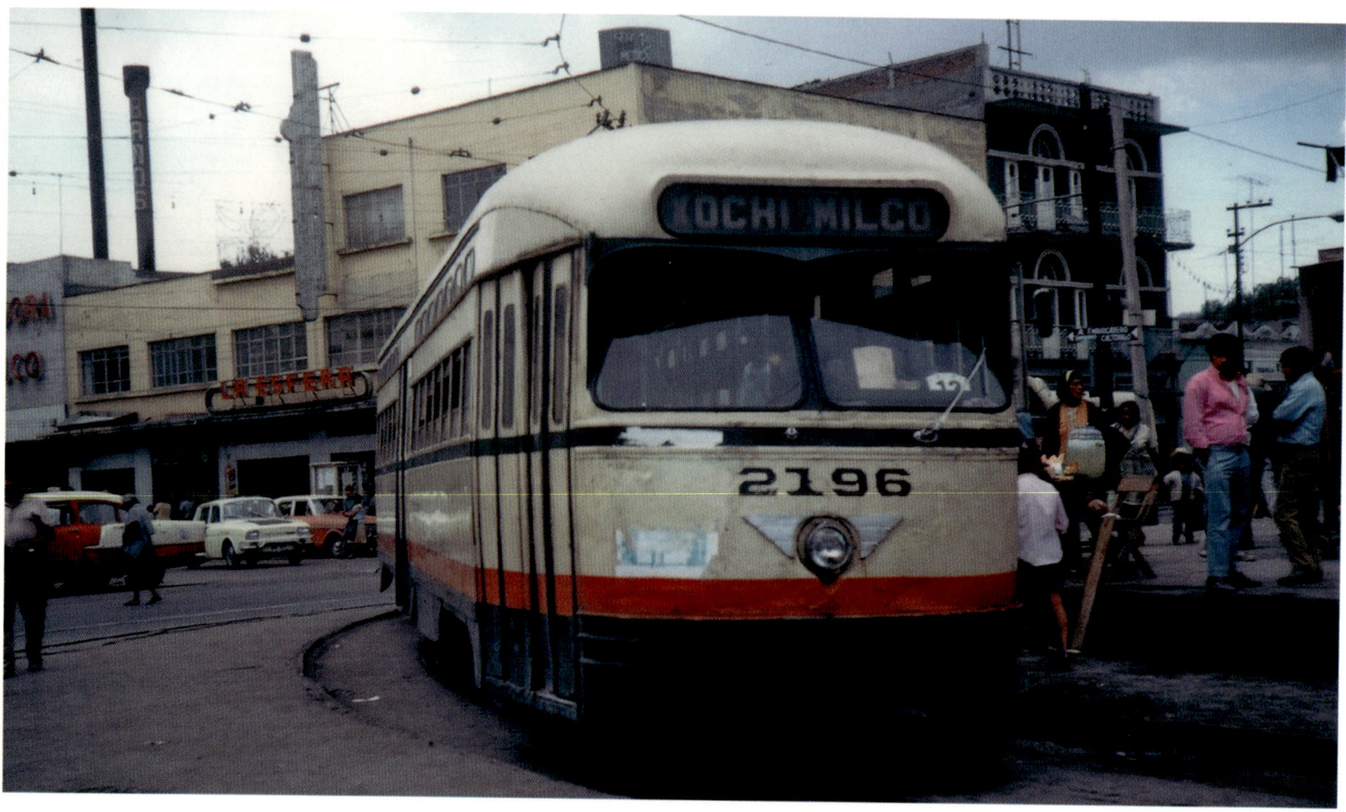

Evidence of the durability of a PCC car is car No. 2196, formerly DSR No. 196, which was one of fifty-three cars (Nos. 181–233) delivered by St. Louis Car Company to DSR between August and October 1949; over twenty-one years later, it was operating in Mexico City on the Xochimilco line on March 20, 1972. (*Kenneth C. Springirth photograph*)

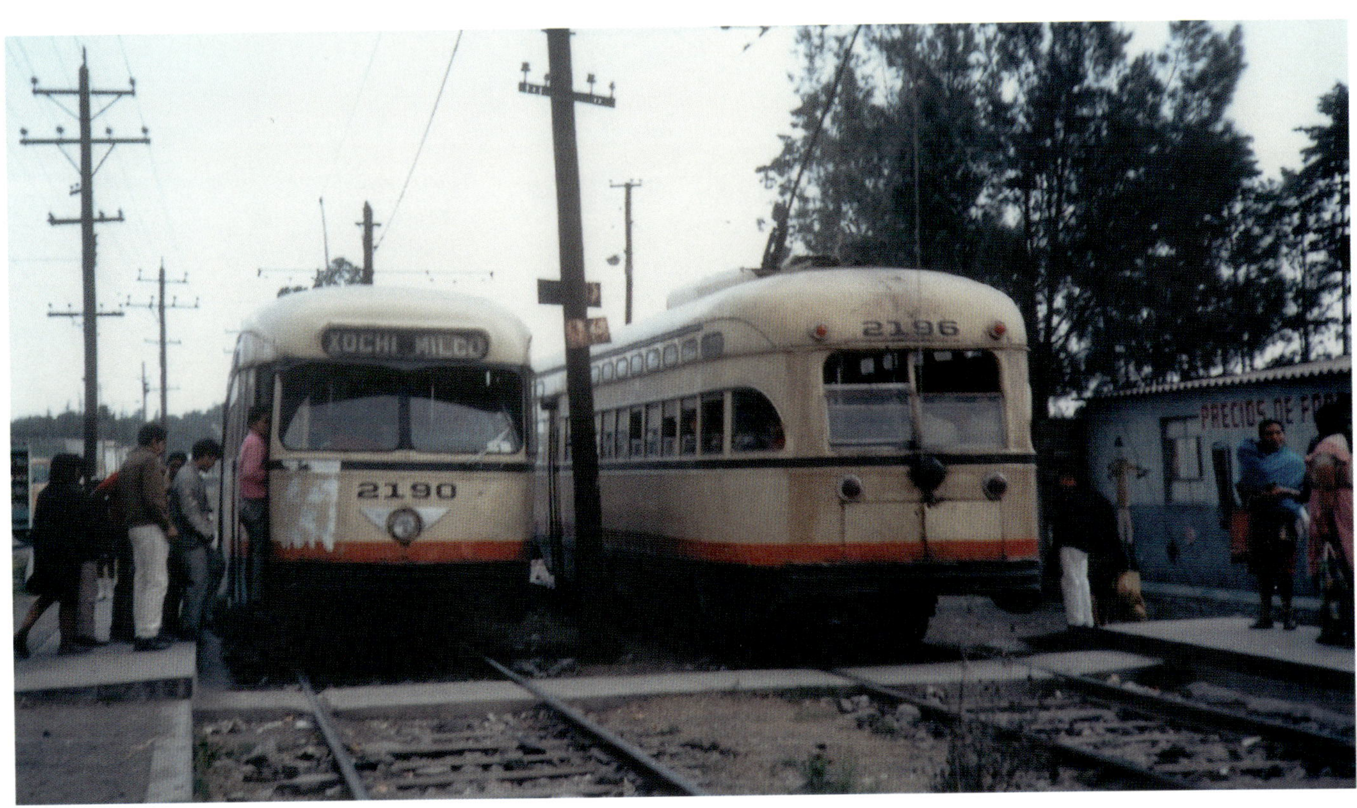

Mexico City's streetcar lines were well patronized as noted in passengers boarding PCC car No. 2190, formerly DSR No. 190, while No. 2196, formerly No. 196, is on the opposite side boarding platform on the Xochimilco line on March 20, 1972. (*Kenneth C. Springirth photograph*)

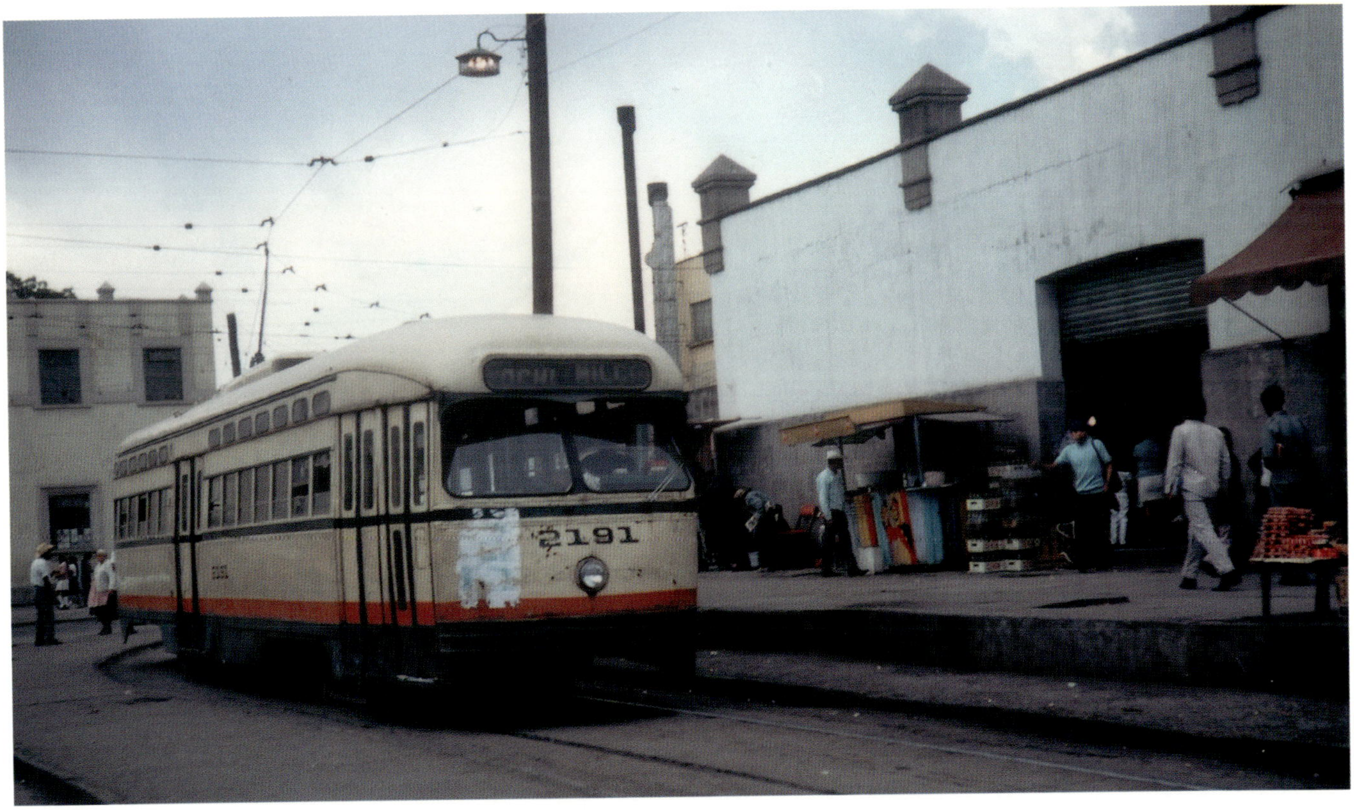

On March 20, 1972, PCC car No. 2191, formerly 191, is traversing a market area on the Xochimilco line. (*Kenneth C. Springirth photograph*)

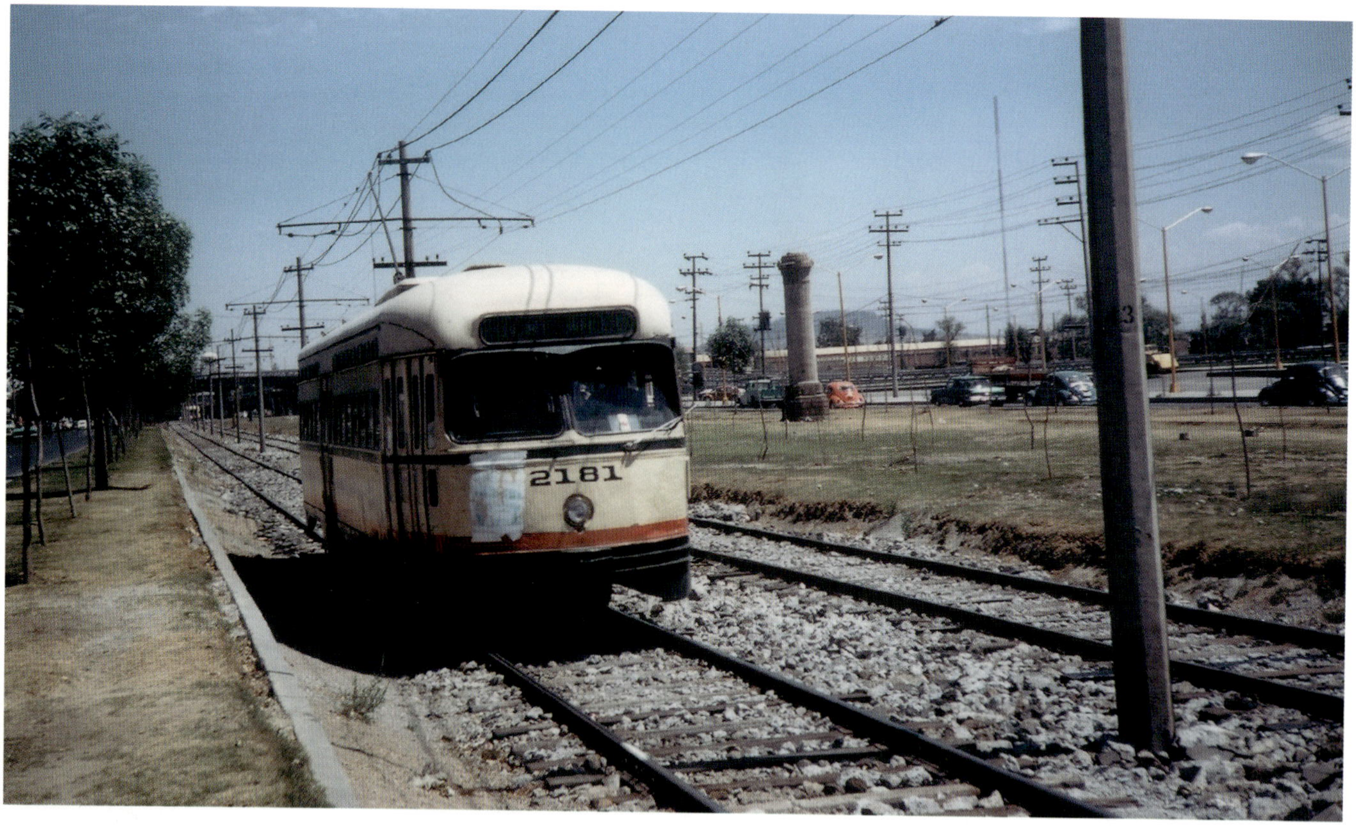

On the private right of way of the Xochimilco line, PCC car No. 2181, formerly DSR No. 181, provides dependable service in this March 20, 1972 view. (*Kenneth C. Springirth photograph*)

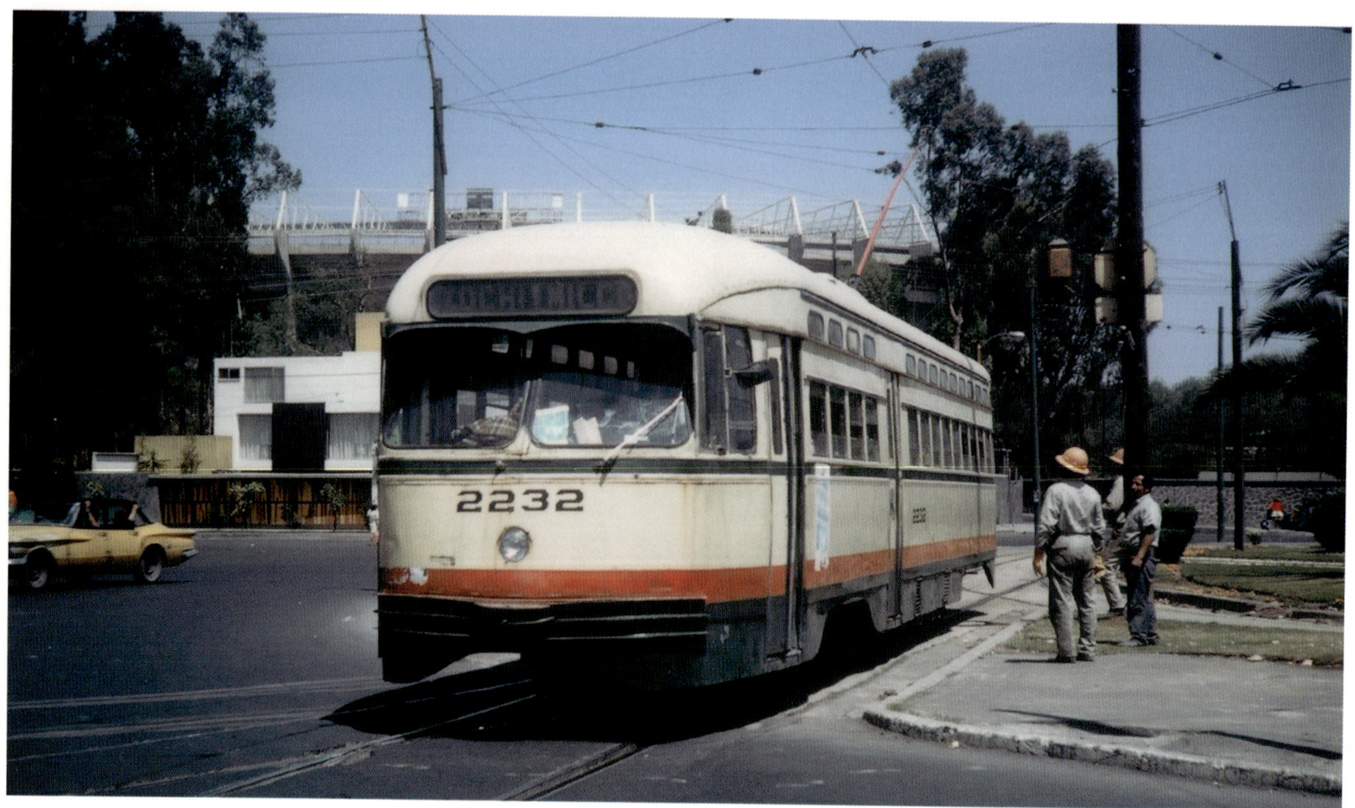

PCC car No. 2232, formerly DSR No. 232, is on the street running portion of the Xochimilco line on March 20, 1972. (*Kenneth C. Springirth photograph*)

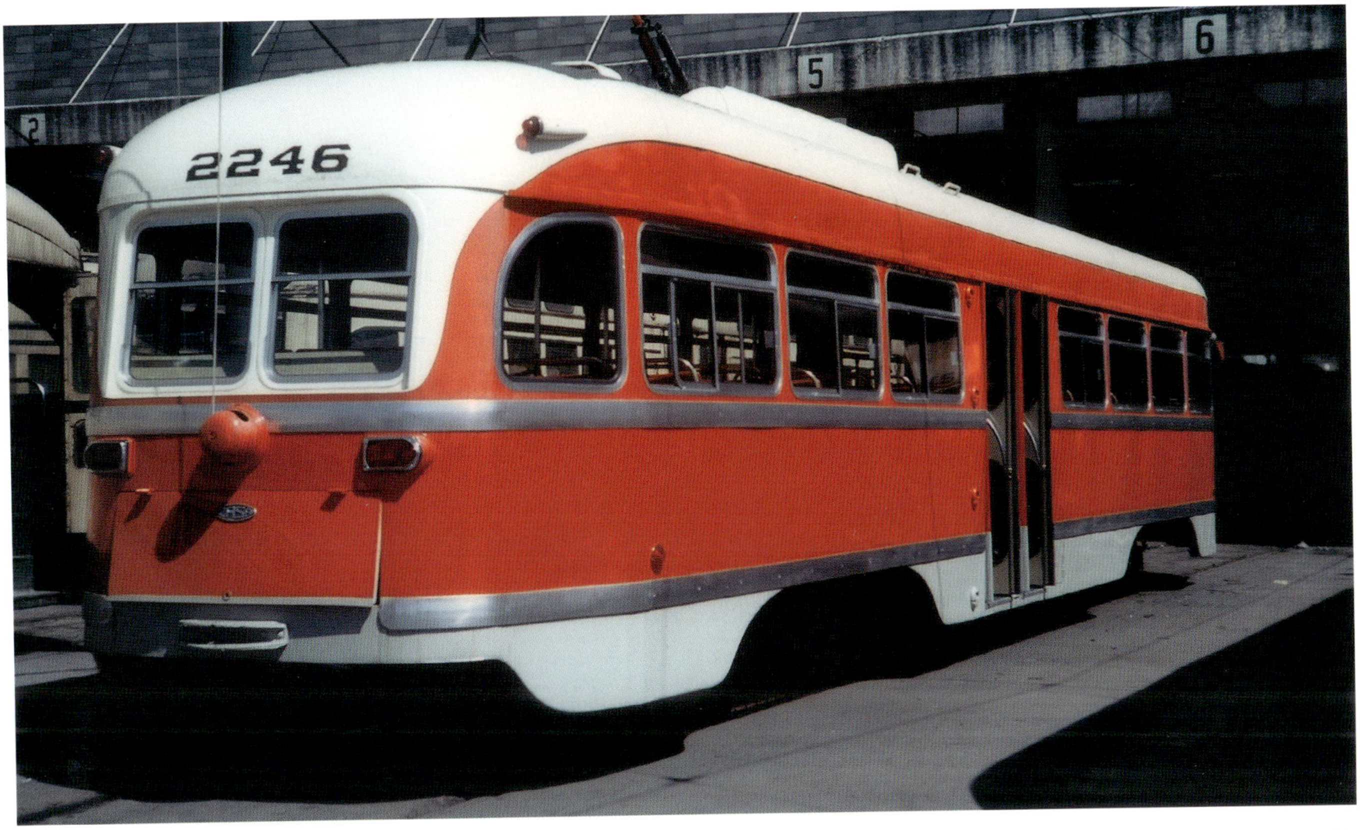

Sharp-looking rebuilt PCC car No. 2246, formerly DSR No. 246, s at the Tetepilco car barn waiting for the next assignment on March 20, 1972. (*Kenneth C. Springirth photograph*)

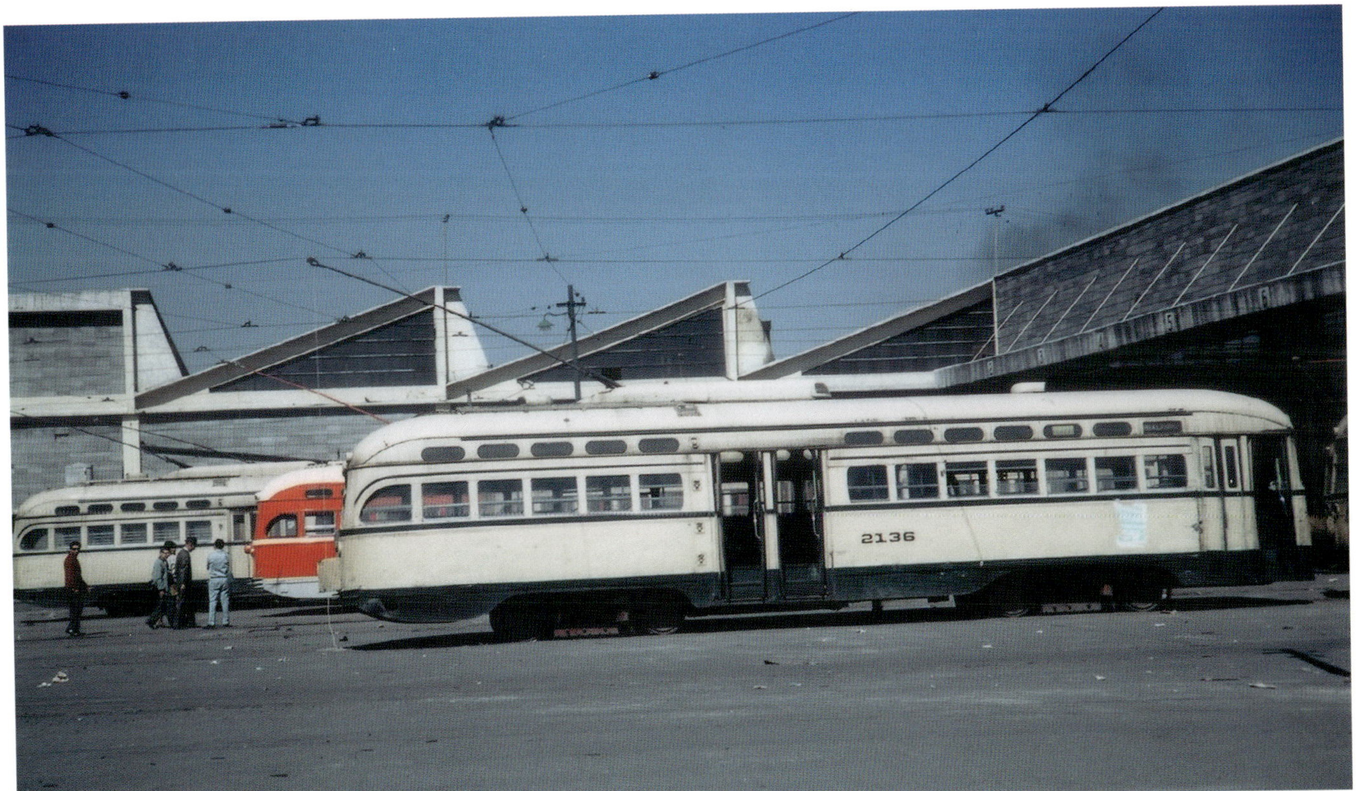

PCC car No. 2136, formerly DSR No. 136, and two other PCC cars are ready for service at the Tetepilco carbarn on February 20, 1972. (*Kenneth C. Springirth photograph*)

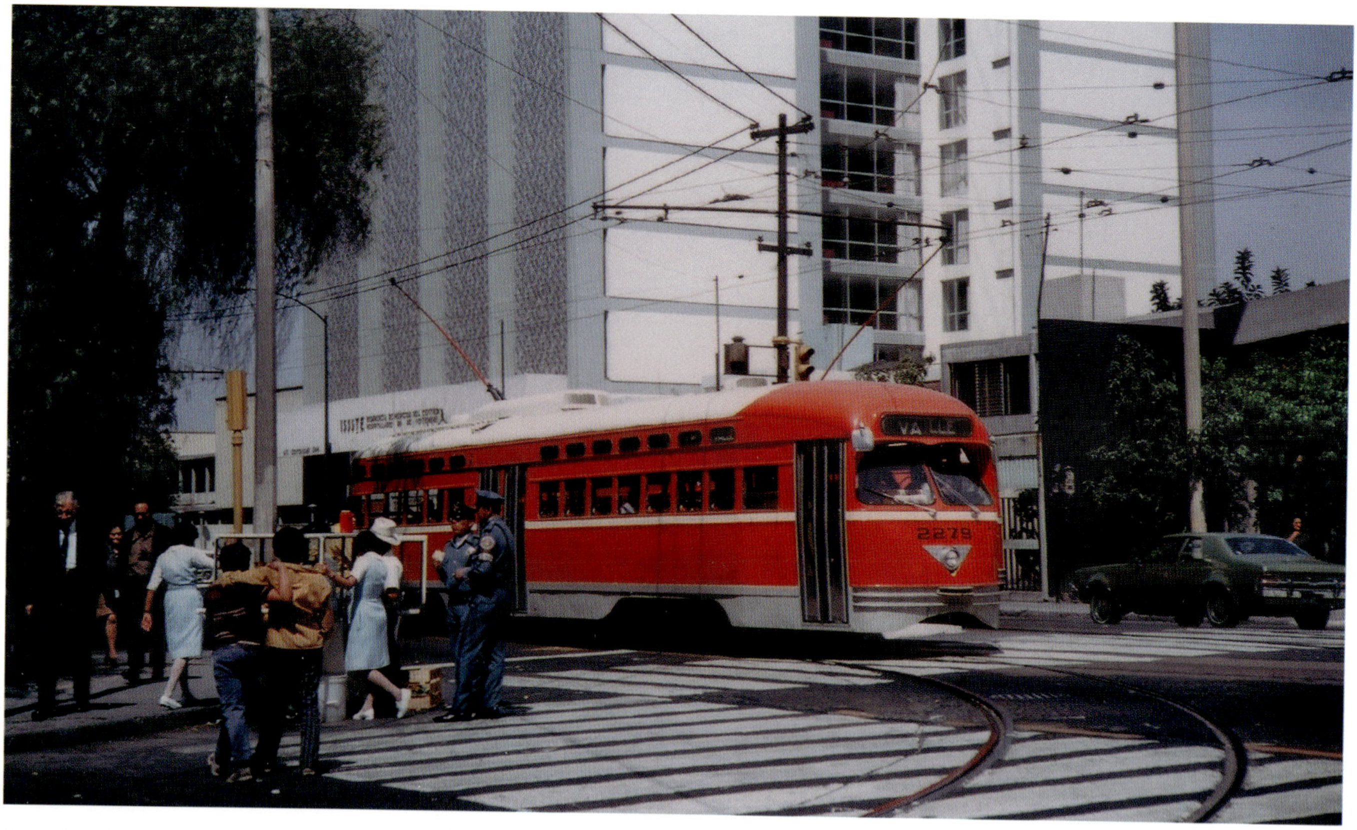

Smartly refurbished PCC car No. 2279, formerly DSR No. 279, is handling a trip on the Valle line on March 20, 1972. (*Kenneth C. Springirth photograph*)

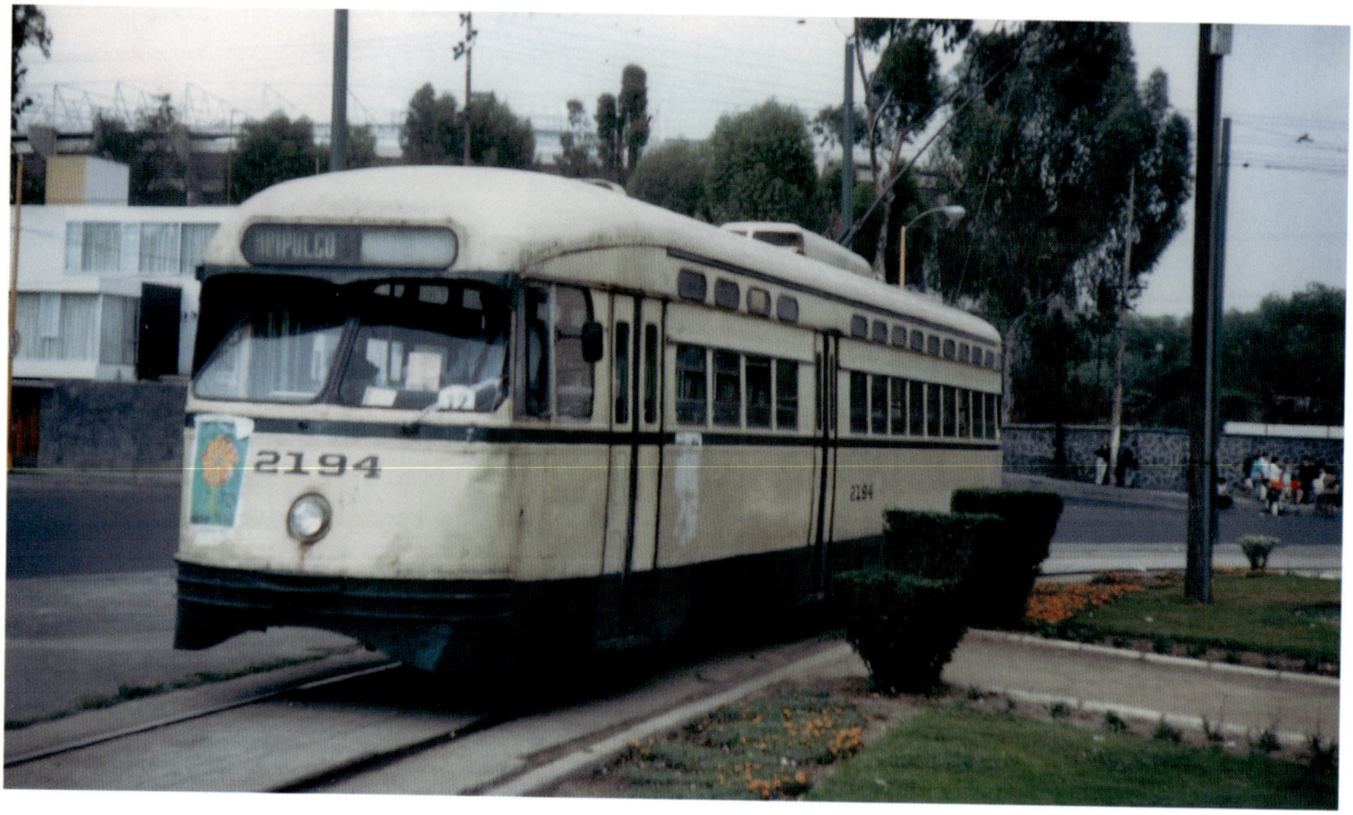

On March 19, 1972, PCC car No. 2194, formerly DSR No. 194, is at a nicely landscaped loop, waiting for departure time. (*Kenneth C. Springirth photograph*)

8

Washington Boulevard Streetcar

Detroit city planner Alexander Pollack had the idea of operating vintage streetcars in downtown Detroit. Following numerous meetings, Detroit Mayor Coleman Young decided that Washington Boulevard would be the location for the streetcar line that would serve as a tourist line and help revitalize downtown. Although Washington Boulevard never had a streetcar line, it once had Detroit's finest stores. Six narrow gauge streetcars that once operated on Lisbon, Portugal's 35.5-inch (the distance 3/8 of an inch from the top of each rail from the inside face of one rail to the inside face of the opposite rail)-narrow gauge system were purchased. The city of Detroit handled the design and construction of the ¾-mile line with funding by Federal, state, and city grants. Service began on September 20, 1976 as a Bi-Centennial project on Washington Boulevard just south of Grand Circus Park to Cobo Hall. During the first week of operation, two streetcars were used and carried over 20,000 riders.

After the first week, ridership averaged about 1,000 per day. In 1978, approval was received to extend the line ¼ mile along Jefferson Avenue to the Renaissance Center, which was completed in 1980. On loan, a 1904 Burton & Ashby Light Railways double-deck streetcar was rebuilt with funding by the Michigan Bell Telephone Company's Yellow Page Division. This line became known as the Detroit Citizens Railway and later the Detroit Downtown Trolley. In 1979, the line carried 75,000 persons. The area through which the line operated continued to decline, causing tourists to avoid the area; additionally, the July 31, 1987 opening of the 2.8-mile elevated automated people mover affected ridership, with a decline to 3,350 for 1997. Originally running on a ten-minute headway, the service was reduced to one car every twenty minutes. The reason so few people rode the streetcar was that there were so few people downtown at that time. Mechanical failures resulted in fewer available cars, and service ended on June 21, 2003. Detroit's heritage streetcar system was the first to be established in 1976, and the first to be abandoned. Economic development did not occur at that time for that area. In February 2004, the streetcar barn was demolished.

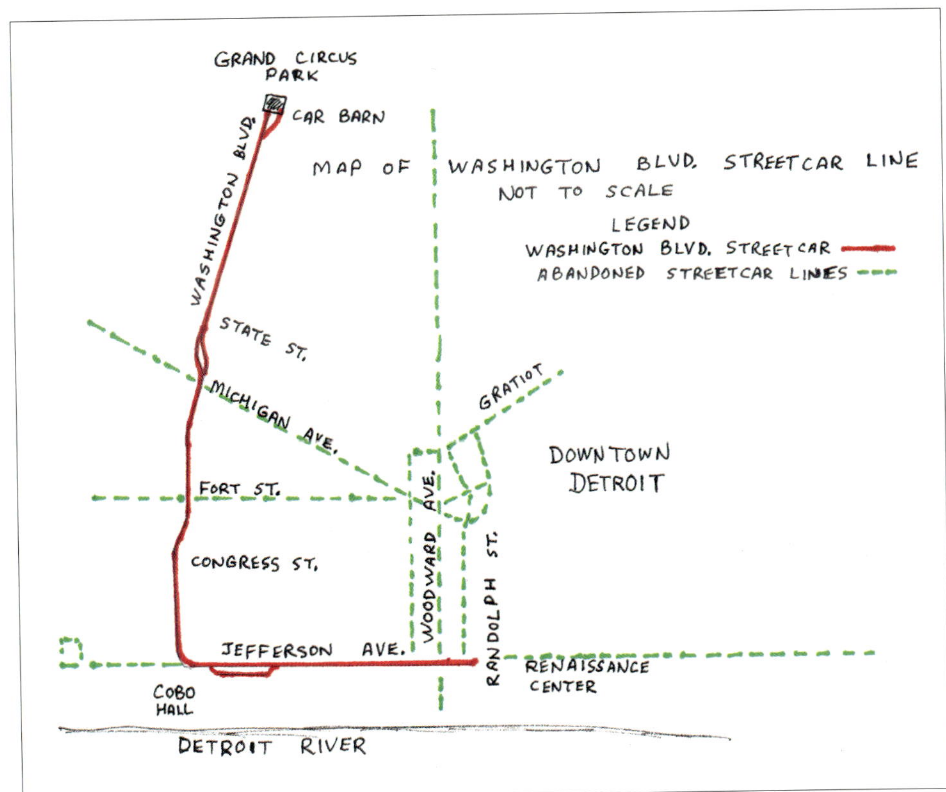

This map shows the completed Washington Boulevard Trolley line. Washington Boulevard never had a trolley line on it. The line became known as the Detroit Citizen's Railway and later Detroit Downtown Trolley.

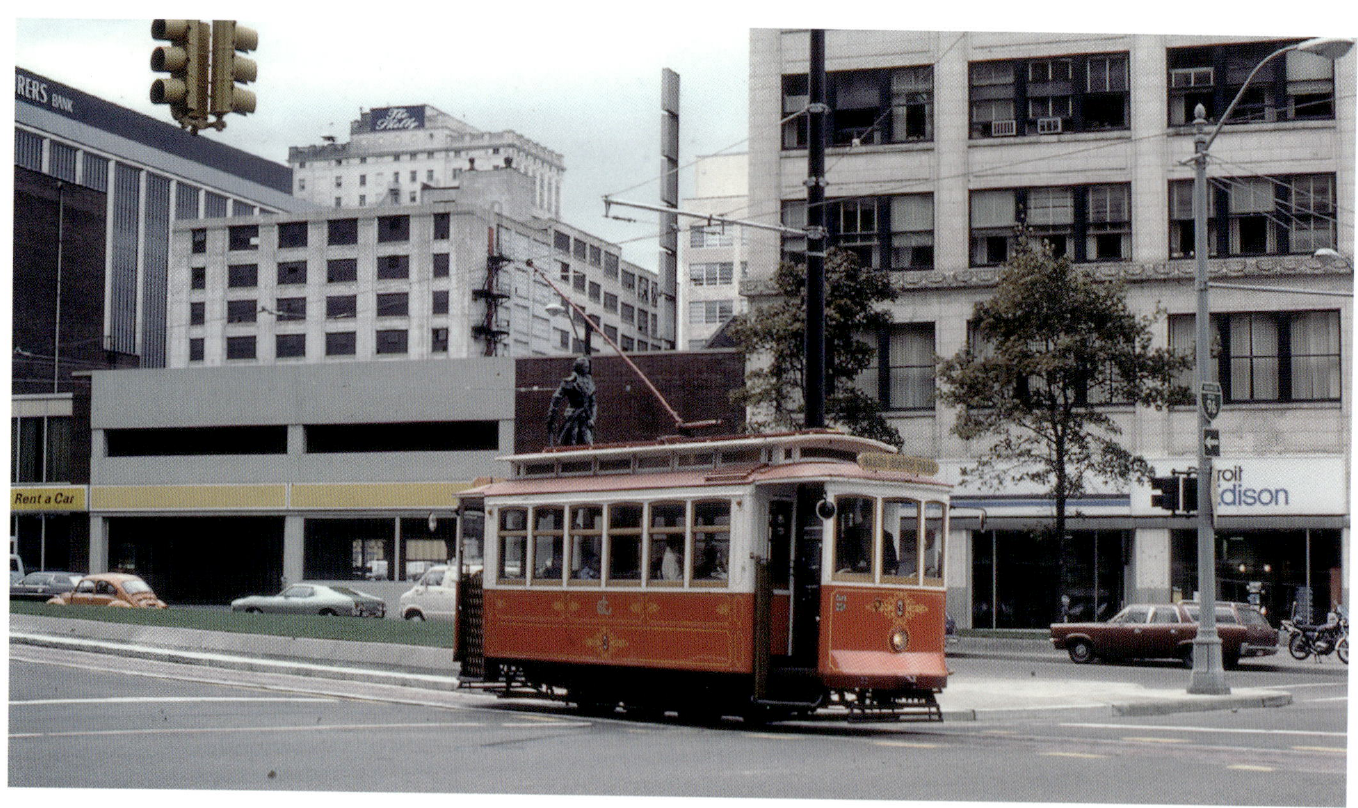

In September 1976, car No. 3, former Companhia Carris de Ferro de Lisboa (CCFL) of Lisbon, Portugal, is on Washington Boulevard at Michigan Avenue. This was one of seventy-five cars (Nos. 400–475) originally ordered from St. Louis Car Company in November 1899; they arrived during 1900–1901. These were four-wheel, twenty-seat closed cars designed to handle Lisbon's hilly routes. (*Clifford R. Scholes collection*)

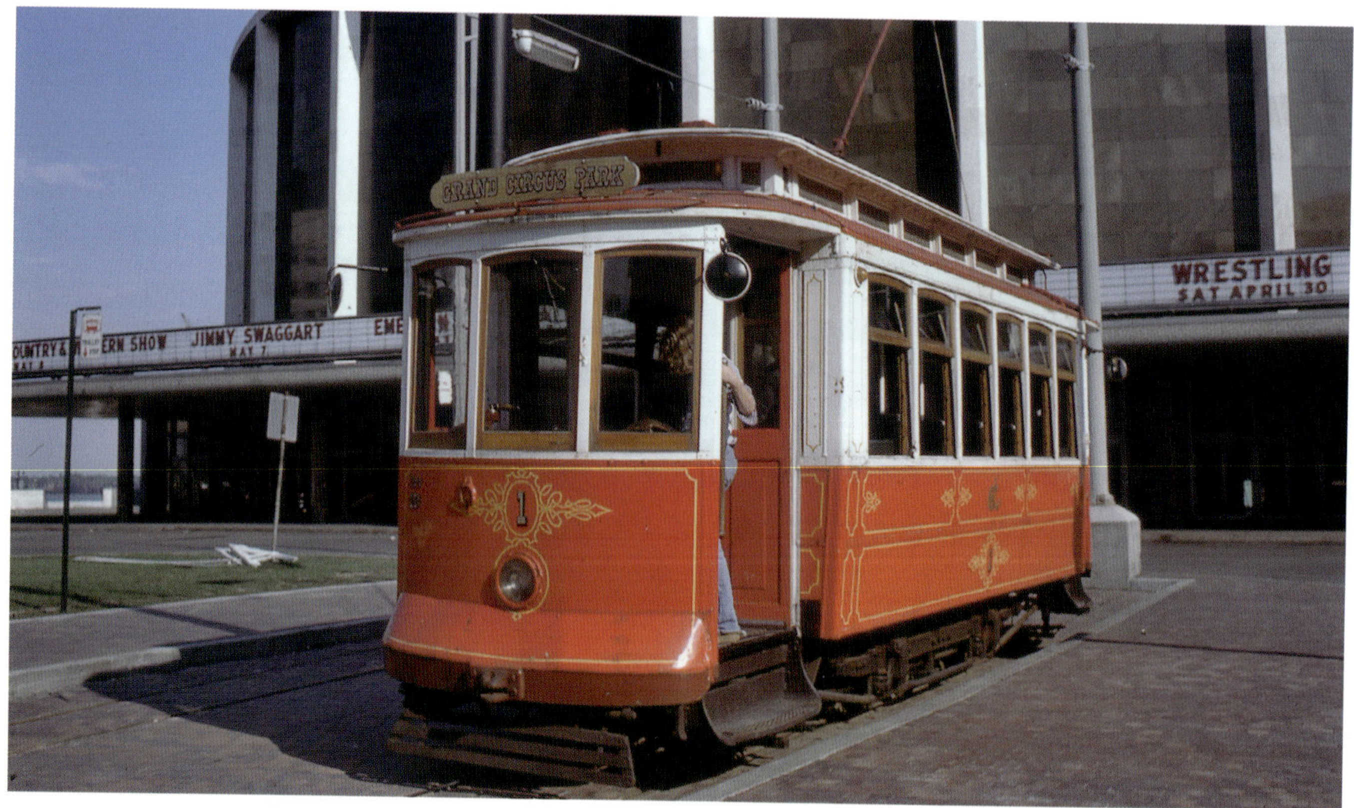

Former Lisbon car No. 1, built in 1899 by St. Louis Car Company, is at the end of the line at Cobo Hall in April 1977. This was in the same series of cars as No. 3. Cobo Hall, opened in 1960, was named after Albert Cobo, the Mayor of Detroit from 1959 to 1957. (*Clifford R. Scholes collection*)

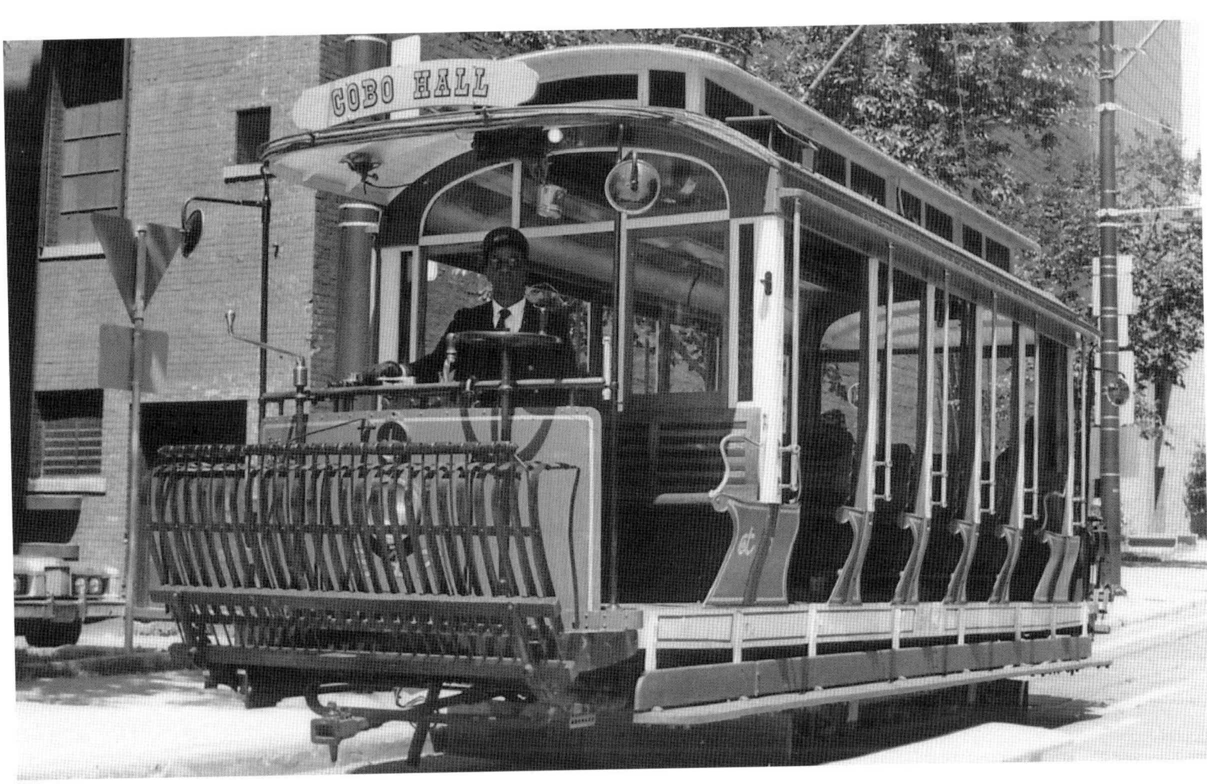

On July 9, 1977, former Lisbon open bench car No. 247 is near the northern terminus of the Washington Boulevard line. This car was built in 1900 by the J. G. Brill Company in Philadelphia for Lisbon, Portugal. It later became a work car and was renumbered 397. The car was restored by the John R. Stevens Associates of Huntingdon, Long Island, during 1975. Floor framing was extensively repaired, new flooring was installed, bulkheads were rebuilt, and many of the body parts were replaced. The car received its original Lisbon number 247. (*Kenneth C. Springirth photograph*)

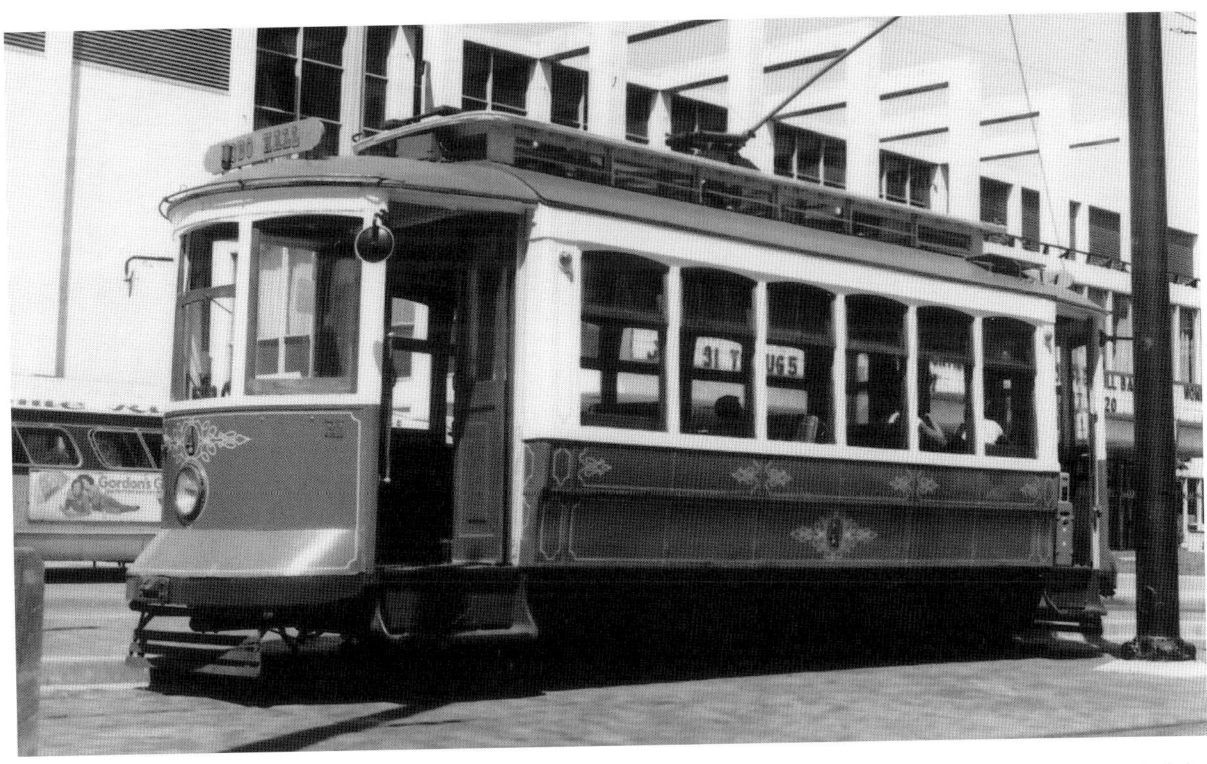

On July 9, 1977, former Lisbon car No. 4 is at the Cobo Hall Terminus. This car was built by St. Louis Car Company in 1925. Built by the City of Detroit, Cobo Hall (a convention center later known as the Cobo Center), opened on August 15, 1960 and was named in honor of former Detroit Mayor Albert Cobo, who had a vision of building a convention center. (*Kenneth C. Springirth photograph*)

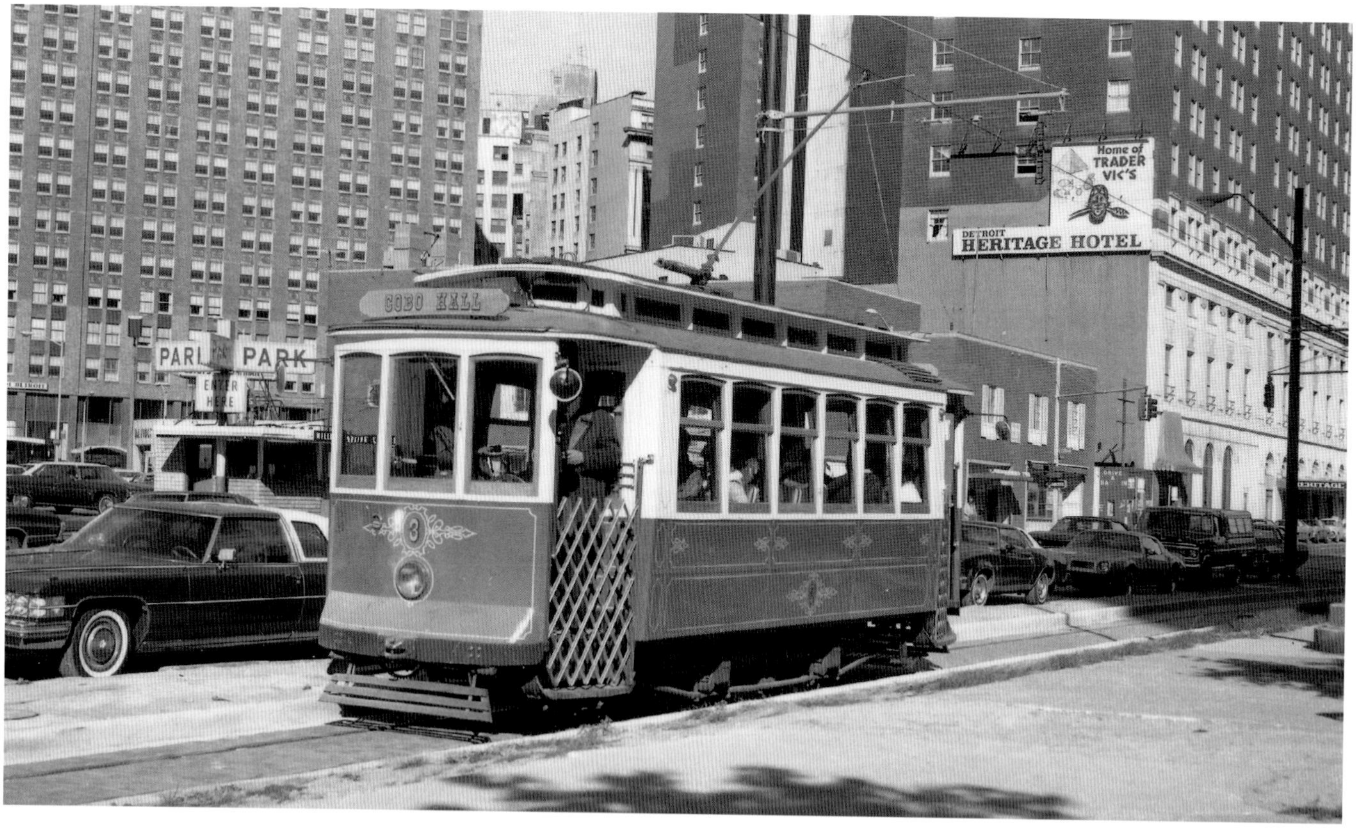

Washington Boulevard, south of Michigan Avenue, is the location of car No. 3 in 1978. The line was operated by Detroit's Department of Transportation. Construction of the line included a concrete curb median that was designed to separate the streetcar from automobile traffic. (*Clifford R. Scholes collection*)

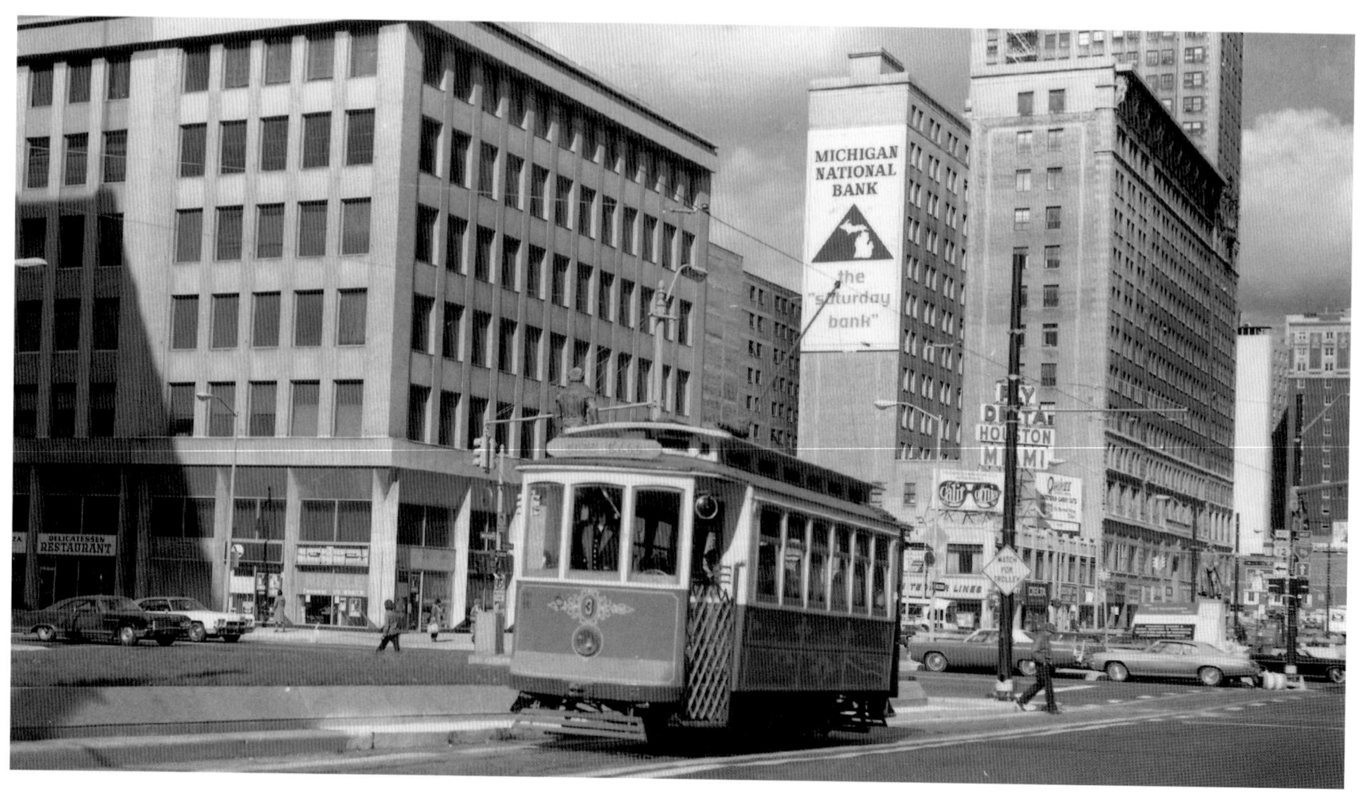

Cobo Hall is the destination for car No. 3 on Washington Boulevard at Grand River Avenue in 1978. (*Clifford R. Scholes collection*)

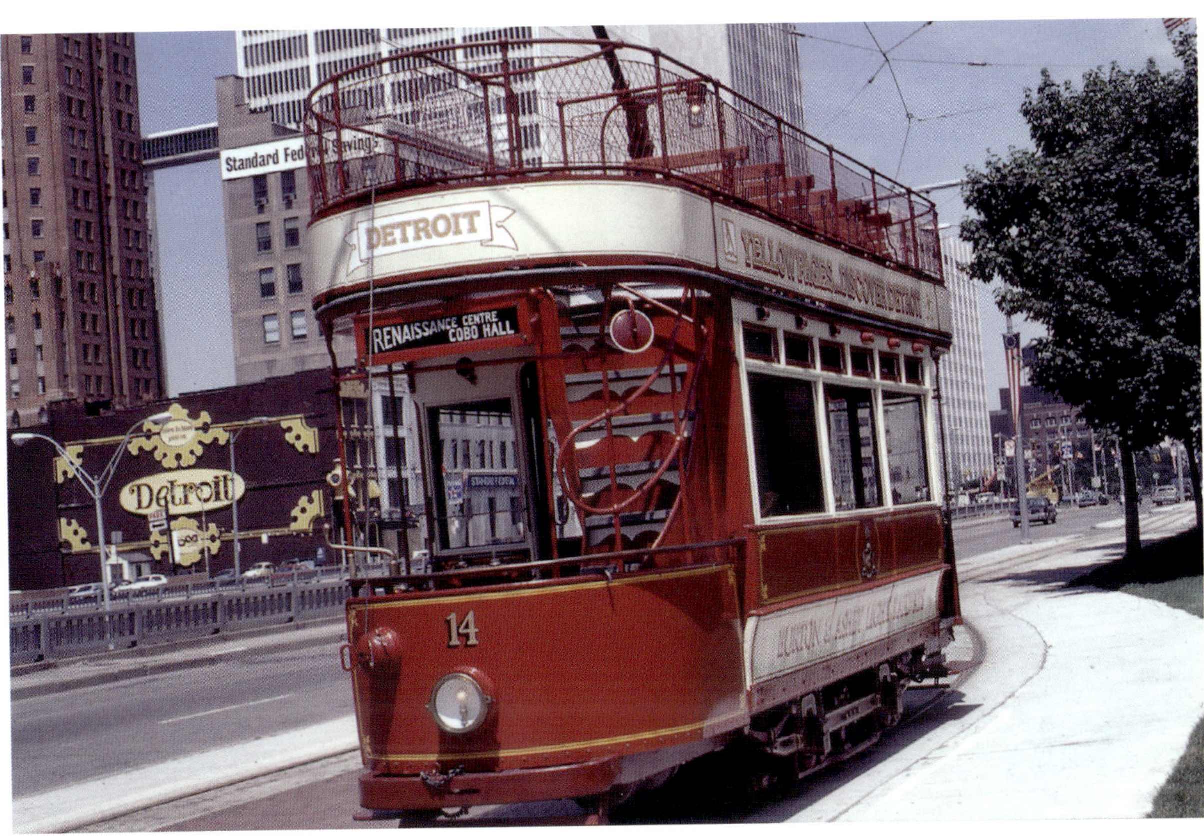

On June 18, 1981, Jefferson Avenue and Shelby Street is the location of former Burton & Ashby Light Railway tramway (streetcar) system open top No. 14, built in 1906 by the Brush Electric Company of Loughborough, England. That system operated between Burton upon Trent and Ashby-de-la-Zouch in England from 1906 to 1927. The car body survived in a garden in Church Gresley and was removed for preservation around 1970. It was exported to Detroit in 1976 and mounted on a Lisbon 35.5-inch gauge truck for the Washington Boulevard line. (*Clifford R. Scholes collection*)

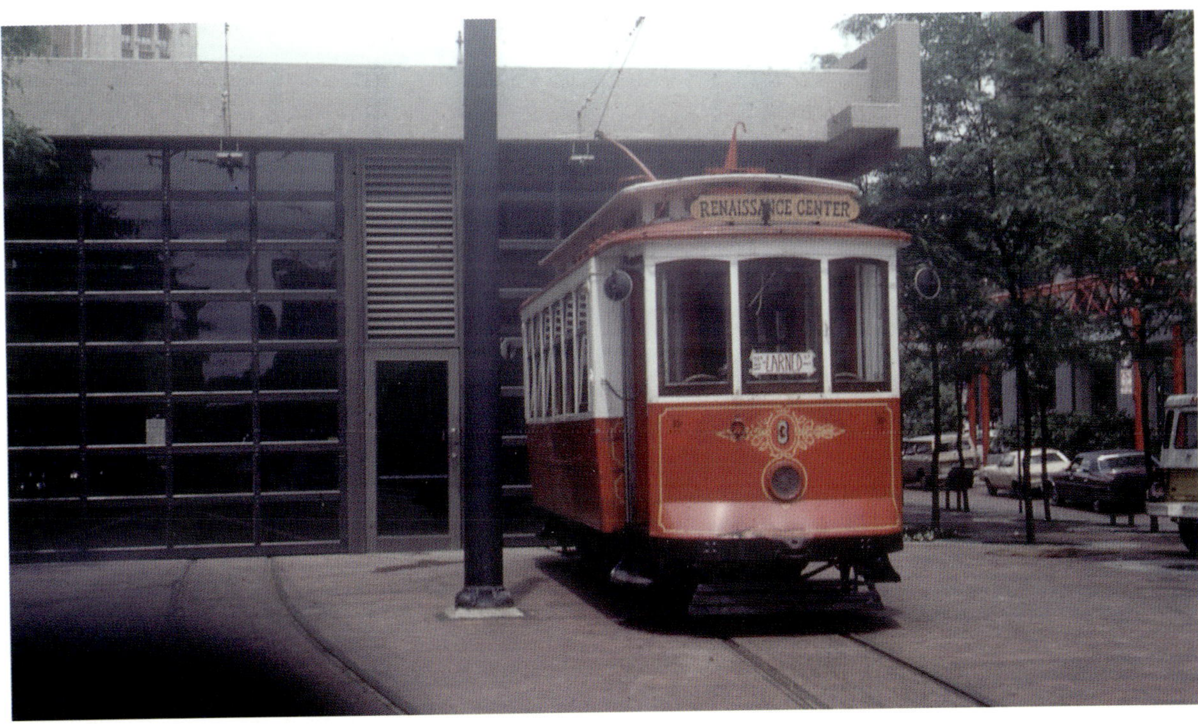

The Washington Boulevard car barn is the location of car No. 3 waiting for the next assignment in May 1982. (*Clifford R. Scholes collection*)

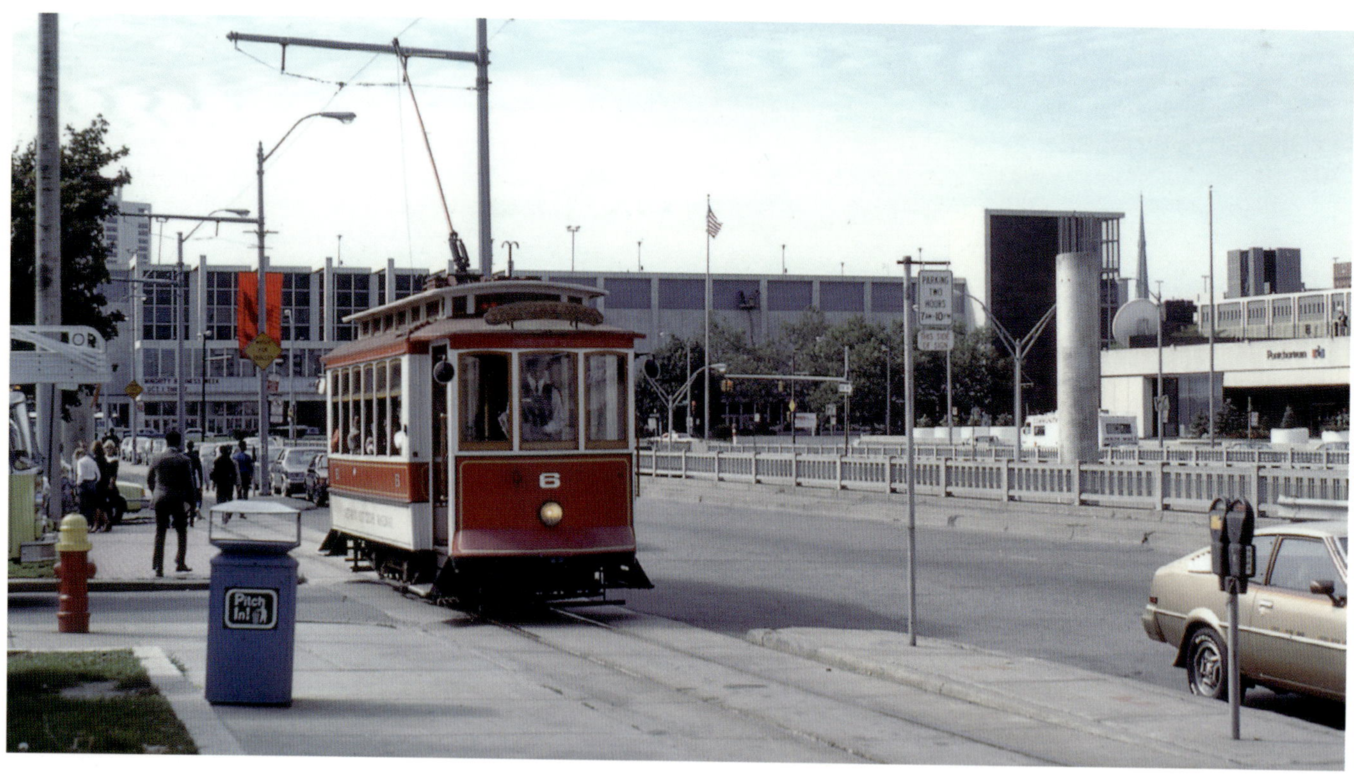

On October 8, 1984, car No. 6 is on Jefferson Avenue at Shelby Street. This was from CCFL of Lisbon, Portugal, and was one of seventy-five cars (Nos. 400–475) originally ordered from St. Louis Car Company in November 1899; they arrived during 1900. (*Jim Smith photograph—Clifford R. Scholes collection*)

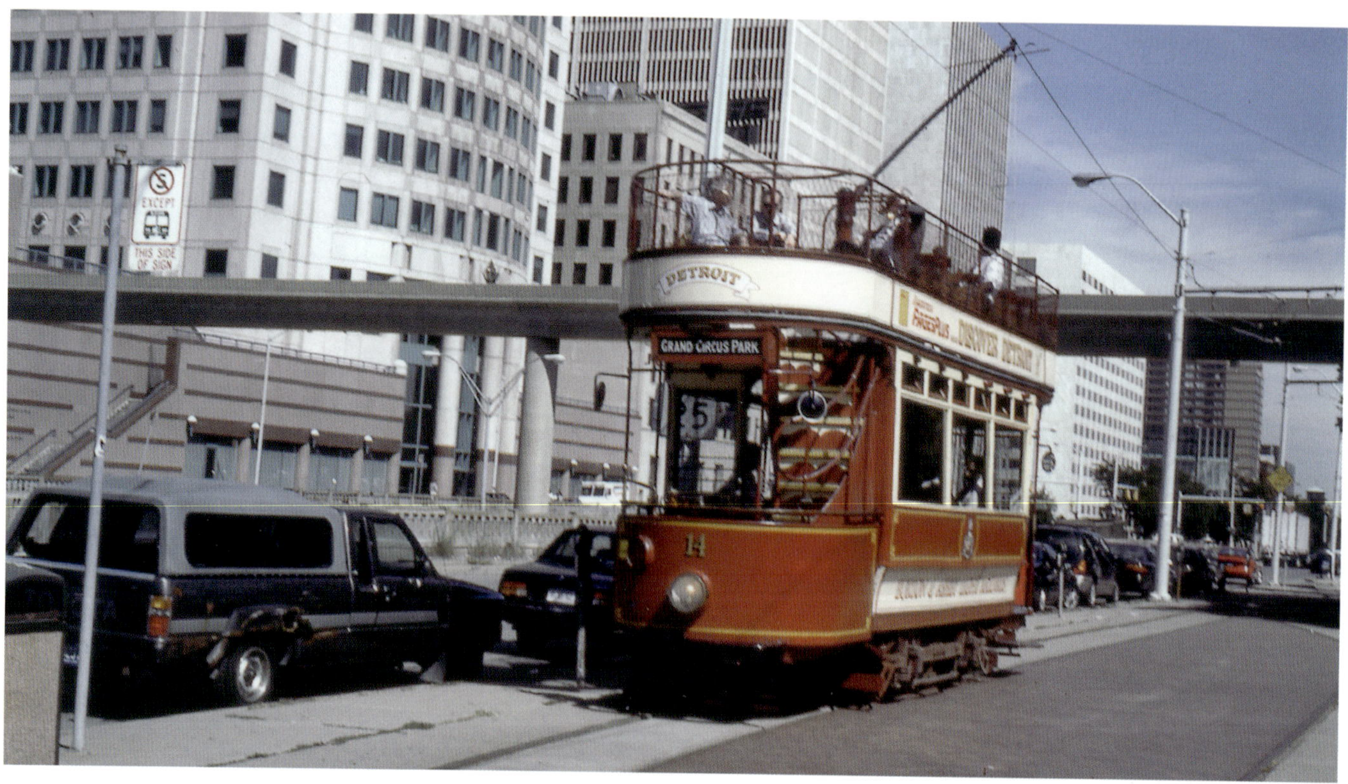

In the bright sunshine of September 1996, car No. 14 is on Jefferson Avenue at Griswold Street. After the Washington Boulevard service ended on June 21, 2003, this car was later stored at a Detroit Department of Transportation facility. In October 2014, the City of Detroit put the car up for sale. It went back to England in 2014, and at the Statfold Barn Railway (located near Tamworth, Staffordshire, England), it was rebuilt with a Clayton battery electric traction package. (*Clifford R. Scholes collection*)

9

The QLINE Streetcar

In 2006, the Detroit Department of Transportation (DDOT) had a study made to look at expanded mass transit options for Woodward Avenue. At the same time, a group of business leaders decided to provide matching private funds to government dollars to develop a $125 million 3.3-mile line through downtown Detroit that would be called the M-1 Rail Line. After a lot of discussion between the investors and the DDOT, the two groups came together on DDOT's plan for a 9.3-mile line connecting the Rosa Parks Transit Center via Woodward Avenue to the State Fair Grounds at Eight Mile Road. There would be nineteen stops served by ten trains, with each train having two cars to seat 150 passengers. The trains would operate in a dedicated right of way in the median of Woodward Avenue between Adams Street at the northern edge of downtown to Eight Mile Road. South of Adams Street, the trains would run in traffic along the sides of Woodward Avenue. To cover the estimated $500 million project cost, the Kresge Foundation provided $35 million in March 2009, the United States Department of Transportation (USDOT) provided $25 million in February 2010, and Detroit City Council approved the sale of $125 million bonds on April 11, 2011. The Federal Transit Administration (FTA) and the City of Detroit signed the environment impact statement on July 1, 2011. A record of decision was signed by the FTA on August 31, 2011 allowing the project to proceed. In December 2011, the federal government withdrew supporting the line in favor of a bus rapid transit system to serve the city and suburbs. After the damage the Recession inflicted on Detroit and industry, a determined group of corporate and philanthropic leaders kept alive the idea of a Woodward streetcar line. The private investors stated they would continue developing their 3.3-mile line under their nonprofit M-1 Rail Consortium. With a new Regional Transit Authority of Southeast Michigan created in 2012, the USDOT released the $25 million to M-1 Rail. The project received the final environmental clearance from the United States government on April 26, 2013, a construction contract was awarded to Stacy & Witbeck on July 31, 2013, and construction officially started on July 28, 2014. The USDOT provided an additional $12.2 million to complete the financing of the project.

On November 4, 2014, Czech-based Inekon was awarded a $30 million contract to build six streetcars. However, the deal collapsed and Brookville Equipment Corporation in Brookville, Pennsylvania, was chosen to build the six streetcars for $32 million, which included spare parts and support services. With about 60 percent of the line constructed without the overhead wire, the articulated three-section, 66.5-foot-long cars were equipped with 750-volt rechargeable lithium ion batteries. Brookville Equipment Corporation had provided streetcars for the Dallas Area Rapid Transit, which also used off-wire technology. The reason for not having overhead wire on much of the route was to minimize the impact on aesthetics of Woodward Avenue, and eliminate the labyrinth of wires that would have occurred at the Penske Technical Center. Construction of the $6.9 million 20,000-square-foot Penske Technical Center was underway on February 15, 2015 to be the M-1 Rail headquarters, operation center, and maintenance facility. On March 24, 1916, Quicken Loans announced that it purchased the naming rights for $5 million, and the line would be called the QLINE; however, M-1 Rail would still exist as the operating organization. The logo's stylized "Q" symbolizes the connectivity the line hopefully achieves. Since the highest number of the previous PCC streetcar was No. 286, the new cars were numbered 287–292. The QLINE, built at an estimated cost of $137 million, officially opened on May 12, 2017. Rides were initially to be free for the first weekend but were extended to one week, later extended to July 1, and still later to September 5, 2017.

In its first six months, from May to October 2017, the QLINE averaged 4,660 riders daily. From November 2017 to April 2018, the average daily ridership dropped to 2,700. The very severe winter may have been a factor. Another factor that may have affected ridership was that streetcars were not arriving on schedule according to published reports.

To succeed, QLINE must help the commuter to get to work or school plus connect with other transportation modes. It is important for QLINE to attract regular riders, and not just riders who will ride it once because it is new. The hope is that ridership will come from new residents, workers coming to the area because of its growing economic development, and tourists. This line is a demonstration of how the public and private partners can work together on a transportation project. It is one piece of a larger regional public transit system that will require additional partners, because it has a logical fit with the bus system and Amtrak. The QLINE does not ensure Detroit's success after losing 61.4 percent of its population between 1950 and 2010; however, it is a beginning point to hopefully bring a well-run regional transit system to a metropolitan area that has never been able to agree on a plan.

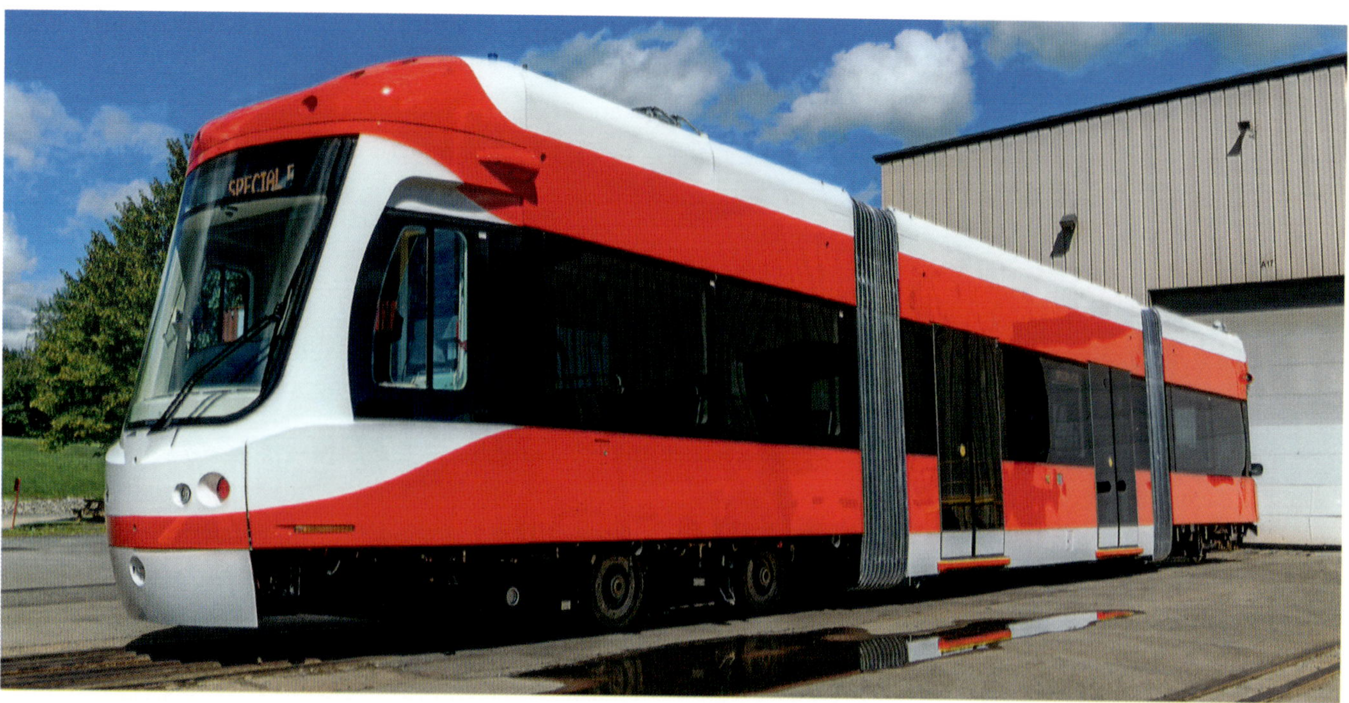

The first Brookville Equipment Corporation streetcar No. 287 for the new QLINE streetcar route in Detroit is shown at their Brookville, Pennsylvania, manufacturing facility in September 2016 in the red and white paint scheme ready to receive the final bottom skirting. The 66.5-foot-long by 8.67-foot-wide Liberty streetcar can comfortably transport 125 passengers and was designed with a battery onboard energy storage system to permit operation without requiring an overhead wire contact system for more than 60 percent of the line. Each of the six streetcars received green vinyl graphics wrap prior to entering service in May 2017. The red/white color is the actual paint finish of each QLINE streetcar. (*Chris Lasher photograph—Brookville Equipment Corporation collection*)

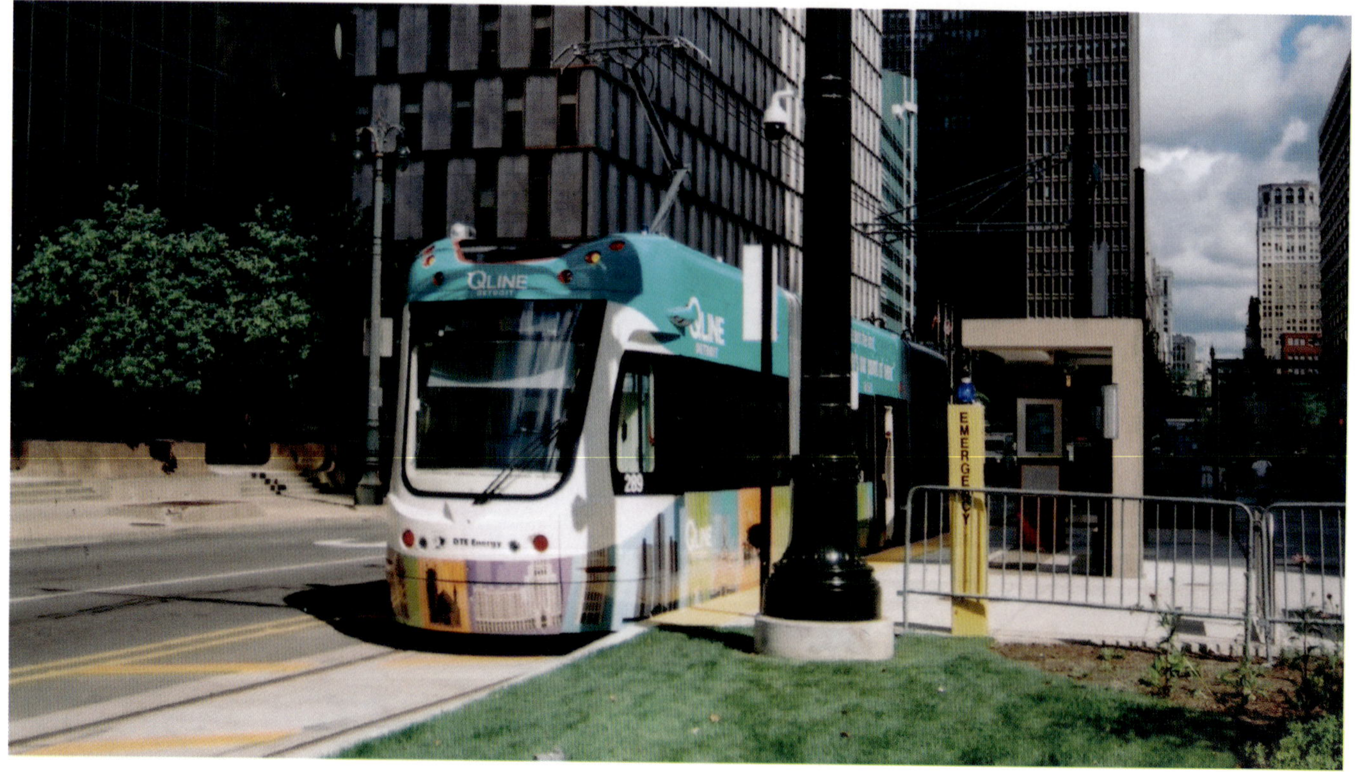

On June 25, 2017, QLINE streetcar No. 289 is at the Congress Street Station. Sixty one years, one month, and four days later, after the final parade of streetcars on the Woodward line on April 8, 1956, streetcars returned to Detroit with the opening of the QLINE on May 12, 2017. The hope is that the QLINE stimulates Detroit's economic activity. (*Kenneth C. Springirth photograph*)

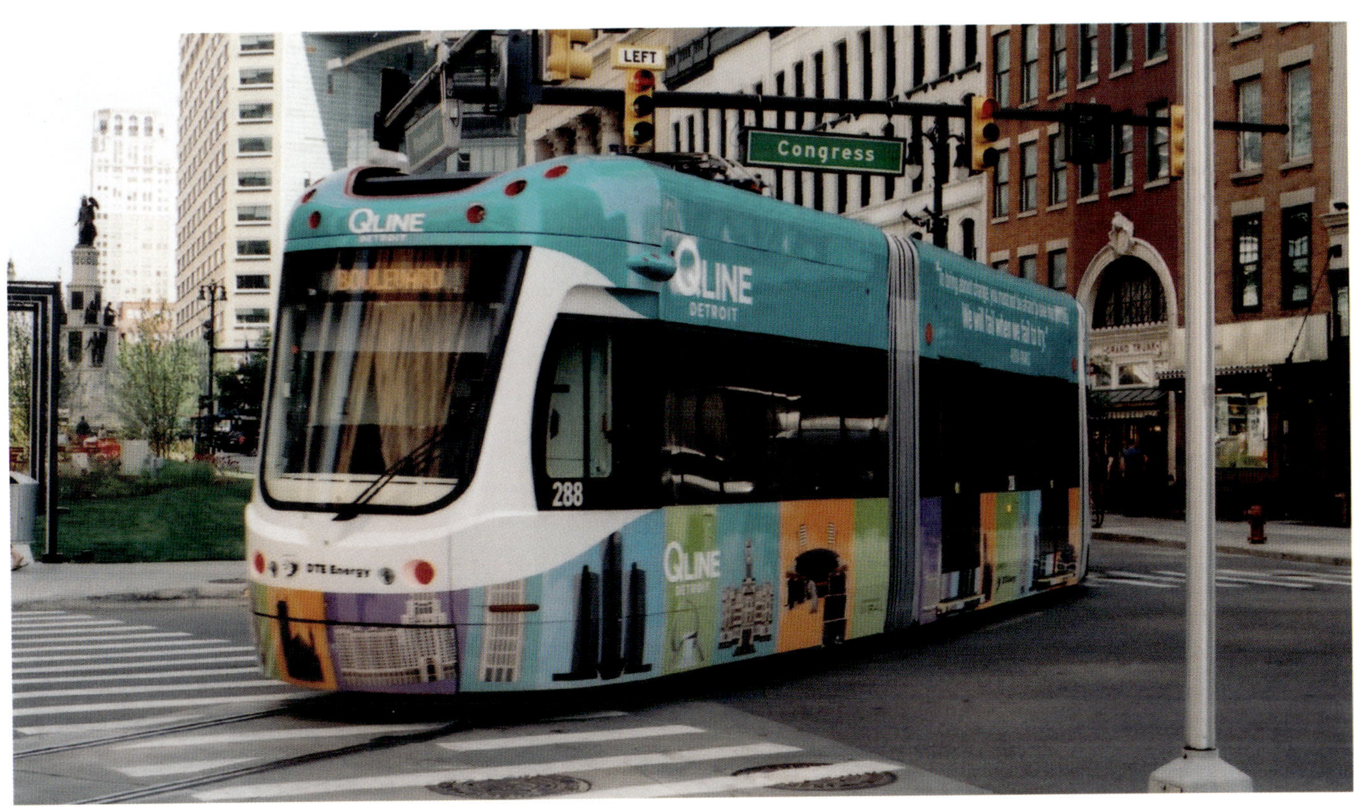

Woodward Avenue and Congress Street is the location of QLINE streetcar No. 288 on June 27, 2017. The six new cars are numbered 287–292 to pick up the next number from the last PCC car number of the previous streetcar system, which was 286. Empty car weight is 83,000 pounds. (*Kenneth C. Springirth photograph*)

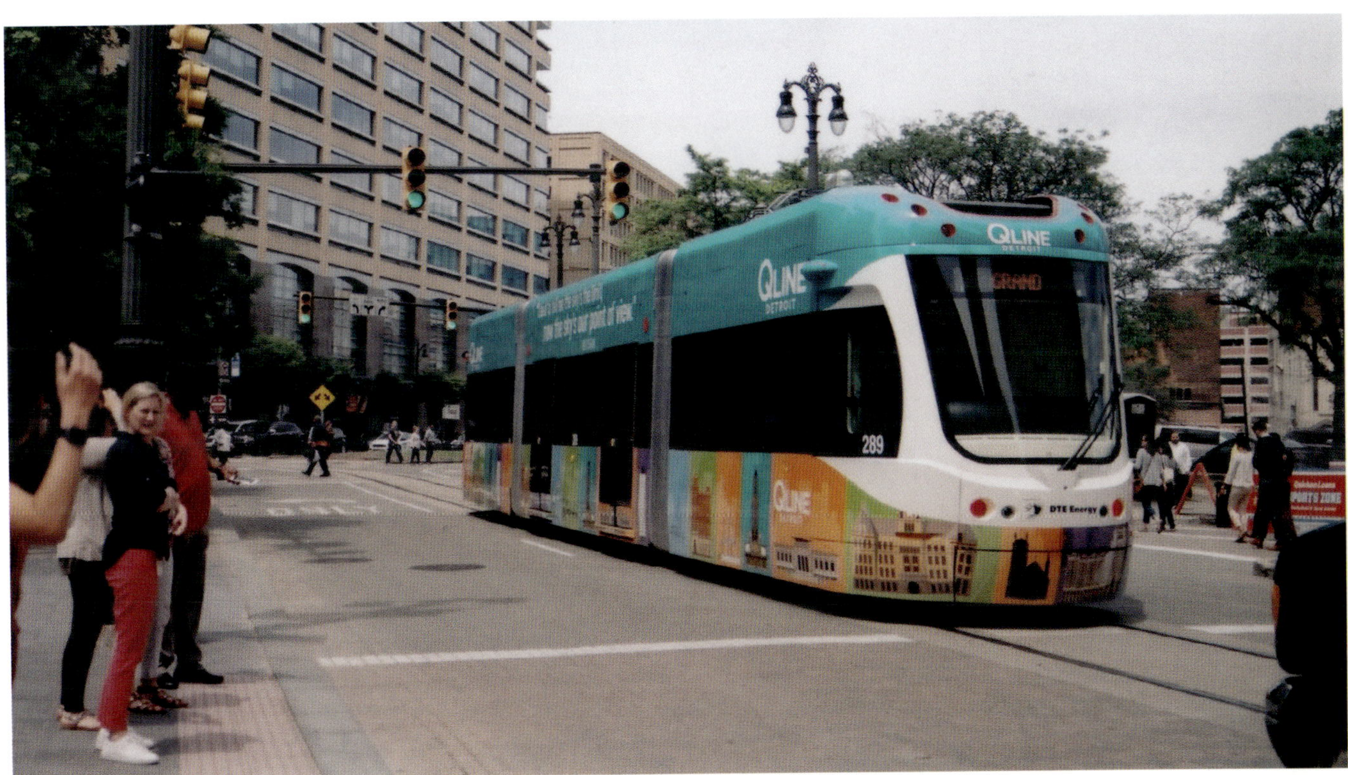

On June 27, 2017, QLINE streetcar No. 289 is passing through Campus Martius (from the Latin for Field of Mars) Park located at the intersection of Woodward and Michigan Avenues. Campus Martius Park is the point of origin of Detroit's coordinate system. For example, seven miles from this point is Seven Mile Road. (*Kenneth C. Springirth photograph*)

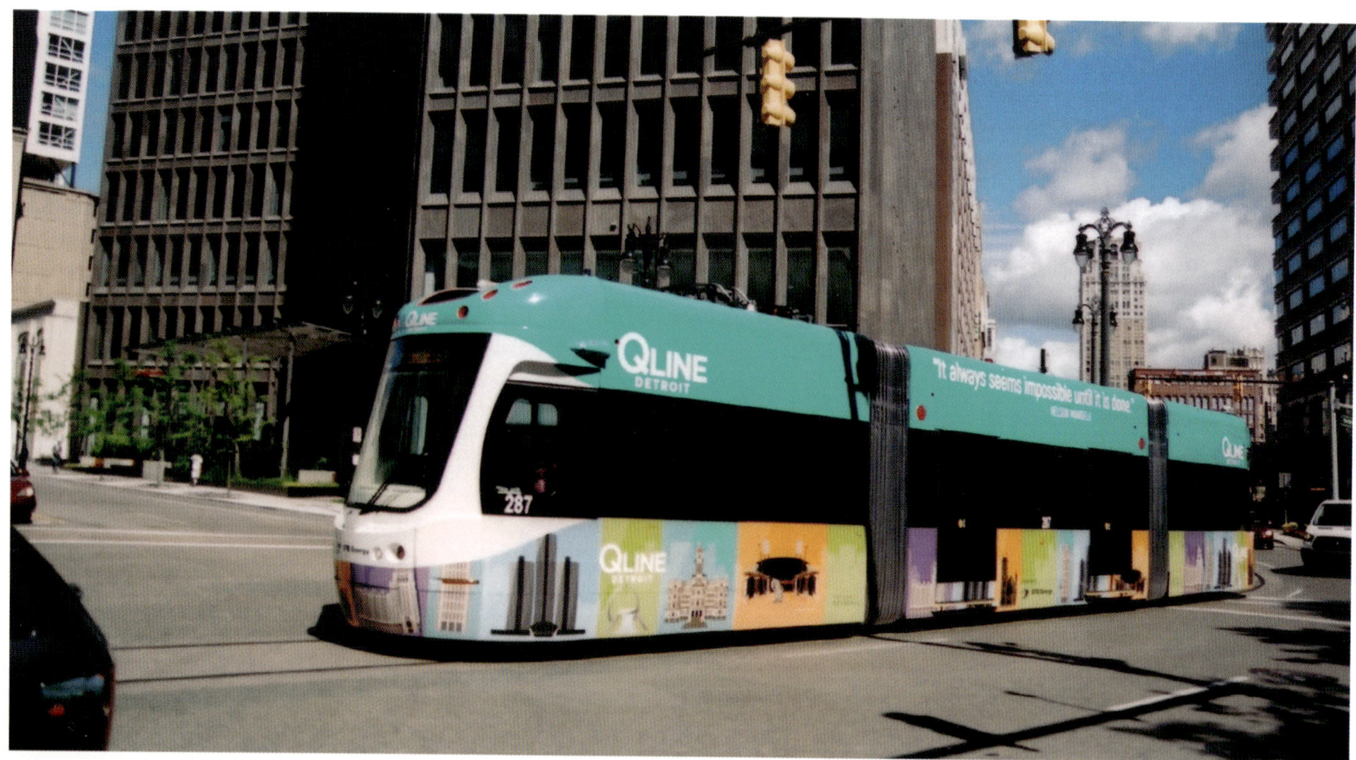

Woodward Avenue and Michigan Avenue is the location of QLINE streetcar No. 287 on a sunny June 28, 2017. Connecting Grand Boulevard with Congress Street in downtown Detroit, the QLINE has station stops at Baltimore Street, Amsterdam Street, Ferry Street, Warren Avenue, Canfield Street, Martin Luther King Boulevard (southbound)/Mack Avenue (northbound), Sproat Street (southbound)/Adelaide Street (northbound), Montcalm Street, Grand Circus, and Campus Martius. (*Kenneth C. Springirth photograph*)

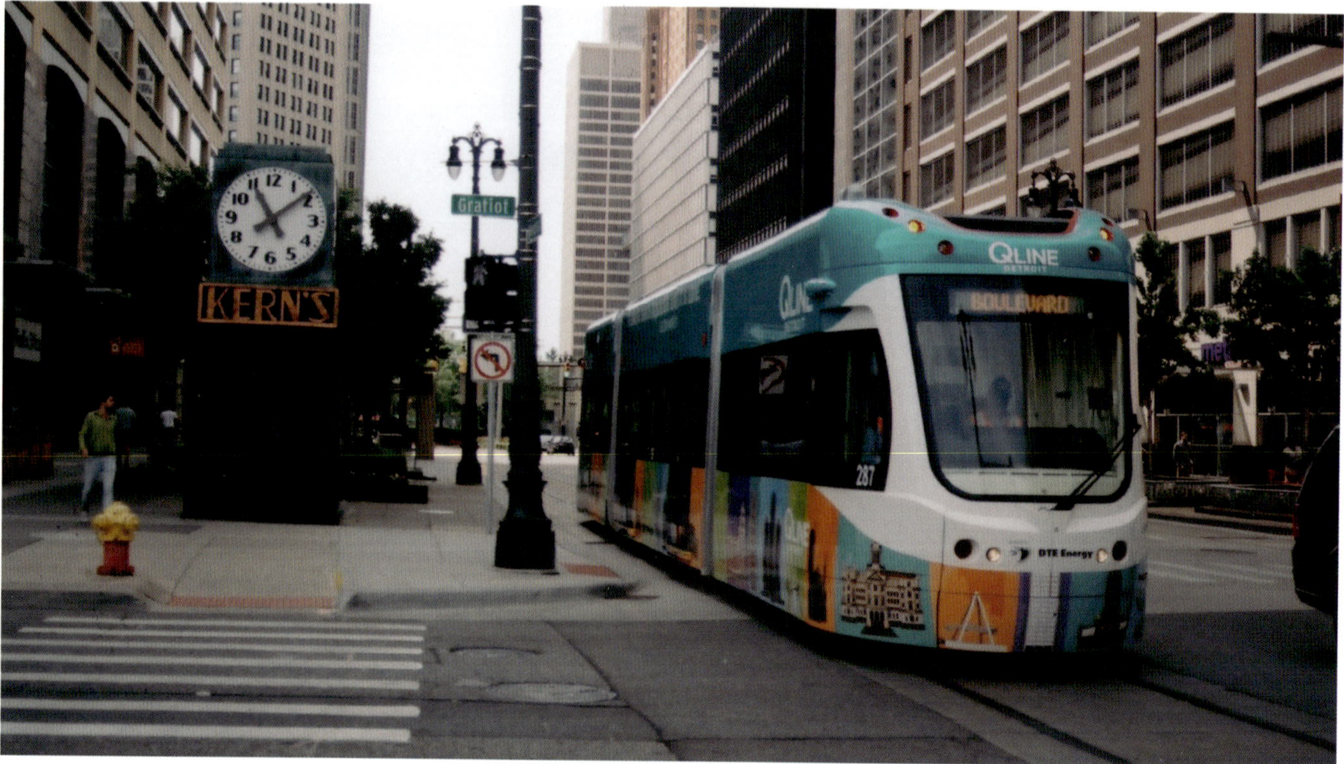

On June 28, 2017, QLINE streetcar No. 287 is northbound on Woodward Avenue, crossing Gratiot Avenue. Running on the standard 56.5-inch track gauge, each car is powered by four 99-KW AC traction motors for a speed of up to 35 mph for the alignment of this line, but it is not necessarily the top speed of the car. An empty car weighs 83,000 pounds. (*Kenneth C. Springirth photograph*)

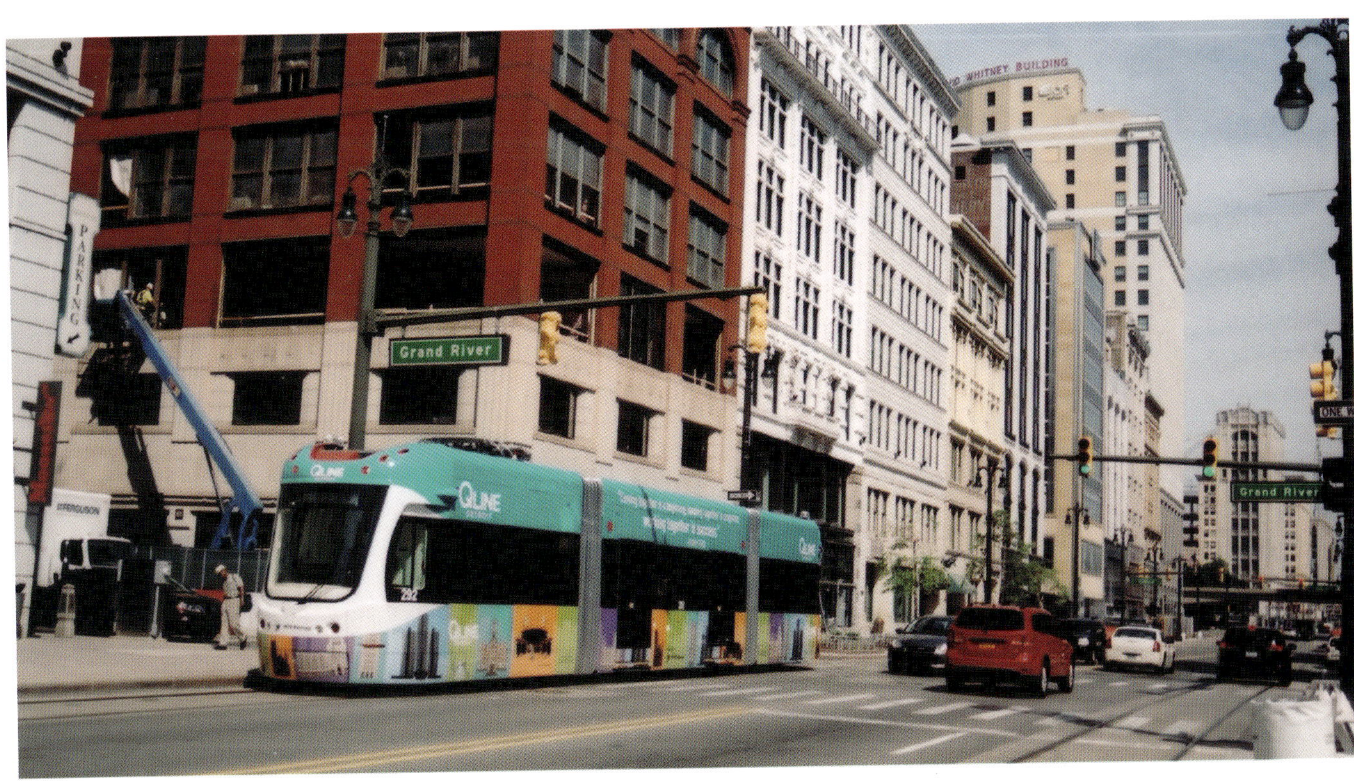

Southbound QLINE streetcar No. 292 is on Woodward Avenue at Grand River Avenue in downtown Detroit on June 27, 2017. M-1 Rail, operator of the QLINE, on June 30, 2016, entered into a five-year, $15.5 million contract with Transdev North America, which includes hiring staff, training and managing streetcar operators, service operation, dispatch, vehicle and track maintenance, and fare enforcement. (*Kenneth C. Springirth photograph*)

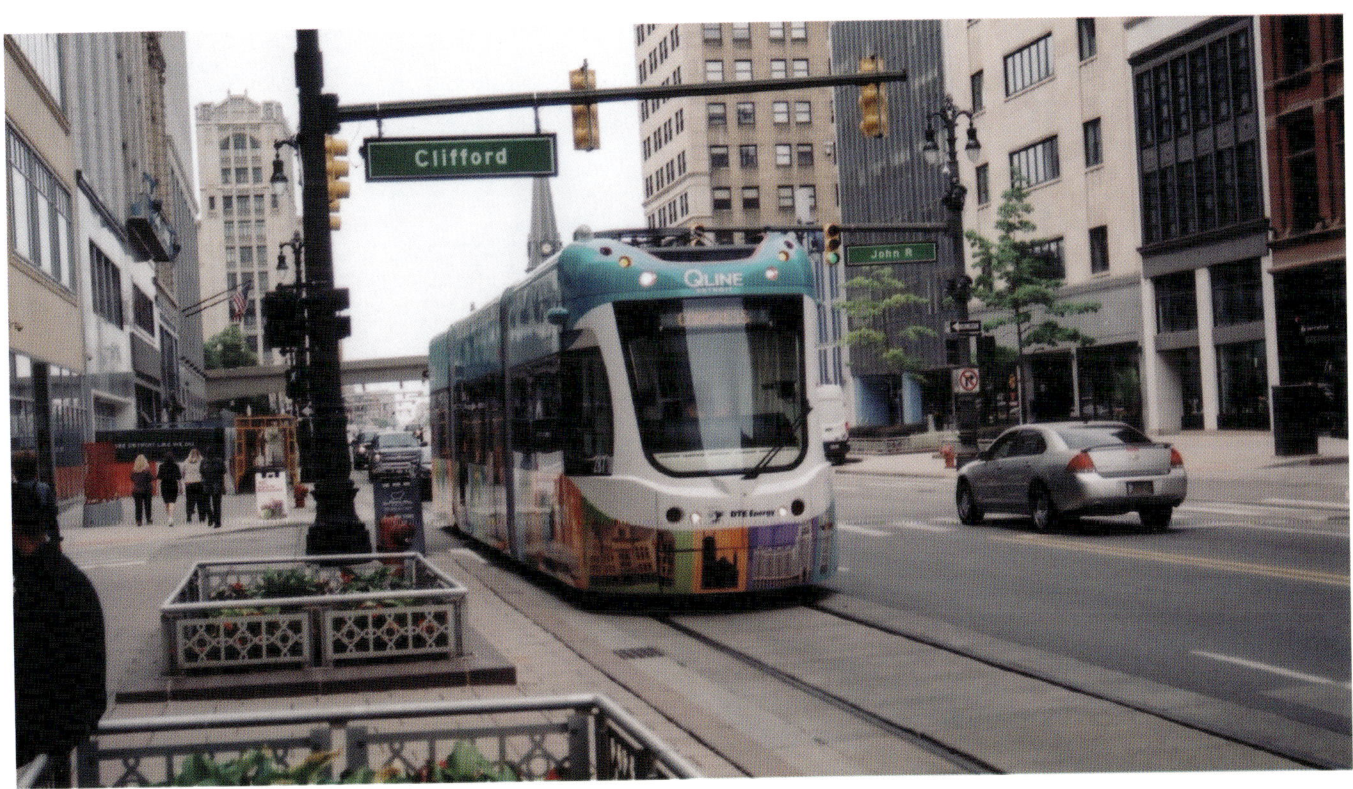

On June 27, 2017, southbound QLINE streetcar No. 287 is on Woodward Avenue at Clifford Street. (*Kenneth C. Springirth photograph*)

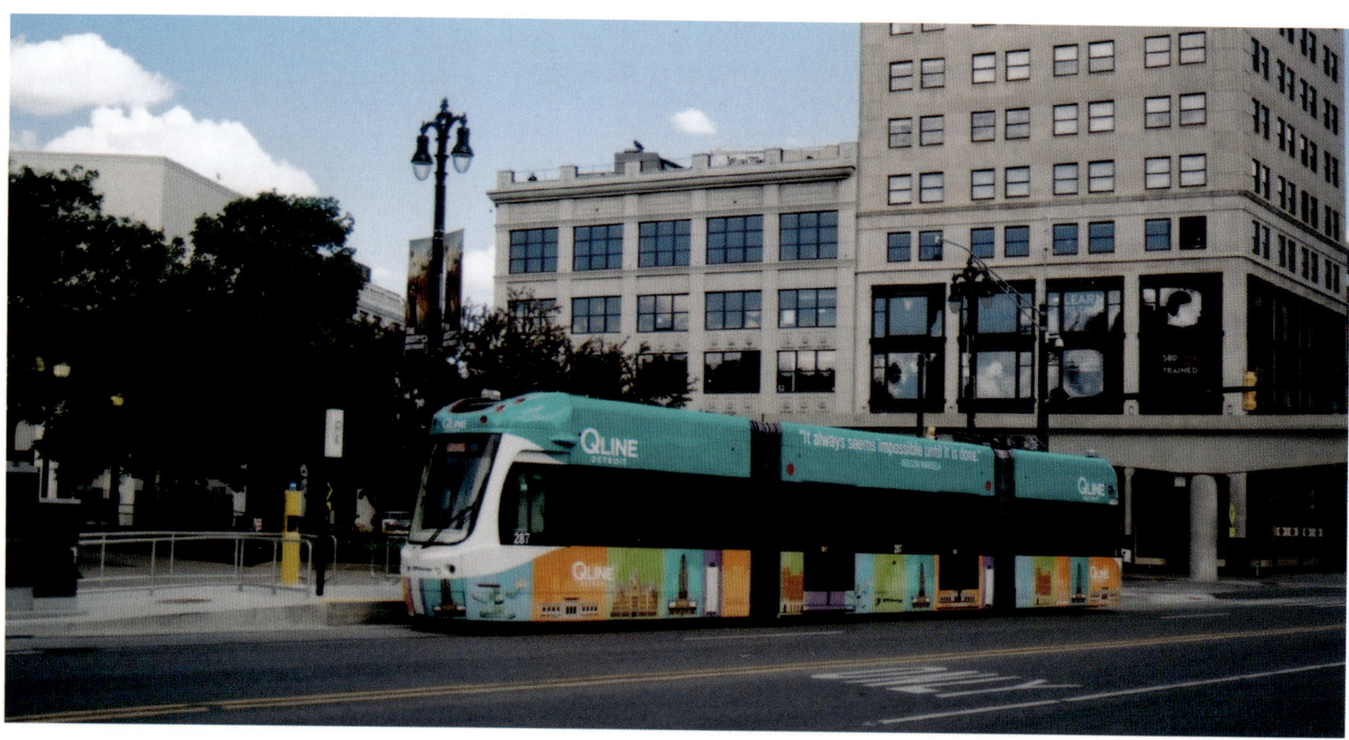

Northbound QLINE streetcar No. 287 is on Woodward Avenue at Grand Circus Station on June 28, 2017. Behind the streetcar is the Detroit People Mover and on the right side of the picture is the David Broderick Tower (a thirty-four-story residential skyscraper completed in 1928 and renovated in 2012) located on the southeast corner of Woodward Avenue and Witherell Street. Not shown in the picture is the David Whitney Building, which is on the southwest corner of Woodward Avenue and Witherell Street and has the People Mover Grand Circus Station providing a transfer point with the QLINE streetcar. (*Kenneth C. Springirth photograph*)

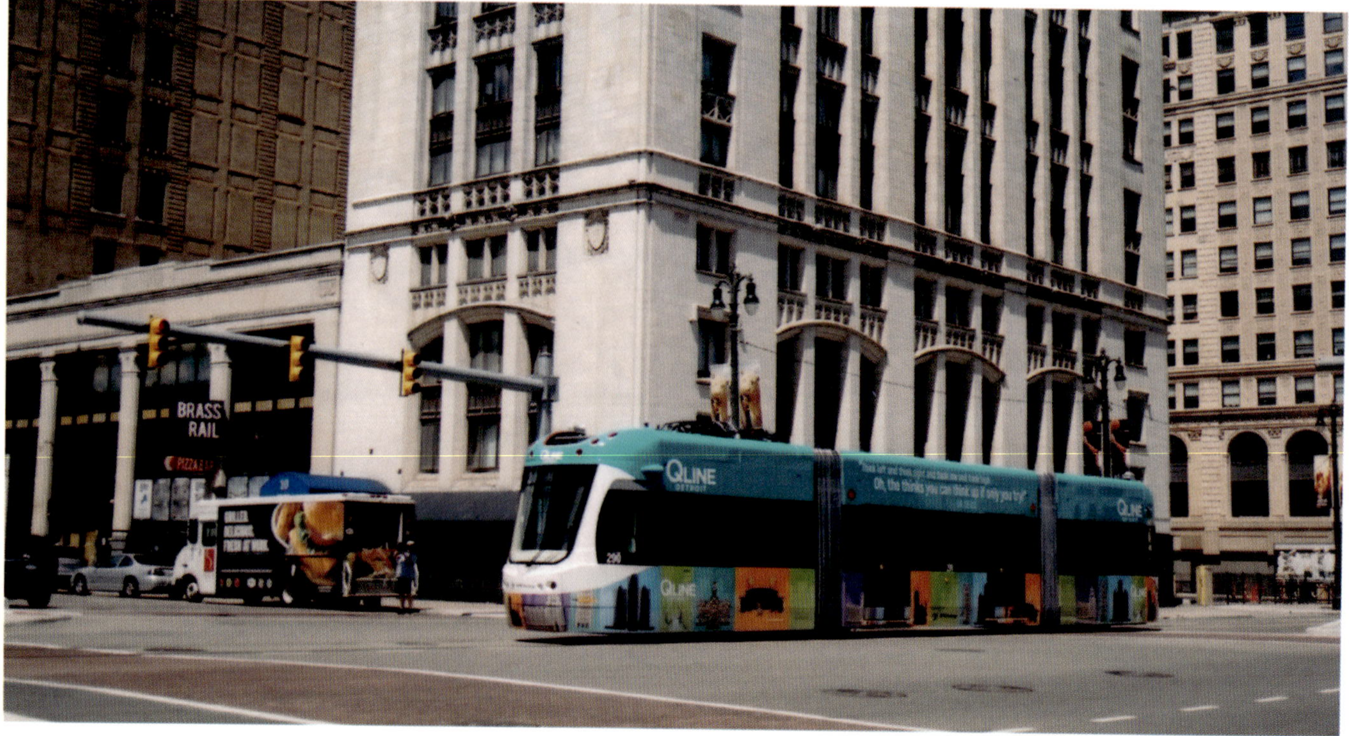

On June 26, 2017, southbound QLINE streetcar No. 290 is on Woodward Avenue, crossing Adams Street and passing by the fourteen-story Fyfe building (with sixty-five residential units and some street level retail) at the northwest corner of Woodward Avenue and Adams Street. The Gothic Revival-style building, characterized by arched windows, was completed in 1919 and named for Richard H. Fyfe, a Detroit merchant who had a successful retail shoe business. (*Kenneth C. Springirth photograph*)

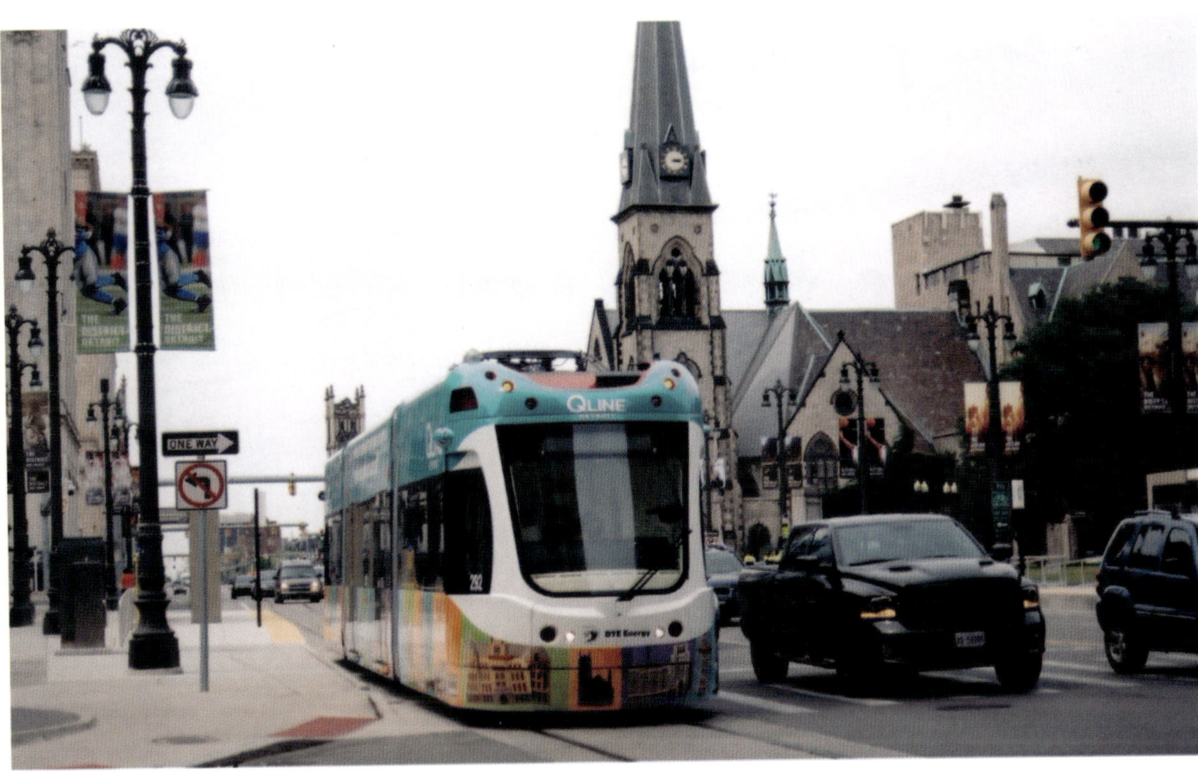

Southbound QLINE streetcar No. 292 is on Woodward Avenue, having passed the light gray rock-faced Central United Methodist Church. Built in 1866, the church's Tudor Revival style with its steeply pitched roof and Gothic Revival-style arched windows placed it in the Michigan State Historic Site on June 6, 1977 and the National Register of historic Places on August 3, 1982. (*Kenneth C. Springirth photograph*)

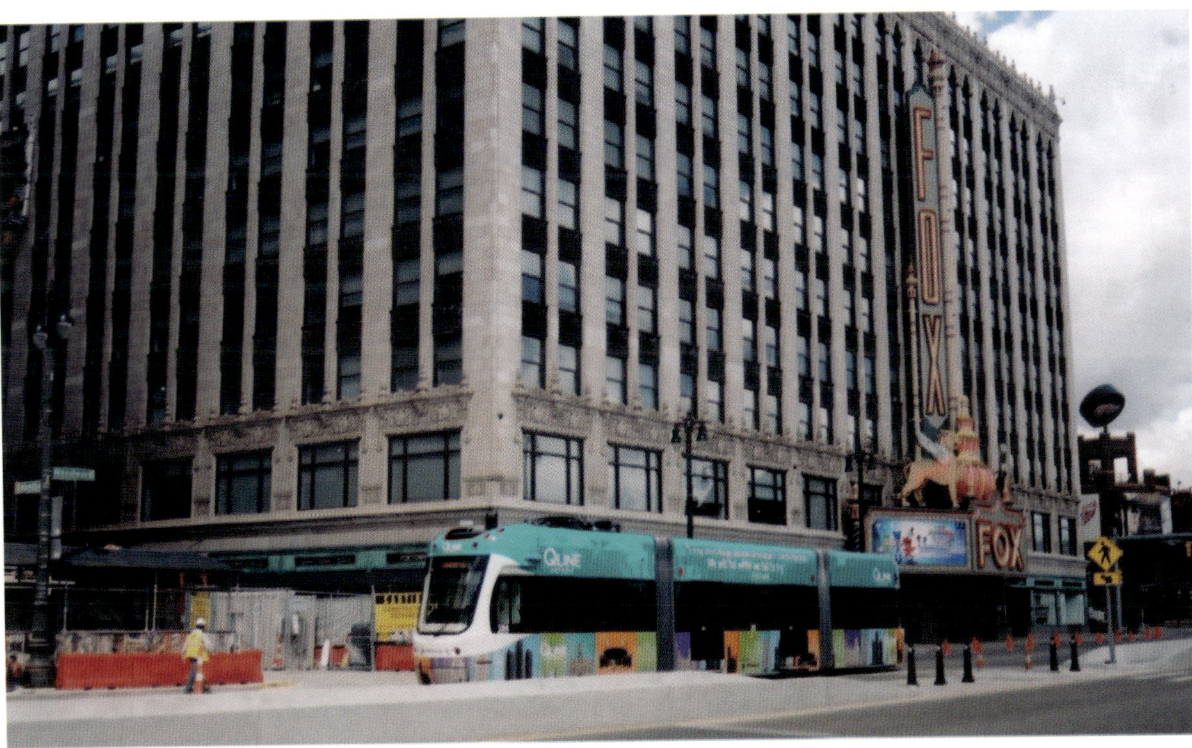

On June 28, 2017, QLINE streetcar No. 288 is gliding on Woodward Avenue at Columbia Street, past the Fox Theatre. Seating over 5,000, the Fox Theatre, Detroit's largest, opened on September 21, 1928. By the 1960s, suburban development threatened its survival. It was listed on the National Register of Historic Places on February 14, 1985. Under new ownership, the Fox Theatre was renovated in 1988, leading the way to redeveloping downtown Detroit. (*Kenneth C. Springirth photograph*)

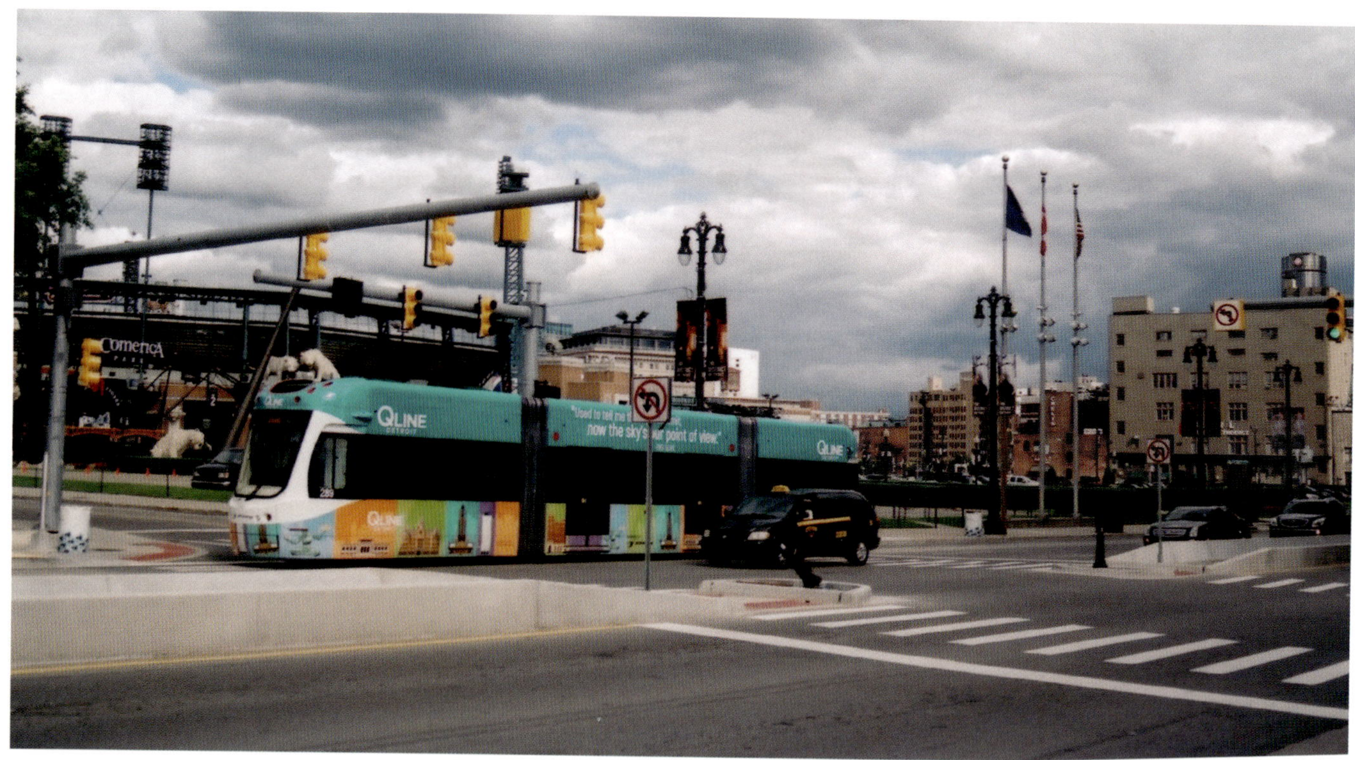

Northbound QLINE streetcar No. 289 is on Woodward Avenue at Montcalm Street on June 26, 2017. Montcalm QLINE station serves the 41,299 seat Comerica Park baseball stadium (named for Comerica Bank) in the background. Opening in 2000 to replace Tiger stadium, this is the home of the Detroit Tigers Major League Baseball Team. The People Mover Grand Circus Park station is a short three-block walk from the stadium. (*Kenneth C. Springirth photograph*)

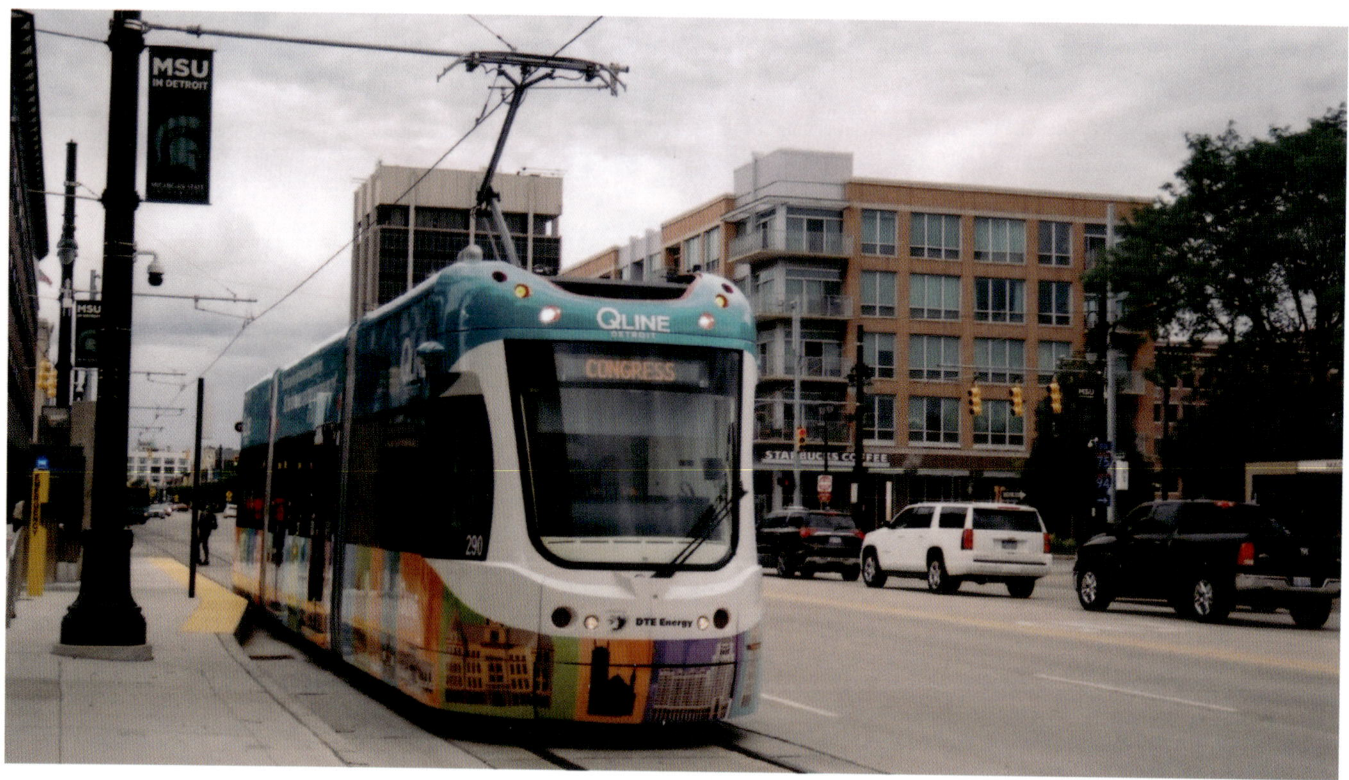

On Woodward Avenue, north of Mack Avenue, QLINE streetcar No. 290 is heading south to downtown Detroit on June 25, 2017. The Mack Avenue station is handy to reach numerous places, including Orchestra Hall (home of the Detroit Symphony Orchestra), Whole Foods Market, Garden Theatre, U of M Detroit Center, Detroit Medical Center, and the Bonstelle Theatre. (*Kenneth C. Springirth photograph*)

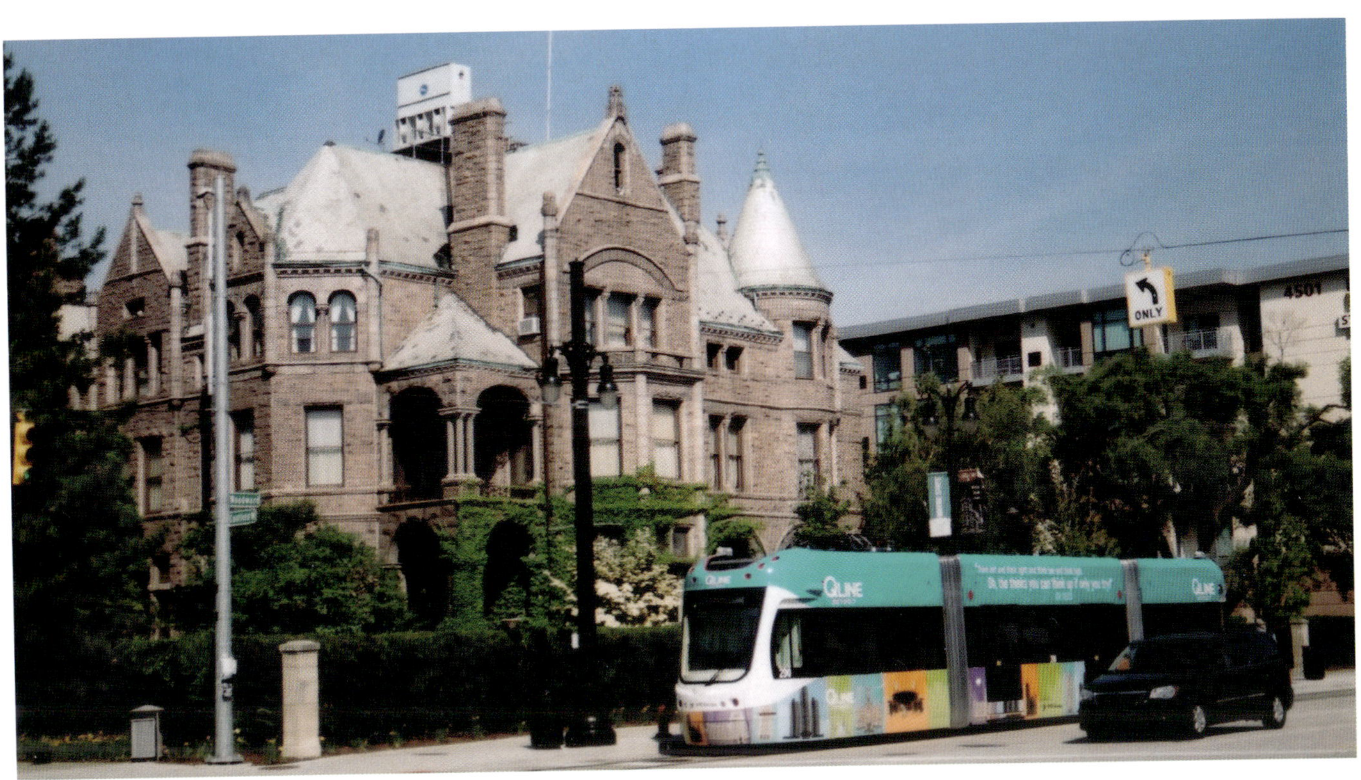

Woodward Avenue at Canfield Street is the location of QLINE streetcar No. 290, passing by the David Whitney House on June 26, 2017. Designed by architect Gordon W. Lloyd in the Romanesque Revival style, characterized by steeply pitched roofs, and completed in 1894, this was the home of David Whitney Jr., one of Michigan's wealthiest residents. After changing hands several times, the forty-two-room (plus ten bathrooms) home became the Upscale Whitney Restaurant in 1986. (*Kenneth C. Springirth photograph*)

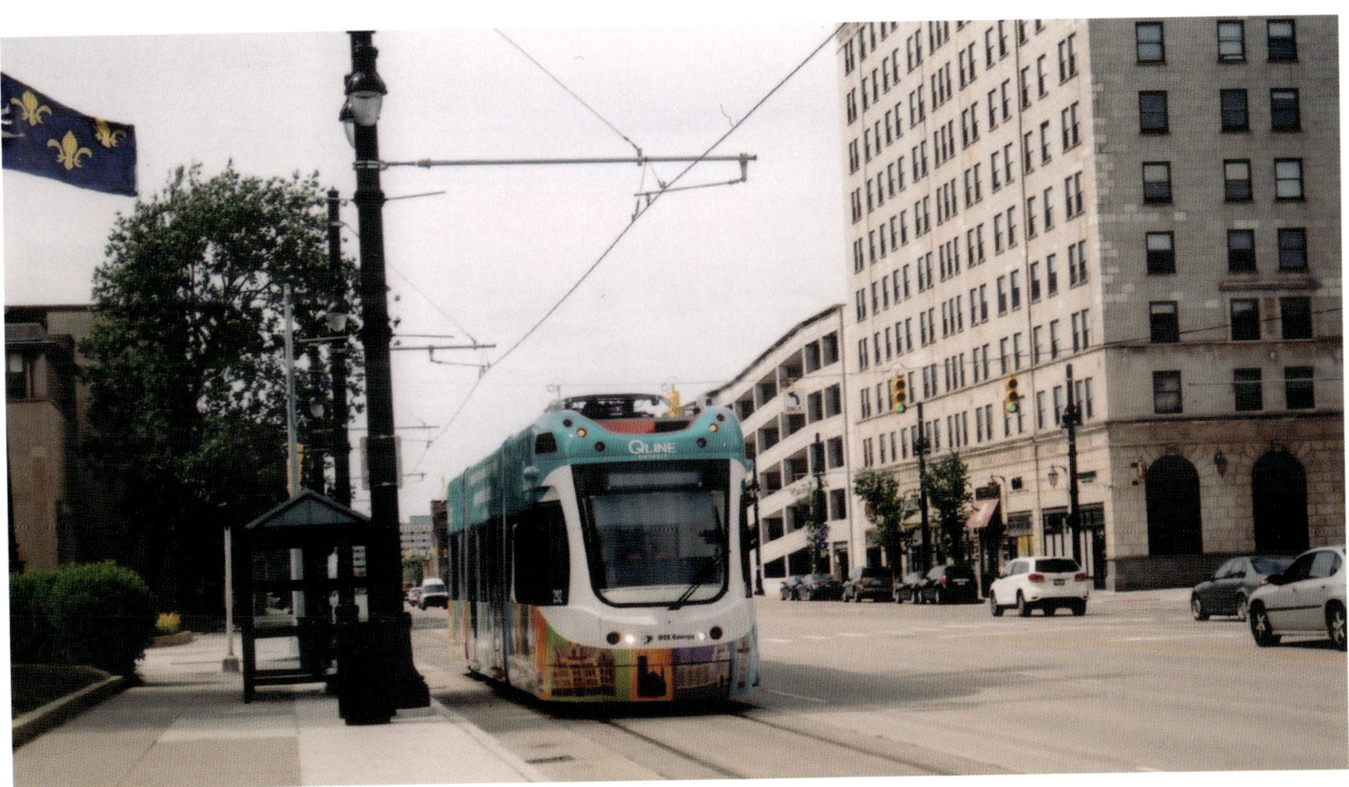

On June 26, 2017, QLINE streetcar No. 292 is on Woodward Avenue at Kirby Street with the high rise Park Shelton Condominiums shown across the street on the right-hand side of the picture. This originally was the Wardell Hotel named for Fred Wardell, the founder of the Eureka Company, and was later converted into luxury condominiums. (*Kenneth C. Springirth photograph*)

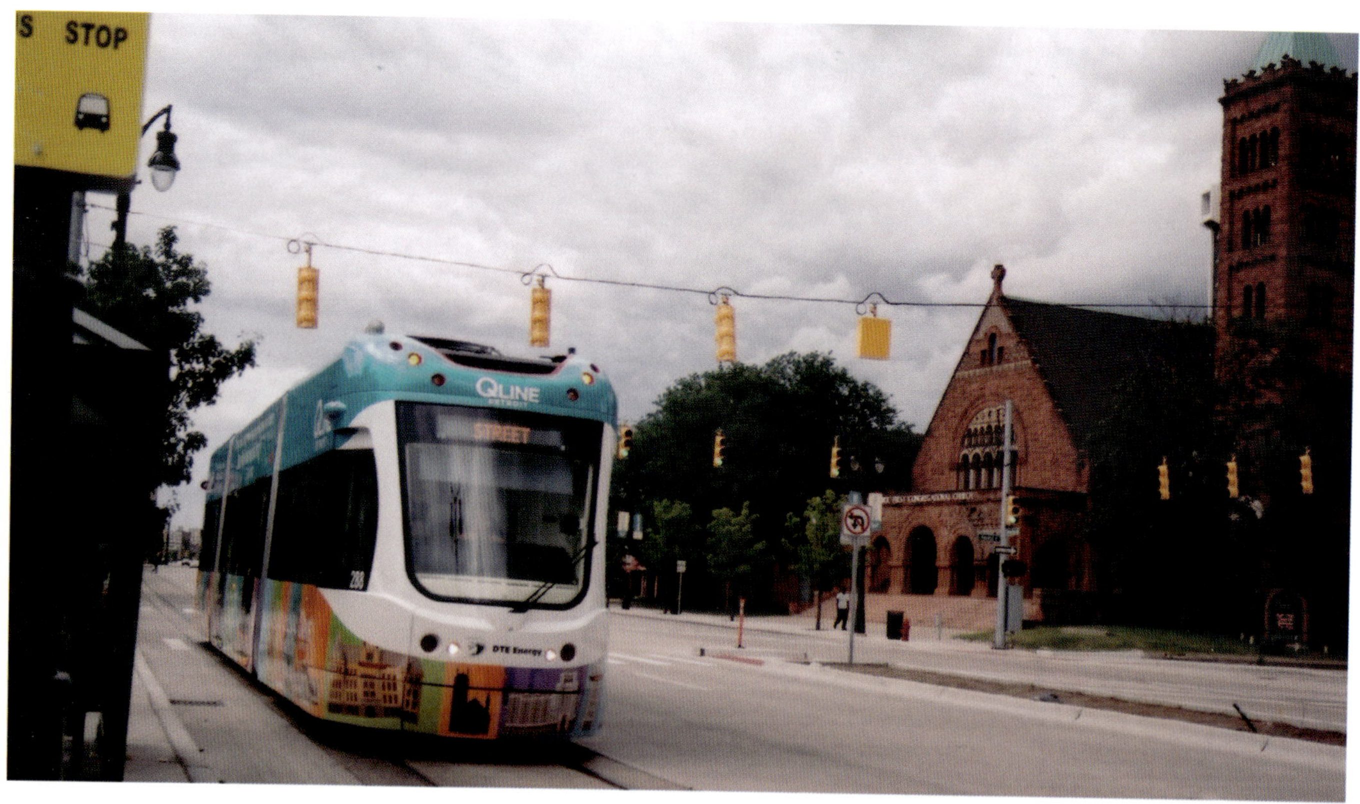

QLINE streetcar No. 288 is on Woodward Avenue at Forest Avenue, passing by the First Congregational Church on June 25, 2017. The red limestone church with a bell tower was built in 1891 in a Romanesque Revival style. It was designated a Michigan State Historic site on July 26,1979 and was listed on the National Register of Historic Places on June 1, 1979. (*Kenneth C. Springirth photograph*)

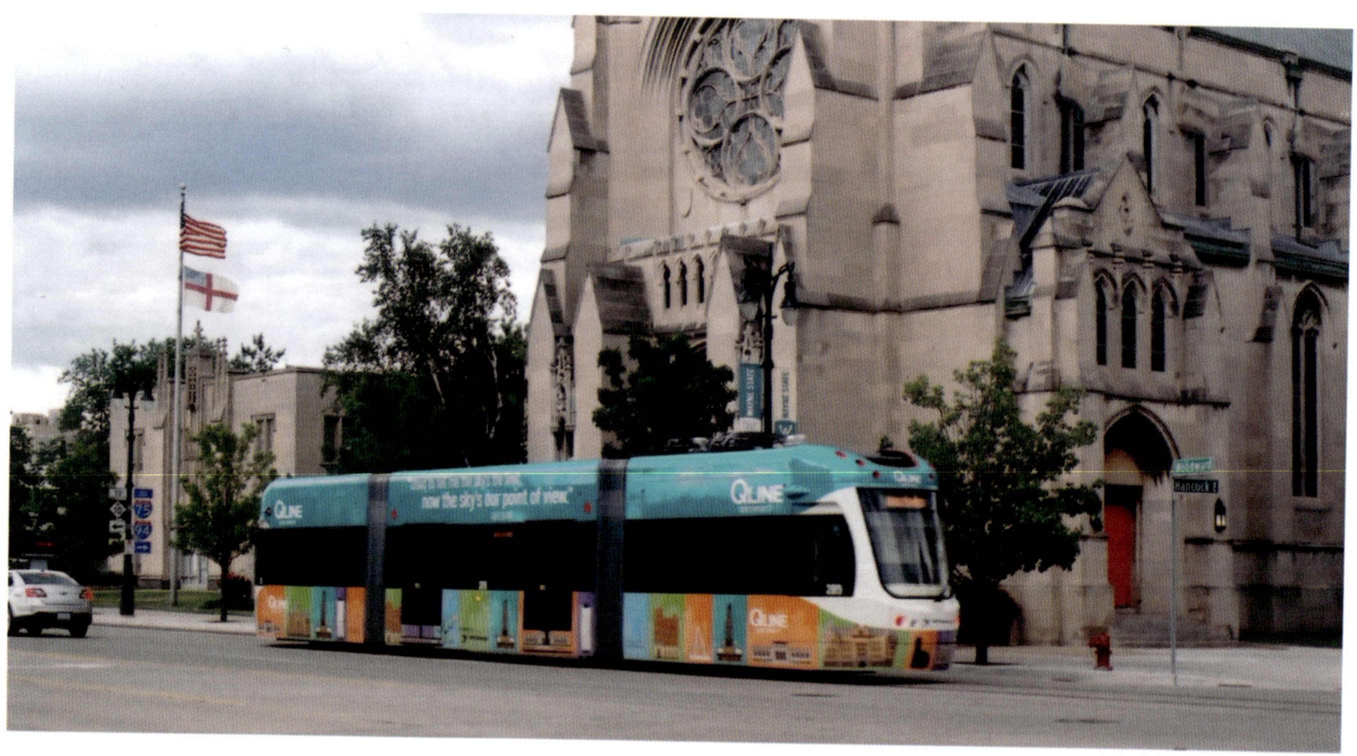

On June 25, 2017, QLINE streetcar No. 289 is on Woodward Avenue at Hancock Street, gliding by the Cathedral of St. Paul. Designed by architect Ralph A. Cram, the Late Gothic Revival-style cathedral (characterized by pointed arches and a steeply pitched roof) was added to the National Register of Historic Places on August 3, 1982. (*Kenneth C. Springirth photograph*)

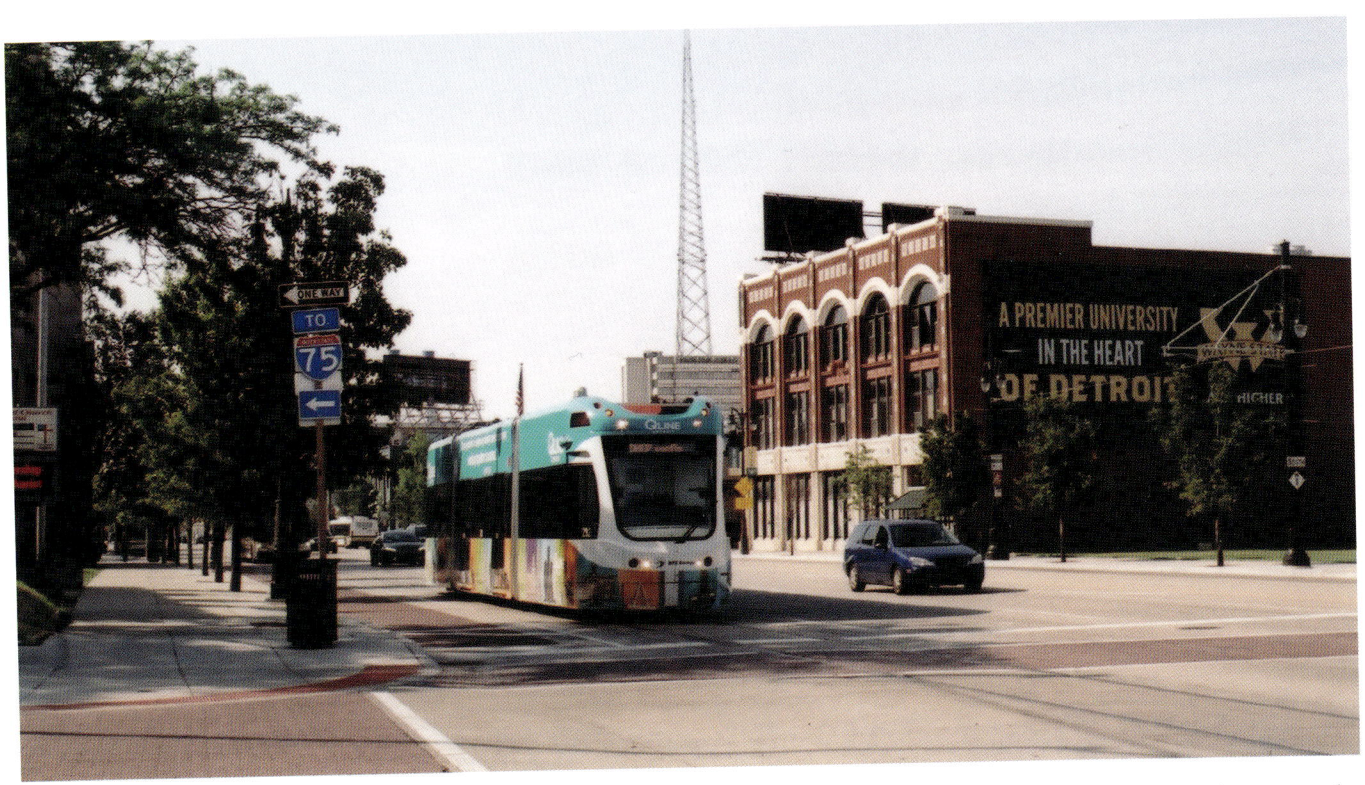

Northbound QLINE streetcar No. 292 is on Woodward Avenue at Warren Avenue with the Leonard N. Simon building across the street to the right of the streetcar. Designed by architect Albert Kahn and completed in 1915, the building originally housed Goodrich Tire Service. Today, the building is part of Wayne State University, housing the Wayne State University Press plus the Stress and Health Lab. In 1994, the building was named the Leonard N. Simons Building in honor of the help Simons provided to the Wayne State University Press. (*Kenneth C. Springirth photograph*)

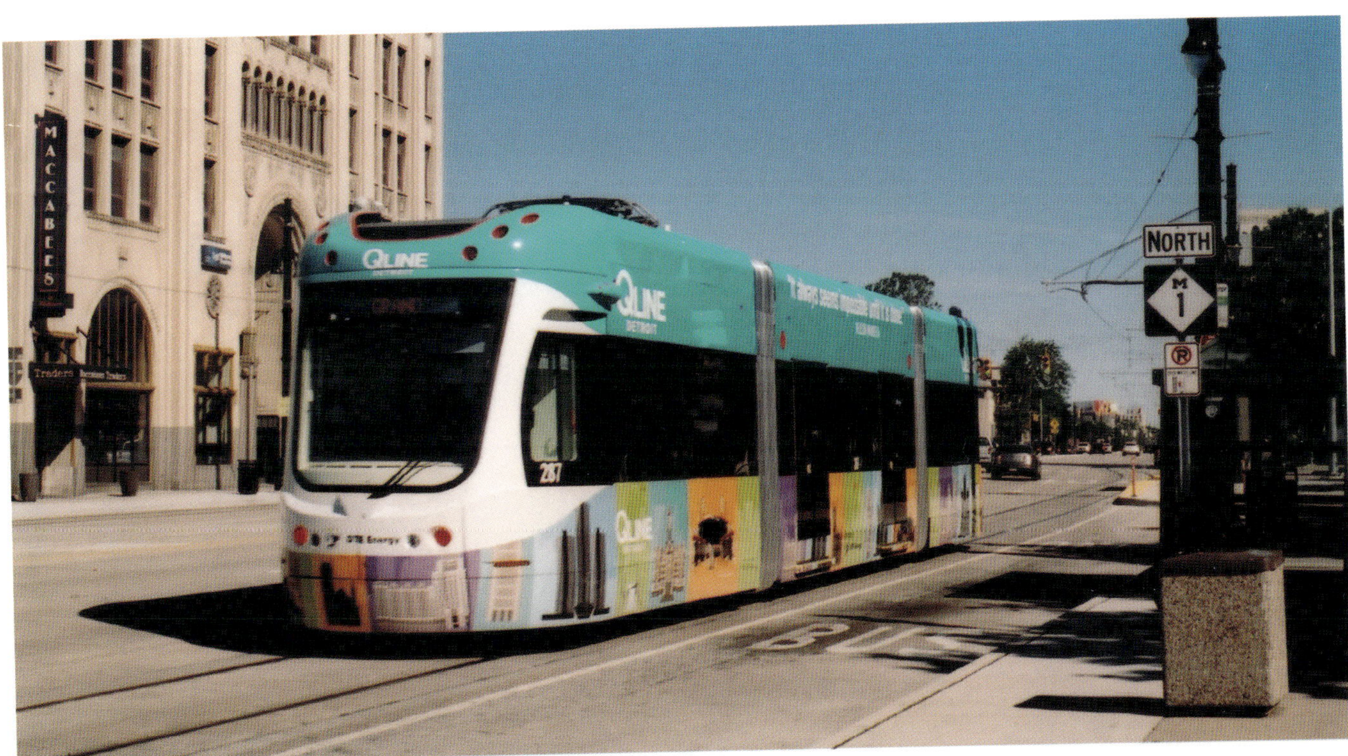

On June 26, 2018, northbound QLINE streetcar No. 287 is passing the fifteen-story limestone-faced Maccabees Building housing the Wayne State University on Woodward Avenue at Warren Avenue. Completed in 1927 for the fraternal organization Knights of the Maccabees, which became the Royal Maccabees Insurance Company, the building served the Detroit Public School from 1960 to 1992. In 2002, Wayne State University purchased the building to house its administrative offices and academic department offices. (*Kenneth C. Springirth photograph*)

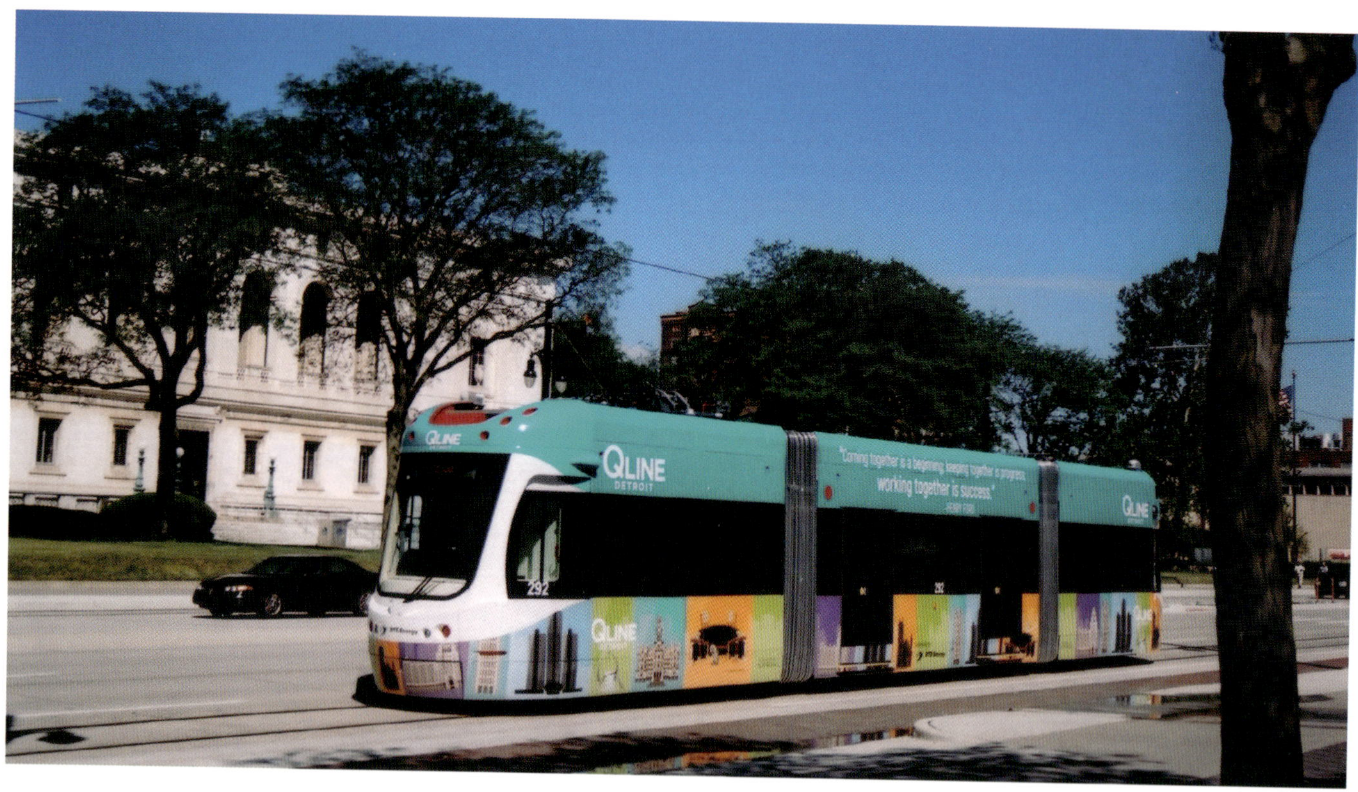

With the Detroit Public Library in the background, QLINE streetcar No. 292 is northbound on Woodward Avenue at Kirby Street on June 26, 2018. Designed by architect Cass Gilbert, the library was constructed with Vermont marble and Serpentine Italian marble trim in an Italian Renaissance style, and it opened on March 21, 1921. (*Kenneth C. Springirth photograph*)

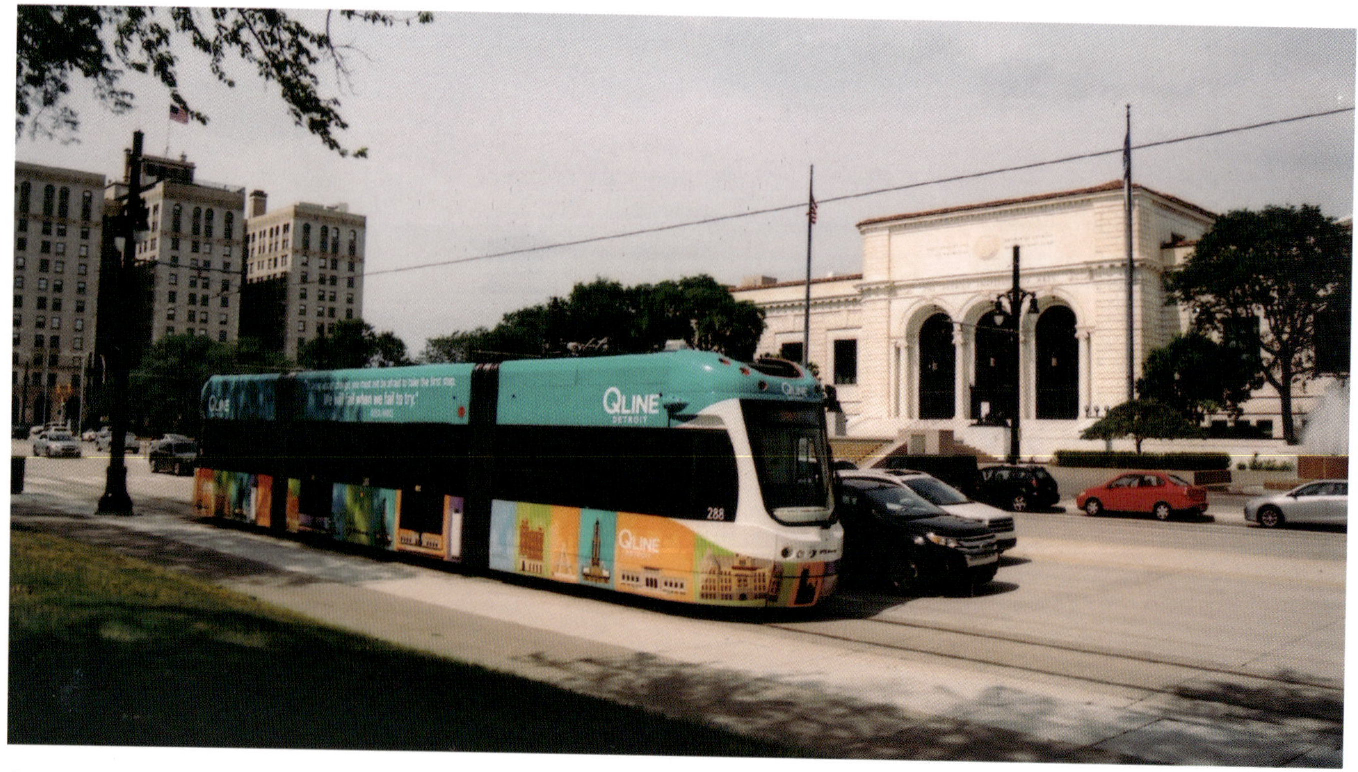

On June 26, 2017, southbound QLINE streetcar no. 288 is passing the white marble exterior material Detroit Institute of Arts on Woodward Avenue between Kirby Street and Putnam Street in Detroit's Cultural Center Historic District. Designed by architect Paul Philippe Cret in a Beaux-Arts, Italian Renaissance style, the building was dedicated on October 7, 1927. (*Kenneth C. Springirth photograph*)

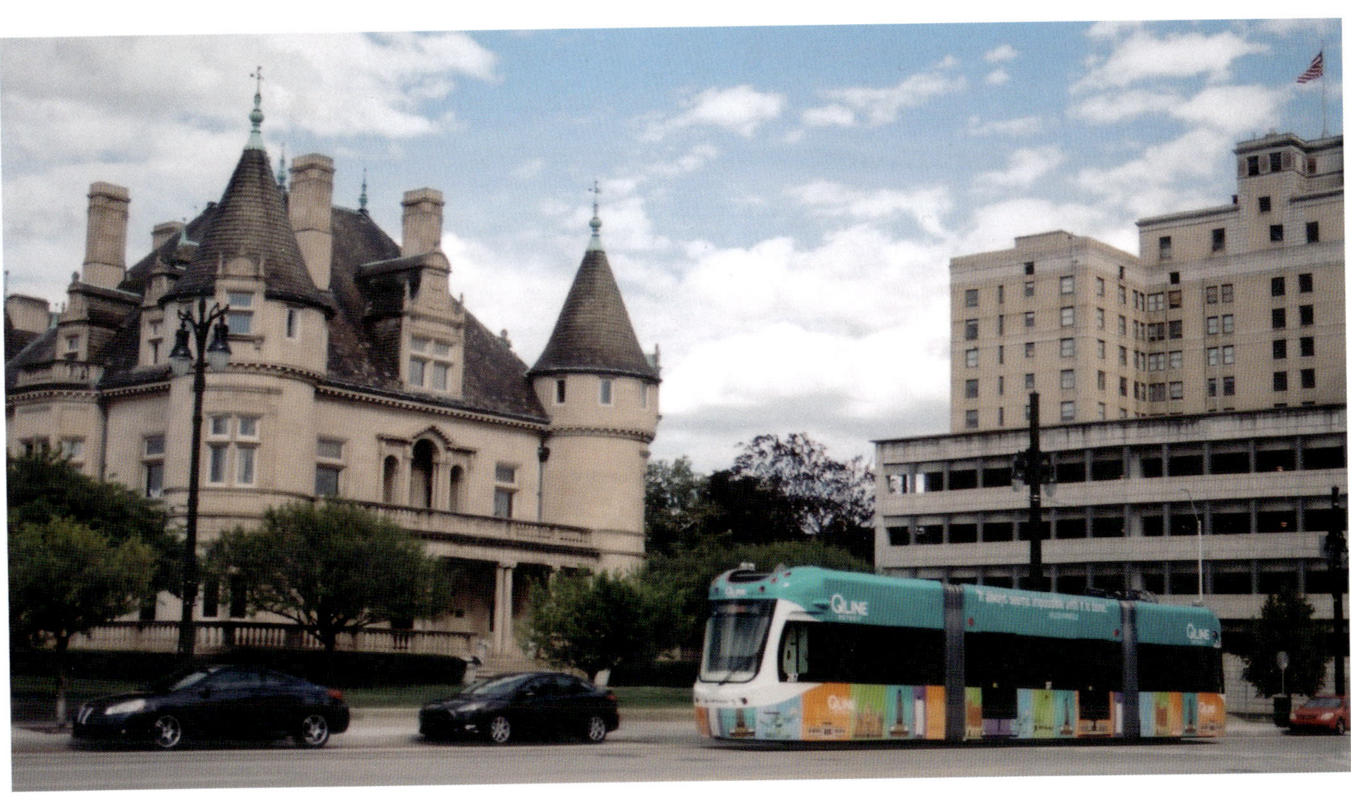

Southbound QLINE streetcar No. 287 is on Woodward Avenue at Ferry Street passing the historic Colonel Frank J. Hecker House. Completed in 1892, this Chateauesque-style home has large corner turrets and a steep hip roof. Later owners used the home for music instruction/sales purposes, a law office, and Royal Dutch Consulate in Detroit. In September 2014, it was purchased by Wayne State University and is now the Tierney Alumni House for the Wayne State University Alumni Association and Office of Alumni Affairs. (*Kenneth C. Springirth photograph*)

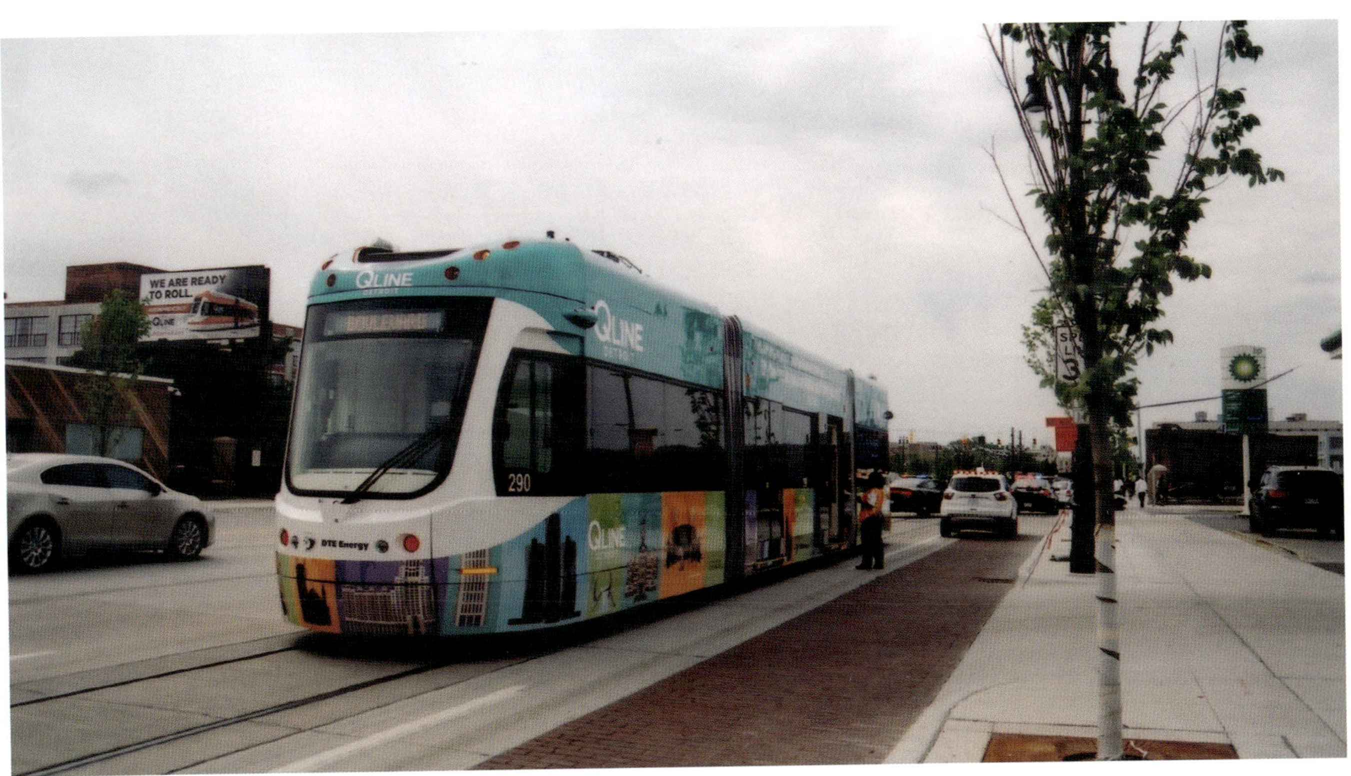

On June 28, 2017, northbound QLINE streetcar No. 290 is on Woodward Avenue at Harper Avenue waiting for police to clear two automobiles damaged ahead in a collision. Across the street is a billboard showing a QLINE streetcar with the words, "WE ARE READY TO ROLL." (*Kenneth C. Springirth photograph*)

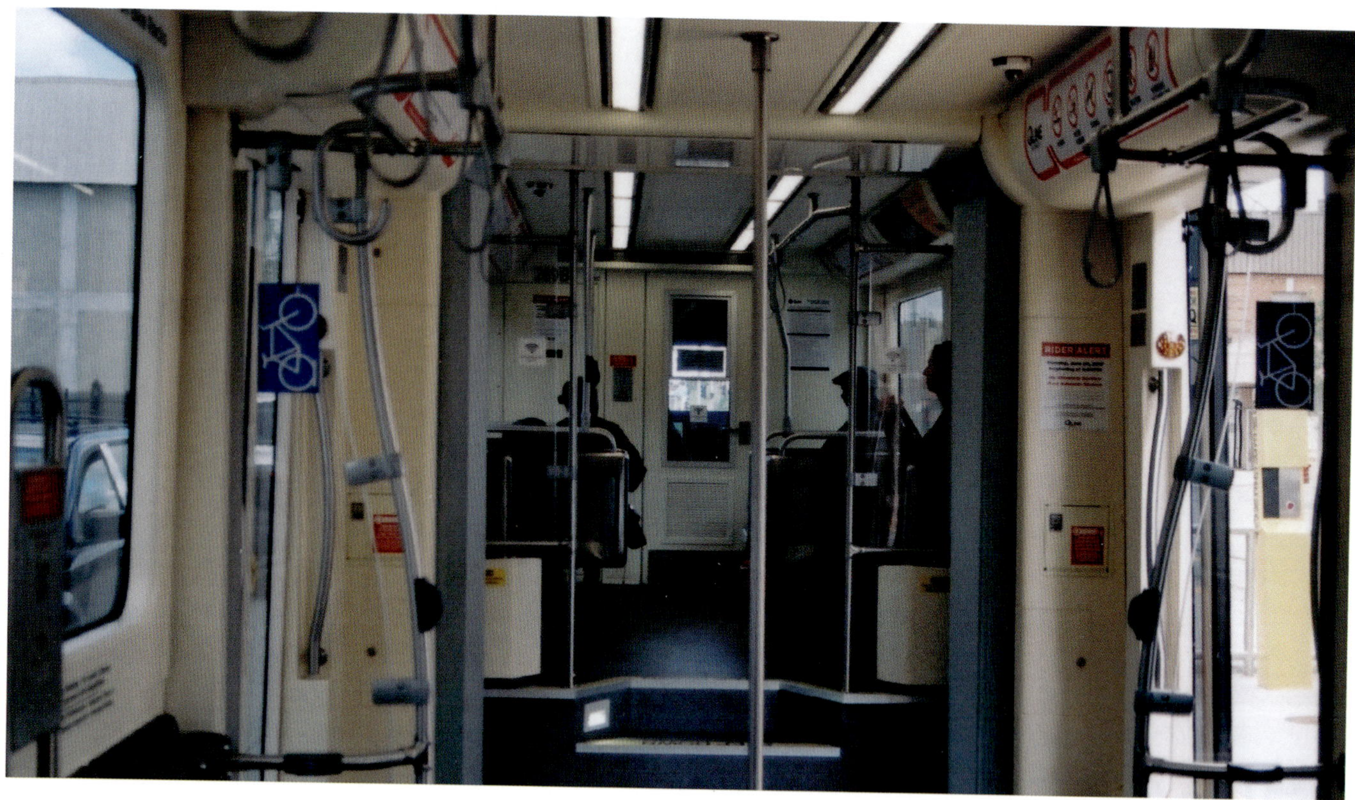

The interior of QLINE streetcar No. 289 on June 25, 2018 includes seating for thirty-two passengers and can accommodate 125 passengers. Each end of the car has an enclosed driver compartment. At the end of the line, the driver goes to the compartment at the other end of the car to head in the other direction. (*Kenneth C. Springirth photograph*)

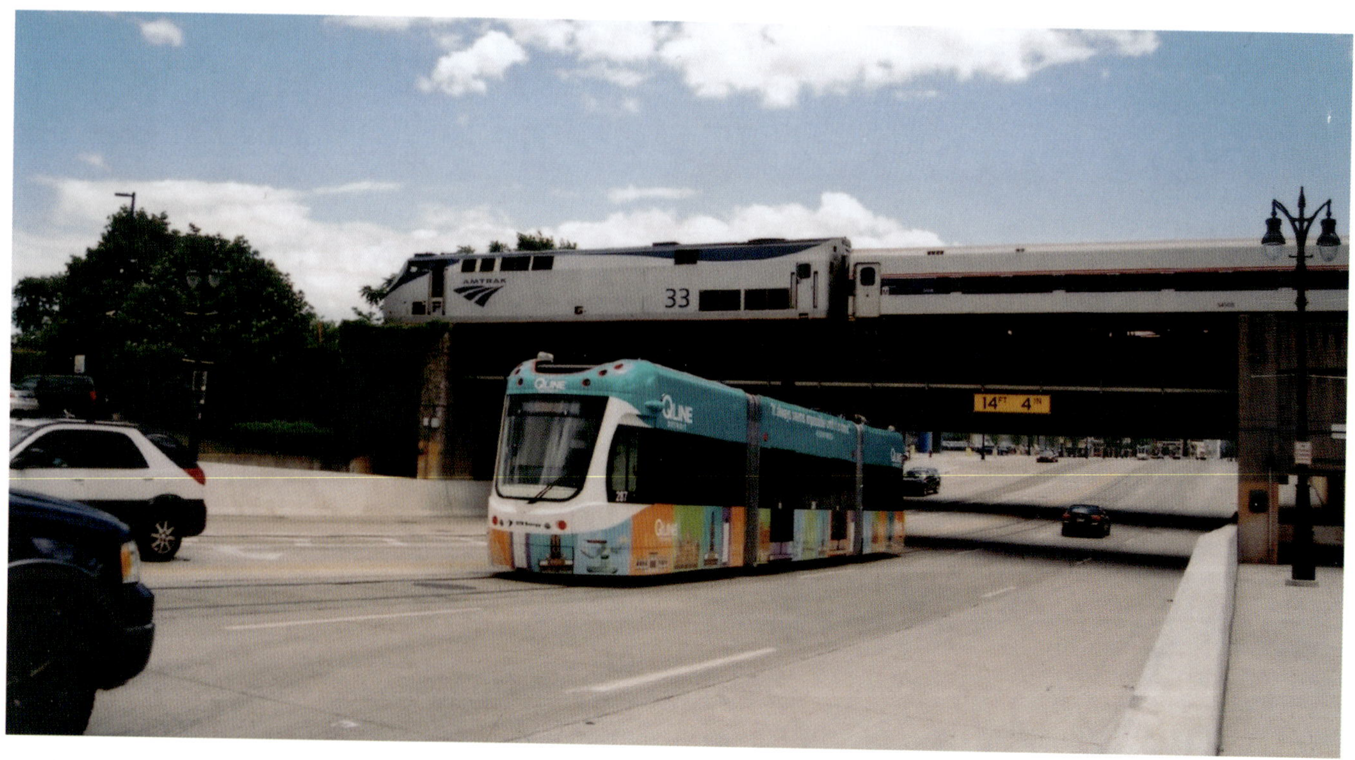

Southbound QLINE streetcar No. 287 is ready to go under the bridge on Woodward Avenue just south of Baltimore Street as Amtrak train No. 350 (Chicago via Detroit to Pontiac, Michigan) was making a passenger stop at Detroit's Amtrak station on June 26, 2017. Powering the train is General Electric type P42DC diesel electric locomotive No. 33 built in December 1996, with its streamlined monocoque car body. (*Kenneth C. Springirth photograph*)

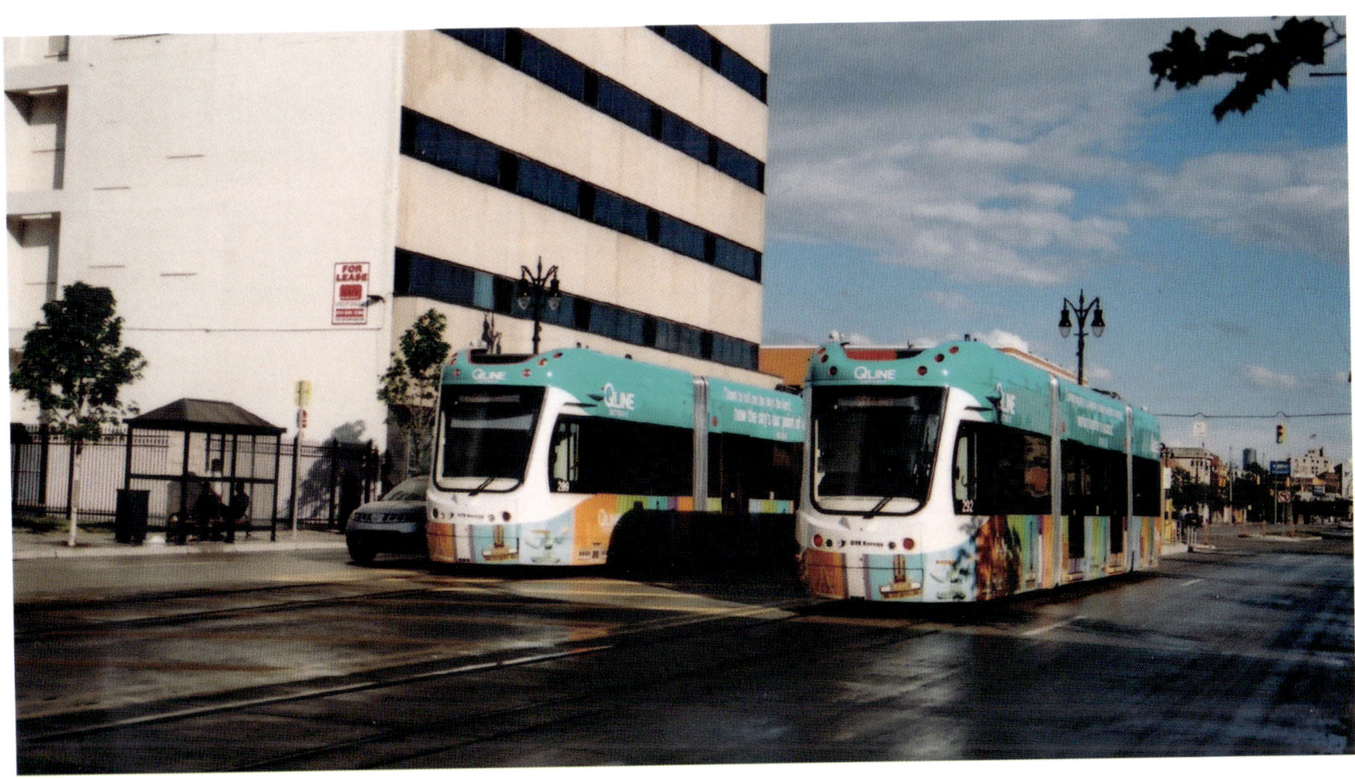

After a short afternoon rain, QLINE streetcars Nos. 289 northbound and 292 southbound are at the Woodward Avenue and Grand Boulevard station on June 26, 2017. The bus shelter on the left is for the Woodward Avenue buses. Within walking distance west on Grand Boulevard is the gorgeous historical thirty-story Fisher Building. The Art Deco-style building opened September 1, 1928. Home to the Fisher Theatre, the building was designated a National Historic Landmark on June 29, 1989. (*Kenneth C. Springirth photograph*)

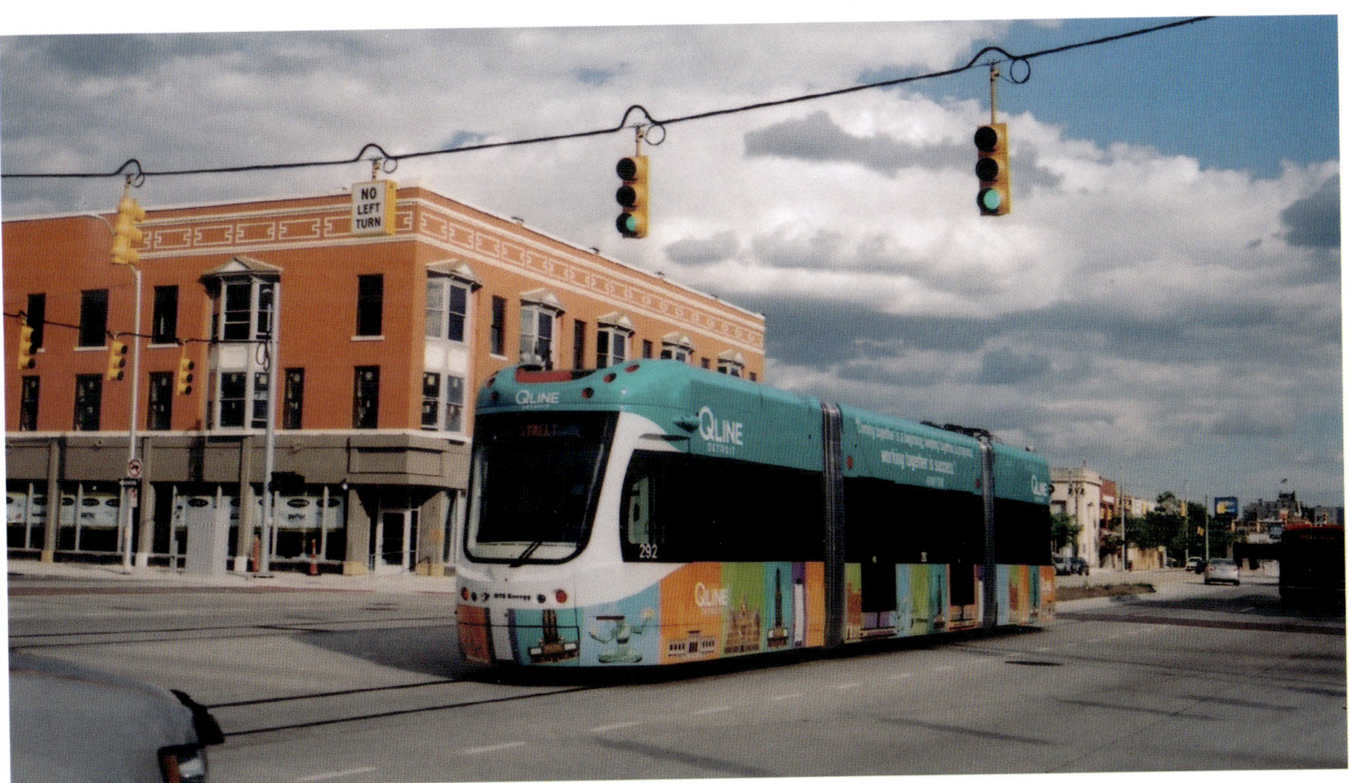

On June 28, 2017, southbound QLINE streetcar No. 292 is on Woodward Avenue crossing Grand Boulevard. This is in the New Center neighborhood, a commercial and residential district about three miles north of downtown Detroit. The QLINE has taken Woodward Avenue from the Detroit River to Grand Boulevard and has provided a major reason for new development. (*Kenneth C. Springirth photograph*)

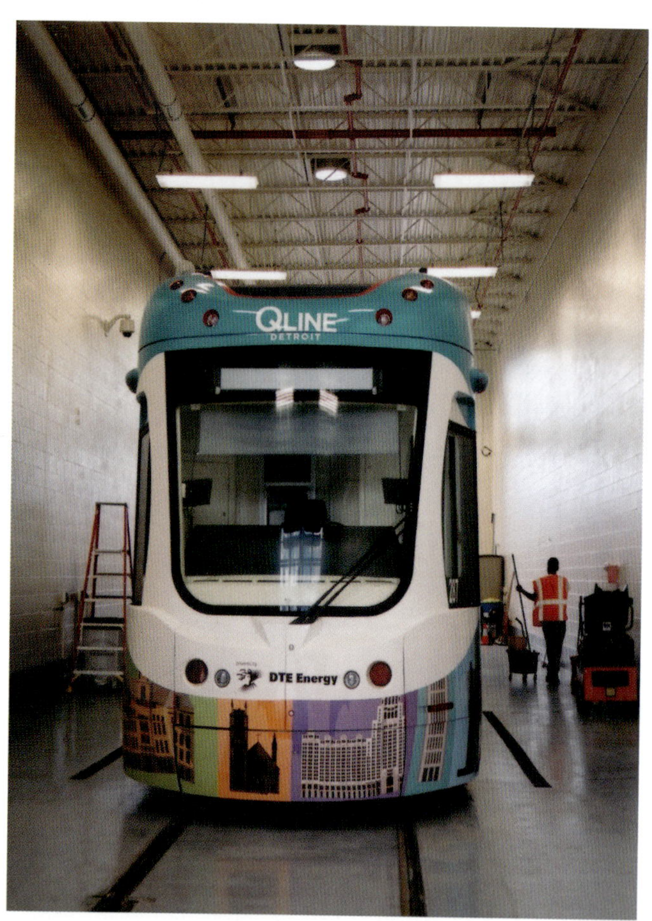

Left: QLINE streetcar No. 287 is inside the Penske Technical Center on June 25, 2017. Named for Roger S. Penske, Chairman of M-1 Rail and Chairman plus CEO of the Penske Automobile Group, this 19,000-square-foot facility is the headquarters with offices, conference rooms, central dispatch, and training rooms for the M-1 rail operators of the QLINE plus handles streetcar maintenance and washing. (*Kenneth C. Springirth photograph*)

Below: On June 26, 2017, QLINE streetcar No. 292 is at the reddish brick Penske Technical Center located on Woodward Avenue between Bethune and Custer Streets, just north of the Grand Boulevard northern terminus of the line. The streetcar storage area is behind the building. This is the nation's first streetcar storage and maintenance facility (car barn) to operate completely off wire. (*Kenneth C. Springirth photograph*)

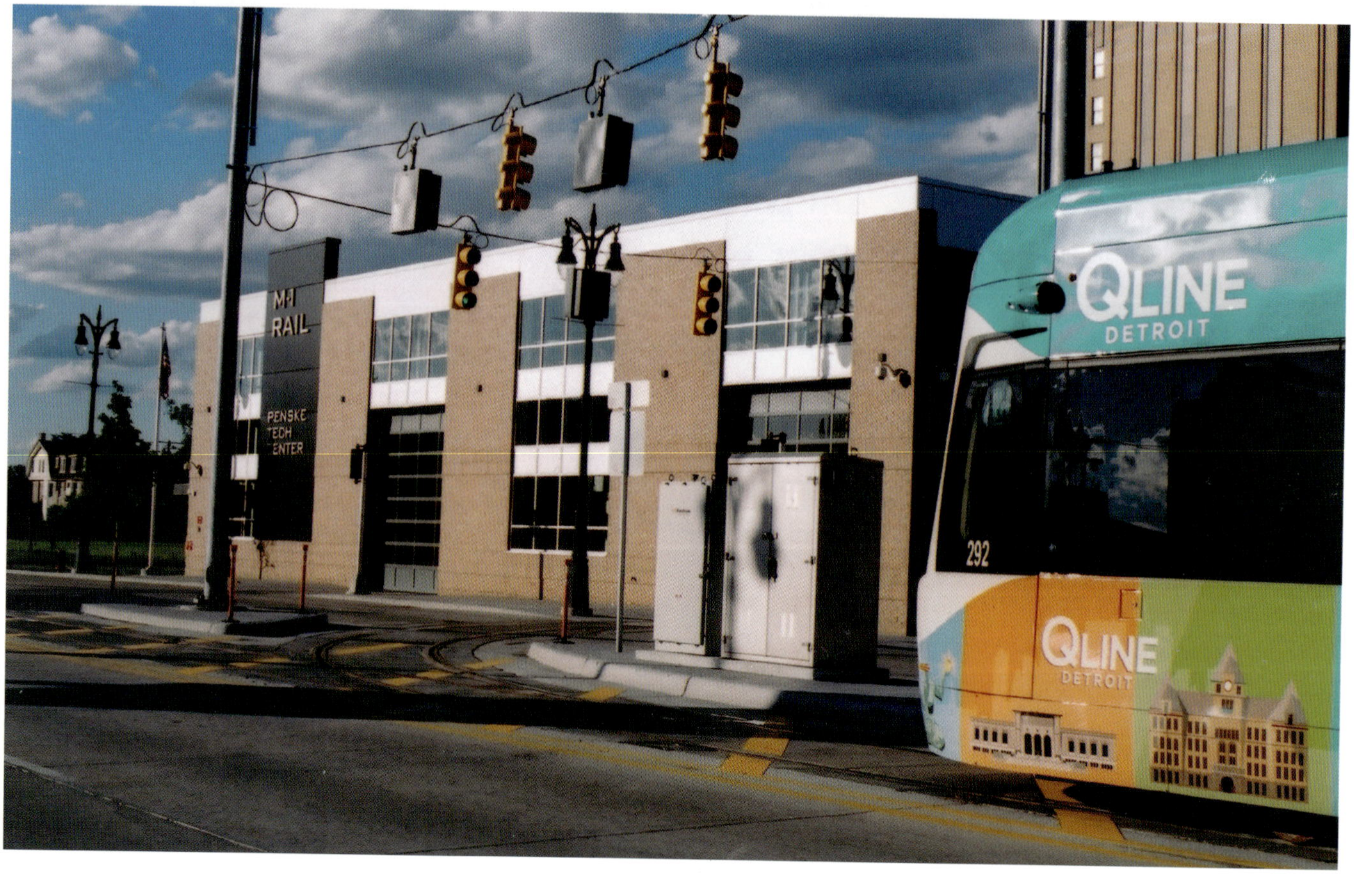